THE BOOK
of
UNDERSTANDING

by

Two Hermits

One who prayed   for   One who wrote
[Brother Michael]   [Brother Anthony]

BenYamin
Geneva   New York

NIHIL OBSTAT AND IMPRIMATUR
  + Donat Chiasson
  Archbishop of Moncton, N.B. Canada

Library of Congress Cataloging-in-Publication Data

Two Hermits (Writer), 1923-
    The Book of Understanding / by Two Hermits.
        p.   cm.
    Includes bibliographical references and index.
    ISBN 0-9627925-3-5 (Soft Cover)
    ISBN 0-9627925-2-7 (Hard Cover)
    1. Spiritual life—Christianity—Quotations, maxims, etc.   2. Spiritual life—Judaism—
    Quotations, maxims, etc.   3. Fear of God—Quotations, maxims, etc.   4. Fear of God
    (Judaism)—Quotations, maxims, etc.   5. Wisdom—Religious aspects—Christianity—
    Quotations, maxims, etc.   6. Wisdom—Religious aspects—Judaism—Quotations,
    maxims, etc.   7. Understanding—Biblical teaching—Quotations, maxims, etc.
    8. God—Knowableness—Quotations, maxims, etc.   9. God (Judaism)—
    Knowableness—Quotations, maxims, etc.
    I. Title.
    BV4501.2.T87   1994   94-24327
    234'.12—dc20   CIP

Published by BenYamin Press
             469 Snell Road
             Geneva, NY 14456 USA
             FAX 1 (315) 789-6000

To
our dear mothers
Helen and Josephine
with
love and gratitude

Contents

PART IV: UNDERSTANDING

ix

Abbreviations

BIBLE VERSIONS

DV .... Douay Version
JB .... Jerusalem Bible
JPSV .... Jewish Publication Society Version [1955]
KJV .... King James [Authorized] Version
NAB .... New American Bible
NAS .... New American Standard Version
NEB .... New English Bible
NIV .... New International Version
NJB .... New Jerusalem Bible
NKJV .... New King James Version
NRSV .... New Revised Standard Version
REB .... Revised English Bible
RSV .... Revised Standard Version
RV .... Revised Version

DEAD SEA SCROLLS

CD .... The Cairo Damascus Document
Q .... Qumrân cave
1QH .... The Hymns of Thanksgiving Scroll
1QHFrag .... The Hymns of Thanksgiving Scroll Fragments
1QM .... The War Scroll
1QMyst .... Book of Mysteries
1QpHab .... Commentary on Habacuc
1QS .... The Scroll of the Rule
1QSb .... Book of Blessings
4QSl .... Angelic Liturgy from Qumrân cave 4
4QEn^c .... Book of Enoch, Fragments from Qumrân cave 4
11QPs^a .... Psalm Scroll from Qumrân cave 11

TALMUDS

PHILO

xv

Spec. .... De Specialibus Legibus
Virt. .... De Virtutibus

PSEUDO PHILO BIBLICAL ANTIQUITIES

Ps.Philo .... Pseudo Philo

ANCIENT CHRISTIAN WRITERS

Collections
PG .... Patrologia Graeca, J.P. Migne
PL .... Patrologia Latina, J.P. Migne

Athenagoras
Emb. .... Embassy

Clement of Alexandria
Paed. .... Paedagogue
Exh. .... Exhortations
Strom. .... Stromata

St. Ephrem
Ad. Init. Prov. .... Homily on Providence

Eusebius
Praep. Evang. .... On the Preparation of the Gospel

St. Gregory of Nazianzus
Orat. .... Orations

St. John Chrysostom
De Anna. Hom. .... Homilies on the Statutes

Justin Martyr
Apol. .... Apology
Dial. .... Dialogue with the Jew Trypho

PROLOGUE

Prologue

Long, long ago, there lived a good and kind-hearted king who had a beautiful and extraordinarily wise daughter named Hakima. One day, while she was still a small child barely able to walk, the king had her brought into the great throne-room where he sat in audience. Placing her on his lap, he received the dignitaries from many lands who came with gifts and tribute to court his favor. There were ambassadors from Egypt, Nubia, Media and Cush; envoys from Lydia, Babylonia, Phrygia and Samarkand. Wealthy Parthians, Elamites, Scythians and rich merchants from far-off Cathay came and vied with one another as their slaves laid before the king gold and silver ingots, caskets of pearls and precious stones, bales of silk and brocades, ivory, ambergris, spikenard ointment and attar of roses in alabaster flasks. Exotically attired retainers of the satraps entered bearing golden cages full of singing birds, and lion cubs held by silver chains. And as the emissaries filed in procession to prostrate themselves before the great monarch, they were astonished to hear the little princess greet them each in his own tongue. No less astounded and delighted was her father the king. The very same day he had a proclamation made to be read throughout his realm summoning all the wise men and learned scribes to the palace. And to the wisest and most scholarly among them he entrusted the education of his daughter. Before many years had gone by they presented themselves to the king and informed him that there was nothing further they could teach the princess for she had surpassed them all in wisdom and learning. From that day onward, the king ruled with Hakima by his side, and because of her wise counsels the land prospered and there was peace everywhere.

Through her guidance the king made good treaties and alliances, and promulgated just laws. Vast irrigation projects made the deserts bloom forth in orchards and vineyards, and kept the fields blanketed with grain. A great merchant fleet was built that traded the kingdom's goods to best advantage because the ships were sent to the right places at the most auspicious times. Rich veins of gold and silver were found and mined throughout the realm, and gem-bearing alluvia were discovered wherever the princess would indicate on the maps. In the same parchments she would trace out new caravan routes along oases less distant from one another. Thus, through her wisdom the king became immensely rich and his treasuries were filled with myriads of gold and silver pieces and coffers full of diamonds, emeralds, rubies, sapphires and pearls. Throughout his domain he had splendid palaces built of the finest marble set with jasper, lapis lazuli, onyx and agate. And in the routes to them pavilions of cloth of gold were assembled with ebony poles, and stocked with every provision. As for herself, the princess had skillful artisans construct at the very end of one of her father's gardens, a small palace of her own design. Leading to it she had the gardeners pattern a verdant maze of meandering hedges and interweaving paths. Those who succeeded going through the labyrinth found themselves before a massive silver door embossed at random with hundreds of silver spheres ranging from the size of a pinhead to that of a large globe. The door had no lock and could only be opened from within unless one pressed simultaneously two separated but identical spheres concealed in the midst of all the varied-sized array. Then, the great door would open and reveal a multi-columned dark passageway that led to a second door made of sandalwood carved throughout with hundreds of small escutcheons of exactly the same shape and design set in concentric rows. In one of these small shields, an extra point had been carved in a little star within the frame. Upon pressing that square, the second door opened and yielded entry to another corridor that traversed a courtyard of fountains and led to the third door. It was a wonder to behold, for on it was painted a marvelous scene of mountains and valleys, cascading streams, and green meadows covered with wildflowers. Here and there, shepherds tended their flocks while in the distant undulating fields of grain, reapers were binding sheaves. There was a blue lake in the foreground and a small village depicted beside it. Not far away were vineyards laden with grapes hanging in purple clusters, and close by were orchards of pomegranate, apricot, and pear trees. Their branches were full of fruits being gathered into baskets by young maidens. It was a beautiful autumnal panorama wrought with perfect symmetry and painstaking detail.

Very unobtrusively in one of the branches, a small pear had been painted topsy-turvy with the stem attached to the broad base. Hidden directly behind it was the spring mechanism that released the catch and opened the door. Further beyond, through successive corridors, four other portals each with their own enigma awaited the answering hand.

Behind the seventh portal were the richly furnished chambers of the princess where she retired in the evenings. Her attendants had access to her chambers by the side entrances of her palace but none were allowed to go through the seven doors and none ventured because only the princess knew how to operate their secret mechanisms. She had purposely devised and had these doors fashioned because she knew the time would come when the king would ask her to betroth one of the many kings and princes who sought her hand. And when the day came that she had to decide among them, she informed her father that she would only marry the one who could go through the portals and answer her question. For she was a very wise woman and she desired a man who would be able to understand her thoroughly and love her. And so, one by one the kings essayed, and the princes attempted, but none went beyond the middle of the maze and the doors remained shut and unravelled.

As the years went by and none of the royal suitors succeeded in going through the labyrinth and opening the doors, the king issued a proclamation throughout his realms giving the princess in marriage to any man, noble or peasant, who would prosper in the undertaking. And to that he added the offer of half his kingdom, for it grieved him to see her sad because her thoughts were not fathomed. Thus, they came from all his domains, young and old, rich and poor, soldiers and commanders, farmers and sailors, mountaineers and valleymen — to no avail. They all got lost in the maze and none of them saw the doors of the princess.

A week's journey from the city of the king, there lived a man who had twelve sons all stalwart and handsome. Some helped their father with the farming, and the others took care of his herds. Yamin, the youngest, shepherded the flocks. He was seventeen years of age at the time of the king's proclamation. Of a ruddy and fair countenance, with an engaging smile and clear blue eyes, he was smaller than his brothers in size but not in brawn nor fleetness. His father loved him above the rest because he was the child of his many years and also because he was very obedient and respectful towards him. From childhood Yamin loved to sit enthralled by the feet of his father and listen to him as he spoke of the old traditions and recounted the wanderings of their tribe. His father taught him to read and to write, and from the Temple scribes obtained for him scrolls containing all the wisdom and counsels of the ancients. He took little Yamin to ride horse with him as he surveyed his lands and herds, and taught him all the lore he had acquired throughout the years, admonishing him to be very observant and notice the similarities and differences in animals, plants and things. He showed him how to track and where to search, and how to be all ears and sharp-eyed to perceive the faintest spoor and hear the merest rustle. And when the father saw how he hungered to learn, and how he struggled to grasp the hidden meaning of what was written in the rolls of parchment, he taught him to ponder throughout the day what seemed inscrutable in them, and patiently wait for the workings of the inner spirit at night to reveal the answer at dawn. And by his father's example, Yamin learned patience, kindness and forbearance, and to put his trust in the Ancient One who lives in the heavens and rewards those who are faithful to His laws. Above all he learned to be true so that he would be able to know and bring forth the Truth from his heart. Thus, the years went by and the father rejoiced to see that his youngest son had become a man of understanding.

Pasturing his father's flocks often took Yamin to the mountain ranges where for many days he would tent alone while the sheep grazed. He was an excellent archer and many were the predatory wolves and snow leopards transfixed by his arrows. One day, high above the plains, he beheld the brother next oldest to him riding home in the distance. Gathering the sheep, he hastened down the valley and hailed his brother towards him. As the brother drew near, he saw from the dejected look in his face that he too had failed to go through the barriers set up by the princess; and he determined to unravel the mysteries of the labyrinth and the doors that had disheartened so many. He then resolved to obtain his father's blessing and venture forth himself toward the city of the king. Making known his intent, on arrival home, he was greeted with derision by his brothers; nevertheless, his father blessed him and sent him on his way with provisions for the journey. With the longbow slung over his shoulders and a coil of rope and the quiver of arrows strapped to the saddle, he rode towards the palace of the wise princess.

On the seventh day before dawn, he came to the walls of the city, entered, and rode on to the king's palace where the guards took him through the gardens to the entrance of the maze. They left him there to bide his time alone, for the sun had not yet risen. Prostrating himself on the ground, he implored the God of the heavens to give him strength and guide his hands. Then, taking an arrow from the quiver, he tied to its shaft one end of the long thin rope and let the rest of the coil dangle to the ground. The other end of the cord he tied around his waist. When the first rays of the sun struck the golden turrets of the palace on the other side of the green maze, Yamin fitted the arrow to the bowstring and drawing it back with all his strength sent it flying high above the hedges trailing the rope behind it. He heard the clang as the arrow struck the silver door, and he saw the cord fall upon the hedges and remain there pointing the way to the egress. Loosening the other end from his waist, and fixing his eyes on the rope dangling high above, he cautiously made his way from shrub to shrub seeking the apertures and following the cord until he reached the other side of the maze. There he saw an awesome sight: thousands of red suns were reflected on the many-sized silver globes. Ascending the marble steps he felt the thick unyielding door and studied the gleaming spheres. He observed their disparity and the seemingly haphazard way they were set upon the massive door. A minuscule globe was beside a large orb and a cherry-sized sphere was set next to a melon-sized ball. No two seemed alike. He was troubled by the disarray until he remembered they were designed by wisdom and he began to search among all the hundreds until he found them — two identical yet separate eye-sized silver spheres. Placing his thumbs upon them he pressed, and the door slowly swung open. He entered a long dark corridor lit here and there by lamps hanging from the columns. At the end of the passageway was the fragrant sandalwood door. He marvelled at the skill of the woodcarver who had wrought the hundreds of identical small shields set in orderly rows. Taking a lamp in hand, he looked at the stars within the frames seeking for that particular one that would point the way in. And when he found it, he pressed the square. As the door opened he heard the sound of falling waters and felt a gentle breeze from the courtyard caress his face. He was hungry for he had fasted since the night before; thus, the first things that caught his eye in the painted door were the fruit-laden trees. He smiled as he saw in one of the branches the odd little pear that was to feed him, for no sooner did he press upon it than the door opened to reveal an alcove with tables of fruits, pastries, sweetmeats, viands, wines and other delicacies.

When he had eaten to his heart's content, he went towards the fourth door. Projecting from its surface were hundreds of small golden bells all of the same size. And as he began to ring each one of them it seemed to him that he heard a distant chorus of maidens shouting with glee, hands clapping and bare feet running to converge behind remote doors. He continued ringing and hearing the same note and pitch in all the bells, except one: the one that he pulled to let himself into the next passageway. It led to a somber door upon which was depicted a stormy scene of heavy black clouds which threatened to pour torrential rains, while far below a raging sea dashed its waves against the cliffs. From a precipitous crag a waterfall cascaded to the sea, and in the distant horizon a caravel struggled against the wind. Yamin peered long at the painting before he ran his finger down the waterfall to feel for the spring mechanism which he knew would be there. For he remembered that wisdom endeavors to unite, and he understood that the cataract was the bridge between the waters above and the waters below. When the door opened he beheld a clear glass portal flanked by two large animals carved out of wood: an ox and an ass. His eyes rejoiced to see them there, and he playfully ran his hands over the eyes of the ox and the ears of the donkey knowing these would yield their secret mechanisms to him for we must have eyes that truly see and ears that really hear if we hope to know and understand wisdom. The glass portal soon responded to his touch letting him in before the last enigma. It was not a door but a thick black fissureless curtain of richest silk that extended from the ceiling to the floor. Seeing it, he drew his dagger from its sheath and pierced the veil rending it from top to bottom.

Then, in all her beauty, the princess stood revealed before him. Around her were all her maidens wide-eyed at his commanding presence while the princess remained regally immobile and impassive. He marvelled at her beauty and the loveliness of her dark eyes and he stared at her speechless. It was then that she softly asked him, "Who shall know wisdom?" Taking her into his arms, he whispered in her ear, "He who shall encompass her by his understanding." She smiled and she kissed him and her maidens heard her sigh with joy, because at last she was understood.

Thus Wisdom and Understanding
were married and lived happily
ever after. And out of their loving
union the Truth was born.

INTRODUCTION

Introduction

"It is the nature of understanding to be very deep, not superficial, it does not display itself openly but loves to hide itself in secrecy."[1] Thus, Job asked: "Where is the place of understanding? Seeing that it is hidden from the eyes of all living and concealed from the birds of the heavens."[2] Furthermore, "there is no searching of His understanding,"[3] and no finding of its place until He beckons when the time comes for it to be known and understood.

Long ago it was said of a patient man that "he will hide his words until his time, and the lips of many shall declare his understanding."[4] The Word of God incarnate came and sowed "His seed."[5] For almost two thousand years He has patiently waited for us to bring forth from His implanted words: "the fruits of understanding"[6] to His glory.

In the plenary sense, to understand is to have full insight into the Truth of a matter. Understanding perceives the very flesh of Truth and its beautiful contours hidden beneath the rich garments and jewels made by Wisdom for its adornment. Understanding esteems the gems in their settings and marvels at the perfect symmetry of the vestures, but it never loses sight of the face of Truth.

Wisdom and knowledge may be heard and read, but "where is the place of understanding? . . . God understands the way to it, and He knows its place."[7] And He taught us that the way to understand is to really listen so that we may "hear and understand,"[8] and become an "understanding hearer."[9] Because to [really] hear is to understand."[10] "All who could hear with understanding"[11] were those who really listened. Thus, the Hebrew word SHAMA' means not only 'to hear,' but 'to understand' as well: "Confound their language so that they may not understand [SHAMA' = literally, 'to hear'];" "They did not know that Joseph understood [SHAMA'] them."[12]

Besides listening attentively, we must also be good if we hope to be given insight into the holy things of God, because "to depart from evil is understanding."[13] Thus, "a righteous person understands."[14] "Blessed are you righteous ones, for to you are revealed the deepest secrets of the Law."[15] Conversely, "the wicked do not understand knowledge"[16] and "evil men do not understand,"[17] for "they are wicked, having no understanding."[18] "If you love to hear, you shall receive understanding,"[19] said the ancients, provided one is good; for true understanding is a gift from God. O Lord, "How can I understand unless You give me understanding?"[20]

But again, "where is the place of understanding?"[2] The place of understanding is in the heart. As the Rabbis said: "the heart is the seat of understanding,"[21] "the Lord has given you a heart not to forget, but to understand"[22] because "God made . . . the heart for understanding."[23] He who is "void of heart"[24] is "void of understanding."[25] When it is said, in the Holy Scriptures, that "Wisdom will enter your heart,"[26] what is really meant is that "Wisdom will enter your understanding"[27] so that you will become not only "wise in heart"[28] but "wise in understanding."[29] But let us not forget that "Wisdom will not enter a deceitful soul, nor dwell in a body that is enslaved by sin."[30] "There is wisdom in the heart of a good man"[31] but not in the heart of an evil one. "Wisdom rests in the heart of him who has understanding,"[32] because Wisdom knows that he has understanding because he is good. For "a good understanding have all those who do His commands."[33] Therefore, "Wisdom rests in the heart of the righteous"[34] and "every man of understanding knows Widsom"[35] because "a man of understanding is faithful to the Law of God,"[36] but "he who is without understanding will not abide with Wisdom."[37]

If we really want to be truly understanding we must not only be good, but also compassionate and patient. "Let not kindness and fidelity leave you, bind them around your neck, write them on the tablet of your heart. So you will find favor and good understanding in the sight of God and man,"[38] and be full of "compassionate understanding."[39] "Righteous men pity and are kind;"[40] "the righteous one is generously merciful and compassionate,"[41] therefore, "the righteous one understands."[42] But "a ruler who is a great oppressor lacks understanding"[43] for "a man of violence does not receive understanding"[44] from God. "Beware, that you be not greatly enraged and be like those who are wanting in understanding."[45] Instead, let us be patient, for "he who is slow to anger is of great understanding;"[46] "be patient and of good understanding."[47]

Long ago it was said that "an understanding man is he who can deduce one thing from another."[48] For true understanding is a great gift which enables us to link things together so that "a text which is not fully explained in its own place is illuminated by another text"[49] found by someone who understands. "By stringing together parable to parable, King Solomon drew out the secrets of the Torah"[50] for he was once "wise . . . and as a flood full of understanding"[51] before he lost his insight by not departing from evil.[52] If we persevere in the way of righteousness we shall be able to keep the gift of understanding and "he who keeps understanding shall find good things"[53] and reduce the complicated to simplicity, bringing what was in the darkness to light.

With the gift of understanding we shall be able to solve things and establish what has been unravelled by our understanding. "The Lord by wisdom has founded the earth, and by understanding He has established the heavens."[54] Thus, "through wisdom is a house built, and by understanding it is established"[55] so that it remains unmoved, surviving every storm. "Everyone who hears these words of Mine, and does them shall be likened to an understanding [PHRONIMŌ] man, who has built his house upon the rock; and the rains fell, and the floods came, and the winds blew and beat upon that house, but it did not fall, because it had been founded on the rock"[56] by the one who understood. For "the understanding . . . has a stability which no argument can shake . . . understanding . . . is defined as a sure and certain apprehension which cannot be shaken by argument."[57] Understanding also enables us to exalt that which has been established, and to praise the Author of all things and Giver of all understanding. "Make me understand the way of Your precepts, then I shall speak [exaltingly] of Your wonderful works."[58] "Grant me understanding, O Lord, in Your Law, and teach me Your ordinances, so that many may hear of Your deeds and people may honor Your glory."[59]

Understanding converts us and persuades us to be good. Thus, the Psalmist prayed: "Give me understanding and I shall keep Your Law, yes, I shall observe it with all my heart."[60] "O Lord, You have put understanding in the heart of Your servant that he may do what is good and right before You, and restrain himself against deeds of wickedness."[61] When God "opens the understanding of men . . . to turn a man from unrighteousness,"[62] He does a wonderful thing — He opens at the same time the doors of His treasury and reveals to the understanding: the precious things of His wisdom and knowledge. He does so to render pale, in comparison, the allurements of sin. In turn, those who are given to understand His beautiful things are to convert and persuade others to be good, "teaching understanding to those whose spirit has gone astray"[63] to draw them to a life of righteousness. Truly, "he who wins souls is wise"[64] and understanding.

There is a great peace in understanding "for the understanding of the Spirit is life and peace."[65] "Learn where understanding [PHRONĒSIS] is . . . so that you may know where is length of days, and life, and where is light of the eyes and peace."[66] Then, let us "be of one understanding, and be at peace"[67] with one another. And let us persevere in the ways of the Lord so that we may keep "that stability and peace of understanding."[68]

If we want good advice we need "the counsel of understanding"[69] from "an understanding counsellor,"[70] because "powerful counsel is rooted in understanding."[71] Thus, it is written: "inquire [for counsel] at the mouth of one who understands."[72] "Seek counsel always from the understanding"[73] for "as the water jar contains water, understanding contains . . . counsel."[74] "From their understanding the godly have devised good counsel"[75] but not sinners, because "the counsel of sinners is not understanding,"[76] it is foolish advice, for they are "void of counsel because there is no understanding in them."[77]

The best counsel we can receive from those who understand is that true understanding is a gift from the Lord. We can "hear wisdom,"[78] and we can "apply . . . our ears to the words of knowledge"[79] but we "receive understanding"[80] from God. Thus, the Psalmist prayed: "O Lord . . . give me understanding;"[81] "give me understanding, O Lord, in Your Law."[82] For "how can I understand unless You give me understanding?"[83] But let us not forget that the Lord gives understanding only to those who are good. "The upright will understand the knowledge of the Most High, and the perfect of way will have understanding of the wisdom of the sons of Heaven,"[84] because "a good understanding have all those who do His commands."[85] But "none of the wicked shall understand,"[86] for theirs is the "confusion of wickedness"[87] brought about by "the foolish reasonings of their unrighteousness."[88]

When Qoheleth said: "I encompassed with my understanding to know, and to search, and to seek out wisdom,"[89] he knew that it is through our understanding that we seek that which we desire to comprehend. It is a characteristic of understanding to seek until it finds and grasps that which it has searched for. Thus, to say: "Wisdom . . . takes hold of those who *seek* her,"[90] is to say "Wisdom . . . takes hold of those who *understand* her."[91] And to say that "in the end you shall *find*,"[92] is to say that "in the end you shall *understand*."[93] Because "understanding loves to learn and to advance to full understanding, and its way [to do that] is to seek the hidden meaning rather than the obvious."[94] Thus, it is written that God "searches out the deep and the heart, for He has understanding,"[95] and He has insight to see and know that which is not visible to the human eye. For "there is no creature that is not manifest in His sight, but all things are naked and laid bare before the eyes of Him to whom we must give account."[96] We "cannot fathom the depths of the human heart,"[97] because "the heart is deep beyond all things."[98] "But the Lord searches all hearts, and understands the inclinations of the thoughts."[99] Wisdom can hide so well that no human being could ever hope to discover her, yet "He has found Wisdom out with His understanding,"[100] and "He has found out all the way to understanding [EPISTĒMĒS]"[101] as well. But "there is no searching of His understanding"[102] and no grasp of its scope, because "His understanding is superior to all wisdom"[103] and "there is no limit to His understanding."[104]

"The understanding grasps"[105] and "the understanding seizes"[106] because "it is the attribute of understanding to apprehend."[107] For "the noble understanding is a fighter and a contestant and is by nature good in struggle."[108] "The understanding which has come down from heaven, though it be fast bound to the constraints of the body nevertheless . . . holding to its own nature of true manhood has the strength to be victor instead of victim in the wrestling bout"[109] with that which it strives to understand. When the wise man said: "My soul wrestled with Wisdom"[110] he meant that he sought to master and know her by the strength of his understanding. Thus, "in common exercise with Wisdom is understanding."[111] We know that "understanding . . . has wide scope and grasps the ends of the universe,"[112] it can also contain galaxies in the vault of its comprehension because "the understanding is a vast and receptive storehouse."[113] But how shall we be able to grasp and embrace Wisdom unless we are good? For "evil men do not understand"[114] and "men without understanding will not be able to seize Wisdom."[115]

When the Holy Scriptures tell us of the understanding of the Lord, they speak of His power. For "God is mighty . . . in the power of understanding."[116] "Great is our Lord and of great power: His understanding is infinite;"[117] "He is wise in understanding, and great in power"[118] because "understanding has mighty power."[119] Thus, the Lord "by His understanding smites through Rahab"[120] because there is power in understanding. "The understanding [SUNESIS] of the powerful [DUNASTON]"[121] is what makes them truly mighty. "Whoever is with understanding is wholly lordly and independent and masterful."[122] "Have you gained power for yourself by your insight and understanding?"[123] If so, be humble, so that you may keep it. Be not like the "proud, understanding nothing."[124] Remember that "he who lifts himself up with pride . . . his wisdom will depart from him,"[125] "neither shall he understand [BIN] . . . because he shall magnify himself above all"[126] by his pride. "Be humble in understanding"[127] for "the one who has both much understanding and humility is called blessed by all who look upon him."[128] "Let a man first grasp the way of humility and then ask God for understanding."[129] "To the way of humility I incline, and thus will my heart gain understanding"[130] because "humility discloses to us the light of understanding."[131] But "we must watch with utmost care lest the wisdom we have received should take away the light of humility."[132] We shall not lose that light if we always keep the fear of the Lord for "whosoever fears the Lord will receive His instruction."[133] Happy indeed are they who are taught by the Lord, because it is from Him that we receive all light and understanding.[134]

1. Philo, *Som.* I.6
2. Job 28:20,21
3. Isaiah 40:28
4. Sirach 1:24
5. St. Luke 8:5
6. Sirach 37:22
7. Job 28:20,23
8. St. Matthew 15:10
9. Isaiah 3:3 (Greek Text)
10. Clement of Alexandria, *Strom.* II.4
11. Nehemiah 8:2
12. Genesis 11:7; 42:23
13. Job 28:28
14. Proverbs 21:12
15. Zohar, *Idra R.* II.26
16. Proverbs 29:7
17. Proverbs 28:5
18. Isaiah 56:11 (Greek Text)
19. Sirach 6:33 (Greek Cursives 248,253)
20. 1QH 12:33 (Dead Sea Scrolls)
21. Midrash Rabbah on Psalm 103.3
22. P.Targum on Deuteronomy 29:4
23. Testament of Naphtali 2:8
24. Proverbs 11:12 (Hebrew Text)
25. Proverbs 11:12 (Greek Text)
26. Proverbs 2:10 (Hebrew Text)
27. Proverbs 2:10 (Greek Text)
28. Exodus 28:3; Job 9:4 (Hebrew Text)
29. Exodus 28:3; Job 9:4 (Greek Text)
30. Wisdom 1:4
31. Proverbs 14:33 (Greek Text)
32. Proverbs 14:33 (Hebrew Text)
33. Psalm 111:10
34. Proverbs 14:33 (Syriac Text)
35. Sirach 18:28
36. Sirach 33:3 (Latin Vulgate)
37. Sirach 6:20
38. Proverbs 3:3-4
39. Baruch 3:20 (Syriac Text)
40. Proverbs 13:9b (Greek Text)
41. Proverbs 21:26 (Greek Text)
42. Proverbs 21:12
43. Proverbs 28:16
44. Sirach 32:18 (Hebrew MS. E)
45. Sirach 13:8 (Hebrew Text)
46. Proverbs 14:29
47. Shepherd of Hermas, *Mand.* VI.33:1
48. Midrash in Libnath Hasappir
49. The 32 Middoth by R. Eliezer ben R. Jose
50. Midrash Rabbah on Song of Songs I.1, Sect. 8
51. Sirach 47:14,15
52. Job 28:28; Sirach 47:19-20; 1 Kings 11:1-9
53. Proverbs 19:8
54. Proverbs 3:19
55. Proverbs 24:3
56. St. Matthew 7:24-25
57. Philo, *Cong.* 140,141
58. Psalm 119:27,104a
59. 11QPsᵃ Col. XXIV.9-10 (Psalm 155) Dead Sea Scrolls
60. Psalm 119:34
61. 1QH 14:8-9 (Dead Sea Scrolls)
62. Job 33:16,17 (Greek Text)
63. 1QS 10:26-11:1 (Dead Sea Scrolls)
64. Proverbs 11:30
65. Romans 8:6 (Literal Translation)
66. Baruch 3:14
67. 2 Corinthians 13:11
68. Philo, *Conf.* 132
69. Psalms of Solomon 17:42
70. 1 Chronicles 26:14
71. Sirach 37:17 (Hebrew Text)
72. Sirach 21:17
73. Tobit 4:18 (Greek Vaticanus B Text)
74. Philo, *Q.Gen.* IV.98
75. Isaiah 32:8 (Greek Text)
76. Sirach 19:22
77. Deuteronomy 32:28; Zadokite Fragment 7:18
78. 2 Baruch 51:4a
79. Proverbs 23:12
80. 2 Baruch 51:4b
81. Psalm 119:33,34,73,125,144,169
82. 11QPsᵃ XXIV.9 (Psalm 155:9) Dead Sea Scrolls
83. 1QH 12:33 (Dead Sea Scrolls)
84. 1QS 4:22 (Dead Sea Scrolls)
85. Psalm 111:10
86. Daniel 12:10
87. 1QS 3:2 (Dead Sea Scrolls)
88. Wisdom 11:15; Romans 1:18,21,22
89. Ecclesiastes 7:25
90. Sirach 4:11 (Greek Text)
91. Sirach 4:11 (Hebrew Text)
92. Sirach 31:22 (Greek Text)
93. Sirach 31:22 (Hebrew Text)
94. Philo, *Decal.* 1

95. Sirach 42:18 (Hebrew Text)
96. Hebrews 4:13
97. Judith 8:14
98. Jeremiah 17:9 (Greek Text)
99. 1 Chronicles 28:9
100. Baruch 3:32
101. Baruch 3:36
102. Isaiah 40:28
103. Odes of Solomon 28:20
104. Psalm 147:5
105. Philo, *Q.Gen*.IV.32
106. Philo, *Q.Gen*.IV.163
107. Philo, *Mig*.78
108. Philo, *Q.Gen*.IV.163
109. Philo, *Her*. 274
110. Sirach 51:19
111. Wisdom 8:18
112. Philo, *Agr*.53
113. Philo, *Deus*.42
114. Proverbs 28:5
115. Sirach 15:7

116. Job 36:5 (Literal Translation)
117. Psalm 147:5
118. Job 9:4 (Greek Text)
119. Corpus Hermeticum, *Libellus* IX.10
120. Job 26:12
121. Sirach 10:3 (Literal Translation)
122. Philo, *Q.Gen*.III.22 (Greek Fragment)
123. Ezekiel 28:4 (Greek Text)
124. 1 Timothy 6:4
125. Pesachim 66b (Babylonian Talmud)
126. Daniel 11:37
127. Sirach 32:3 (Hebrew Text)
128. R. Joseph Kimchi's, *Shekel Hakodesh* 67
129. Tanna debe Eliyahu Zuṭṭa p.31 [Edit. Friedman]
130. R. Joseph Kimchi's *Shekel Hakodesh* 79
131. St. Gregory, *Morals on the Bk of Job* XXV.30
132. ibid. XXVII. 75
133. Sirach 32:14a (Greek Text)
134. Psalm 119:130

THE FEAR OF THE LORD

THE BEGINNING

of all

WISDOM, UNDERSTANDING AND KNOWLEDGE

is

THE FEAR OF THE LORD*

*Re: The Fear of the Lord:

YIRAH and YARE, the usual Hebrew words for "the fear [YIRATH] of the Lord," have actually the connotation of "reverential fear" i.e., to regard something or someone with deep respect and veneration. Thus YARE is also the Hebrew word for "awe" and "great wonder" such as the astonishment expressed in the exclamation: "Wow!" After awakening from the vivid dream of a ladder going up to the heavens with the Lord at the pinnacle, and the angels of God ascending and descending upon it, Jacob exclaimed: "how awesome [YARE] is this place! This is none other than the house of God, and this is the gate of heaven!" (Genesis 28:17).

There are other Hebrew words that convey the usual sense of "fear" or "dread" viz., PACHAD, EMAH, MAGOR, MEGURAH, CHATH, CHITTITH and MORA, all of which would exempt one from being happy and peaceful at the *same time*. But "happy [ASHER] is everyone who fears [YARE i.e., 'reverences'] the Lord and walks in His ways" (Psalms 128:1; 112:1) because "the fear [YIRAH] of the Lord leads to life and he who has it rests satisfied" (Proverbs 19:23) and peaceful.

PROLOGUE
TO
THE FEAR OF THE LORD

NOTE

Each quotation used in the Prologue sections of THE FEAR OF THE LORD and WISDOM has a numbered alphabetical character beside it in the left margin indicating where the same quotation *along with its source* can be found in the section immediately following each Prologue.

Example:

C-3 found in the Prologue
to THE FEAR OF THE LORD =

Segment C, quote No. 3 in the "Scriptural, Apocryphal, Patristic, and Rabbinic Texts on the Fear of the Lord" section (pp. 19-46)

A-5 found in the Prologue
to WISDOM =

Segment A, quote No. 5 in the "Scriptural, Apocryphal, Patristic, and Rabbinic Texts on Wisdom" section (pp. 59-99)

A-1 'Come, O children, listen to me, I will teach you the fear of the Lord.'

What is the fear of the Lord but a holy awareness that God exists, that He is the Lord and Creator of the universe and all the galaxies hurling through space.

B-7 To become aware of the infinite majesty and power of God, is to be filled with awe and to exclaim in wonder: 'What is man . . . ?'

What are we before the Lord God of all the heavens and the earth?

In the very instant that we know that He is, our intellect shall be humbled, and we shall perceive the boundless wisdom and knowledge of God found in all His works.

G-44 For 'the fear of the Lord is the instruction of wisdom.'
G-46,F-56 'The fear of the Lord is the beginning of wisdom,' and 'the beginning of knowledge' as well; because 'whosoever fears the Lord will receive
G-43 His instruction.'

G-42 'You will fear Me, and you will receive instruction . . . says the Lord.'

G-8 'Who is the man who fears the Lord? him shall He teach . . . .'
And him shall He make to understand His hidden things, because
G-26 'the secret of the Lord is for those who fear Him; He makes known to them' what He conceals from those who do not fear Him: the proud unbelievers.

G-1 Thus it is that 'the fear of the Lord is wisdom and instruction, and faith and meekness are His delight.'

G-17,14 'Those who believe and fully know the Truth,' know that 'You have given Your understanding, O Lord, to Your believers' who are made
G-19 'wise unto salvation through faith,' and through meekness.

G-10,8 'His mysteries are revealed to the meek,' because 'the meek will He guide . . . and the meek will He teach': the hidden things of His wisdom.

G-40 'Understand the fear of the Most High, and meditate upon His commandments continually, and He shall make your heart to understand, and make you wise in that which you desire.'

C-17,G-9 'Get wisdom in the fear of the Lord quickly,' and 'in the meekness of wisdom' you shall understand, that those who fear the Lord reverence Him and keep His commandments.

D-1	'By the fear of the Lord men depart from evil.'
D-12	Because, 'the fear of the Lord is to hate evil, pride, arrogancy, and the evil way, and the perverted mouth.' And all other things that offend Him, and keep us away from His love.
D-11	'The Lord hates all abomination, and they who fear God love it not.'
D-5	'Fear God, and depart from all sin, and do that which is pleasing in His sight.'
D-2,6	'Fear the Lord, and depart from evil,' for 'to depart from evil is a thing pleasing to the Lord; and to forsake unrighteousness is an atonement' before Him.
C-6	'There is One wise and greatly to be feared: the Lord sitting upon His throne.'
C-3	'The Lord of Hosts, He is the king of glory.'
C-1	'Sanctify the Lord of Hosts Himself; and let Him be your fear, and let Him be your dread.'
C-9	'Behold, God is the judge, fear Him! Depart from all your sins, and forget your iniquities never more to meddle with them.'
C-10	'Do not fear those who kill the body but cannot kill the soul; rather fear Him who can destroy both body and soul in hell.'
C-12	'Fear Him who after He has killed has power to cast into hell, yes, I tell you, fear Him!'
C-13	'Fear Him who has all power to save and to destroy.'
C-16	For 'it is a fearful thing to fall into the hands of the living God.'
D-18	'If you want to do evil, fear the Lord and you will not do it.'
D-14	'For nothing more effectively preserves us from all sin than the fear of punishment, and the fear of God.'
D-19	'The fear of God reproves us all the time and chases away sin and suppresses vice. The fear of God renders a man prudent and attentive. Where there is no fear there is a dissolute life. Where there is no fear there is a life of crime.'
D-20	'The fear of the Lord drives out sins, and where it is present it turns away wrath.'
D-17	O, 'that His fear may be before your eyes, that you do not sin.'

F-1	'He who fears God neglects nothing.'
F-2	'If you fear the Lord you will do everything well.'

F-7   'They who fear the Lord will seek that which is well-pleasing to Him.' And what pleases the Lord is that we love one another, and do good.

F-40   'Fear God, and depart from all sin, and do that which is good before the Lord your God.'

F-38,39   'He who fears God will do good,' because 'the fear of God is not to omit the good that should be done.'

F-33   'Fear the Lord and love your neighbor . . . for he who fears God and loves his neighbor shall be shielded by the fear of God . . . He is helped by the Lord through the love which he has towards his neighbor.'

F-34   'Remember the fear of the Lord, and do not be angry with your neighbor.'

F-35   'The fear of God overcomes hatred, for fearing lest one should offend the Lord, one will do no wrong to anyone even in his thoughts.'

F-37   Neither will one be jealous of others, for 'deliverance from envy comes by the fear of God.'

F-41   'Blessed is he who fears God and serves Him . . . blessed is he who judges a judgment justly to the widow and orphan, and helps everyone who has been wronged, clothing the naked with garments, and feeding the hungry with bread.' For he truly fears, and best reverences the Lord, who has compassion toward those in need.

The fear of the Lord softens our hearts so that we may be filled by the Lord with loving care for one another.

E-44   'Happy the man who always fears God, but he who hardens his heart will fall into evil.'

The prophets knew that it is the fear of the Lord which makes our hearts tender towards one another. Thus Isaiah cried out:

L-1   'O Lord, why have You made us err from Your ways and hardened our heart, so that we do not fear You?'

May the Lord deliver us from a heart so hardened that it cannot fear.

L-2   And may He spare us from 'an evil heart of unbelief . . . hardened through the deceitfulness of sin.'

D-1   Truly, 'by the fear of the Lord men depart from evil' and their hearts are made soft again.

	We go from the fear of the Lord to the love of God.
A-10,F-22	'Fear the Lord your God,' and you shall 'love the Lord your God' and be loved by Him.
F-44	'The fear of the Lord is the first step to be accepted by Him and . . . obtains His love.' For when we reverence the Lord we depart from evil and do good,
F-45	'in every nation any one who fears Him and does what is right, is acceptable to Him.'
F-24	'Fear of God is the gateway to Him. Only he who has gone through that gate can truly love Him, and in the manner in which only He can be loved,' said a holy Jew.
F-23	'Fear of God is the beginning of wisdom and it takes us to the love of God, and from slaves that we are, it makes us children and beloved by God,' said a Christian saint.
F-31	'O fear the Lord, all ye His holy ones.'
F-32	'O love the Lord, all ye His godly ones.'
F-25	If it is said that 'they who fear the Lord are a sure seed, and they who love Him are an honorable plant,' it is because the fear of the Lord grows to become the love of Him.
E-9 F-50	'They who fear the Lord keep His commandments,' and they are the ones who love the Lord, 'for this is the love of God, that we keep His commandments.'
F-51	'He who has My commandments and keeps them, he it is who loves Me . . . and I will love him and manifest Myself to him.'
F-47	'For every one who does the Lord's Law will be loved by Him,' and the Lord reveals Himself to those whom He loves.
F-52	'Ye who fear the Lord, love Him, and your hearts shall be enlightened,'
F-53	for 'the Love of the Lord surpasses all things for illumination' —
F-54	'the illumination that fulfills all desire.'
F-55	And 'in illumination what we receive is knowledge': the knowledge of God. But it all begins with the fear of the Lord, and the keeping of His commandments.
L-3	'Hereby do we know that we know Him, if we keep His commandments' through His holy fear.
F-56 F-59	Truly, 'the fear of the Lord is the beginning of knowledge' because 'the fear of the Lord is the beginning of His love.'

F-28   'Behold, the eyes of the Lord are upon those who fear Him.'

F-12   'As a father pities his children, so the Lord pities those who fear Him, for He knows our frame; He remembers that we are dust.'

F-10   'He will fulfill the desire of those who fear Him; He will hear their cry and save them.'

F-11   For 'the Lord hears the prayer of everyone who fears God.'

F-8   'The Lord takes pleasure in those who fear Him.'

F-9   'Those who fear Him, He cherishes,' because they who fear the Lord have their eyes upon Him.

L-4   'Behold, as the eyes of servants look to the hand of their master, as the eyes of a maid to the hand of her mistress', so do the eyes of those who fear the Lord look towards Him, eager to serve Him with all their heart and soul.

L-5   For to fear the Lord is not only to be aware of Him and kneel in awe before His glory, but it is also to know that 'the Lord is righteous in all His ways, and kind in all His deeds.'

They who fear the Lord learn to know that He created us through His lovingkindness so that we may rejoice in Him. And they respond to His love by giving themselves wholeheartedly to God.

A-16   'Fear the Lord your God, that you may keep all His statutes and His commandments.'

E-8   Revere Him, so that you may always be aware of the Lord and strive to walk in perfection before Him, for 'where there is fear of God there is observance of precepts.'

A-17   'Fear the Lord your God that you may walk in all His ways,' and be full of joy the day you shall discover Him.

F-18   For 'those who have the fear of God . . . seek after Him'; and

F-21   'they who fear the Lord will find Him' waiting for them with outstretched arms, at the end of His ways.

And having found Him, they who fear the Lord shall embrace Him, whom they sought with all their love.

L-6   'Cleave to the Lord your God,' all you who love Him, and never let Him go.

H-9   But remember: 'Life with God belongs to those who fear Him — and keep His commandments.'

THE FEAR OF THE LORD

SCRIPTURAL, APOCRYPHAL, PATRISTIC,

RABBINIC, AND OTHER ANCIENT TEXTS

on

THE FEAR OF THE LORD

A

EXHORTATIONS

Invitation

1 "Come, O children, listen to me, I will teach you the fear of the Lord" (Psalm 34:11).

2 "And his children answered . . . and said, 'Speak, O father, for we listen.' He said unto them, 'I give you no command except in regard to the fear of the Lord: Him shall you serve, and to Him shall you cleave' " (Testament of Naphtali 1:4-5, Hebrew Text; Deuteronomy 10:20).

3 "My children, let all your works be done in order with good intent in the fear of God" (Testament of Naphtali 2:9, Greek Text).

We are to fear the Lord the same way that we are to love Him: with all our heart and soul

4 "Fear the Lord your God with all your heart" (Testament of Levi 13:1).

5 "Fear God in all your heart" (Sirach 7:29, Hebrew Text).

6 "With all your soul fear the Lord" (Sirach 7:31, Latin Vulgate).

We are commanded by the Lord to fear Him

7 "You shall fear your God: I am the Lord" (Leviticus 19:14,32; 25:17).

8 "You shall fear the Lord your God, and serve Him" (Deuteronomy 6:13).

9 "The Lord commanded us to do all these statutes, and to fear the Lord our God for our good always" (Deuteronomy 6:24).

10 "You shall fear the Lord your God; you shall serve Him and cleave to Him" (Deuteronomy 10:20).

11 "You shall walk after the Lord your God and fear Him, and keep His commandments and obey His voice, and you shall serve Him and cleave to Him" (Deuteronomy 13:4).

12 "Fear the Lord and serve Him in sincerity and in truth" (Joshua 24:14).

13 "Fear the Lord and serve Him in truth with all your heart" (1 Samuel 12:24).

14 "The Lord your God you shall fear, and He shall deliver you out of the hand of all your enemies" (2 Kings 17:39).

15 "Know then in your heart that, as a man chastises his son, the Lord your God chastises you. That you should keep the commandments of the Lord your God, and walk in His ways and fear Him" (Deuteronomy 8:5-6).

16 "Fear the Lord your God that you may keep all His statutes and His commandments" (Deuteronomy 6:2).

17 "Fear the Lord your God that you may walk in all His ways, and may love Him, and may serve the Lord your God with all your heart and with all your soul" (Deuteronomy 10:12).

18 "Oh that they had such a heart in them that they would fear Me, and keep all My commandments always, that it might be well with them, and with their children forever!" (Deuteronomy 5:29).

B

MEANS OF OBTAINING THE FEAR OF THE LORD

Prayer

1 "Teach me Your way, O Lord, and I will walk in Your truth; make my heart one to fear Your name" (Psalm 86:11).

2 "I will give them one heart, and one way, that they may fear Me forever . . . I will put my fear in their hearts, that they shall not depart from Me" (Jeremiah 32:39,40; Baruch 3:7).

Seeing the wonderful order, beauty, and immensity of God's Creation

3 "Observe the heavens . . . and every work of the Most High, and fear Him and work no evil in His presence" (Enoch 101:1).

4 "I will praise You, for I am fearfully and wonderfully made, marvelous are Your works, that my soul knows right well" (Psalm 139:14).

5 "From the greatness and beauty of created things is the Maker of them discovered" (Wisdom 13:5; Romans 1:20).

6 "Lift up your eyes on high and see: Who created these? . . . Have you not known? Have you not heard? The Lord is the everlasting God, the Creator of the ends of the earth" (Isaiah 40:26,28).

7   "When I see Your heavens, the work of Your fingers, the moon and the stars which You have established; what is man?" (Psalm 8:3-4).

8   "Fear before Him who created the foundations of the earth" (Targum on Isaiah 40:21).

Hearing and understanding the words of God

9   "I will make them hear My words, that they may learn to fear Me all the days that they shall live upon the earth, and that they may teach their children so" (Deuteronomy 4:10).

10   "You shall read this Law before Israel in their hearing . . . that they may hear, and that they may learn to fear the Lord your God, and be careful to do all the words of this Law, and that their children who have not known it may hear and learn to fear the Lord your God" (Deuteronomy 31:11,12,13).

11   "He shall write for himself in a book a copy of this Law . . . and it shall be with him and he shall read it all the days of his life, that he may learn to fear the Lord his God, and may keep all the words of this Law and these statutes, to do them" (Deuteronomy 17:18,19).

12   "One of the priests . . . came and dwelt in Bethel, and taught them how they should fear the Lord" (2 Kings 17:28).

13   "He has put a new song in my mouth, even praise to our God: many shall see it and fear, and shall trust in the Lord" (Psalm 40:3).

14   "And all men shall fear, and shall declare the work of God for they shall understand [SAKAL]* what He has done" (Psalm 64:9).

15   "When I understand [BIN], I am afraid of Him" (Job 23:15).

16   "Will you not understand so as to fear before Him who created the foundations of the earth?" (Targum on Isaiah 40:21).

17   Conversely: "Those who do not understand the Lord, who do not fear God" (2 Enoch 48:8).

Doing the commandments of God found in His Law

18   "Now, these are the commandments, the statutes, and the judgments which the Lord your God commanded to teach you, that you may do them . . . that you may fear the Lord your God" (Deuteronomy 6:1,2).

---

*SAKAL is the verbal form of the noun SEKEL ("skillful understanding"). All words derived from this verbal form will for the sake of uniformity be indicated by the verbal root SAKAL.

19 "Observe to do all the words of this Law that are written in this book that you may fear this glorious and fearful name: The LORD your God" (Deuteronomy 28:58).

20 "Then Zerubbabel the son of Shealtiel, and Joshua the son of Josedech the high priest, with all the remnant of the people obeyed the voice of the Lord their God, and the words of Haggai the prophet, as the Lord God had sent him and the people did fear before the Lord" (Haggai 1:12).

Seeing God's power manifested in His miracles

21 "For the Lord your God dried up the waters of the Jordan for you until you passed over, as the Lord your God did to the Red Sea, which He dried up for us until we passed over, so that all the people of the earth may know that the hand of the Lord is mighty; that you may fear the Lord your God forever" (Joshua 4:23-24).

22 "So Samuel called upon the Lord, and the Lord sent thunder and rain that day; and all the people greatly feared the Lord" (1 Samuel 12:18).

23 "So they took up Jonah and threw him into the sea [see vv.4,12]; and the sea ceased from its raging. Then the men feared the Lord exceedingly, and they offered a sacrifice to the Lord" (Jonah 1:16).

Seeing and experiencing the judgment of God and His justice

24 "The earth feared and was still, when God arose to judgment, to save all the meek of the earth" (Psalm 76:8,9).

25 "He shall judge the poor of the people, He shall save the children of the needy, and shall break in pieces the oppressor. They shall fear You as long as the sun and moon endure throughout all generations" (Psalm 72:4-5).

26 "According to their deeds, so will He repay, wrath to His adversaries, requital to His enemies; to the islands He will repay recompense. So they shall fear the name of the Lord" (Isaiah 59:18,19).

27 "Render to each, whose heart You know, according to all his ways . . . that they may fear You and walk in Your ways all the days that they shall live in the land" (2 Chronicles 6:30,31).

Seeing God's bountiful response
to our tithing and giving alms

28   "You shall tithe all the produce of your seed, which comes forth from the field year after year. And before the Lord your God, in the place which He will choose, to make His name dwell there, you shall eat the tithe of your grain, of your wine, and of your oil, and the firstlings of your herd and flock; that you may learn to fear the Lord your God always" (Deuteronomy 14:22-23).

29   "This people have a stubborn and rebellious heart; they have turned aside and gone away. They do not say in their hearts, 'Let us fear the Lord our God, who gives the rain in its season, the autumn and the spring rain and reserves for us the appointed weeks of the harvest'" (Jeremiah 5:23-24).

30   "He gave alms, and he increased in the fear of the Lord God" (Tobit 14:2).

C

THE TITLE OF GOD MANIFESTED IN ALL HIS POWER AND MAJESTY IS: "THE LORD OF HOSTS." IT IS ALSO HIS TITLE AS THE KING ENTHRONED TO DO JUDGMENT, AND TO SAVE; HENCE TO BE FEARED.

1   "Sanctify the Lord of Hosts Himself, and let Him be your fear and let Him be your dread" (Isaiah 8:13).

2   "I am a great King, says the Lord of Hosts, and My name is feared among the nations" (Malachi 1:14).

3   "The Lord of Hosts, He is the King of glory" (Psalm 24:10).

4   "Thus says the Lord the King . . . the Lord of Hosts" (Isaiah 44:6; 6:5).

5   "The Lord sits enthroned as King forever" (Psalm 29:10).

6   "There is One wise and greatly to be feared: the Lord sitting upon His throne" (Sirach 1:8).

7   "O Lord of Hosts, who tries the righteous, who sees the reins and the heart" (Jeremiah 20:12).

8   "O Lord . . . You sit on the throne judging righteously" (Psalm 9:1,4).

9   "Behold, God is the Judge, fear Him! depart from all your sins, and forget your iniquities never more to meddle with them" (2 Esdras 16:67).

10   "Do not fear those who kill the body but cannot kill the soul; rather fear Him who can destroy both body and soul in hell" (St. Matthew 10:28).

11   "Fear none but Him" (Proverbs 7:2, Greek Text).

12   "Fear Him who after he has killed has power to cast into hell, yes, I tell you, fear Him!" (St. Luke 12:5).

13   "Fear Him who has all power to save and to destroy" (Shepherd of Hermas, *Mand.* XII.6.49:3).

14   "There is one Lawgiver and Judge, He who is able to save and to destroy" (St. James 4:12).

15   "They who fear the Lord understand His judgment" (Sirach 32:16, Hebrew Text, MS.E).

16   "It is a fearful thing to fall into the hands of the living God" (Hebrews 10:31).

17   "Quickly [SPOUDE] get wisdom in the fear of the Lord!" (Testament of Levi 13:7).

D

THROUGH THE FEAR OF THE LORD WE DEPART FROM EVIL AND ARE RESTRAINED FROM SINNING. THE FEAR OF THE LORD LEADS US TO REPENTANCE AND PRESERVES US FROM WRATH.

Fear of God and departing from evil

1   "By the fear of the Lord men depart from evil" (Proverbs 16:6).

2   "Be not wise in your own eyes; fear the Lord and depart from evil" (Proverbs 3:7).

3   "And from his infancy he taught him to fear God, and to abstain from all sin" (Tobit 1:10, Latin Vulgate).

4   "And all nations shall turn, and fear the Lord God truly, and shall bury their idols" (Tobit 14:6, Greek Vaticanus Text).

5   "Fear God and depart from all sin and do that which is pleasing in His sight" (Tobit 4:21, Greek Vaticanus Text).

6   "To depart from evil is a thing pleasing to the Lord; and to forsake unrighteousness is an atonement" (Sirach 35:3, Hebrew Text [32:3 Greek Text]).

7   "Where there is not fear [of God] there is no wisdom" (Pirke Aboth 3:21).

8   "A wise man fears [God] and departs from evil" (Proverbs 14:16).

9   "He who keeps the Law is a wise son" (Proverbs 28:7).

10   "The highway of the upright is to depart from evil and he who keeps His way preserves his soul" (Proverbs 16:17).

11   "The Lord hates all abomination and they who fear God love it not" (Sirach 15:13).

12   "The fear of the Lord is to hate evil, pride, arrogancy, and the evil way and the perverted mouth" (Proverbs 8:13).

13   "The tongue . . . shall not have rule over them who fear God, neither shall they be burned by its flame" (Sirach 28:18,22).

Fear of God restrains

14   "Nothing more effectively preserves us from all sin than the fear of punishment and the fear of God" (St. Jerome in *Liber Scintillarum*, 12:42 [PL 88, pp.597-817]).

15   "I will put the fear of Me in their hearts so that they will not turn away from Me" (Jeremiah 32:40).

16   "Nothing guards our heart better than the fear of God" (Origen in *Commentary to Psalm* 140:3).

17   "God is come to prove you so that His fear may be before your eyes, that you do not sin" (Exodus 20:20).

18   "If you want to do evil, fear the Lord and you will not do it, but, on the other hand, if you want to do good, fear the Lord and you will do it" (Shepherd of Hermas, *Mand.* VII.37:4).

19   "The fear of God reproves us all the time and chases away sin, and suppresses vice. The fear of God renders a man prudent and attentive. Where there is no fear, there is a dissolute life. Where there is no fear, there is a life of crime" (St. Isidore, *Synonyma* 2:26 [PL 83:825-868].

20   "The fear of God drives away sins, and where it is present it turns away wrath" (Sirach 1:21, Greek Cursives 248,70,106,253; ibid. 1:27, Latin Vulgate).

Fear of God and repentance

21 "Fear [of God] . . . leads to repentance and hope" (Clement of Alexandria, *Strom.* II.c.9).

22 "He who fears the Lord will repent from his heart" (Sirach 21:6).

23 "Those men who draw near to Him through fear, He converts" (Clement of Alexandria, *Exh.* IX.87.3).

24 "Fear fell upon them all . . . many . . . now came and openly confessed their evil deeds" (Acts 19:17,18).

25 "Let us, as far as in us lies, practice the fear of God and strive to keep His commandments that we may rejoice in His judgments" (Clement of Alexandria, *Strom.* VII, ending).

E

THEY WHO FEAR THE LORD OBEY HIM AND KEEP HIS COMMANDMENTS, WALKING IN HIS WAYS AND SERVING HIM FAITHFULLY. THE GOOD ARE THEY WHO FEAR THE LORD.

Fear of God and Obedience

1 "They who fear the Lord will not disobey His word" (Sirach 2:15).

2 "Disobey not the fear of the Lord and do not come to Him with a double heart" (Sirach 1:28).

3 "Obey . . . in singleness of heart, fearing God, and whatsoever you do, do it wholeheartedly, as to the Lord" (Colossians 3:22,23).

4 "Obedient . . . with fear and trembling in singleness of your heart as unto Christ; not in the way of eye-service, as men pleasers, but as servants of Christ, doing the will of God from the heart" (Ephesians 6:5,6).

5 "Fear the Lord and the king and do not disobey either" (Proverbs 24:21).

Fear of God and the keeping of His commandments

6 "Whosoever fears Him and keeps His commandments will live to God" (Shepherd of Hermas, *Mand.* VII.37:4).

7 "O that there was such a heart in them, that they would fear Me, and keep all My commandments always" (Deuteronomy 5:29).

8 "Where there is fear of God there is observance of precepts" (St. Gregory of Nazianzus, *Orat.* 39.8 [PG 36, p.344]).

9 "They who fear the Lord keep His commandments" (Sirach 2:21, Latin Vulgate).

10 "Blessed is every one who fears the Lord and walks in His ways" (Psalm 128:1).

11 "Nothing is better than the fear of the Lord, and there is nothing sweeter than to keep the commandments of the Lord" (Sirach 23:27).

12 "Blessed is the man who fears the Lord and delights greatly in His commandments" (Psalm 112:1).

13 "I am a companion to all who fear You: to those who keep Your precepts" (Psalm 119:63).

14 "God asks nothing but for you to . . . fear Him . . . and to walk in every way that will lead you to please Him, to serve Him not half-heartedly but with the whole soul filled with the determination to love Him and to cling to His commandments and to honor justice" (Philo, *Spec.* I.299,300).

Fear of God and service to Him

15 "You shall fear the Lord your God and serve Him" (Deuteronomy 6:13).

16 "You shall reverence the Lord your God and Him only shall you serve" (St. Matthew 4:10; St. Luke 4:8).

17 "Fear the Lord and serve Him in sincerity and in Truth" (Joshua 24:14).

18 "Fear the Lord and serve Him in Truth with all your heart" (1 Samuel 12:24).

19 "You shall fear the Lord your God; you shall serve Him and cleave to Him" (Deuteronomy 10:20).

20 "If you will fear the Lord your God and serve Him and obey His voice and not rebel against the commandment of the Lord" (1 Samuel 12:14).

21 "Serve ye the Lord with fear and rejoice unto Him with trembling" (Psalm 2:11).

22 "Let us have grace whereby we may serve God well pleasingly with reverence and awe" (Hebrews 12:28).

23 "Blessed is he who fears God and serves Him" (2 Enoch 42:6, B Text).

Fear of God and fidelity to Him

24 "To fear the Lord . . . was created with the faithful in the womb" (Sirach 1:14).

25 "He was a faithful man and feared God more than many" (Nehemiah 7:2).

Fear of God and righteousness

26 "Behold, the fear of the Lord is wisdom" (Job 28:28, Hebrew Text).

27 "Behold, godliness [THEOSEBEIA] is wisdom" (Job 28:28, Greek Text).

28 "A righteous man, and one who fears God" (Acts 10:22).

29 "Be with a man who fears God continually whom you know to be one who keeps the commandments" (Sirach 37:12, Hebrew Text).

30 "Be continually with a godly [EUSEBOUS] man whom you know to keep the commandments of the Lord" (Sirach 37:12, Greek Text, Cursive 248).

31 "Be continually with a holy man whom you shall know to observe the fear of God" (Sirach 37:12 [12], Old Latin and Latin Vulgate Texts).

32 "Let your living be with a righteous man who fears to sin before God and whose heart is as your heart." (Sirach 37:12, Syriac Text).

33 "No evil shall happen to him who fears the Lord" (Sirach 33:1).

34 "No evil shall happen to the righteous" (Proverbs 12:21).

35 "The eye of the Lord is upon those who fear Him" (Psalm 33:18).

36 "The eyes of the Lord are upon the righteous" (Psalm 34:15).

Conversely, the wicked and the proud and hardened of heart, do not have the fear of the Lord.

37 "It shall not be well with the wicked, neither shall he prolong his days, which are as a shadow, because he does not fear before God" (Ecclesiastes 8:13).

38 "The wicked one . . . there is no fear of God before his eyes" (Psalm 36:1).

39 "A man that is wicked . . . he does not understand the fear of the Lord" (Sirach 23:23,31, Latin Vulgate).

40 "There is no one righteous, no, not even one, there is no one who understands . . . there is no fear of God before their eyes" (Romans 3:10,11,18).

41 "They are not humbled unto this day neither have they feared, nor walked in My Law, nor in My statutes" (Jeremiah 44:10).

42 "Be not high-minded but fear [God]" (Romans 11:20).

43 "Fools hate knowledge . . . they shall not find me because they hated knowledge, and did not choose the fear of the Lord" (Proverbs 1:22,28,29).

44 "Happy the man who always fears [God] but he who hardens his heart shall fall into evil" (Proverbs 28:14).

45 "For this reason godliness and peace are far removed because every one has abandoned the fear of God and has lost the clear vision which faith affords" (First Clement, *Epistle to Corinthians* 3:4).

F

THEY WHO FEAR THE LORD STRIVE TO DO HIS WILL AND PLEASE HIM. THE FEAR OF THE LORD LEADS US TO TRUST IN HIM AND MOVES US TO SEEK HIM SO THAT WE MAY KNOW AND SERVE HIM BETTER. THE FEAR OF GOD LEADS US TO THE LOVE OF THE LORD AND THE LOVE OF OUR NEIGHBOR. IT RENDERS US ACCEPTABLE TO GOD AND MERITS FOR US HIS FRIENDSHIP AND INSTRUCTION.

Fear of God and diligence

1 "He who fears God neglects nothing" (Ecclesiastes 7:19, Latin Vulgate).

2 "If you fear the Lord you will do everything well" (Shepherd of Hermas, *Mand.* VII.37:1).

3 "Thus shall you do in the fear of the Lord, faithfully and with a perfect heart" (2 Chronicles 19:9).

4 "Let the fear of the Lord be with you and do all things with diligence" (2 Chronicles 19:7, Latin Vulgate).

5 "Let all your works be done in order with good intent in the fear of God" (Testament of Naphtali 2:9).

Fear of God and pleasing Him

6 "Fear God and depart from all sin and do that which is pleasing in His sight" (Tobit 4:21, Greek Vaticanus and Alexandrinus Texts).

7   "They who fear the Lord will seek that which is wellpleasing to Him" (Sirach 2:16).

8   "The Lord takes pleasure in those who fear Him" (Psalm 147:11).

9   "Those who fear Him, He cherishes" (Psalms of Solomon 13:11, Syriac Text).

10 "He will fulfill the desire of those who fear Him; He will hear their cry and save them" (Psalm 145:19).

11 "The Lord hears the prayer of every one who fears God" (Psalms of Solomon 6:8).

12 "As a father pities his children, so the Lord pities those who fear Him, for He knows our frame; He remembers that we are dust" (Psalm 103:13,14).

Fear of God and trust in Him

13 "The Lord takes pleasure in those who fear Him; in those who hope for His mercy" (Psalm 147:11).

14 "The man who fears God and trusts in Him has possession of the whole fountain of joy" (St. Chrysostom, *De Anna. Hom.* XVIII.6 [PG 54]).

15 "You who fear the Lord, trust in the Lord" (Psalm 115:11).

Fear of God and seeking Him

16 "Do you not fear God and hasten to learn about Him?" (Clement of Alexandria, *Exh.* IX.82.3).

17 "We follow You with all our heart, we fear You and seek Your face" (Prayer of Azarias v.18).

18 "Those who have the fear of God, and seek after Him and Truth" (Shepherd of Hermas, *Mand.* X.1.40:6).

19 "Send Your fear upon all the nations that do not seek after You" (Sirach 36:2, Latin Vulgate).

20 "Send Your fear upon all the nations who have not known You" (Sirach 36:2, Syriac Text).

21 "They who fear the Lord will find Him" (Sirach 6:16).

Fear of God leads to the love of God

22 "Fear the Lord your God . . . love the Lord your God" (Deuteronomy 6:2,5).

23 "Fear of God is the beginning of wisdom and it takes us to the love of God, and from slaves that we are, it makes us children and beloved by God" (St. Gregory of Nazianzus, *Orat.* 21.6 [PG 36]).

24 "Fear of God is the gateway to Him. Only he who has gone through that gate can truly love Him, and in the manner in which only He can be loved" (Martin Buber, *For the Sake of Heaven* p.46).

25 "They who fear the Lord are a sure seed and they who love Him are an honorable plant" (Sirach 10:19, Greek Cursive 248).

26 "They who fear the Lord will not disobey His Word and they who love Him will keep His ways" (Sirach 2:15).

27 "They who fear the Lord will seek that which is well pleasing to Him and they who love Him will be filled with the Law" (Sirach 2:16).

28 "The eyes of the Lord are upon those who fear Him" (Sirach 34:19, Latin Vulgate).

29 "The eyes of the Lord are upon those who love Him" (Sirach 34:16, Greek Text).

30 "And now, Israel, what does the Lord your God require of you but to fear the Lord your God that you may walk in all His ways, and may love Him, and may serve the Lord your God with all your heart and with all your soul" (Deuteronomy 10:12, Hebrew Text).

31 "O fear the Lord, all ye His holy [QADOSH] ones" (Psalm 34:9).

32 "O love the Lord, all ye His godly [CHASID] ones" (Psalm 31:23).

Fear of God leads to love of our neighbor, and to good deeds

33 "Fear the Lord and love your neighbor . . . for he who fears God and loves his neighbor . . . shall be shielded by the fear of God . . . he is helped by the Lord through the love which he has towards his neighbor" (Testament of Benjamin 3:3,4,5).

34 "Remember the fear of God, and do not be angry with your neighbor" (Sirach 28:8, Latin Vulgate).

35 "The fear of God overcomes hatred for fearing lest one should offend the Lord, one will do no wrong to anyone even in his thoughts" (Testament of Gad 5:4,5).

36 "Where there is fear of God there is no envy" (St. Chrysostom, *De Anna. Hom.* XV.2).

37 "Deliverance from envy comes by the fear of God" (Testament of Simeon 3:4).

The fear of God leads to good deeds done
in a spirit of love towards our neighbor

38 "He who fears God will do good" (Sirach 15:1).

39 "The fear of God is not to omit the good that should be done" (St. Gregory, *Morals on Job*, Book I.3).

40 "Fear God and depart from all sin and do that which is good before the Lord your God" (Tobit 4:21, Greek Sinaiticus Text).

41 "Blessed is he who fears God and serves Him . . . blessed is he who judges a judgment justly to the widow and orphan, and helps every one who has been wronged, clothing the naked with garments, and feeding the hungry with bread" (2 Enoch 42:6,7-9 B Text, Slavonic).

42 "Where there is fear of God there is zeal in almsgiving, and intensity of prayer, and tears warm and frequent, and compunction. Nothing makes virtue more to increase and flourish than the perpetual fear of God" (St. Chrysostom, *De Anna. Hom.* XV.2 [PG 54]).

43 "He who fears God while he does the deeds of love, the bride Love is, as it were brought to the bridegroom Fear" (Clementine Homilies, Hom. XII.32 [PG 2]).

Fearing God and doing good works
makes us acceptable to the Lord

44 "The fear of the Lord is the first step to be accepted by Him" (Sirach 19:18, Greek Cursive 248).

45 "In every nation, he who fears Him and works righteousness, is acceptable to Him" (Acts 10:35).

Fear of God makes us beloved by Him,
and recipients of His Knowledge

46 "If you will, you can keep the commandments and perform acceptable faithfulness" (Sirach 15:15).

47 "For every one who does the Lord's Law will be loved by Him" (Testament of Joseph 11:1).

48 "Practice the fear of God and strive to keep His commandments" (Clement of Alexandria, *Strom.* VII.c.18).

49 "They who fear the Lord, keep His commandments" (Sirach 2:21, Latin Vulgate).

50 "For this is the love of God, that we keep His commandments" (1 John 5:3).

51 "He who has My commandments and keeps them, he it is who loves Me . . . and I will love him and manifest Myself to him" (St. John 14:21).

52 "You who fear the Lord, love Him, and your hearts shall be enlightened" (Sirach 2:10, Latin Vulgate).

53 "The love of the Lord surpasses all things for illumination" (Sirach 25:11, Greek Cursive 248).

54 "The illumination that fulfills all desire" (St. Gregory of Nazianzus, *Orat.* 39.6 [PG 36]).

55 "In illumination what we receive is knowledge" (Clement of Alexandria, *Paed.* I.6.29:3).

56 "The fear of the Lord is the beginning of knowledge" (Proverbs 1:7).

57 "From reverence comes knowledge, and from knowledge comes love" (Shepherd of Hermas, *Vision* III.8.16:7).

58 "With all your soul fear the Lord and . . . with all your strength love Him who made you" (Sirach 7:31,32, Latin Vulgate).

59 "The fear of the Lord is the beginning of His love" (Sirach 25:12, Greek Cursive 248).

G

THE HUMILITY, MEEKNESS AND FAITH OF THOSE WHO FEAR THE LORD, MAKES THEM DEAR TO HIM. AND BECAUSE THEY WHO FEAR THE LORD SEEK HIM, THEY ARE THE ONES WHOM THE LORD INSTRUCTS SO THAT THEY MAY LEARN TO KNOW AND LOVE HIM. THUS THE FEAR OF THE LORD LEADS TO WISDOM, UNDERSTANDING AND KNOWLEDGE.

The humility, meekness and faith of those who fear God
pleases Him and He teaches them His hidden things

1 "The fear of the Lord is wisdom and instruction; and faith and meekness are His delight" (Sirach 1:27; Berakoth 58b, BT).

2 "Hear the word of the Lord, you who tremble at His word" (Isaiah 66:5).

3 "Thus says the Lord . . . 'This is the man to whom I will look, he that is humble and contrite in spirit and trembles at My word'" (Isaiah 66:1,2).

4   "To the humble He shows favor" (Proverbs 3:34).

5   "His secret [SODH] is revealed to the humble" (Sirach 3:19, Hebrew Text).

6   "With the humble is wisdom" (Proverbs 11:2).

7   "The man Moses was very meek, more than all the men that were on the face of the earth . . . 'My servant Moses, he is faithful [AMAN] in all My house. With him I speak mouth to mouth clearly, and not in dark speech' " (Numbers 12:3,7,8).

8   "The meek will He guide in judgment, and the meek will He teach His way . . . Who is the man who fears the Lord? him shall He teach" (Psalm 25:9,12).

9   "In the meekness of wisdom" (St. James 3:13).

10 "His mysteries [MUSTERION] are revealed to the meek" (Sirach 3:19, Greek Sinaiticus Text and Cursives 248,106,253).

11 "Without faith it is impossible to please God" (Hebrews 11:6).

12 "Jesus . . . marvelled and said to those who followed Him, 'truly, I say to you, not even in Israel have I found such faith!' " (St. Matthew 8:10).

13 "O Lord . . . teach me good judgment and knowledge for I have believed" (Psalm 119:65,66).

14 "You have given Your understanding, O Lord, to Your believers" (Odes of Solomon 4:3).

15 "Through faith we understand" (Hebrews 11:3).

16 "Believe and understand" (Isaiah 43:10).

17 "Those who believe and fully know the truth" (1 Timothy 4:3).

18 "Believe . . . that you may know and continue to know" (St. John 10:38).

19 "The holy Scriptures which are able to make you wise unto salvation through faith in Christ Jesus" (2 Timothy 3:15).

20 "You . . . reveal what is hidden to the pure who in faith have submitted themselves to You and Your Law" (2 Baruch 54:5).

21 "The secrets of righteousness: the inheritance of faith" (Enoch 58:5).

22 It is "to men of faith" that the heavenly secrets are revealed (3 Enoch 48 D,v.10; Zohar I.37b; Alphabet of Rabbi Akiba 3:29).

23 "There is no knowledge without faith" (Clement of Alexandria, *Strom.* V.c.1).

24   "If you do not believe neither will you at all understand" (Isaiah 7:9, Greek, Syriac and Old Latin Texts).

25   "Before all, faith and the fear of God must take lead in your heart, then you will understand these things" (Theophilus, *Ad Autolycum* I.7).

The Lord reveals His secrets to those who believe and fear Him, and He manifests Himself to them

26   "The secret [SODH] of the Lord is for those who fear Him; He makes known to them His covenant" (Psalm 25:14).

27   "The Lord . . . shows Himself to those who have faith in Him" (Wisdom 1:1,2, Syriac and Latin Vulgate).

28   "Those who do faithfully [EMUNAH] are His delight" (Proverbs 12:22).

They who fear God seek after Him and strive to please Him. Having sought the Lord, they are instructed by Him and they understand.

29   "We follow You with all our heart, we fear You and seek Your face" (Prayer of Azarias v.18).

30   "The ones who have fear of God . . . seek after Him" (Shepherd of Hermas, *Mand.* X.1.40:6).

31   "They who fear the Lord will seek that which is well pleasing unto Him" (Sirach 2:16).

32   "He is a rewarder of those who diligently seek Him" (Hebrews 11:6).

33   "They who seek Him diligently will find favor" (Sirach 35:14, Greek Text).

34   "He who seeks God will receive instruction and he who overtakes [NASAG] Him early [SHACHAR] will receive an answer ['ANAH] and he who seeks God's good pleasure [CHEPHETS] will receive learning [LEQACH]" (Sirach 32:14, Hebrew Text).

35   "They who seek the Lord understand all things" (Proverbs 28:5).

36   "To those who sought Him, He has made to understand wisdom, and taught them the way of judgment" (Targum to Isaiah 40:14).

37   "It is great understanding [TEBUNAH] to do His good pleasure" (Sirach 15:15, Hebrew Text).

They who desire to obtain wisdom through the
instruction of the Lord must first have His holy Fear.
The fear of the Lord is the beginning and end of all wisdom.

38   "The truest [ALESTHESTATE] beginning of wisdom is the desire for instruction" (Wisdom 6:17).

39   "He will fulfill the desire of those who fear Him" (Psalm 145:19).

40   "Understand the fear of the Most High, and meditate upon His commandments continually and He shall make your heart to understand, and make you wise in that which you desire" (Sirach 6:36, Hebrew Text).

41   "Great is the wisdom of His instruction!" (Clement of Alexandria, *Paed.* I.8.74:3).

42   "You will fear Me and you will receive instruction . . . says the Lord" (Zephaniah 3:7,8).

43   "Whosoever fears the Lord will receive His instruction" (Sirach 32:14a, Greek Text).

44   "The fear of the Lord is the instruction of wisdom" (Proverbs 15:33).

45   "Where there is no fear [of God], there is no wisdom" (Pirke Aboth 3:21).

46   "The fear of the Lord is the beginning of wisdom: a good understanding have all they who do His commands" (Psalm 111:10).

47   "The fear of the Lord is the beginning of wisdom, and the knowledge of the holy is understanding" (Proverbs 9:10).

48   "The root of wisdom is to fear the Lord and the branches thereof are long life" (Sirach 1:20).

49   "The fear of the Lord is a crown of wisdom making peace and perfect health to flourish" (Sirach 1:18).

50   "The fear of the Lord is the fullness of wisdom" (Sirach 1:16).

51   "The fear of the Lord is all wisdom, and in all wisdom is the performance of the Law and the knowledge of His omnipotency" (Sirach 19:20, Greek Cursive 248).

52   "He who fears Me and fulfills the words of the Law, he has all wisdom and Law in his heart" (Midrash Rabbah to Deuteronomy 11.6).

53   "The perfect completion [SUNTELEIA] of the fear of the Lord is wisdom attained [PROSLEPHIS]" (Sirach 21:11, Greek Cursive 248).

54   "The perfection of the fear of God is wisdom and understanding" (Sirach 21:13, Latin Vulgate).

55   "Behold, the fear of the Lord, that is wisdom; and to depart from evil is understanding" (Job 28:28).

> WE MAY ATTAIN TO WISDOM THROUGH THE FEAR OF GOD,
> BUT WISDOM IN ALL HER RADIANT GLORY IS THE GIFT
> OF GOD TO THOSE WHO LOVE HIM SO THAT THEY MAY
> BEHOLD HIM IN HER LIGHT. THE LIGHT OF THE
> KNOWLEDGE OF GOD IS ALSO FOR THOSE WHO
> LOVE THE LORD AND DESIRE TO SEE HIM.

Glorious Wisdom is full of Light

56   "Wisdom is radiant and never fades away, she is easily seen by those who love her" (Wisdom 6:12).

57   "Wisdom is the brightness of eternal light, the unspotted mirror of the working of God, and the image of His goodness" (Wisdom 7:26).

58   "Wisdom is fairer than the sun and above all the order of the stars; being compared with light she is found superior" (Wisdom 7:29).

59   "Love the light of wisdom" (Wisdom 6:23, Latin Vulgate).

60   "I loved Wisdom . . . and chose to have her rather than light, because her radiance never ceases" (Wisdom 7:10).

61   "I will . . . bring the knowledge of wisdom to light" (Wisdom 6:22).

The light of knowledge

62   "He makes the teaching of knowledge appear as light" (Sirach 24:27, Greek Cursive 248).

63   "Lighting up the light of knowledge as the sun the day" (Testament of Levi 18:3).

64   "When the knowledge of the Existent One shines, it wraps everything in light" (Philo, *Ebr.* 44).

65   "Divine light is identical with knowledge" (Philo, *Mig.* 39).

66   "As light disperses the darkness, His knowledge will disperse . . . ignorance" (Philo, *Jos.* 06).

67   "She compares delusion to darkness and the knowledge of God to the sun and light" (Clement of Alexandria, *Exh.* VIII.77.3).

68   "He has poured forth from the fount of His knowledge, the light that enlightens me" (1QS 11:3, Dead Sea Scrolls).

69 "A torch to shine upon the world in knowledge" (1 QSb 4:27, Dead Sea Scrolls).

70 "Light ye for yourselves the light of knowledge" (Hosea 10:12, Greek and Syriac Texts and Targum).

> *"The brightness of wisdom . . . and the light of knowledge"*
> *[Sepher Ha Tappuach], are outright gifts of God to those*
> *who love Him, so that they may be able to behold Him.*

71 "Men . . . with wisdom . . . shall advance, even till they come to the sight of God" (Sirach 15:8, Latin Vulgate).

72 "If you desire Wisdom keep the commandments and the Lord shall give her unto you" (Sirach 1:25).

73 "For this is the love of God, that we keep His commandments" (1 John 5:3).

74 "He has given wisdom freely to those who love Him" (Sirach 1:10).

75 "To the godly He has given wisdom" (Sirach 43:33 and 50:29, Greek Cursives 248,55,70,254).

76 "For the chosen there shall be light . . . there shall be bestowed upon the chosen: wisdom" (Enoch 5:7,8).

77 "The love of the Lord is glorious wisdom, He imparts it to whom He appears, that they might behold Him" (Sirach 1:10c,d, Greek Cursives 70, 253).

78 "To the man who is good in His sight, God gives wisdom, and knowledge, and joy" (Ecclesiastes 2:26).

79 "Ye who fear the Lord, love Him and your hearts shall be enlightened" (Sirach 2:10, Latin Vulgate),

80 With "the light of knowledge" (Testament of Levi 4:3).

81 "Love . . . the Lord Jesus Christ" (1 Corinthians 16:22).

82 "Jesus Christ . . . has called you out of the darkness into His marvelous light" (1 Peter 2:5,9).

83 "The light of the knowledge of the glory of God in the face of Jesus Christ" (2 Corinthians 4:6).

84 "A holy man continues in wisdom as the sun" (Sirach 27:12, Latin Vulgate).

85 "Let those who love [`AHAB] Him be as the sun when he goes forth in his might"! (Judges 5:31).

86 "Those who are understanding [SAKAL-SUNIENTES] shall shine as the

brightness of the firmament; and they who turn many to righteousness, as the stars forever and ever" (Daniel 12:3, Hebrew and Greek Texts).

Even though we may have attained and been given all wisdom and understanding and knowledge, we must humbly realize that we cannot retain these His gifts unless we keep the fear of the Lord with us always.

87   "They who are wise shall be humble" (Enoch 5:8).

88   "A man who has learnt everything, only if he has the fear of sin is it all his" (Midrash Exodus Rabbah 30.14).

89   "Every one whose fear of sin precedes his wisdom, his wisdom endures" (Pirke Aboth 3:12).

90   "A [truly] wise man will fear [God] in everything" (Sirach 18:27).

91   "It is the quality of the righteous that although they have received God's assurance, they have never cast off the fear of Him" (Tanchuma B. Hukkat, 65b).

92   "But continued immoveable in the fear of God" (Tobit 2:14, Latin Vulgate).

93   "Be with a man who fears God continually, whom you know to be one who keeps the commandments" (Sirach 37:12, Hebrew Text).

94   "Be in the fear of the Lord all day long" (Proverbs 23:17).

95   "Happy the man who fears [God] always" (Proverbs 28:14).

96   "He who fears Me and carries out the precepts of the Law, in the heart of such a man is the entire Law and all wisdom" (Pesikta de Rab Kahana, Sup.I.2).

H

THE FEAR OF THE LORD GIVES US JOY, AND THE PROMISE OF LIFE IN THIS WORLD AND IN THE WORLD TO COME.

1   "The fear of the Lord delights the heart, and gives joy and gladness, and a long life" (Sirach 1:12).

2   "The fear of the Lord is . . . gladness and a crown of rejoicing" (Sirach 1:11).

3   "The man who fears God and trusts in Him, has possession of the whole fountain of joy" (St. Chrysostom, *De Anna. Hom.* XVIII.6 [PG 54]).

4   "The fear of the Lord leads to life, and he who has it rests satisfied, and shall not be visited with evil" (Proverbs 19:23).

5   "The fear of the Lord is a crown of wisdom making peace and perfect health to flourish" (Sirach 1:18).

6   "Fear the Lord your God . . . that your days may be prolonged . . . the Lord God commanded us . . . to fear the Lord our God, for our good always, that He might preserve us alive" (Deuteronomy 6:2,24).

7   "For the fear of the Lord is life" (Sirach 50:29, Hebrew Text).

8   "The fear of the Lord is a fountain of life that one may depart from the snares of death" (Proverbs 14:27).

9   "Whoever fears Him, and keeps His commandments will live to God . . . life with God belongs to those who fear Him, and keep His commandments" (Shepherd of Hermas, *Mand.* VII.37:4,5).

10   "For you who fear My name, the sun of righteousness shall arise with healing in its wings" (Malachi 4:2).

11   "Whosoever fears the Lord, it shall go well with him at the end; on the day of his death he shall find favor" (Sirach 1:13).

12   "The spirit of those who fear the Lord shall live, for their hope is in Him who saves them" (Sirach 34:13).

13   "They who fear the Lord shall rise to life eternal, and their life shall be in the light of the Lord, and they shall no more come to an end" (Psalms of Solomon 3:16[12]).

Conversely

14   "It will not be well with the wicked, neither shall he prolong his days, [which are] like a shadow, because he does not fear before God" (Ecclesiastes 8:13).

15   "He who is without fear [of the Lord] shall dwell in places where knowledge is not seen" (Proverbs 19:23, Greek Text).

I

THE FEAR OF THE LORD GIVES US COURAGE, IT PROTECTS AND DELIVERS US FROM EVIL.

1   "In the fear of the Lord is strong confidence" (Proverbs 14:26).

2   "He who fears the Lord shall tremble at nothing, and shall not be afraid, for He is his hope" (Sirach 34:16, Latin Vulgate).

3   "The fear of the Lord produces absence of fear" (Clement of Alexandria, *Strom.* II.c.9).

4   "Phineas, the son of Eleazar . . . had zeal in the fear of the Lord, and stood up with good courage of heart" (Sirach 45:23).

5   "The angel of the Lord encamps around those who fear Him and delivers them" (Psalm 34:7).

6   "You have given a banner to those who fear You" (Psalm 60:4).

7   "Nothing guards our heart better than the fear of God" (Origen in *Comm. to Psalm* 140:3).

8   "Sanctify the Lord of Hosts Himself, and let Him be your fear and let Him be your dread, and He shall be as a sanctuary" (Isaiah 8:13,14).

9   "The eyes of the Lord are upon them who fear Him, He is their powerful Protector and a strong support, a defence from the heat, and a cover from the sun at noon" (Sirach 34:19, Latin Vulgate; see also Malachi 4:2).

10 "He who fears God shall come forth from them all [troubles]" (Ecclesiastes 7:18).

11 "It will be well with those who fear God, because they fear before Him" (Ecclesiastes 8:12).

12 "No evil shall happen to him who fears the Lord, but in his temptation he shall be delivered again and again" (Sirach 33:1).

13 "The fear of the Lord drives away sins, and where it is present it turns away wrath" (Sirach 1:21, Greek Cursives 248,70,106,253; ibid. 1:27, Latin Vulgate).

14 "His salvation is close to them who fear Him" (Psalm 85:9).

15 "Whoever among you fears God, to you is the word of this salvation sent" (Acts 13:26).

16 "There is no want in the fear of the Lord and it does not need to seek help" (Sirach 40:26).

17   "O fear the Lord, you His holy ones, for there is no want to those who fear Him" (Psalm 34:9).

J

THE FEAR OF THE LORD IS THE CROWN OF THE HUMBLE AND MEEK. THERE IS GREAT GLORY IN THE FEAR OF GOD BECAUSE THE LORD HONORS THOSE WHO FEAR HIM. THE FEAR OF THE LORD IS HIS TREASURY, AND IN IT ARE ALL HIS OTHER GIFTS TO US.

1   "The crown of humility is the fear of God" (Derek Eretz Zuta V.4, BT).

2   "The fear of the Lord is the imprint of humility" (Shabbath I.5,f.3c,1.17 [JT]).

3   "The fruit of humility is the fear of the Lord" (Proverbs 22:4, Latin Vulgate).

4   "The fear of God goes before the obtaining of authority" (Sirach 10:21, Greek Cursives 248,106).

5   "He who rules over men must be just, ruling in the fear of God" (2 Samuel 23:3).

6   "You shall choose out of all the people able men, who fear God, men of truth who hate covetousness; and place such men over the people as rulers of thousands" (Exodus 18:21).

7   "The seed of men who fear God shall be honored" (Sirach 10:23, Latin Vulgate).

8   "He who fears the Lord is honored among His people" (Sirach 10:20, Hebrew Text).

9   "Let your glorying be in the fear of the Lord" (Sirach 9:16).

10   "Whether he be rich, noble, or poor, their glory is the fear of the Lord" (Sirach 10:22).

11   "This is great wealth, this is treasure: if we have the fear of God, we lack nothing, if we do not have it though we have royalty itself, we are the poorest of all men. Nothing is like the man who fears the Lord, for 'the fear of the Lord surpasses all things' [Sirach 25:11], let us do everything we can to obtain this fear" (St. Chrysostom *Hom.* III.24 [on the Epistle to the Philippians re 1:18-20]).

12   "The great man, and the judge, and the mighty man shall be glorified, yet there is none of them greater than he who fears the Lord" (Sirach 10:24).

13   "The fear of the Lord is honor, glory and happiness and a crown of joyfulness" (Sirach 1:11).

14   "Much experience is the crown of old men, and the fear of the Lord is their glory" (Sirach 25:6).

15   "They who remain shall know that there is nothing better than the fear of the Lord, and that there is nothing sweeter than to observe the commandments of the Lord" (Sirach 23:27).

16   "How great is he who finds wisdom, but there is no one above him who fears the Lord" (Sirach 25:10).

17   "There is none greater than he who fears God, he shall be more glorious in time to come" (2 Enoch 43:3, Slavonic A Text).

18   "He who fears the Lord shall be great forever" (Judith 16:16).

19   "As he that is chief is honorable among brothers, so are they who fear the Lord in His eyes" (Sirach 10:20).

20   "He [God] honors them who fear the Lord" (Psalm 15:4).

21   "The God-fearing man, the whole world was created for his sake, he is equal in worth to the whole world" (Berakoth, 6b, BT).

22   "The fear of the Lord is His treasury" (Isaiah 33:6).

K

THE FEAR OF THE LORD IS HIS GREAT GIFT TO US SO THAT WE MAY BE FILLED WITH AWE BEFORE HIM AND REJOICE IN THE GREATNESS OF HIS WORKS. THE LORD PLACES THE TREASURE OF HIS HOLY FEAR IN OUR HEARTS, THAT WE MAY SING PRAISES TO HIS GLORY.

1   "For this cause You have put Your fear in our hearts, to the intent that we should call upon Your name and praise You" (Baruch 3:7).

2   "Make my heart one to fear Your name, I will praise You, O Lord my God, with all my heart, and I will glorify Your name forevermore" (Psalm 86:11,12).

3   "Who shall not fear You, O Lord, and glorify Your name?" (Revelation 15:4).

4   "You who fear the Lord, praise Him" (Psalm 22:23).

5   "Tobit increased in the fear of the Lord God, and praised Him" (Tobit 14:2).

6   "Praise our God, all you His servants who fear Him, both the little and the great!" (Revelation 19:5).

7   "You who fear the Lord praise God with understanding" (Psalms of Solomon 2:37[33]).

L

MISCELLANEOUS TEXTS FOR THE PROLOGUE

1   "O Lord, why have You made us err from Your ways, and hardened our heart, so that we do not fear You?" (Isaiah 63:17).

2   "Take heed, brethren, lest there be in you an evil heart of unbelief in departing from the living God; but exhort one another daily while it is called 'Today', lest any of you be hardened through the deceitfulness of sin" (Hebrews 3:12-13).

3   "Hereby do we know that we know Him, if we keep His commandments" (1 John 2:3).

4   "Behold, as the eyes of servants look to the hands of their master, as the eyes of a maid to the hand of her mistress; so our eyes look to the Lord our God" (Psalm 123:2).

5   "The Lord is righteous in all His ways, and kind in all his deeds" (Psalm 145:17).

6   "You are to cleave to the Lord your God, as you have done to this day" (Joshua 23:8).

PROLOGUE
TO
WISDOM

B-2	'All wisdom comes from the Lord and is with Him forever.'
B-4	'With Him is wisdom and strength, He has counsel and understanding.'
B-7	'Great is the wisdom of the Lord, He is mighty in power and beholds all things, and His eyes are upon those who fear Him, and He knows
A-5	every work of man.' 'Who of those who are born has ever found the beginning or end of Your wisdom?'
B-10	'Among all the wise ones of the nations, and in all their kingdoms,
B-9	there is no one like You': 'the only wise God.'
B-23	'O Lord, how manifold are Your works! In wisdom You have made them all; the earth is full of Your possessions.'
B-19	'The Lord by wisdom has founded the earth, and by understanding He has established the heavens.'
C-14	'The Lord has made all things, and to the godly He has given wisdom';
C-22	'He has given wisdom to those who love Him.'
C-12	'God gives to a man who is good in His sight wisdom, and knowledge, and joy.'
C-45	'O God . . . give me Wisdom who sits by Your throne.'
B-5	For 'with You is Wisdom, who knows Your works and was present when You made the world, and who understands what is pleasing in Your sight.'
B-6	'Wisdom does not depart from the place of Your throne, nor turns away from Your presence.'
B-16	'The Lord Himself created Wisdom.'
B-15	'Wisdom came forth from God.'
B-17	'Wisdom came out of the mouth of the Most High and covered the earth like a mist.'
B-24	'The wisdom which is in this world . . . is the work of God.'
C-46	'O God . . . send Wisdom forth out of the holy heavens, and dispatch her from the throne of Your glory, that being present she may labour with me, and that I may know that is pleasing to You. For Wisdom knows and understands all things, and she will guide me in my actions prudently and guard me in her glory.'
C-41	'For what man can know the counsel of God? Or who can conceive what the Lord wills?':
C-42	'Unless You have given Wisdom, and sent Your Holy Spirit from on high.'

C-48	'If any of you lacks wisdom, let him ask God, who gives to all men generously and without reproaching, and it will be given him.'
C-47	'I prayed, and understanding was given me; I called upon God, and the spirit of wisdom came to me.'
D-1	Then I knew, that 'the source of wisdom is the Word of God.'
D-12	And that 'he who has knowledge of the Law will obtain wisdom', provided that he keeps and does what the Law of the Lord commands.
C-29	Because 'all wisdom is in the performance of the Law.'
C-31	Thus it is written: 'Through Your commandments You have made me wiser.'
C-30	'The love of Wisdom is the keeping of her Laws.'
D-34	'They who have rejected the Word of the Lord, what
D-35	wisdom is in them?' 'He is not wise who hates the Law.'
D-16	'A wise man hates not the Law,' but loves it, for he knows that,
D-10	'wisdom is contained in the teaching of the Law, by means of which we learn divine things reverently, and human things profitably.'
D-18	'The Holy Scriptures are able to make you wise unto salvation through faith' in Him.
D-30	'Blessed is the one who meditates on these things, and the person who lays them to heart shall become wise.'
D-25	'Let your understanding be upon the commands of the Lord, and meditate continually on His commandments, and He shall establish your heart and make you wise in that which you desire.'
C-28	'If you desire Wisdom, keep the commandments, and the Lord shall give her unto you.'
V-6	'Love Wisdom.'
E-1	For 'the Lord of all things Himself loved Wisdom' and
V-7	'In the love of Wisdom is good delight.'
T-8	'Come to Wisdom with all your soul, and keep her ways with all your might.'
C-30	Remember that 'the love of Wisdom is the keeping of her Laws.'
V-6	'Love Wisdom, and she shall keep you' for you have kept her wise words.
E-21	'Be therefore wise in God . . . that the Lord may love you' for
E-20	'Wisdom obtains His love';
E-2	And 'the Lord loves those who love Wisdom.'

We seek whom we love.

V-18   'Wisdom is easily seen by those who love her, and found by those who seek her' with all the love of their hearts.

V-14   'Wisdom is near to those who seek her, and he that gives his desire to her shall find her.'

V-15   For 'Wisdom hastens to make herself known to those who desire her.'

V-16   'Whoever rises early to seek her will have no difficulty, for he will find her sitting at his doors.'

V-17   Because 'Wisdom goes about seeking those who are worthy of her, and she graciously appears to them' who look for her, with love and desire in their eyes and in their hearts.

V-12   I heard Wisdom cry: 'Come to me all you who desire me, and be filled with my fruits.'

V-30   And so, I desired Wisdom, and 'I went about seeking how to take her for myself,'

V-28   because 'my soul longed with desire for Wisdom,' and

V-29   'My inmost being yearned for Wisdom to look upon her.'

V-25   'I desired to make Wisdom my spouse, and I became enamoured of her beauty' —

V-32   'but I knew that I could not take her unless God gave her to me.' Therefore I determined to keep the ways of the Lord, for God gives Wisdom only to those who are worthy of her.

C-28
P-12   'If you desire Wisdom, keep the commandments and the Lord shall give her unto you' and 'you shall embrace her.'

But first of all fear the Lord!

C-24   For 'the fear of the Lord is the beginning of wisdom.'

And be good.

C-12   Because to one 'who is good in His sight, God gives wisdom, and knowledge, and joy.'

Be true, and speak the truth.

C-40   For 'men who speak the truth shall be found with Wisdom.'

And be pure.

W-2,C-38   For 'the Wisdom that is from above is first of all chaste' — 'and

C-33   sinners shall not see her' — 'because Wisdom will not enter a deceitful soul, nor dwell in a body enslaved to sin.'

U-52   'Through purity I found Wisdom,' and saw her in:

W-18   'wise souls pure as virgins.'

V-4   'Follow after and pursue the genuine and unmated virgin: the Wisdom of God.'

53

U-47	'O the happiness of a man who finds wisdom!'
C-46,N-4	For 'Wisdom knows and understands all things' and 'Wisdom orders all things graciously.'
B-5	But most of all because 'Wisdom . . . understands what is well pleasing', before the eyes of the Lord.
X-1	And 'it is Wisdom who teaches the knowledge of God' to us.
C-46	'O God . . . send Wisdom forth out of the holy heavens . . . that being present she may labour with me . . . and so shall my works be acceptable' to You.
N-32,5	For 'wisdom is profitable to direct' every endeavor, and 'wisdom harmonizes and fits together to bring about equality and unity' in all that we do.
N-50	'Wisdom is right guidance.'
N-11	And 'Wisdom who is the artificer of all things' shall teach us how to do something beautiful for God.
P-18	'Wisdom is radiant.'
U-33	'If riches be a possession to be desired in life, what is richer than Wisdom who works all things gainfully?' Or what is more
P-2	desirable than: 'His glorious wisdom'?
E-19	'Wisdom is an unfailing treasure for mankind.'
U-20	'Wisdom is better than jewels, and all things that you can desire are not to be compared to her.'
	Wisdom is incomparable.
E-19	Because 'those who get wisdom obtain friendship with God';
E-18	'Wisdom makes them beloved by God.'
E-4	'Even if one be perfect among the children of men, yet if the wisdom which comes from You be not with him, he shall be held of no account.'
E-3	'For God loves nothing so much as the man who lives with Wisdom.'
	Wisdom may walk with the good and perfect but Wisdom lives only with those who desire to give glory to God.
Q-6	They who live with Wisdom shall truly know her 'and the excellence of the knowledge of Wisdom is that it gives life to him who has it.'
Q-3	'He who loves wisdom loves life' and has it now and forever, because,
R-3	'By means of wisdom we shall obtain immortality.'

Q-1 R-1	Wisdom cried out: 'In me is all grace of the way and of the truth, in me is all hope of life, and of virtue.' 'I being eternal am given to all my children, to those who are named by Him.'
N-30, Q-3 Q-9	'Wisdom teaches her children' and 'Wisdom inspires life into her children,' and feeds them 'the bread of life and understanding' day by day.
R-2,4	'In kinship with Wisdom there is immortality,' for 'in the keeping of Wisdom's Laws is the assurance of incorruption, and incorruption makes us to be near to God.'
T-2,E-27 Y-1 R-b,a	'Wisdom's ways are everlasting commandments,' and 'it shall be our righteousness if we observe to do all these commandments before the Lord our God, as He has commanded us.' 'Whoever . . . keeps His commandments will live to God,' because 'righteousness is immortal,' and 'righteousness leads to life.'
V-19, T-8 V-21 Q-4	'Draw near to Wisdom,' and 'come unto Wisdom with all your soul.' 'And when you have taken hold of Wisdom, do not let her go,' for 'Wisdom is a tree of life to those who take hold of her,' and they shall increase in strength.
Q-12 Q-13	'Wisdom will strengthen him' who holds her fast, because 'Wisdom herself shall be made strong in him, and he shall not be moved.'
Q-11 Q-14	Thus, 'Wisdom strengthens the wise more than ten mighty men.' 'A wise man is strong,' indeed.
 C-36	If we want to lay hold upon Wisdom we must depart from evil, for 'To depart from evil is understanding'; and it is through our understanding that we shall be able to grasp, hold fast, and know Wisdom.
Y-2, G-12 E-16 C-34,35 C-38	'Understand first' that 'every man of understanding knows Wisdom,' because 'a man of understanding is faithful to the Law of God.' 'The wicked do not understand,' and 'evil men do not understand' that 'men without understanding will not be able to seize Wisdom.'
V-21 V-23 V-24	'When you have taken hold of Wisdom, do not let her go.' 'Cleave unto Wisdom that you may prove yourself wise.' For 'he who masters Wisdom shall teach her.'
D-9 D-8	There was a Man who mastered Wisdom, and in Him 'are hidden all the treasures of wisdom and knowledge.' Cleave to Jesus: 'the Power of God, and the Wisdom of God.'

WISDOM

SCRIPTURAL, APOCRYPHAL, PATRISTIC,

RABBINIC AND OTHER ANCIENT TEXTS

on

WISDOM

A

INTRODUCTION

1   'What Wisdom is, and how she came into being, I will declare, and will not conceal from you mysteries, but will trace Wisdom out from the beginning of creation, and bring into light the knowledge of her" (Wisdom 6:22).

2   "Who can find out the height of heaven, and the breadth of the earth, and the deep, and Wisdom?" (Sirach 1:3).

3   "To whom has the root of Wisdom been revealed? Or who has known her devices?" (Sirach 1:6).

4   "Unto whom has the knowledge of Wisdom been manifest? And who has understood her wide experience?" (Sirach 1:7, Greek Cursives 23,55,70,106, 253, and Old Latin Texts).

5   "Who of those who are born has ever found out the beginning or end of Your wisdom?" (2 Baruch 14:9).

B

ALL WISDOM COMES FROM GOD AND IS WITH HIM FOREVER. ONLY GOD IS TRULY WISE, AND BY HIS WISDOM HE HAS FOUNDED AND ESTABLISHED THE EARTH.

From God is all wisdom; and Wisdom is with Him forever.

1   "Where does wisdom come from?" (Job 28:20).

2   "All wisdom comes from the Lord and is with Him forever" (Sirach 1:1).

3   "The Lord of wisdom" (Enoch 63:2).

4   "With Him is wisdom and strength, He has counsel and understanding" (Job 12:13).

5   "With You is Wisdom who knows Your works and was present when You made the world, and who understands what is pleasing in Your sight" (Wisdom 9:9).

6   "Wisdom does not depart from the place of Your throne nor turn away from Your Presence" (Enoch 84:3).

7   "Great is the wisdom of the Lord, He is mighty in power and beholds all things, and His eyes are upon those who fear Him, and He knows every work of man" (Sirach 15:18-19).

8   "Blessed be the name of God forever and ever, for wisdom and might are His" (Daniel 2:20).

God alone is truly wise.

9   "The only wise God" (Romans 16:27).

10   "Among all the wise ones of the nations, and in all their kingdoms, there is no one like You" (Jeremiah 10:7).

11   "God alone is wise, from whom comes wisdom" (Clement of Alexandria, *Paed.* I.10.93:3).

God created Wisdom, and poured her forth upon all His works.

12   "Wisdom has been created before all things" (Sirach 1:4).

13   "He created me [Wisdom] from the beginning before the world, and from eternity I shall not cease to exist" (Sirach 24:9).

14   "The Lord possessed me [Wisdom] at the beginning of His way, before His works of old" (Proverbs 8:22).

15   "Wisdom came forth from God" (Sirach 15:10, Latin Vulgate).

16   "The Lord Himself created Wisdom, and saw her, and numbered her, and poured her out upon all His works" (Sirach 1:9).

17   "Wisdom came out of the mouth of the Most High and covered the earth like a mist" (Sirach 24:3).

18   "Wisdom is a vapour of the power of God, and a pure effluence of the glory of the Almighty, therefore no defiled thing comes into her" (Wisdom 7:25).

By His wisdom He has founded and established the earth.

19   "The Lord by wisdom has founded the earth, and by understanding He has established the heavens" (Proverbs 3:19).

20   "In Your wisdom You have founded the world" (1QH 1:7, Dead Sea Scrolls).

21 "He has established the world by His wisdom" (Jeremiah 10:12; 51:15).

22 "Establishing the world by His wisdom" (11QPsᵃ XXVI.7, Dead Sea Scrolls).

23 "O Lord how manifold are Your works! In wisdom You have made them all; the earth is full of Your possessions" (Psalm 104:24).

24 "The wisdom which is in the world . . . is the work of God." (Philo, *Q.Gen.* I.11).

C

IT IS GOD WHO GIVES WISDOM TO MAN. HE GRANTS WISDOM TO THE RIGHTEOUS WHO REVERENCE HIM AND WHO KEEP HIS COMMANDMENTS. IF WE DESIRE WISDOM WE SHOULD PRAY TO THE LORD TO GIVE US THE GIFT OF HIS WISDOM.

1 "Who has put wisdom in the inward parts?" (Job 38:36).

2 "Who has given understanding and wisdom to everything that moves in the earth and in the sea?" (Enoch 101:8).

3 "Who . . . makes us wiser than the birds of the heavens?" (Job 35:11).

It is God who gives us wisdom.

4 "The Lord gives wisdom; out of His mouth comes knowledge and understanding" (Proverbs 2:6).

5 "Wisdom, insight and understanding of words come from the Lord" (Sirach 11:15, Hebrew Text).

6 "He has created and given to man the power of understanding the word of wisdom" (Enoch 14:3).

7 "It is from God that a physician is wise" (Sirach 38:2, Hebrew Text).

8 "God gave Solomon wisdom and understanding exceeding much" (1 Kings 4:29).

9 "The Lord gave Solomon wisdom as He promised him, and there was peace" (1 Kings 5:12).

10 "I [Wisdom] therefore, being eternal, am given [by God] to all my children who are named by Him" (Sirach 24:18, Greek Cursives 248,70).

11 "God gives wisdom to the wise, and knowledge to them who know understanding" (Daniel 2:21).

God gives wisdom to the righteous

12 "God gives to a man who is good in His sight wisdom, and knowledge, and joy" (Ecclesiastes 2:26).

13 "Unto the godly He gives wisdom" (Sirach 50:29, Greek Cursives 248,55,70, 254).

14 "Everything has the Lord made, and to the godly He has given wisdom" (Sirach 43:33).

15 "The discourse of the godly is always with wisdom" (Sirach 27:11).

16 "Wisdom . . . entering into *holy* souls makes them beloved by God and prophets" (Wisdom 7:24,27).

17 "There is wisdom in the *good* heart of a man" (Proverbs 14:33, Greek Text).

18 "There shall be bestowed upon the chosen: wisdom" (Enoch 5:8).

19 "Behold, godliness is wisdom" (Job 28:28, Greek Text).

20 "For this is the love of God, that we keep His commandments" (1 John 5:3).

21 "He who has My commandments and keeps them, he it is who loves Me" (St. John 14:21).

22 "He has given wisdom to those who love Him" (Sirach 1:10b).

23 "The love of the Lord is glorious wisdom, He imparts it to those to whom He appears so that they might behold Him" (Sirach 1:10c,d, Greek Cursives 70,253).

The Lord gives Wisdom to the righteous
who reverence Him and do His commandments.

24 "The fear of the Lord is the beginning of wisdom" (Proverbs 9:10; Psalm 111:10).

25 "Where there is no fear [of God], there is no wisdom" (Pirke Aboth 3:21).

26 "To fear the Lord is the beginning of Wisdom; she [Wisdom] is created with the faithful in the womb" (Sirach 1:14).

27 "They who fear the Lord keep His commandments" (Sirach 2:21, Latin Vulgate).

28 "If you desire Wisdom, keep the commandments and the Lord shall give her unto you" (Sirach 1:25).

29 "All wisdom is in the performance of the Law" (Sirach 19:20).

30 "The love of Wisdom is the keeping of her Laws" (Wisdom 6:18).

31 "Your commandments have made me wiser than my enemies for they are ever with me" (Psalm 119:98).

32 "Keep therefore and do them [His Commandments], for this is your wisdom and your understanding in the sight of the nations" (Deuteronomy 4:6).

Conversely

33 "Wisdom will not enter a deceitful soul, nor dwell in a body enslaved to sin" (Wisdom 1:4).

34 "The wicked do not understand" (Proverbs 29:7).

35 "Evil men do not understand" (Proverbs 28:5).

36 Because "to depart from evil is understanding" (Job 28:28).

37 "A good understanding have all those who do His commands" (Psalm 111:10).

38 "Men without understanding will not be able to seize Wisdom, and sinners shall not see her" (Sirach 15:7, Greek Text, Literal Translation).

39 "Wisdom is far from pride and men who are liars cannot remember her" (Sirach 15:8).

40 "But men who speak the truth shall be found with Wisdom" (Sirach 15:8, Latin Vulgate).

We should pray to the Lord for the gift of wisdom.

41 "For what man can know the counsel of God? Or who can conceive what the Lord wills?" (Wisdom 9:13).

42 "Who has known Your counsel unless You have given Wisdom and sent Your Holy Spirit from on high? And thus the paths of those on earth were set straight, and men were taught the things that are pleasing to You and were saved by Your Wisdom" (Wisdom 9:17-18).

43 "Wisdom . . . understands what is pleasing in Your sight" (Wisdom 9:9).

44   "While I was still young before I went on my travels, I sought Wisdom openly in my prayer. Before the temple I asked for her, and I will seek her out even to the end" (Sirach 51:13-14).

45   "I prayed to the Lord and begged Him, and with my whole heart I said, O God . . . give me Wisdom who sits by Your throne, and do not reject me from among Your children" (Wisdom 8:21; 9:1,4).

46   "O God . . . send Wisdom out of the holy heavens and dispatch her from the throne of Your glory that being present she may labour with me, and that I may know what is pleasing to You. For wisdom knows and understands all things and she will guide me in my actions prudently and guard me in her glory. And so shall my works be acceptable" (Wisdom 9:1,10-12).

47   "I prayed and understanding was given me; I called upon God and the spirit of wisdom came to me" (Wisdom 7:7).

48   "If any of you lacks wisdom, let him ask of God who gives to all men generously, and without reproaching, and it will be given him" (St. James 1:5).

49   "That the God of our Lord Jesus Christ, the Father of glory, may give you the spirit of wisdom and revelation in the knowledge of Him" (Ephesians 1:17).

50   "God give you wisdom in your heart" (Sirach 45:26).

51   "May He grant you wisdom of heart, and may there be peace" (Sirach 50:23, Hebrew Text).

52   And may the Lord say: "Behold . . . I have given you a wise and understanding heart" (1 Kings 3:12).

53   "Wisdom and knowledge are granted to you" (2 Chronicles 1:12).

54   "I have given wisdom to you, and to your children" (Enoch 82:2).

55   "From You comes victory, from You comes wisdom, and Yours is the glory" (1 Esdras 4:59).

56   "Blessed are You who have given me wisdom" (1 Esdras 4:60).

57   "Till the present day such wisdom has never been given by the Lord of Spirits as I have received according to my understanding" (Enoch 37:4).

D

GOD USUALLY GIVES WISDOM TO US THROUGH HIS WORD, AND HIS LAW AND COMMANDMENTS.

1 "The source of wisdom is the Word of God on High" (Sirach 1:5, Greek Cursives 248,23,55,70,106,253; ibid. Latin Vulgate, Syro-Hexaplar and Sahidic Texts).

2 "They found it to be a dictum of God that it is the divine Word from which all kinds of instruction and wisdom flow in a perpetual stream" (Philo, *Fug.* 137).

3 "In the beginning was the Word, and Word was with God, and the Word was God" (St. John 1:1).

4 "The Word was made flesh, and dwelt among us, and we beheld His glory, glory as of the only begotten from the Father, full of grace and truth" (St. John 1:14).

5 "We have heard, what we have seen with our eyes, what we have looked upon, and our hands have handled, concerning the Word of life . . . His [God's] Son, Jesus Christ" (1 John 1:1,3).

6 "His name [Jesus, the Lamb of God] is called: the Word of God" (Revelation 19:13).

7 "The Father, the Word [Jesus, Son of God], and the Holy Spirit are One" (1 John 5:7).

8 "Christ, the Power of God and the Wisdom of God" (1 Corinthians 1:24).

9 "Christ, in whom are hid all the treasures of wisdom and knowledge" (Colossians 2:2,3).

10 "Wisdom . . . is contained in the teaching of the Law, by means of which we learn divine things reverently, and human things profitably" (4 Maccabees 1:16,17).

11 "Wisdom is the knowledge of divine and human things and their causes" (4 Maccabees 1:16).

12 "He who has knowledge of the Law will obtain wisdom" (Sirach 15:1, Greek Cursive 248).

13 "All wisdom is in the performance of the Law" (Sirach 19:20).

14 "The love of Wisdom is the keeping of her Laws" (Wisdom 6:18).

15   "He who keeps the Law is a wise son" (Proverbs 28:7, Latin Vulgate).

16   "A wise man hates not the law" (Sirach 33:2).

17   "They read the Holy Scriptures and seek wisdom" (Philo, *Cont.* 28).

18   "The Holy Scriptures are able to make you wise unto salvation through faith which is in Christ Jesus" (2 Timothy 3:15).

19   "If you desire Wisdom, keep the commandments and the Lord shall give her unto you" (Sirach 1:25).

20   "Your commandments have made me wiser than my enemies for they are ever with me" (Psalm 119:98).

21   "Through Your precepts I get understanding" (Psalm 119:104).

22   "I understand more than the ancients because I keep Your precepts" (Psalm 119:100).

23   "Keep therefore and do them [His commandments, precepts and statutes], for this is your wisdom and your understanding in the sight of the nations, who will hear all these statutes and say, 'surely this great nation is a wise and understanding people'" (Deuteronomy 4:6).

24   "A good understanding have all those who do His commandments" (Psalm 111:10).

25   "Let your understanding be upon the ordinances of the Lord and meditate on His commandments continually and He shall establish your heart, and make you wise in that which you desire" (Sirach 6:37).

26   "He who keeps the Law gets the understanding thereof" (Sirach 21:11).

27   "Observe to do according to all the Law which Moses My servant commanded you: do not turn from it to the right or to the left so that you may understand [SAKAL]" (Joshua 1:7).

28   "Keep the charge of the Lord your God, to walk in His ways, to keep His statutes, and His commandments, and His judgments, and His testimonies as it is written in the Law of Moses, that you may understand [SAKAL]" (1 Kings 2:3).

29   "Do all that is written in the Law . . . then you shall have good understanding [SAKAL]" (Joshua 1:8).

30   "Blessed is the man who meditates on these things, and he who lays them to heart shall become wise" (Sirach 50:28, Hebrew Text).

31   "Who is wise and will keep these things? They will understand the lovingkindness of the Lord" (Psalm 107:43, Literal Translation).

32   "The Law of the Lord is perfect, restoring the soul; the testimony of the Lord is sure, making wise the simple" (Psalm 19:7).

33   "I have more understanding than all my teachers, because Your testimonies are my meditation" (Psalm 119:99).

Conversely

34   "They who have rejected the Word of the Lord, what wisdom is in them?" (Jeremiah 8:9).

35   "He is not wise who hates the Law" (Sirach 33:2, Hebrew Text).

E

GOD LOVES WISDOM, AND HE LOVES THE TRULY WISE, FOR THEY ARE GOOD.

1   "The Lord of all things Himself loved Wisdom" (Wisdom 8:3).

2   "The Lord loves those who love Wisdom" (Sirach 4:14).

3   "God loves nothing so much as the man who lives with Wisdom" (Wisdom 7:28).

4   "Even if one be perfect among the children of men, yet if the Wisdom which comes from You be not with him, he shall be held of no account" (Wisdom 9:6).

5   "Wisdom . . . no defiled thing comes into her" (Wisdom 7:25).

6   "Wisdom is devoid of great evils, ignorance, and lack of discipline" (Philo, *Q.Gen.* IV.138).

7   "There is no [truly] wise man who is evil" (Sirach 19:22, Syriac Text).

8   "Wisdom will not enter a deceitful soul, nor dwell in a body enslaved to sin" (Wisdom 1:4).

9   "Wisdom rests in the heart of the righteous" (Proverbs 14:33, Syriac Text).

10   "There is wisdom in the good [AGATHOS] heart of a man" (Proverbs 14:33, Greek Text).

11 "Wisdom is known with the just and faithful" (Sirach 1:16, Latin Vulgate).

12 "With men of truth is wisdom" (Sirach 1:15, Syriac Text).

13 "The wisdom of the wise nothing can take away except the blindness of ungodliness, and the callousness that comes from sin" (Testament of Levi 13:7).

14 "A wise heart that has understanding will abstain from sins" (Sirach 3:32, Latin Vulgate).

15 "Whoever keeps the Law is an understanding son" (Proverbs 28:7, Literal Translation).

16 "A man of understanding is faithful to the Law" (Sirach 33:3, Latin Vulgate).

17 "Wisdom rests in the heart of him who has understanding" (Proverbs 14:33, Hebrew Text).

18 "Generation by generation entering into holy souls, wisdom makes them beloved by God and prophets" (Wisdom 7:27).

19 "Wisdom is an unfailing treasure for mankind, and those who get wisdom obtain friendship with God" (Wisdom 7:14).

20 "Wisdom obtains His love" (Sirach 19:18, Greek Cursive 248).

21 "Be therefore wise in God . . . and prudent, knowing the order of His commandments and the Laws of every Word, that the Lord may love you" (Testament of Naphtali 8:10).

It is because they are righteous that God
loves the truly wise and gives them the gift of wisdom.

22 "He loves righteousness" (Psalm 33:5).

23 "The righteous God loves righteousness" (Psalm 11:7).

24 "The Lord loves the righteous" (Psalm 146:8).

25 "The Lord . . . loves him who follows after righteousness" (Proverbs 15:9).

26 "The Lord loves holy hearts, and all blameless persons are acceptable before Him" (Proverbs 22:11, Greek Text).

27 "It shall be our righteousness, if we observe to do all these commandments before the Lord our God, as He has commanded us" (Deuteronomy 6:25).

28 "Righteousness is by the Law" (2 Baruch 67:6).

29 "Everyone who does the Law of the Lord shall be loved by Him" (Testament of Joseph 11:2, Armenian Text).

30 "If you keep My commandments you will abide in My love" (St. John 15:10).

31 "They who love Him will strictly keep His commandments" (Sirach 2:15, Greek Sinaiticus, Syro-Hexaplar and Armenian Texts).

32 "All wisdom is in the performance of the Law" (Sirach 19:20).

33 "The love of Wisdom is the keeping of her Laws" (Wisdom 6:18).

34 "God gives to a man who is good in His sight, wisdom, and knowledge and joy" (Ecclesiastes 2:26).

35 "Let a man first do good deeds, and then ask God for knowledge of Torah [the Law], let a man first act as righteous and upright men act, and then let him ask God for wisdom, let a man first grasp the way of humility, and then ask God for understanding" (Tanna debe Eliyahu Rabbah p.31, ed. Friedmann, 1902).

36 "Wisdom and knowledge and piety towards the Lord, these are the treasures of righteousness" (Isaiah 33:6, Greek Text).

37 "I saw the fountain of righteousness which was inexhaustible, and around it were many fountains of wisdom, and all the thirsty drank from them and were filled with wisdom" (Enoch 48:1).

38 "All these matters will be understood by everyone who seeks for the wisdom of God and is pleasing to Him through faith and righteousness and good deeds" (Theophilus of Antioch, *Ad Autolycum* II.38).

F

JUST AS THE RIGHTEOUS AND WISE ARE PLEASING TO GOD, SO DOES A WISE SON MAKE HIS FATHER REJOICE.

1 "He who keeps the Law is a wise son" (Proverbs 28:7, Latin Vulgate).

2 "A wise son makes a father glad" (Proverbs 15:20).

3 "He who begets a wise son will rejoice in him" (Proverbs 23:24).

4 "Be wise, my son, and make my heart glad" (Proverbs 27:11).

5 "My son, if your heart is wise, my heart too will be glad" (Proverbs 23:15).

6 "He who loves wisdom makes his father rejoice" (Proverbs 29:3).

G

SILENCE AND WISDOM

1   "Be silent and I shall teach you wisdom" (Job 33:33).

2   "Oh that you would keep silent, and it would be your wisdom!" (Job 13:5).

3   "The wise shall be silent but the foolish shall speak" (2 Baruch 70:5).

4   "At an inopportune time do not display your wisdom" (Sirach 32:4, Hebrew Text).

5   "The wise man is silent until the right time, but a fool takes no note of the time" (Sirach 20:7, Hebrew Text).

6   "There is one who keeps silence and is found wise" (Sirach 20:5).

7   "Even a fool when he keeps silent is considered wise and he who shuts his lips is esteemed a man of understanding [BIN]" (Proverbs 17:28).

8   "The words of wise men heard in quietness are better than the shouting of a ruler among fools" (Ecclesiastes 9:17).

9   "A fool utters all his mind [literally "wind"] but a wise man keeps it in till afterwards" (Proverbs 29:11).

10   "A man of understanding is silent" (Proverbs 11:12).

11   Because "A man of understanding [BIN] has wisdom" (Proverbs 10:23 [KJV]).

12   "Every man of understanding knows wisdom" (Sirach 18:28).

H

HEARING AND WISDOM

The truly wise have wisdom because
they listen and ponder what is said.

1   "An attentive ear is the desire of a wise man" (Sirach 3:29).

2 "And a good ear will hear wisdom with all desire" (Sirach 3:31, Latin Vulgate).

3 "The heart of the wise seeks instruction" (Proverbs 15:14, Latin Vulgate).

4 "Hear instruction and be wise and do not refuse it" (Proverbs 8:33).

5 "Hear, my son, and be wise, and direct your heart in the way" (Proverbs 23:19).

6 "He who hears counsel is wise" (Proverbs 12:15).

7 "Hear counsel and receive instruction that you may be wise" (Proverbs 19:20).

8 "Hear wisdom and be wise, and do not separate yourself from it" (Proverbs 8:33, Greek Text).

9 "My son . . . incline your ear to wisdom, and apply your heart to great understanding" (Proverbs 2:1,2).

10 "My son, pay attention to my wisdom, and bow down your ear to my understanding" (Proverbs 5:1).

11 "I bowed down my ear a little and received wisdom and got much learning" (Sirach 51:16).

12 "A wise man will hear and increase in learning" (Proverbs 1:5).

13 "Bow down your ear and hear the words of the wise and apply your heart to my knowledge" (Proverbs 22:17).

14 "Let a wise man hear me" (Job 34:34).

15 "A wise son hears his father's instruction" (Proverbs 13:1).

16 "How good it is when a son accepts what his father says" (Instruction of Ptah-hotep Line 237, Egyptian Papyrus [Circa 2450 B.C.]).

17 "The fear of the Lord is the instruction of wisdom" (Proverbs 15:33).

18 "The fear of the Lord is the beginning of wisdom" (Proverbs 9:10; Psalm 111:10).

19 "Whoever gives ear to Wisdom shall judge the nations, and he who draws near to her shall dwell in security" (Sirach 4:15).

20 "He who walks with wise men will be wise" (Proverbs 13:20).

21 Wisdom says: "Now therefore, hear me, O you children, for happy are they who keep my ways" (Proverbs 8:32).

22 "The ear that listens to Wisdom rejoices" (Sirach 3:27, Hebrew Text).

Conversely

23 "No one hears Your wisdom, and [therefore] no one understands Your mighty works" (1QH 10:2,3, Dead Sea Scrolls).

**Pondering over what is heard gives
understanding to the truly wise.**

24 "Happy is the man who meditates on wisdom" (Sirach 14:20, Hebrew Text).

25 "He who meditates Wisdom's ways in his heart, shall also have understanding in her secrets" (Sirach 14:21, Greek Text).

26 "To ponder upon wisdom is perfect understanding" (Wisdom 6:15).

I

THE HUMBLE AND POOR ARE ALWAYS READY TO LISTEN; THUS, IT IS THEY WHO ARE REALLY WISE.

1 "They who give heed unto Him are the poor of the flock" (Zadokite Fragment 1:9 [MS. B1]).

2 "The poor of the flock . . . knew that it was the Word of the Lord" (Zechariah 11:11).

3 "The poor man who knows . . . ." (Ecclesiastes 6:8).

4 "A poor wise man . . . by his wisdom delivered the city" (Ecclesiastes 9:15).

5 "The poor man's wisdom" (Ecclesiastes 9:16).

6 "A poor and wise child" (Ecclesiastes 4:13).

7 "The wisdom of the poor shall lift up his head, and make him sit in the midst of nobles" (Sirach 11:1, Hebrew Text).

8 "The humble . . . they are most pleasing in God's sight" (St. Chrysostom, *In Matthew*, Homily 65.6 [PG 58, p. 625]).

9 "God gives to a man who is good in His sight wisdom, and knowledge, and joy" (Ecclesiastes 2:26).

10 "With the humble is wisdom" (Proverbs 11:2).

11 "His secret is revealed to the humble" (Sirach 3:19, Hebrew Text).

12 "Faith and meekness are His delight" (Sirach 1:27).

13 "Learn from Me for I am meek and humble in heart" (St. Matthew 11:25).

14 "The meek will He guide in judgment, and the meek will He teach His way" (Psalm 25:9).

15 "Be meek to hear the Word [of God] so that you may understand and return a true answer with wisdom" (Sirach 5:13, Latin Vulgate).

16 "The meekness of wisdom" (St. James 3:12, Literal Translation).

17 "His mysteries are revealed to the meek" (Sirach 3:19, Greek Sinaiticus Text and Cursives 248,106,253).

Conversely

18 "They obeyed not, neither inclined their ear, but made their neck stiff, that they might not hear, nor receive instruction" (Jeremiah 17:23).

19 "A proud and scornful man will not accept teaching" (Sirach 32:18, Hebrew Text).

20 "They who have rejected My Law and stopped their ears that they might not hear wisdom or receive understanding" (2 Baruch 51:4).

21 "A rebellious house, who have eyes to see but do not see, and they have ears to hear but do not hear; for they are a rebellious house" (Ezekiel 12:2).

22 "Wisdom is far from men of pride, and liars cannot remember her" (Sirach 15:8).

23 "Men of pride shall not see Wisdom" (Sirach 15:7, Hebrew Text).

24 "A scoffer seeks wisdom and does not find it" (Proverbs 14:6).

25 "He who lifts himself up with pride . . . his wisdom will depart from him" (Pesachim 66b, BT).

26 "When the scoffer is punished the simple is made wise" (Proverbs 21:11a).

J

THE WISDOM OF THE ANCIENTS

1   "With the ancient is wisdom, and in length of days: understanding" (Job 12:12).

2   "The ancients of Gebal and their wise men" (Ezekiel 27:9).

3   "He will seek out the wisdom of all the ancients" (Sirach 39:1).

4   "Days should speak, and multitude of years should make wisdom known" (Job 32:7).

5   "My son, receive instruction from your youth up, and in your old age you shall attain wisdom" (Sirach 6:17, Hebrew D Text).

6   "The perfect completion [SUNTELEIA] of the fear of the Lord is wisdom attained [PROSLEPHIS]" (Sirach 21:11, Greek Text, Cursive 248).

7   "To instruct his princes at his pleasure and to teach his ancients wisdom" (Psalm 104:22, Greek and Latin Vulgate Texts; Psalm 105:22, Syriac Text).

K

WISE WOMEN

1   "Send for wise women that they may come" (Jeremiah 9:17).

2   "And Joab sent to Tekoah and fetched from there a wise woman" (2 Samuel 14:2).

3   "Then the woman wisely came to all the people" (2 Samuel 20:22).

4   "A valiant woman . . . she opens her mouth with wisdom and in her tongue is the teaching of kindness" (Proverbs 31:10,26).

5   "Her wise ladies answered her, yes, she repeats her words to herself" (Judges 5:29).

6   "A wise and good woman" (Sirach 7:19).

L

WISDOM OF THE ANGELS

1 "My lord is wise, according to the wisdom of an angel of God to know all things that are in the earth" (2 Samuel 14:20).

2 "As an angel of God, so is my lord the king to discern good and evil" (2 Samuel 14:17).

3 "The upright will understand the knowledge of the Most High, and the perfect of way will have understanding of the wisdom of the sons of Heaven [Angels]" (1QS 4:22, Dead Sea Scrolls).

M

SOLOMON'S WISDOM

1 "I have given you [Solomon] a wise and understanding heart" (1 Kings 3:12; 5:12).

2 "God gave Solomon wisdom and understanding exceeding much, and largeness of heart, like the sand that is on the seashore" (1 Kings 4:29).

3 "And Solomon's wisdom excelled the wisdom of all the children of the east, and all the wisdom of Egypt. For he was wiser than all men . . . and men came from all peoples to hear the wisdom of Solomon, and from all the kings of the earth, who had heard of his wisdom" (1 Kings 4:30,31,34).

4 "Solomon surpassed all the kings of the earth for riches and for wisdom. And the whole earth sought the presence of Solomon to hear his wisdom, which God had put in his heart" (1 Kings 10:23-24).

5 "The queen of the South . . . came from the ends of the earth to hear the wisdom of Solomon . . . ." (St. Matthew 12:42).

6 "When the queen of Sheba had seen all the wisdom of Solomon . . . there was no more spirit in her" (1 Kings 10:4,5).

7   "Then she said to the king, 'the report was true which I heard in my own land about your words and your wisdom, but I did not believe their reports until I came and my own eyes had seen it; and behold, half the greatness of your wisdom was not told me' " (2 Chronicles 9:5,6).

N

WITH WISDOM ONE IS ABLE TO WORK SKILLFULLY AND TO BUILD WELL. THE WISDOM OF GOD IS NEEDED TO BE ABLE TO RULE AND GUIDE WISELY AND TO JUDGE RIGHTLY. WITH THE GRACIOUS AND CHOICE WORDS OF WISDOM ONE IS ABLE TO ALLURE AND TO CONVERT OTHERS.

Wisdom is needed to be able to work skillfully

1   "O Lord how manifold are Your works! In wisdom You have made them all" (Psalm 104:24).

2   "He has adorned the splendors of His wisdom . . . O how desirable are all His works" (Sirach 42:21,22).

3   "O God . . . You organized man by Your wisdom" (Wisdom 9:1,2).

4   "Wisdom orders [DIOIKEI] all things graciously" (Wisdom 8:1).

5   "Wisdom harmonizes and fits together to bring about equality and unity" (Philo, *Q.Gen.* IV.144).

6   "Wisdom works all things gainfully" (Wisdom 8:5).

7   "In the labours of Wisdom's hands are infinite riches" (Wisdom 8:18).

8   "Wisdom . . . knows Your works . . . and understands what is pleasing in Your eyes" (Wisdom 9:9).

9   "Wisdom knows and understands all things" (Wisdom 9:11).

10   "O God . . . send Wisdom forth out of the holy heavens, and from the throne of Your glory send her, that she may be with me and work, and that I may know what is pleasing to You" (Wisdom 9:1,10).

11   "Wisdom who is the artificer of all things taught me" (Wisdom 7:22).

12 "Send me therefore a man wise to work in gold, and in silver, and in brass and in iron, and in purple, and crimson and blue, and who knows how to engrave with the wise men" (2 Chronicles 2:7).

13 "They are all the work of wise men" (Jeremiah 10:9).

14 "All kinds of wise men for every kind of work" (1 Chronicles 22:15).

15 "With you for all the work will be every willing wise [ḤAKAM] man" (1 Chronicles 28:21).

16 "Bezaleel and Aholiab, and every wise hearted man in whom the Lord put wisdom and understanding to know how to work all manner of work for the service of the sanctuary" (Exodus 36:1).

17 "And every wise hearted man among them who were performing the work of the tabernacle made ten curtains of fine twined linen and blue and purple and scarlet stuff, with cherubim skillfully worked" (Exodus 36:8, Literal Translation).

18 "All the women whose heart stirred them up in wisdom spun the goat's hair" (Exodus 35:26, Literal Translation).

19 "All the women who were wise hearted did spin with their hands, and brought that which they had spun both of blue and of purple and scarlet and of fine linen" (Exodus 35:25, Literal Translation).

20 "All who are wise hearted, whom I have filled with the spirit of Wisdom that they may make Aaron's garments" (Exodus 28:3).

Wisdom is needed to build well.

21 "The wise artisan" (Isaiah 3:3).

22 "The artisan built it by his wisdom" (Wisdom 14:2).

23 "Through wisdom is a house built" (Proverbs 24:3).

24 "Every wise woman builds her house" (Proverbs 14:1).

25 "Wisdom has built her house, she has hewn out her seven pillars" (Proverbs 9:1).

26 "As a wise master builder, I have laid the foundation" (1 Corinthians 3:10).

The Wisdom of God teaches how to rule and guide wisely.

"Unless the rulers and the ruled loved wisdom, it is impossible to make the states blessed" (Plato, *Republic* V.18).

27   "God . . . is the Guide [ODĒGOS] of Wisdom and the Director [DIORTHŌTĒS] of the wise" (Wisdom 7:15).

28   "It is Wisdom who teaches the knowledge of God, and is the chooser of His works" (Wisdom 8:4, Latin Vulgate).

29   "All things that are either secret or manifest I learned to know, for Wisdom the artificer of all things taught me" (Wisdom 7:21,22).

30   "Wisdom teaches her children" (Sirach 4:11a, Hebrew and Syriac Texts).

31   "Wisdom orders all things graciously" (Wisdom 8:1).

32   "Wisdom is profitable to direct [KASHER = "to make right"]" (Ecclesiastes 10:10).

33   "O God . . . You organized man by your wisdom that he should have dominion over the creatures made by You, and rule the world in holiness and righteousness" (Wisdom 9:1,2,3).

34   "I appointed him [Adam] as ruler to rule on earth having rule by My wisdom" (2 Enoch 30:12, Slavonic A Text).

35   "Because of wisdom . . . I [King Solomon] shall govern people and nations shall be subject to me" (Wisdom 8:13,14).

36   "All that belongs to Wisdom is of royal origin and is sovereign and ruling by nature" (Philo, *Q.Gen.* III.44).

37   "By me [Wisdom] kings reign, and princes decree justice. By me princes rule, and nobles, even all the judges of the earth" (Proverbs 8:15,16).

38   "We pronounce wisdom to be kingship for we pronounce the wise man to be king" (Philo, *Mig.* 197).

39   "Desire for wisdom leads to a kingdom" (Wisdom 6:20).

40   "Take wise and understanding and experienced men from your tribes, and I will make them rulers over you" (Deuteronomy 1:13).

41   "Let Pharaoh look for a man understanding and wise, and set him over the land of Egypt" (Genesis 41:33).

42   "If you then delight in thrones and scepters, O you monarchs of the people, honour Wisdom that you may reign forever" (Wisdom 6:21).

43   "A wise king is the upholding of the people" (Wisdom 6:26, Latin Vulgate).

44   "A wise king winnows the wicked and brings the threshing wheel over them" (Proverbs 20:26).

45 "Love the light of wisdom all you who bear rule over peoples" (Wisdom 6:23, Latin Vulgate).

46 "Unto you therefore O sovereigns are my words that you may learn wisdom, and not fall away" (Wisdom 6:9).

47 "Wisdom guided them along a marvelous way" (Wisdom 10:17).

48 "Thy wise men, O Tyre, who were in thee, were thy pilots" (Ezekiel 27:8).

49 "A wise man is . . . as a pilot in a ship or a ruler in a city, or a general in war, or again as a soul in a body" (Philo, *Abr.* 272).

50 "Your life you have ordered [DISPOSUISTI] in wisdom" (2 Esdras 13:54).

51 "Your Law is life and Your wisdom is right guidance" (2 Baruch 38:2).

The Wisdom of God is needed for good judgment.

52 "Whoever gives ear to Wisdom shall judge the nations, and he who draws near to her shall dwell securely" (Sirach 4:15).

53 "He shall judge peoples and nations in the wisdom of his righteousness" (Psalms of Solomon 17:31).

54 "O Lord God . . . give me now wisdom and knowledge to go out and come in before this people, for who can judge [SHAPHAT] this Your people, that is so great? God answered Solomon, 'Because this was in your heart, and you have not asked possessions, wealth, honor, or the life of those who hate you, and have not even asked long life, but have asked wisdom and knowledge for yourself that you may judge [SHAPHAT] My people over whom I have made you king, wisdom and knowledge are granted to you' " (2 Chronicles 1:9,10,11,12).

55 "Wisdom shall guard me in her glory, and so shall my works be acceptable and I shall judge Your people righteously, and I shall be worthy of my father's [King David's] throne" (Wisdom 9:11-12).

56 "They saw that the wisdom of God was in him [Solomon] to do judgment" (1 Kings 3:28).

57 "And you, Ezra, according to the wisdom of God which is in your hand, appoint magistrates and judges who may judge all the people" (Ezra 7:25).

58 "A wise judge shall instruct his people, and the government of a man of understanding is well ordered" (Sirach 10:1).

59 "By me [Wisdom] . . . princes decree justice" (Proverbs 8:15,16).

60 "God give you wisdom in your heart to judge His people in righteousness, that their good things be not abolished, and that their glory may endure forever" (Sirach 45:26).

61 "Is there not among you one wise man who will be able to judge [DIAKRINAI] between his brethren?" (1 Corinthians 6:5).

With the gracious and choice words of Wisdom one is able to pacify, allure and convert others.

62 "The words of a wise man's mouth are gracious" (Ecclesiastes 10:12).

63 "The wise man by a few words makes himself beloved" (Sirach 20:13, Hebrew Text).

64 "He that is wise [SOPHOS] in words [LOGOIS] will promote himself [to honour], and a man of understanding will please great men" (Sirach 20:27).

65 "By the word is wisdom known, and understanding by the answer of the tongue" (Sirach 4:24, Hebrew Text).

66 "The Preacher was wise . . . the Preacher sought to find pleasing words, and to write words of truth correctly" (Ecclesiastes 12:9,10).

67 "The wrath of a king is as messengers of death, but a wise man will pacify it" (Proverbs 16:14).

68 "Scornful men set a city on fire, but wise men turn away wrath" (Proverbs 29:8).

69 "Now there was found in it [a besieged city] a poor wise man, and he by his wisdom delivered the city" (Ecclesiastes 9:15).

70 "He shall be filled with the spirit of understanding, he shall pour forth the words of his wisdom . . . many shall commend his understanding" (Sirach 39:6,9).

71 "Do not reject the discourse of the wise, and busy yourself with their riddles because from them you will learn doctrine so that you may stand in the presence of princes" (Sirach 8:8, Hebrew Text).

72 "By wisdom shall praise be uttered" (Sirach 15:10).

73 "The wise ruler of the people shall be praised for his words" (Sirach 9:17).

74 "Wise [SOPHOI] were their words [LOGOI] in their instruction" (Sirach 44:4).

75 "Persuasive words of wisdom" (1 Corinthians 2:4).

76 "He who wins souls is wise" (Proverbs 11:30).

77 "I will give you utterance and wisdom which none of your opponents will be able to resist or refute" (St. Luke 21:15; Acts 6:10).

O

WISDOM AND PEACE

1 "Wisdom's ways are ways of pleasantness, and all her paths are peace" (Proverbs 3:17).

2 "May he grant you wisdom of heart, and may there be peace among you" (Sirach 50:23, Hebrew Text).

3 "The Lord gave Solomon wisdom as He promised him; and there was peace" (1 Kings 5:12).

4 "After him [David] rose up a wise son and for his sake he dwelt in peace" (Sirach 47:12, Syriac Text).

5 "Solomon . . . how wise you were in your youth . . . you were beloved for your peace" (Sirach 47:13,14,16).

6 "Wisdom and knowledge shall be the stability of your times" (Isaiah 33:6).

7 "The wisdom from above is . . . peaceable" (St. James 3:17).

P

WISDOM IS GLORIOUS AND RADIANT; SHE MAKES THE FACE OF THE WISE SHINE.

Glory and Wisdom.

"Wisdom shall be a glory to him" (Testament of Levi 13:8).

83

1   "Wisdom is . . . a pure emanation of the glory of the Almighty" (Wisdom 7:25).

2   "His [God's] glorious wisdom" (1QS 4:18, Dead Sea Scrolls).

3   "Great wealth of glory is wisdom" (Testament of Levi, Line 94 [13:7], Cambridge Aramaic Fragment).

4   "Riches and glory are with me [Wisdom]" (Proverbs 8:18).

5   "In her [Wisdom's] left hand are riches and glory" (Proverbs 3:16).

6   "My [Wisdom's] branches are the branches of glory and grace . . . and my flowers are the fruit of glory and riches" (Sirach 24:16,17).

7   "The wise shall inherit glory" (Proverbs 3:35).

8   "Wisdom will place on your head a garland of grace, she will present you with a crown of glory" (Proverbs 4:9).

9   "Wisdom . . . exalts to glory those who hold her fast" (Sirach 1:19).

10 "To Him who gives me wisdom I will give glory [DOXA]" (Sirach 51:17).

11 "The wisdom of God . . . the hidden wisdom which God ordained before the ages to our glory" (1 Corinthians 2:7).

12 "Exalt Wisdom and she shall exalt you, she will bring you to glory when you shall embrace her" (Proverbs 4:8; Berakoth 48a, BT).

13 "He shall rely upon Wisdom . . . he shall put his trust in her . . . and Wisdom shall exalt him" (Sirach 15:4,5, Hebrew Text).

14 "Honour Wisdom that you may reign forever" (Wisdom 6:21).

15 "Let not the wise man glory in *his* [earthly] wisdom" (Jeremiah 9:23).

16 "Wisdom shall praise herself and shall glory in the midst of her people" (Sirach 24:1).

17 "Wisdom shall guide me . . . and guard me in her glory [DOXA]" (Wisdom 9:1,10-12).

Wisdom is radiant.

18 "Wisdom is radiant and never fades away" (Wisdom 6:12).

19 "I loved Wisdom . . . and chose to have her rather than light, because her radiance never ceases" (Wisdom 7:10).

20 "Wisdom is the brightness of eternal light, the unspotted mirror of the working of God, and the image of His goodness" (Wisdom 7:26).

21 "Wisdom is fairer than the sun and above all the order of the stars; being compared with light she is found superior. For after it [the light of day] succeeds the night, but no wickedness can overcome Wisdom" (Wisdom 7:29-30).

22 "Wisdom reaches mightily [like the rays of the sun] from one end of the earth to the other, and she orders all things graciously" (Wisdom 8:1).

23 "Bring the knowledge of wisdom to light" (Wisdom 6:22).

24 "Love the light of wisdom" (Wisdom 6:23, Latin Vulgate).

25 "Wisdom illuminates all who understand her" (Sirach 4:11, Syriac Text).

Wisdom makes the face of the wise to shine.

26 "A man's wisdom makes his face to shine" (Ecclesiastes 8:1).

27 "Wisdom shines in the face of the wise" (Proverbs 17:24, Latin Vulgate).

28 "A holy man continues in wisdom as the sun" (Sirach 27:1, Latin Vulgate).

Wisdom gives the wise: words that are lucid to enlighten others.

29 "The word of him who is of the Lord is very lucid . . . the word of the wise man is luminous" (Philo, *Q.Gen.* II.4).

Q

WISDOM AND LIFE AND STRENGTH

Wisdom and Life.

"Seek wisdom so that you may live" (Proverbs 9:6, Greek Alexandrinus Text).

1 "In me [Wisdom] is all grace of the way and of the truth, in me is all hope of life, and of virtue" (Sirach 24:25, Latin Vulgate).

2 "The wisdom of the flesh is death but the wisdom of the spirit is life and peace" (Romans 8:6).

3 "Wisdom inspires life into her children and protects those who seek after her . . . he who loves Wisdom, loves life" (Sirach 4:12-13, Latin Vulgate).

4   "Wisdom is a tree of life to those who take hold of her" (Proverbs 3:18).

5   "He who finds me [Wisdom] finds life and obtains favor from the Lord; but he who misses me injures himself; all who hate me love death" (Proverbs 8:35-36).

6   "The excellence of the knowledge of wisdom is that it will give life to him who has it" (Ecclesiastes 7:13, Greek Text).

7   "Long life is in Wisdom's right hand" (Proverbs 3:16).

8   "Wisdom's branches are long life" (Sirach 1:20).

9   "Wisdom shall feed him [the God-fearing man] with the bread of life and understanding" (Sirach 15:3a, Latin Vulgate).

10   "The teaching of the wise is a fountain of life, that one may depart from the snares of death" (Proverbs 13:14).

Wisdom and Strength

11   "Wisdom strengthens the wise more than ten mighty men" (Ecclesiastes 7:19).

12   "Wisdom will strengthen him" (Sirach 4:20, Latin Vulgate).

13   "Wisdom shall be made strong in him, and he shall not be moved" (Sirach 15:3b, Latin Vulgate).

14   "A wise man is strong, a man of knowledge increases strength" (Proverbs 24:5).

15   "A wise man scales the city of the mighty, and brings down the stronghold in which they trust" (Proverbs 21:22).

16   "He who has so great a power must necessarily be filled with all-powerful wisdom" (Philo, *Q.Gen*. II.13).

Wisdom and health, and the preservation of life.

17   "By Wisdom they were healed, whoever have pleased You O Lord, from the beginning" (Wisdom 9:19, Latin Vulgate).

18   "The tongue of the wise is health" (Proverbs 12:18).

19   "Wisdom preserved the first formed father of the world . . . and brought him out of his fall" (Wisdom 10:1).

20   "Wisdom delivered out of troubles those who served her" (Wisdom 10:9).

21 "Wisdom delivered a holy people and a blameless seed from a nation of oppressors" (Wisdom 10:15).

22 "When the impious were perishing, Wisdom saved the righteous man, escaping the descending fire on Pentapolis" (Wisdom 10:6).

23 "Wisdom protected him from his enemies, and kept him safe from those who lay in wait for him" (Wisdom 10:12).

24 "Men were taught the things pleasing to You and were saved by Wisdom" (Wisdom 9:18).

25 "The Holy Scriptures are able to make you wise unto salvation through faith which is in Christ Jesus" (2 Timothy 3:15).

26 "He who walks wisely will be delivered" (Proverbs 28:26).

R

WISDOM AND IMMORTALITY

a. "Righteousness leads to life" (Proverbs 11:19).

b. "Righteousness is immortal" (Wisdom 1:15).

1 "I [Wisdom] being eternal am given to all my children who are named by Him" (Sirach 24:18, Greek Cursives 248,70).

2 "In kinship with Wisdom there is immortality" (Wisdom 8:17).

3 "By means of Wisdom I shall obtain immortality" (Wisdom 8:13).

4 "The love of Wisdom is the keeping of her Laws, and in the keeping of the Laws [of Wisdom] is the assurance of incorruption, and incorruption makes us to be near to God" (Wisdom 6:18-19).

S

THE SPIRIT OF WISDOM

1 "The spirit of Wisdom" (Isaiah 11:2).

2   "In Wisdom is an understanding spirit" (Wisdom 7:22, Greek Text).

3   "Wisdom is a spirit that loves man" (Wisdom 1:6).

4   "In Him dwells the spirit of wisdom, and the spirit which gives insight, and the spirit of understanding and of might" (Enoch 49:3).

5   "Joshua the son of Nun was full of the spirit of wisdom" (Deuteronomy 34:9).

6   "All who are wise hearted whom I have filled with the spirit of wisdom" (Exodus 28:3).

7   "For in wisdom is the spirit of understanding: holy, one, manifold, subtle, eloquent, active, undefiled, sure, sweet, loving that which is good, quick which nothing hinders, beneficent" (Wisdom 7:22, Latin Vulgate).

8   "That the God of our Lord Jesus Christ, the Father of glory, may give you the spirit of wisdom and revelation in the knowledge of Him" (Ephesians 1:17).

9   "I prayed and understanding was given me; I called upon God and the spirit of wisdom came to me" (Wisdom 7:7).

T

THE WAYS OF WISDOM

1   "Blessed are they who keep my [Wisdom's] ways" (Proverbs 8:32).

2   "Wisdom . . . her ways are everlasting commandments" (Sirach 1:5, Greek Cursives 23,55,70,106,248).

3   "Wisdom's ways are ways of pleasantness, and all her paths are peace" (Proverbs 3:17).

4   "None of these [non-Israelites] have known the way of Wisdom or remembered her paths" (Baruch 3:23).

5   "Now therefore hear me [Wisdom], O you children, for blessed are they who keep my ways" (Proverbs 8:32).

6   "He who meditates Wisdom's ways in his heart shall also have understanding in her secrets" (Sirach 14:21).

7   "I have taught you in the way of Wisdom, I have led you in upright paths" (Proverbs 4:11).

8   "Come to Wisdom with all your soul, and keep her ways with all your might" (Sirach 6:26).

9   "Pursue Wisdom as a hunter, and lie in wait in her ways" (Sirach 14:22).

U

GOD HIDES HIS WONDERFUL WISDOM AS A TREASURE
SO THAT WE MAY SEEK IT AND BRING IT TO LIGHT.
HAVING FOUND IT WE MUST NOT HIDE WISDOM
BUT SHARE IT WITH OTHERS TO HIS GLORY.

Wisdom is hidden

1   "Where does wisdom come from? . . . it is hidden from the eyes" (Job 28:20,21).

2   "We speak the wisdom of God in a mystery, the hidden wisdom which God ordained before the ages to our glory" (1 Corinthians 2:7).

3   "Christ, in whom are hidden all the treasures of wisdom and knowledge" (Colossians 2:2,3).

4   "He brings forth the things that are hidden [TA'ALUMAH] to light" (Job 28:11).

5   "O that God . . . would show you the hidden things [TA'ALUMAH] of wisdom" (Job 11:6).

6   "The secrets of wisdom" (Enoch 51:3).

7   "Wisdom is not manifest to many" (Sirach 6:22).

8   "Wisdom is drawn out of secret places" (Job 28:18, Latin Vulgate).

9   "Who has put wisdom in the inward parts?" (Job 38:36).

10   "Who of those who are born has ever found out the beginning or end of Your wisdom?" (2 Baruch 14:9).

11   "O, the depth of the riches both of the wisdom and knowledge of God!" (Romans 11:33).

12   "In the hidden [SATHAM], You shall make me know wisdom" (Psalm 51:6).

The treasures and riches of Wisdom.

"A man who is rich in wisdom" (Targum on Ecclesiastes 5:11).

13   "Wisdom is an unfailing treasure for mankind" (Wisdom 7:14).

14   "Thousands of treasures of wisdom" (Sirach 41:12, Hebrew Text).

15   "The treasures of wisdom beneath Your throne" (2 Baruch 54:13).

16   "Great wealth of glory is Wisdom and a goodly treasure to all who find her" (Testament of Levi, Cambridge Aramaic Fragment, Line 94 [13:7]).

17   "They [the righteous] have acquired for themselves treasures of wisdom" (2 Baruch 44:14).

18   "The parables of understanding are in the treasures of wisdom" (Sirach 1:24).

19   "Wisdom is more precious [YAQAR] than jewels, and all things that you can desire cannot be compared to her" (Proverbs 3:15).

20   "Wisdom is better than jewels, and all things that you can desire cannot be compared to her" (Proverbs 8:11).

21   "Wisdom . . . cannot be gotten for pure gold, nor can silver be weighed as its price. It cannot be valued in the gold of Ophir, in precious onyx, or sapphire. Gold and crystal cannot equal it, nor can it be exchanged for jewels of fine gold" (Job 28:12,15-17).

22   "The price of wisdom is above pearls" (Job 28:18).

23   "How much better to get wisdom than gold!" (Proverbs 16:16).

24   "Receive Wisdom's instruction rather than silver, and knowledge rather than choicest gold" (Proverbs 8:10).

25   "Riches and honor are with me [Wisdom], enduring wealth and righteousness. My fruit is better than gold, even pure gold, and my yield than choice silver" (Proverbs 8:18-19).

26   "I [Wisdom] will fill their treasuries" (Proverbs 8:21).

27   "Wisdom shall heap upon him [the God-fearing man] a treasure of joy and gladness, and shall cause him to inherit an everlasting name" (Sirach 15:6, Latin Vulgate).

28   "In her [Wisdom's] left hand are riches and glory" (Proverbs 3:16).

29   "There came to me with Wisdom all good things together and innumerable riches in her hands" (Wisdom 7:11).

30 "I preferred Wisdom to scepters and thrones and I accounted riches as nothing in comparison with her. Neither did I liken her to a priceless gem, because all gold is but a little sand in her sight, and silver will be accounted as clay before her" (Wisdom 7:8-9).

31 "For gold and silver and every possession perishes, but the wisdom of the wise nothing can take away, except the blindness of ungodliness and the callousness that comes from sin. For if one keeps oneself from these evil things, then even among his enemies shall wisdom be a glory to him" (Testament of Levi 13:7,8).

32 "The crown of the wise is their riches" (Proverbs 14:24; see v.18).

33 "If riches are a possession to be desired in life, what is richer than Wisdom who works all things gainfully" (Wisdom 8:5).

34 "In the labors of Wisdom's hands are infinite riches" (Wisdom 8:18).

35 "Wisdom stood by him [Jacob] and made him rich" (Wisdom 10:11).

36 "Only the wise man is rich, and all things belong to the wise man" (Philo, *Q.Gen.* IV.182).

37 "O the depth of the riches both of the wisdom and knowledge of God!" (Romans 11:33).

We should seek the Wisdom of God.

38 "Where shall Wisdom be found?   And where is the place of Understanding?" (Job 28:12).

39 "Search and seek and wisdom shall be made known to you" (Sirach 6:27).

40 "He who devotes himself to the study of the Law of the Most High will seek out the wisdom of all the ancients, and will be concerned with prophecies; he will preserve the discourse of notable men and penetrate the subtleties of parables; he will seek out the hidden meanings of proverbs and be at home with the enigmas of parables" (Sirach 39:1-3).

41 "From my youth I sought after Wisdom" (Sirach 51:15).

42 "My heart was stirred to seek Wisdom" (Sirach 51:21).

43 "I and my heart compassed to know and to search out and to seek Wisdom and the explanation of things" (Ecclesiastes 7:25).

44 "Wisdom I loved and diligently sought her from my youth" (Wisdom 8:2).

45 "I went about seeking how to take Wisdom for myself" (Wisdom 8:18).

46 "A wise man will not leave wisdom when it is hidden [but he will seek it out]" (Sirach 32:18, Syriac Text).

Finding Wisdom

47 "O the happiness of a man who finds wisdom!" (Proverbs 3:13).

48 "How great is he who has found wisdom!" (Sirach 25:10).

49 "Child and city establish a name, but above them both is he who has found wisdom" (Sirach 40:19, Hebrew Text).

50 "My son, from your youth up choose instruction, and until you are old you will keep finding wisdom" (Sirach 6:18).

51 "If in your youth you have not gathered Wisdom, how will you find her in your old age?" (Sirach 25:3, Syriac Text).

52 "Through purity I found Wisdom" (Sirach 51:20, Greek and Hebrew texts).

Having found the treasures of wisdom, we should bring them to light.

53 "I do not hide wisdom's riches" (Wisdom 7:13).

54 "The wise man does not hide wisdom" (Sirach 32[35]:18, MS. E, Hebrew Text).

55 "Wise men have declared from their fathers, and have not hidden it [wisdom]" (Job 15:18).

56 "What Wisdom is and how she came to be, I will declare, and will not conceal from you mysteries, but will trace Wisdom out from the beginning of creation, and bring to light the knowledge of her" (Wisdom 6:22).

57 "Do not hide your wisdom in her beauty" (Sirach 4:23, Greek Cursives 70,106,248,253).

58 "Hidden wisdom and concealed treasure that is not seen, what profit is there in either of them?" (Sirach 41:14).

59 "Truly, wisdom which is not published is as a treasure buried in the dust of the earth" (R. Joseph Kimchi's *Shekel Hakodesh* 42).

60 "Better is a man who hides his folly than a man who hides his wisdom" (Sirach 20:31; 41:15).

61 "Even from those who come after us we will not withhold the beginning of wisdom" (Enoch 37:3).

62 "Behold I have not laboured for myself only but for all those who seek wisdom" (Sirach 24:34, Greek Text; Idem. 33:18, MS. E, Hebrew Text).

63 "Without wisdom it is not possible to praise the Creator of all things" (Philo, *Q.Gen*. I.6).

V

WISDOM IS PRESENTED TO US NOT ONLY AS A DESIRABLE TREASURE, BUT ALSO AS A BEAUTIFUL WOMAN WHOM GOD LOVES AND WANTS US TO LOVE AND LONG FOR.

1 "The Lord of all things Himself loved Wisdom" (Wisdom 8:3).

2 "And who is to be considered the daughter of God but Wisdom, who is the first-born mother of all things and most of all of those who are greatly purified in soul?" (Philo, *Q.Gen*. IV.97).

3 "It is Wisdom's name that the holy oracles proclaim by 'Bathuel', a name meaning, 'Daughter of God', yes, a true born and ever virgin daughter" (Philo, *Fug*. 50).

4 "Follow after and pursue the genuine and unmated virgin, the Wisdom of God" (Philo, *Q.Gen*. II.3).

5 "Pursue Wisdom as a hunter and lie in wait in her ways" (Sirach 14:22).

6 "Love Wisdom, and she shall keep you" (Proverbs 4:6).

7 "In the love of Wisdom is good delight" (Wisdom 8:18).

8 "Wine and music gladden the heart, but the love of Wisdom is above them both" (Sirach 40:20).

9 "The Lord loves those who love Wisdom" (Sirach 4:14).

10 "God loves nothing so much as the man who lives with Wisdom" (Wisdom 7:28).

11 "I Wisdom . . . love those who love me, and those who seek me early shall find me" (Proverbs 8:12,17).

12 "Come to me [Wisdom] all you who desire me, and be filled with my fruits" (Sirach 24:19).

13 "Come to Wisdom with all your soul, and keep her ways with all your might" (Sirach 6:26).

14 "Wisdom is near to those who seek her, and he who gives his desire to her shall find her" (Sirach 51:26, Hebrew Text).

15 For "Wisdom hastens to make herself known to those who desire her" (Wisdom 6:13, RSV).

16 "Whoever rises early to seek Wisdom will have no difficulty, for he will find her sitting at his doors" (Wisdom 6:14).

17 "For Wisdom goes about seeking those who are worthy of her, and she graciously appears to them" (Wisdom 6:16).

18 "Wisdom is easily seen by those who love her, and found by those who seek her" (Wisdom 6:12).

19 "Draw near to Wisdom . . . and when you draw close to her, do it as a hero and as a mighty man" (Sirach 1:22, Greek Sinaiticus Text).

20 "Wisdom will bring you to glory when you shall embrace her" (Proverbs 4:8; Berakoth 48a, BT).

21 "And when you have taken hold of Wisdom do not let her go" (Sirach 6:27).

22 "Happy are those who hold her [Wisdom] fast" (Proverbs 3:18).

23 "Cleave unto Wisdom that you may prove yourself wise" (Sirach 2:3, Syriac Text).

24 For "he who masters Wisdom shall teach her" (Sirach 15:10, Hebrew Text).

25 "I loved Wisdom and sought her from my youth, and I desired to make Wisdom my spouse, and I became enamoured of her beauty" (Wisdom 8:2).

26 "I loved Wisdom . . . and chose to have her rather than light, because her radiance never ceases" (Wisdom 7:10).

27 "I preferred Wisdom to scepters and thrones, and I accounted riches as nothing in comparison with her" (Wisdom 7:8-9).

28 "My soul longed with desire for Wisdom" (Sirach 51:19, Hebrew Text).

29 "My inmost being yearned [literally, "burned with desire"] for Wisdom to look upon her" (Sirach 51:21, Hebrew Text).

30 "I went about seeking how to take Wisdom for myself" (Wisdom 8:18).

31 "I determined to take Wisdom to live with me" (Wisdom 8:9).

32 "But I knew that I could not take her [Wisdom] unless God gave her to me, and it was a mark of understanding to know whose gift she was" (Wisdom 8:21).

33 "If you desire Wisdom, keep the commandments and the Lord shall give her unto you" (Sirach 1:25).

34 "For God gives to a man who is good in His sight: Wisdom" (Ecclesiastes 2:26).

We should desire to be wise, because it is through wisdom that we shall know the will of God and be able to please Him in accomplishing it.

35 "Wisdom knows and understands all things" (Wisdom 9:11).

36 "Wisdom . . . knows Your works . . . and understands what is pleasing in Your eyes, and right in Your commandments" (Wisdom 9:9).

37 "O God . . . send Wisdom forth out of the holy heavens . . . send her, that she may be with me and work, and that I may know what is pleasing to You" (Wisdom 9:1,10).

38 "O my son . . . desire to be wise" (Story of Ahikar 2:60, Arabic Text).

39 "Desire that you may be filled with the knowledge of His will in all wisdom and spiritual understanding, that you may walk worthy of the Lord, fully pleasing to Him" (Colossians 1:9,10).

40 Jesus said: "I have kept My Father's commandments and I abide in His love" (St. John 15:10).

41 "I always do what is pleasing to Him" (St. John 8:29).

42 "Christ, the Power of God and the Wisdom of God" (1 Corinthians 1:24).

43 "Christ, in whom are hidden all the treasures of wisdom and knowledge" (Colossians 2:2,3).

W

THE WISDOM OF GOD IS CHASTE, AND IT IS THE PURE IN HEART WHO SHALL SEE AND POSSESS HER.

1 "The genuine and unmated virgin: the Wisdom of God" (Philo, *Q.Gen.* II.3).

2 "The wisdom that is from above is first of all chaste [AGNĒ]" (St. James 3:17).

3 "Wisdom . . . pervades and penetrates all things by reason of her pureness" (Wisdom 7:24).

4 "Wisdom is the brightness of eternal light, the unspotted mirror of the working of God, and the image of His goodness" (Wisdom 7:26).

5 "Vice shall not prevail against Wisdom" (Wisdom 7:30).

6 "Nothing fights so hard against another thing as does Wisdom against sensual pleasure" (Philo, *Q.Gen.* IV.41).

7 "The nature of the flesh is alien to Wisdom so long as it is familiar with sensual desire" (Philo, *Q.Gen.* I.90).

8 "Wisdom . . . by reason alike of her own modesty and the glory of Him who begot her, has obtained a nature free from every defiling touch" (Philo *Fug.* 50).

9 "Continence . . . loves the wisdom of discipline" (Philo, *Q.Gen.* IV.243).

10 "The plan which is not entertaining impure thoughts comes and is called wisdom" (Midrash Genesis Rabbah 90.3).

11 "Love Wisdom with a love that is guileless and pure and genuine" (Philo, *Virt.* 62).

12 "I found Wisdom in purity [KATHARISMŌ], and through her guidance I obtained understanding" (Sirach 51:20, Greek Text).

13 "Through purity [TAHOR] I found Wisdom" (Sirach 51:20, Hebrew Text).

14 "With the chaste [TSANA' = 'chaste' in Rabbinic Hebrew] is wisdom" (Proverbs 11:2).

15 "The virgin daughter of Jephthah she is more wise than her father, and a maiden of understanding more than all the wise who are here" (Ps. Philo, *Biblical Antiquities*, XL.4).

16   "Virgins who have kept their chastity not under compulsion, like some Greek priestesses, but of their own free will in their ardent yearning for Wisdom. Eager to have Wisdom for their life mate, they have spurned the pleasures of the body, and desire no mortal offspring but those immortal children [Truths] which only the soul that is dear to God can bring to birth" (Philo, *Cont.* 68).

17   "Wise souls pure as virgins" (Clement of Alexandria, *Strom.* V.c.3).

18   "Wisdom . . . is the firstborn mother . . . of those who are greatly purified in soul" (Philo, *Q.Gen.* IV.97).

19   "We speak wisdom among those who are perfect [TELEIOS]; a wisdom however, not of this world, nor of the rulers of this world, who are passing away; but we speak of the wisdom of God in a mystery, the hidden wisdom which God predestined before the ages to our glory. The wisdom which none of the rulers of this age has understood; for if they had understood it, they would not have crucified the Lord of glory" (1 Corinthians 2:7-8).

Conversely

20   "Sinners shall not see Wisdom" (Sirach 15:7, Greek Text, Literal Translation).

21   "For Wisdom will not enter a deceitful soul, nor dwell in a body enslaved to sin" (Wisdom 1:4).

X

WISDOM IS A GREAT TEACHER, AND SHE TEACHES HER CHILDREN HOW TO TEACH OTHERS WHAT THEY HAVE LEARNED FROM HER. BEING WISE, HER CHILDREN KNOW HOW TO JUSTIFY WISDOM BEFORE THE EYES OF THE WORLD. WISDOM EXALTS THOSE WHO EXALT HER.

1   "It is Wisdom who teaches the knowledge of God, and is the chooser of His works" (Wisdom 8:4, Latin Vulgate).

2   "The children of Wisdom are the congregation of the just" (Sirach 3:1, Latin Vulgate).

3   "Wisdom teaches her children" (Sirach 4:11a, Hebrew and Syriac Texts).

4   "All things that are either secret or manifest, I learned to know, for Wisdom the artificer of all things taught me" (Wisdom 7:21,22).

5   "The heart of the wise teaches his mouth, and adds learning [LEQACH] to his lips" (Proverbs 16:23).

6   "When the wise is instructed, he receives knowledge" (Proverbs 21:11b).

7   "The lips of the wise disperse [through teaching] knowledge" (Proverbs 15:7).

8   "Because the Preacher was wise, he also taught the people knowledge" (Ecclesiastes 12:9).

9   "Let the Word of Christ dwell in you richly, as you teach and admonish one another in all wisdom" (Colossians 3:16).

10   "Admonishing every man, and teaching every man in all wisdom that we may present every man perfect in Christ Jesus" (Colossians 1:28).

11   "And on the Sabbath He [Jesus] began to teach in the synagogue; and many who heard Him were astonished, saying, "where did this man get these things? And what is this wisdom given to Him?"" (St. Mark 6:2).

12   "Defend Wisdom and she shall exalt you" (Proverbs 4:8, Greek Text).

13   "Wisdom is justified by all her children" (St. Luke 7:35).

14   "Wisdom exalts her children" (Sirach 4:11, Greek Text).

15   "Wisdom exalts to glory those who hold her fast" (Sirach 1:19).

16   "He shall rely on Wisdom . . . he shall put his trust in her . . . and Wisdom shall exalt him" (Sirach 15:4,5, Hebrew Text).

17   "Exalt Wisdom and she shall exalt you" (Proverbs 4:8; Berakoth 48a, BT).

18   "Wisdom . . . bears witness to those who understand her" (Sirach 4:11b, Hebrew Text, Literal Translation).

19   "Honour Wisdom that you may reign forever" (Wisdom 6:21).

20   "Every one who acknowledges Me [Jesus Christ] before men, I also will acknowledge before My Father who is in heaven" (St. Matthew 10:32).

21 "Christ, the Power of God and the Wisdom of God" (1 Corinthians 1:24).

22 "Christ, in whom are hid all the treasures of wisdom and knowledge" (Colossians 2:2,3).

Y

MISCELLANEOUS TEXTS
FOR THE PROLOGUE

1 "Whoever fears Him and keeps His commandments will live to God" (Shepherd of Hermas, *Mand.* VII.37:4).

2 "Do not find fault before examining the evidence; understand [NOĒSON] first, and then reprove" (Sirach 11:7).

THE
LADDER
OF
UNDERSTANDING

NOTE

In Part III: THE LADDER OF UNDERSTANDING, references to previous sections can be identified in the following manner:

Examples:

[FL/B:3-5]   =   See Part I: THE FEAR OF THE LORD; segment B,
                  quotation Nos. 3 to 5 in the "Scriptural,
                  Apocryphal, Patristic and Rabbinic Texts on
                  the Fear of the Lord" section.

[W/N: 35-40]   =   See Part II: WISDOM; segment N, quotation Nos. 35
                  to 40 in the "Scriptural, Apocryphal, Patristic
                  and Rabbinic Texts on Wisdom" section.

THE FOUNDATION

THE FOUNDATION

THE FEAR OF THE LORD

The Ladder of Understanding has many rungs, and it is ascended step by step. The foundation upon which it stands is the fear of the Lord:

> "Before all . . . fear of God must take lead in your heart, then you will understand these things" (Theophilus, *Ad Autolycum* 1.7).

> "If you take the fear of God as your starting point you will never miss the goal" (Letter of Aristeas v. 189).

> "First one should fear God and then ascend to Wisdom" (Zohar Ḥadash, Ki Tissa, 45c-45d).

THE FIRST RUNG

ḤOKHMAH

[WISDOM]

The first rung, next to the foundation, is wisdom, for where you find the fear of the Lord — there you also find wisdom [FL/G:44-55]. There would be no ladder without wisdom, for it is through wisdom that we are given the ability to build and join things together in an orderly manner and for a good purpose [W/N:1:26]. "Wisdom harmonizes and fits together to bring about equality and unity" [W/N:5] in all the things she does. The Hebrew word for wisdom is CHOKMAH and it is related to the words for "to fasten" or "hook together": CHOK, CHOKKAH, CHAK. If Wisdom is said to be "hidden from the eyes", and "like her name she is not manifest to many" [W/U:1,7], it is because she is like the invisible string which holds together in perfect array the pearls in a necklace, or as the hidden golden setting displaying the jewels in a brooch. Wisdom holds things together beautifully, yet remains imperceptible herself, except to those who are aware of her hidden presence. So well does Wisdom organize, that she may be compared to a plan made up of many methods towards a definite goal. In an ancient Accadian Text excavated in Sippar, the word for "plan" is related to the Hebrew word for "wise", CHAKIM:

> "Who knows the will of the gods in heaven? Who understands the plans [CHA-AK-KIM] of the under-world gods?" (*Ludlul Bel Nemeq*, Sippar Text 37+381, Lines 36-37).

As the Rabbis were to say later on: "The plan which is not entertaining impure thoughts comes and is called wisdom" (Genesis Rabbah 90.3).

THE SECOND RUNG

BIN
[BASIC UNDERSTANDING]

The second rung of the ladder is BIN: the Hebrew word designating the basic ability to understand. As human beings we all have the capacity to understand. "Man . . . without understanding [BIN] is like the beasts that perish" (Psalm 49:20). That is why the psalmist cried out in exasperation: "Understand [BIN] you beastly ones among the people" (Psalm 94:8). Fundamentally, BIN is the ability "to distinguish between" — "to make a separation between", hence it is related to the Hebrew word for "between" [BEIN]:

> "Distinguish between [BEIN] the unclean and the clean" (Leviticus 11:47).

> "And God separated between [BEIN] the light and the darkness" (Genesis 1:4).

> "From between [BEIN] the two cherubim that are upon the ark of the Testimony I will speak with you all" (Exodus 25:22).

But BIN not only enables us to distinguish between or differentiate, it also makes manifest to us what is not immediately perceptible. We see a good example of this in the first book of Kings, in the incident of the woman whose own child had been removed from her bosom while she was asleep, and a dead child substituted in its place. When she arose to feed her baby and found the dead child in her bosom, she thought at first that it was her own, but the light of day revealed to her what had really happened. With "understanding" [BIN] she distinguished that the dead child was not hers, and with the same understanding, she conjectured that her roommate had accidentally suffocated her own child that night [1 Kings 3:19], and in despair made the surreptitious substitution. Thus, it is literally written:

> "When I arose in the morning to suckle my child, behold, it was dead; but when I had understood [BIN] it in the morning, behold, it was not my son which I did bear" (1 Kings 3:21).

The word BIN is variously translated in the English version of this text as: "considered" [KJV, RV]; "considered him more diligently" [DV]; "looked at him closely" [RSV, NEB, NIV]; "looked at him carefully" [JB, NAS]; and "examined him" [NAB]; but none of these has the full force of the Hebrew "understood [BIN] it", which tells us that through BIN the woman distinguished it was not her child, and also realized that her roommate having discovered she had suffocated her child:

"Arose at midnight, and took my son from beside me, while your maidservant slept, and laid it in her bosom, and laid her dead son in my bosom" (1 Kings 3:20).

With BIN we can also detect the counterfeit, and those who feign to be what they are not:

"As the palate tries the taste of a thing, so an understanding [BIN] heart the taste of a lie" (Sirach 36:24b, Hebrew Text).

"The rich man is wise in his own eyes but a poor man who has understanding [BIN] searches him out" (Proverbs 28:11).

We see this aspect of BIN brought to the fore in the book of Ezra when Ezra made the people pass in review before him so that he could separate from among them true members of the tribe of Levi to serve as ministers in the Temple that was to be reconstructed in Jerusalem. As he scrutinized them he discerned with the perspicacity of his understanding [BIN] that there were no true Levites among them:

"I gathered them together . . . and I understood [BIN] the people and the priests and I found no sons of Levi there" (Ezra 8:15.)

BIN, in the Hebrew text, means more that just "reviewed" [KJV, RV, NEB]; "sought among" [DV]; "observed" [JB, NAS]; "perceived" [NAB]; and "checked among the people" [NIV]. Isaiah also literally says: "They that see you will scrutinize you and understand [BIN] you" (Isaiah 14:16). In other words 'they shall discern who you really are' with their understanding [BIN]. As the wise man said in the book of Proverbs:

"I understood [BIN] among the youths, a young man void of understanding" (Proverbs 7:7).

Although God created us with the capacity for basic "understanding [BIN]", it needs to be perfected in us so that we can understand to the fullest capability of our understanding [BIN]. It is the Lord who perfects our understanding [BIN], and He does so when we are sincere towards Him and strive to be good, and ask Him to make us understand as we should so that we can then:

"Understand [BIN] the Law" (Nehemiah 8:7).
"Understand [BIN] the reading of the Law" (Nehemiah 8:8).
"Understand [BIN] the Word of the Lord" (Sirach 36[33]:3, Hebrew Text).

"Understand [BIN] His counsel" (Micah 4:12).

"Understand [BIN] prudence" (Proverbs 8:5).

"Understand [BIN] His judgment" (Sirach 32:16, Hebrew Text, MS. E).

"Understand [BIN] the wondrous works of God" (Job 37:14; Zadokite Fragments 1:1,2; 2:14-15 [MS. A]).

"Understand [BIN] all Your marvels and the power of Your might" (1QS 11:19-20, Dead Sea Scrolls).

"Understand [BIN] the parables of the wise" (Sirach 3:29, Hebrew Text, MS. A).

"Understand [BIN] the words of understanding [BINAH]" (Proverbs 1:2).

For it is one thing to "understand" [BIN] ordinary things, circumstances and people, but it is another thing to have "understanding [BIN] in words" (1 Samuel 16:18) as David did, and to have "understand [BIN] in all visions and dreams" (Daniel 1:17) as Daniel had. We have to start at the bottom of the ladder and first of all fear the Lord, for we must be good before we can truly understand [BIN]. "Apply your understanding [BIN] to the fear of the Most High and meditate upon His commandments continually, and He will make your heart to understand [BIN] and make you wise in that which you desire" (Sirach 6:36, Hebrew Text). Truly, "they who fear the Lord understand [BIN] His judgment" [FL/C:15], and His Law, and His counsel, and His wisdom, because He has made their hearts to really understand:

> "Who is wise and will observe these things? They shall understand [BIN] the lovingkindness of the Lord" (Psalm 107:43).

> "Who is wise and he shall understand [BIN] these things? Who is understanding [BIN] and he shall know them?" (Hosea 14:9).

Certainly not the wicked for:

> "The wicked they know not, neither will they understand [BIN], they walk on in darkness" (Psalm 82:4,5).

> "The wicked do not understand [BIN] knowledge" (Proverbs 29:7).

> "The wicked . . . they do not understand [BIN] the works of the Lord, nor the work of His hands" (Psalm 28:3,5).

To really understand [BIN] is a very great thing inasmuch as it helps us understand what evils we must avoid as Nehemiah did when he "understood [BIN] of the evil that Eliashib did" (Nehemiah 13:7 [Hebrew Text, Literal

Translation]); but it also makes us aware of our unseen faults and unconscious errors that keep us away from the path to perfection. For "who can understand [BIN] his errors" (Psalm 19:12), unless the Lord perfects our understanding? O Lord "teach me . . . and cause me to understand [BIN] wherein I have erred" (Job 6:24). For "how can a man understand [BIN] his own way?" (Proverbs 20:24) unless the Lord helps him to really understand, and be upright and prudent:

> "The upright, he understands [BIN] his way" (Proverbs 21:29).

> "The wisdom of the prudent is to understand [BIN] his way" (Proverbs 14:8).

> "The prudent man understands [BIN] where he is going" (Proverbs 14:15).

Let us ask the Lord, as the Psalmist did, to give us true understanding that we may understand and fulfill all His instruction:

> "O Lord . . . give me understanding [BIN]" (Psalm 119:33,34,73,125,144,169).

> "Make me to understand [BIN] the way of Your precepts" (Psalm 119:27).

> For "through Your precepts I get understanding [BIN]" (Psalm 119:104 [see v. 100]).

> "Give me understanding [BIN] O Lord in Your Law" (11QPs[a] XXIV.9 [Psalm 154:9, Dead Sea Scrolls]).

> "Give me understanding [BIN] that I may learn Your commandments" (Psalm 119:73).

> "Give me understanding [BIN] and I shall keep Your Law, yes, I shall observe it with all my heart" (Psalm 119:34).

We are helpless to understand [BIN] as we should unless the Lord makes us understand and teaches us for:

> "How can dust and ashes . . . understand [BIN] His works?" (1QH 12:27,28, Dead Sea Scrolls).

> "How then is man, this nothing possessing but breath, to understand [BIN] Your marvelous deeds unless You teach him?" (1QH 7:32,33, Dead Sea Scrolls).

Never forget that "the renewing of your understanding" (Romans 12:2) depends on God.

> "Whom shall He make to understand [BIN] doctrine?" (Isaiah 28:9).

The little ones who ask Him, of course.

THE THIRD RUNG

BINAH

[INSIGHT]

After we have truly understood to the full capacity of our basic understanding [BIN], we are ready to climb the third rung of the ladder: BINAH. "Pay close attention to have knowledge [DAATH] of understanding [BINAH]" (Proverbs 4:1), and understand that BINAH is a wonderful gift of God that will enable us "to understand [BIN] the words of understanding [BINAH]" (Proverbs 1:2), and "the parables of understanding [BINAH]" (Sirach 6:35 [Hebrew Text, MS D]), and "the secrets of understanding [BINAH]" (Sirach 9:15, Hebrew Text). Although BIN is proper to us as human beings, BINAH is not. All BINAH, and "all wisdom comes from the Lord and is with Him forever" (Sirach 1:1). "The spirit of wisdom and understanding [BINAH]" (Isaiah 11:2), comes from the Lord and we receive it as a gift from Him. We must never forget that it is *His* "understanding [BINAH]" (1QH 14:12 [Dead Sea Scrolls]), and that if we possess BINAH it is only because we have received it from Him: "these things I have known because of Your understanding [BINAH], for You have uncovered my ears to Your marvelous Mysteries" (1QH 1:21, Dead Sea Scrolls), that I may truly understand [BINAH] Your holy things. For "the knowledge of the holy is understanding [BINAH]" (Proverbs 9:10), and if we are to praise Him as we should, we need to understand [BINAH] His holy and mysterious things: "the secrets of understanding [BINAH]" (Sirach 9:15, Hebrew Text). Thus it is written:

> "He has given man understanding [BINAH] so that
> He may be glorified in His mighty work" (Sirach 38:6,
> Hebrew Text; see Sirach 17:6-10, Greek Text).

> "I give You thanks, O Lord, who have put understanding [BINAH] in the heart of Your servant . . . that
> he might praise Your name" (1QH 14:8,9,10, Dead Sea
> Scrolls).

> "We know these things because of Your understanding [BINAH]" (1QM 10:16, Dead Sea Scrolls).

"Where there is no understanding, there is no knowledge" (Pirke Aboth 3:21) of holy things.

We will not receive "His understanding" [BINAH], unless we are good and do all His commandments:

> "Keep [the commandments, statutes, judgments]
> therefore, and do them, for this is your wisdom and
> your understanding [BINAH] in the sight of the
> nations" (Deuteronomy 4:6).

And also "forsake the foolish and live and go in the way of understanding [BINAH]" (Proverbs 9:6); for "to depart from evil is understanding [BINAH]" (Job 28:28). Thus it is written that evil men have no understanding [BINAH]:

> "They [the wicked] have not known the mystery to come and have not understood [BINAH] past things" (1Q Myst. 1:3 [Book of Mysteries], Dead Sea Scrolls).

> "It is because of their sins that You have hidden the fount of understanding [BINAH] and the secret of Truth" from them (1QH 5:25,26, Dead Sea Scrolls).

> "Men of deceit . . . a people without understanding [BINAH]" (1QH 2:16,19, Dead Sea Scrolls).

Long, long ago, during the time of their innocence, Adam and Eve were endowed with BINAH which they lost after the Fall, but in the beginning "the Lord . . . gave them a heart to understand and He filled them with the knowledge of understanding" (Sirach 17:1,6,7) which is why Agur said in the book of Proverbs:

> "Surely, I am more brutish than any man [ISH] and have not the understanding [BINAH] of Adam. [For] I have not learned wisdom nor have I knowledge of the holy" (Proverbs 30:2-3, Literal Translation).

For "the knowledge of the holy is understanding [BINAH]" (Proverbs 9:10); the understanding that comes through the Lord's "spirit of Wisdom and Understanding [BINAH]" (Isaiah 11:2).

We know we can obtain this great gift from the Lord by keeping and doing His commandments (Deuteronomy 4:6) and by departing from evil (Job 28:28). Do we not remember that God gives wisdom to those who are good [W/C:12-32]? Let us take every precaution to remain good, because "to depart from evil is understanding [BINAH]" (Job 28:28); the understanding that the Lord gives to those who persevere in their righteousness. "Acquire wisdom, acquire understanding [BINAH]! Do not forget, nor turn away from the words of my mouth" (Proverbs 4:5). To have wisdom is a great thing, but it is an even greater thing to have understanding [BINAH], because with BINAH we draw closer to the knowledge of God. For "God . . . gives wisdom to the wise and knowledge to those who know [YADA'] understanding [BINAH]" (Daniel 2:21). Do we want to know understanding [BINAH]? "Pay close attention to have knowledge of understanding [BINAH]" (Proverbs 4:1).

"Wisdom is the first [RESHITH] thing [you must get], therefore get wisdom, and with all your getting get understanding [BINAH]" (Proverbs 4:7). "Cry out for understanding [BINAH]" (Proverbs 2:3), because with understanding [BINAH] you will be able to do wonderful things.

Understanding [BINAH] helps us to keep the Law of the Lord and do what is right before Him:

> "The Lord give you understanding [SAKAL] and insight [BINAH], . . . that you may keep the Law of the Lord your God" (1 Chronicles 22:12).

> "I give You thanks, O Lord, who have put understanding [BINAH] into the heart of Your servant that he may do what is good and right before You, and that he may show himself stout-hearted against the crimes of ungodliness, and that he might praise Your name, and choose all that You love, and loathe all that You hate" (1QH 14:8-11, Dead Sea Scrolls).

It is through BINAH that we know our human limitations:

> "And I, because of Your understanding [BINAH] have knowledge that the righteousness of man is not in the hand of flesh and that man is not master of his way" (1QH 15:12,13, Dead Sea Scrolls).

Without understanding [BINAH] we can easily go astray:

> "A people without understanding [BINAH] so that they might be lost in their straying" (1QH 2:19, Dead Sea Scrolls).

> "They have fallen to their destruction for lack of understanding [BINAH]" (1QH 4:7, Dead Sea Scrolls).

> "For this is a people without understanding [BINAH], they are a nation void of counsel for there is no understanding [BINAH] among them" (Zadokite Fragment [CD] 5:16,17, MS. A).

> "Great in folly and lacking in understanding [BINAH] was he [Rehoboam] who made the people revolt by his [senseless] counsel" (Sirach 47:23, Hebrew Text).

> "They [the wicked] have not known the Mystery to come, and have not understood [BINAH] past things, and they have not known that which would befall them and have not saved their soul from the Mystery to come" (1Q Myst. 1:3,4 [Book of Mysteries, Dead Sea Scrolls]).

"I am but a creature of clay and a thing kneaded with water, a foundation of shame, and a fount of defilement, a crucible of iniquity and fabric of sin, a spirit of straying and perverse, void of understanding [BINAH]" (1QH 1:21-23, Dead Sea Scrolls).

O "that this vermin that is man may be raised from the dust to Your secret of Truth, and from the spirit of perversity to Your understanding [BINAH], that he might stand before You with the everlasting host" (1QH 11:12-13, Dead Sea Scrolls).

With BINAH we get understanding of the times and know what to do:

"Men who had understanding [BINAH] of the times to know what Israel ought to do" (1 Chronicles 12:32).

Because with understanding [BINAH] we can interpret the signs of the times and take the necessary precautions to meet any contingency. We know that "Daniel had understanding [BIN] in all visions and dreams" (Daniel 1:17), but one day he saw a vision that was beyond his BIN type of understanding and Daniel then knew: "as I was understanding [BIN] it" (Daniel 8:5, Literal Translation) that his basic understanding [BIN] was not sufficient to be able to interpret such a profound vision. On that day, he sought for [BINAH] from the Lord, and in His great kindness, the Lord sent him the angel Gabriel under the appearance of a man; first of all, to make Daniel really understand [BIN], and later to give him the gift of understanding [BINAH]:

"And it came to pass that I, even I Daniel [who was given 'understanding in all visions and dreams'] had seen the vision and sought [BAQASH] understanding [BINAH], then, behold, there stood before me one who had the appearance of a man. And I heard the voice of a man between the banks of Ulai, and He called out and said: 'Gabriel, make this man to understand [BIN] the vision'" (Daniel 8:15-16).

Later on, to give him even greater understanding of the vision:

"He [Gabriel] made me understand [BIN], and spoke with me, and said, 'O Daniel, I am now come forth to give you skillful understanding [SAKAL] and insight [BINAH]'" (Daniel 9:22, Literal Translation).

Thereafter, "Daniel . . . understood [BIN] the thing and had understanding [BINAH] of the vision" (Daniel 10:1) and could interpret these things. With understanding [BINAH] comes the ability to announce and interpret mysterious things:

"That he may announce them unto creatures because
of his understanding [BINAH] and be an interpreter
of these things" (1QH 18:11, Dead Sea Scrolls).

It is a good thing to be wise, but it is a better thing to have understanding
[BINAH], because a man with understanding [BINAH] can figure out and solve
the riddles of the wise. When King Solomon commenced to build the Temple in
Jerusalem, he sent a message to Hiram, King of Tyre, asking him to send him a
wise man [wisdom is needed for skillful work, see W/N:1-26] able to do fine
metal work and work with colored fabrics, and also knowing how to engrave so
that he could work along with Solomon's wise engravers:

"Send me [Solomon] now a wise [CHAKAM] man to
work in gold, and in silver, and in brass, and in irons,
and in purple, and crimson, and blue fabrics, who
knows how to engrave with the wise men who are
with me in Judah and in Jerusalem" (2 Chronicles 2:7).

And King Hiram sent him a man who was not only wise but also knowing in
understanding [BINAH], thus able to figure out and execute any project given
him by the wise men of Solomon:

"I have sent a wise [CHAKAM] man knowing
[YADA] understanding [BINAH] . . . knowing how to
work in gold, and in silver, in brass, in iron, in stone,
and in timber, in purple, in blue, and in fine linen, and
in crimson; also able to engrave any manner of
engraving, and to figure out [CHASHAB] any device
which is given to him" (2 Chronicles 2:13,14).

King Hiram gave King Solomon more than he asked for, he sent him a man of
understanding [BINAH]. And a man of understanding can put a hundred wise
men of this world to shame. For one may be seemingly wise by spouting the wise
sayings of others, "but a poor man who has understanding searches him out"
(Proverbs 28:11) and detects his ignorance. And an eloquent man may be famous
and esteemed for his pretended learning, "but the man of understanding knows
when he slips" (Sirach 20:7) and is able to unmask him. Even where there is real
wisdom, a man of understanding excels, for "if a man of understanding hears a
wise word he will commend it and *add* unto it" (Sirach 21:15), because he has
understanding. The "wise man knowing in understanding [BINAH]" that King
Hiram sent to King Solomon not only knew "how to work in gold, and in silver,
in brass [and] in iron," but also "in stone, and in timber . . . and in fine linen." He
was not only able to "engrave any manner of engraving," but he was also able
"to figure out any device which is given to him."

"There is a wisdom that abounds in evil, and there is no understanding" (Sirach 21:15, Latin Vulgate) nor real wisdom, because evil abounds. Such is "the wisdom of this world which is foolishness with God" (1 Corinthians 3:19), because "to depart from evil is understanding" (Job 28:28) and any wisdom that abounds in evil is not from above, and the "wisdom that descends not from above is earthly, sensual, devilish" (St. James 3:15) and foolish before God. Be aware that there are some who are "wise [CHAKAM] to do evil" (Jeremiah 4:22), but that kind of wisdom is not from above but "devilish." For "the wisdom that is from above is first of all chaste, then peaceable, gentle, reasonable, full of mercy and good fruits, unwavering and without hypocrisy" (St. James 3:17); the hypocrisy of those "professing themselves to be wise" and become "fools" (Romans 1:22), because all they possess is "the wisdom of this world," and "of the princes of this world that is coming to nothing" (1 Corinthians 2:6) before the great wisdom of God.

Know, that a man of understanding [BINAH] is truly wise, because he knows Wisdom personally and intimately: "Every man of understanding knows Wisdom" (Sirach 18:28). "A man of understanding has Wisdom" (Proverbs 10:23) because "Wisdom rests in the heart of him who has understanding" (Proverbs 14:33). Wisdom loves to rest in his heart because "a man of understanding is faithful to the Law of God" (Sirach 33:3, Latin Vulgate), and we know that "Wisdom will not enter into a deceitful soul, nor dwell in a body enslaved to sin" (Wisdom 1:4, RSV). "Who is wise and shall understand these things? Who is understanding and he shall know them?" (Hosea 14:9). Greater than the wisdom of Solomon is the understanding of the Lord [St. Matthew 12:42; St. Luke 11:31]. Do we not remember how from the very beginning "all who heard Him were astonished at His understanding and His answers"? (St. Luke 2:47). The answers that manifested the great power of His understanding before His opponents and demolished their arguments (St. Mark 11:27-33; St. Luke 20:20-40; St. Mark 7:1-23; St. Matthew 12:1-8, 22-30; 22:41-46; St. Mark 3:22-28; St. Luke 13:10-17; 14:1-6). No wonder "they dared not ask Him any more questions" (St. Mark 12:34; St. Luke 20:40), "and all bore witness to Him and marvelled at the gracious words that proceeded from His mouth" (St. Luke 4:22), for "Wisdom is known through speech" (Sirach 4:24a, Greek Text), "and by the reply [`ANAH] of the tongue one has knowledge of understanding" (Sirach 4:24b, Hebrew Text). "Understand first, and then rebuke" (Sirach 11:7). The gift of understanding [BINAH] enables us to reply effectively as Zophar said: "my understanding [BINAH] makes me reply [`ANAH]" (Job 20:3). "Do not miss the discourse of the aged; for they also learned from their fathers, because from them you shall learn understanding so as to be able to give answer in time of need" (Sirach 8:9).

Before we can give a good answer we must be able to hear and understand what is said. BINAH enables us to hear so acutely, that we can perceive by the ear the voice of words:

> "If now you have understanding [BINAH], hear this:
> give ear to the voice [QOL] of my words" (Job 34:16).

Thus when the Lord afflicted His people, He sent against them:

> "A fierce people, a people of deeper speech than you
> can hear [and understand, i.e. BIN]; and of a foreign
> tongue which you cannot understand [BINAH]"
> (Isaiah 33:19).

Meaning that no matter how acutely they listened with their ears and understanding [BINAH], it would be beyond their understanding [BINAH]. "We know these things because of Your understanding [BINAH]" (1QM 10:16, Dead Sea Scrolls). "Through Your understanding [BINAH] . . . You have uncovered my ears to Your marvelous Mysteries" (1QH 1:21, Dead Sea Scrolls). For by the gift of His understanding [BINAH] we shall be able to hear and understand the "choice words ['EMER] of understanding [BINAH]" (Proverbs 1:2), and "the choice words ['EMER] of knowledge" (Proverbs 19:27; 23:12), and even "the parables of understanding" [BINAH], and "the secrets of understanding [BINAH]" (Sirach 6:35, Hebrew Text MS. D; ibid. 9:15, Hebrew Text), so that we may give glory to God: "For He has given man understanding [BINAH] so that He may be glorified in His mighty work" (Sirach 38:6, Hebrew Text).

Let us take heart, for though the Lord said:

> "Behold, I will precede to do a marvelous work
> among this people, a marvelous work and a wonder:
> for the wisdom of their understanding [BIN] men
> shall be hidden" (Isaiah 29:14).

He also said:

> "In the latter days you shall understand [BIN] with
> understanding [BINAH]" (Jeremiah 23:20).

And then:

> "They who erred in spirit shall know understanding
> [BINAH], and they that murmured shall learn doc-
> trine" (Isaiah 29:24).

THE FOURTH RUNG

S E K E L

[SKILLFUL UNDERSTANDING WITH THE ABILITY TO TEACH WELL]

When we shall have understood [BIN] as we should, and been given insight [BINAH] of His holy things, we shall then be ready to climb to the fourth rung of the ladder and receive there, the gift of SEKEL from the Lord. SEKEL is that wonderful gift which enables us to accomplish things well, and prosper in all our undertakings, because we have done them with "skillful understanding" [SEKEL]. SEKEL is good understanding in action. It is the understanding we need in all our doings and goings, so that we may succeed. Pray "that you may understand [SAKAL] in all that you do" (Deuteronomy 29:9), and "understand [SAKAL] wherever you may go" (Joshua 1:7), for if you "understand [SAKAL] in all you do and wherever you may turn" (1 Kings 2:3), you will certainly prosper. Maybe, that is why most English versions of the Bible rendered Deuteronomy 29:9: "that you may prosper in all you do" [KJV, NAS, NIV]; "that you may be successful in all you do" [NEB, NAB]; and "thrive in all you do" [JB]. The older translations faithfully rendered it: "that you may understand in all you do" [Greek Text, Latin Vulgate, and DV], so that we may not lose sight of the necessary ingredient for success in all our works: the gift of understanding [SEKEL].

SAKAL not only gives us success in all our doings and goings, but it also enables us to teach well and help others understand:

> "They who understand [SAKAL] among the people shall make the many to understand [BIN]" (Daniel 11:33).

> "For the man of understanding [SAKAL], that he may make to understand [BIN] and teach all the sons of light concerning the nature of all the sons of men" (1QS 3:13, Dead Sea Scrolls).

It takes SEKEL to be able to teach others about SEKEL:

> "Hezekiah spoke to the hearts of all the Levites who made [the people] to understand [SAKAL] about the good understanding [SEKEL] of the Lord" (2 Chronicles 30:22, Literal Translation).

> "Instruction in understanding [SAKAL] and apt proverbs by Simeon etc." (Sirach 50:27, Hebrew Text).

To have "understanding" [SEKEL] is also to have discernment and thus be able to teach others the significance of a text:

"They [the Levites] read the Book of the Law of God,
interpreting [PARASH], and giving the meaning
[SEKEL], and causing them [the people] to understand [BIN] the reading" (Nehemiah 8:8).

With the insight of SEKEL, we understand why the inspired scribes wrote
such things as these:

"Blessed is he who understands [SAKAL] towards the
poor, the Lord will deliver him in the day of evil"
(Psalm 41:1, Literal Translation).

"The righteous man understands [SAKAL] the house
of the wicked, for their evil the wicked are overthrown" (Proverbs 21:12).

If we understand [SAKAL], we shall know that to "understand [SAKAL]
towards to poor," is to act with understanding towards them, that is, to come to
their aid and fill their needs even before they have to ask. It is also to understand
that they who help the poor give to the Lord Himself [St. Matthew 25:35-40,45;
Proverbs 14:31; 19:17; 2 Corinthians 8:9], and receive as their reward the gift of
faith [St. James 2:5; 2 Corinthians 8:14], and the knowledge of God. Thus it is
written: "The righteous one knows [YADA'] the cause of the poor, but the wicked
[who oppress the poor] do not understand [BIN] knowledge [DAATH]"
(Proverbs 29:7).

Again, "the righteous man understands [SAKAL] the house of the
wicked" (Proverbs 21:12) and what he "understands" [SAKAL] about the wicked
man's house, is that on the day "the wicked are overthrown" (Proverbs 12:7a;
21:12), "the house of the wicked shall be overthrown" (Proverbs 14:11a), "but the
house of the righteous shall stand" (Proverbs 12:7b), and "the tent of the upright
shall flourish" (Proverbs 14:11b).

Good teachers make good directors. The gift of SEKEL shall also enable us
to guide others skillfully and unerringly towards the Truth. When the prophet
Jeremiah spoke of an excellent troop of marksmen, he said that: "their arrows
shall be as of an understanding [SAKAL] mighty man; none shall return in vain"
(Jeremiah 50:9). Thus, when the Lord promised to give us good spiritual guides,
He said: "I will give you shepherds after My own heart who shall feed you with
knowledge and understanding [SAKAL]" (Jeremiah 3:15). They shall be able to
do so because His good shepherds shall possess those gifts themselves. But, as
for the foolish shepherds who no longer follow the Lord, they are "the shepherds" who "have become brutish and have not sought the Lord, therefore they
shall not understand [SAKAL] and all their flocks shall be scattered" (Jeremiah
10:21), because they do not have the understanding [SEKEL] needed to guide
them well. Woe to them, "they shall be greatly ashamed, for they shall not under-

stand [SAKAL], their everlasting confusion shall never be forgotten" (Jeremiah 20:11). But let us take heart for:

> "Behold, the days are coming, says the Lord, when I will raise up for David a righteous branch, and He shall reign as King and understand [SAKAL], and shall execute justice and righteousness in the earth" (Jeremiah 23:5).

We need understanding [SEKEL] not only to be able to teach, interpret and guide, but also to be able to give an intelligent answer:

> "O my God . . . there is no just man beside You to understand [SAKAL] Your Mysteries, and to answer a word" (1QH 12:11,19,20, Dead Sea Scrolls).

> "What shall I say unless You open my mouth? And how shall I reply unless You make me understand [SAKAL]?" (1QH 10:7, Dead Sea Scrolls)

Therefore, "receive understanding [SEKEL] so that you may be able to reply in time of need" (Sirach 8:9, Hebrew Text).

We should desire to have SEKEL, that we may be able to have "understanding [SAKAL] in all wisdom" (Daniel 1:4), and "understanding [SEKEL] in all learning" (Daniel 1:17), so that we may understand the marvelous deeds and Mysteries of the Lord, and His wonderful Truth:

> "What am I that You should teach me the secret of Your Truth and give me understanding [SAKAL] of Your marvelous deeds?" (1QH 11:3,4, Dead Sea Scrolls).

> "I give You thanks, O Lord, for You have given me understanding [SAKAL] of Your Truth, and have made me know Your marvelous Mysteries" (1QH 7:26,27, Dead Sea Scrolls).

> "Your mercy is obtained by all the sons of Your good pleasure; for You have made known to them Your secret of Truth and given them understanding [SAKAL] of all Your marvelous Mysteries" (1QH 11:9,10, Dead Sea Scrolls).

But above all we should desire to have SEKEL, because it is through the gift of SEKEL that we shall begin to understand and know the Lord Himself:

"O God of knowledge . . . that they may know You according to the measure of their understanding [SEKEL]" (1QH 1:26,31, Dead Sea Scrolls).

"From my youth You have appeared to me in the understanding [SEKEL] of Your judgment" (1QH 9:31, Dead Sea Scrolls).

"And I, gifted with understanding [SEKEL], I have knowledge of You O my God" (1QH 12:11, Dead Sea Scrolls).

"To Your children of Truth You have given understanding [SEKEL], and they shall know You forever and ever" (1QH 10:27, Dead Sea Scrolls).

SEKEL leads us to the knowledge of God because it impels us to seek Him whose marvelous works and Mysteries we have understood, so that we may know the Author of them. What the Lord desires from us is the knowledge of God:

"The Lord looked down from heaven upon the sons of man to see if there were any who understand [SAKAL] and seek God" (Psalms 14:2; 53:2).

"Thus says the Lord: 'Let not the wise man glory in his wisdom, let not the mighty man glory in his might, let not the rich man glory in his riches; but let him who glories, glory in this — that he understands [SEKEL] and knows Me, that I am the Lord'" (Jeremiah 9:23,24).

How can we obtain SEKEL? By being good — by keeping and doing His commandments, and meditating on them:

"Be careful to do according to all the Law which Moses My Servant commanded you; do not turn away from it to the right or to the left, so that you may understand [SAKAL] wherever you may go" (Joshua 1:7).

"This book of the Law shall not depart from your mouth, but you shall meditate on it day and night, so that you may be careful to do according to all that is written in it; for then you will make your way prosperous and then you will understand [SAKAL]" (Joshua 1:8).

"Keep therefore the words of this covenant and do them, that you may understand [SAKAL] in all that you do" (Deuteronomy 29:9).

"Keep the charge of the Lord your God, to walk in the Law of Moses so that you may understand [SAKAL] in all that you do and wherever you may turn" (1 Kings 2:3).

"He did that which was right in the sight of the Lord . . . he trusted in the Lord God of Israel . . . he clung to the Lord and did not depart from following Him but kept His commandments . . . and the Lord was with him and he understood [SAKAL] wherever he went" (2 Kings 18:3,5,6,7).

"A good understanding [SEKEL] have all those who do His commandments" (Psalm 111:10).

"I understand [SAKAL] more than all my teachers because Your testimonies are my meditation" (Psalm 119:99).

Therefore, the foolish, the wicked, the idolaters and mockers, and those who do not follow the Lord are not given understanding [SEKEL]:

"Fools, when will you understand [SAKAL]?" (Psalm 94:8).

"None of the wicked will understand [BIN] but those who understand [SAKAL] will understand [BIN]" (Daniel 12:10).

"They [the idolaters] have not known nor understood [BIN], for He has smeared over their eyes so that they cannot see and their hearts so that they cannot understand [SAKAL]" (Isaiah 44:18).

"You have kept their ["the scoffers"] heart from understanding [SEKEL]" (Job 17:4).

"They [the detractors] shall be greatly ashamed for they shall not understand [SAKAL], their everlasting confusion shall never be forgotten" (Jeremiah 20:11).

"The shepherds . . . have not sought the Lord; therefore they shall not understand [SAKAL]" (Jeremiah 10:21).

We can also obtain understanding [SEKEL] by being obedient, and carrying out the good counsels of our parents:

> "My son, do not forget my teaching, and let your heart keep my commandments . . . do not let mercy and truth leave you; bind them around your neck, write them on the tablet of your heart. So you will find favour and good understanding [SEKEL] in the sight of God and man" (Proverbs 3:1,3-4).

> "My son, hear me and receive my understanding [SEKEL], and set your heart upon my words" (Sirach 16:22, Hebrew Text).

It is the humble, patient and long-suffering who understand [SAKAL]:

> "Be humble in understanding [SEKEL]" (Sirach 32[35]:3, Hebrew Text).

> "The spirit of humility and forbearance, of abundant mercy and eternal goodness, of skillful understanding [SEKEL] and insight [BINAH] and almighty wisdom [are grouped together]" (1QS 4:3, Dead Sea Scrolls).

> "The understanding [SEKEL] of a man makes him slow to anger, and it is his glory to overlook an offense" (Proverbs 19:11).

> In "an evil time" — "the understanding [SAKAL] person shall keep silence" (Amos 5:13b,a).

> For "he who refrains his lips is understanding [SAKAL]" (Proverbs 10:19).

That is why, in Holy Scripture, it is often the poor humble servants who have understanding [SEKEL]. The Lord gives them skillful understanding so that through SEKEL they may find favor before their masters, and be exalted:

> "A poor man who is understanding [SAKAL] is not to be despised, nor is any man of violence to be honored" (Sirach 10:23, Hebrew Text).

> For "a man of violence does not receive understanding [SEKEL]" (Sirach 32:18, Hebrew Text, MS. E).

> "There is a poor man who is honored for his understanding [SEKEL]" (Sirach 10:30, Hebrew Text).

"An understanding [SAKAL] servant shall have rule over a son who causes shame" (Proverbs 17:2).

"The King's favour is towards an understanding [SAKAL] servant, but his wrath is against him who causes shame" (Proverbs 14:35).

"Unto a servant who is understanding [SAKAL], will nobles do service" (Sirach 10:25, Hebrew Text).

"Let your soul love an understanding [SAKAL] servant, and do not defraud him of his liberty" (Sirach 7:21, Hebrew Text).

"Behold My Servant shall understand [SAKAL], He shall be exalted and extolled, and be very high" (Isaiah 52:13).

If we pray for the grace of repentance and turn away from our iniquities we shall understand [SAKAL]:

"All this evil has come upon us, yet we have not made our prayer before the Lord our God, that we might turn away from our iniquities and understand [SAKAL] Your truth" (Daniel 9:13).

Let us listen attentively to the words of the wise and the aged, that we may receive "instruction in SEKEL" (Sirach 50:27, Hebrew Text) from them:

"The proverbs of Solomon . . . to receive the instruction of understanding [SAKAL], righteousness, judgment and uprightness" (Proverbs 1:1,3).

"Do not despise the tradition of the aged which they have heard from their fathers because from them you will receive understanding [SEKEL]" (Sirach 8:9, Hebrew Text).

"Love Wisdom" (Proverbs 4:6), and "come to Wisdom with all your soul, and keep her ways with all your might" (Sirach 6:26). Then, Wisdom will abide with you and you shall truly understand [SAKAL], because "she will feed 'you' with the bread of understanding [SEKEL]" (Sirach 15:3, Hebrew Text). "Happy the husband of an understanding [SAKAL] wife" (Sirach 25:8, Hebrew Text), for if she is "an understanding [SAKAL] woman, her good grace is above pearls" (Sirach 7:19, Hebrew Text). "A friend and a companion will each give support at the right time, but an understanding [SAKAL] wife is above both" (Sirach 40:23, Hebrew Text) because from her we can learn to understand, and "he who is understanding [SAKAL] may be profitable to himself" (Job 22:2), for "understanding [SEKEL] is a well-spring of life unto him who has it" (Proverbs 16:22).

Above all let us pray to Him if we want SEKEL, for all "wisdom, skillful understanding [SEKEL], and understanding [BIN] of things are from the Lord" (Sirach 11:15, Hebrew Text), and "He does not lack any understanding [SEKEL]" (Sirach 42:20, Hebrew Text).

> May "the Lord give you skillful understanding [SEKEL] and insight [BINAH]" (1 Chronicles 22:12).

> And "May He enlighten your heart with understanding [SEKEL] of life" (1QS 2:3, Dead Sea Scrolls).

If you now have understanding [SEKEL], praise the Lord:

> "Sing ye praises with understanding [SAKAL]" (Psalm 47:7).

THE FIFTH RUNG

TEBUNAH

[GREAT UNDERSTANDING]

After we have understood [SAKAL], we can ascend and receive at the fifth rung of the ladder, a very great gift of God: TEBUNAH, which is the infinite understanding of the Lord Himself. It is not easy to ascend to the fifth, and we shall not be able to scale it unless we have first walked righteously before the Lord day after day, and have been very patient and kind towards one another. For "a man of great understanding [TEBUNAH] walks uprightly" (Proverbs 15:21), and in a time of stress "a man of great understanding [TEBUNAH] holds his peace" (Proverbs 11:12), for "he who is slow to anger has great understanding [TEBUNAH]" (Proverbs 14:29). Indeed, "he who has a cool spirit is a man of great understanding [TEBUNAH]" (Proverbs 17:27). "To the way of humility I incline, and thus my heart will gain great understanding [TEBUNAH]," said Rabbi Joseph Kimchi in his work: *Shekel Hakodesh* 79.

The Lord does not entrust His TEBUNAH to anyone, but to the very good and patient, because the great understanding [TEBUNAH] of God is a gift of great power given only to those who are able to wield it wisely. It is because "a man of great understanding [TEBUNAH] has wisdom" (Proverbs 10:23), that he has had TEBUNAH confided to him. They who have wisdom know that the greatest wisdom is to keep the commandments of God, and to do His will in all things, for we thereby please the Lord and prove our love for Him. "If you desire [TEBUNAH], keep the commandments for it is great understanding [TEBUNAH] to do His good pleasure" (Sirach 15:15, Hebrew Text). Whoever desires to receive His TEBUNAH must strive through right conduct to draw near to the Lord. For "the Lord gives wisdom," but "out of His mouth comes knowledge and great understanding [TEBUNAH]" (Proverbs 2:6), for those who are close to Him. Knowing the sacredness of the Lord's TEBUNAH, the Jewish scribes who translated the Holy Scriptures into Greek rendered "great understanding [TEBUNAH] shall keep you" (Proverbs 2:11) into "holy understanding shall keep you" (ibid., Greek Text).

What is it that we shall be able to do with His TEBUNAH beyond that which BIN, BINAH, and SEKEL can accomplish for us?

Let us first know what the Lord can do with His TEBUNAH:

> "O give thanks to the Lord of lords . . . to Him who by
> great understanding [TEBUNAH] made the heavens"
> (Psalm 136:3,5).

"He . . . has stretched out the heavens by His great understanding [TEBUNAH]" (Jeremiah 10:12; 51:15).

"The Lord by wisdom has founded the earth, and by great understanding [TEBUNAH] He has established the heavens" (Proverbs 3:19).

"Great is our Lord, and mighty in power; His great understanding [TEBUNAH] is infinite" (Psalm 147:5).

"He divides the sea by His power, and by His great understanding [TEBUNAH] He crushes the proud one [RAHAB]" (Job 26:12).

When we behold the glory of the heavens above, we can see what the Lord can do with His TEBUNAH. That is why, when the Lord showed Moses "patterns of things in the heavens" that He desired to have His people fashion for the glory of His Sanctuary (Hebrews 9:23; 8:5; Exodus 25:9-40); He sent to Moses a man called Bezaleel having beforehand "filled him with the Spirit of God, in wisdom, and in great understanding [TEBUNAH], and in knowledge, and in all manner of workmanship" (Exodus 31:3; 35:31), so that Bezaleel could fashion the heavenly things the Lord desired for His Sanctuary. The Lord gave Bezaleel "great understanding [TEBUNAH] to have knowledge how to do all manner of work for the service of the Sanctuary . . . according to all that the Lord had commanded" Moses (Exodus 36:1), for it takes great understanding [TEBUNAH] to be able to do all these things well, as the Lord desires.

If "it is Wisdom who teaches the knowledge of God" (Wisdom 8:4, Latin Vulgate), it is Great Understanding [TEBUNAH] who helps us express what we have learned from Wisdom. "All things that are either secret or manifest I learned to know, for Wisdom the artificer of all things taught me" (Wisdom 7:21,22), "and when I had greatly understood [TEBUNAH] it, I set it down in writing" (Sirach 39:32 [Hebrew Text MS. B]) to help others understand.

Wisdom gives us the words, and Great Understanding [TEBUNAH] contrives for us the right answers, for "by the word is Wisdom known, and great understanding [TEBUNAH] by the reply of the tongue" (Sirach 4:24, Hebrew Text, MS. A).

"Does not Wisdom cry out and Great Understanding [TEBUNAH] put forth her voice?" (Proverbs 8:1), she does, so that we may hear and understand her better, for Great Understanding [TEBUNAH] seeks to make intelligible the mysterious cry of Wisdom. And does not Wisdom herself know that a voice is clearer than a cry? Because it is written that "Wisdom cries out abroad [CHUTS = "outside"] but "she puts forth her voice in the streets" (Proverbs 1:20) to be better heard and understood where the people are. Again, "Wisdom cries out at the head of the noisy places" to gain attention, but "in the opening of the gates in the city she utters her words" (Proverbs 1:21) to be better understood by the people waiting there. "Does not wisdom cry out [QARA`]? . . . 'unto you, O men, I cry out [QARA`], and my voice is to the sons of men'" (Proverbs 8:1,4), yes, her clearer voice is for the little ones who desire to understand her. Cry out for Wisdom, and "put forth your voice for great Understanding [TEBUNAH]" (Proverbs 2:3), and she will come to you, for she will know by your voice that you are now ready to understand her.

It is a wonderful thing to have great understanding [TEBUNAH], because through TEBUNAH we can help others understand His holy things. Furthermore, it is through great understanding [TEBUNAH] that we shall be able to uphold and establish His Truth, for "by great understanding [TEBUNAH] it is established" (Proverbs 24:3) just as the Lord "established the heavens"— "by His great understanding [TEBUNAH]" (Proverbs 3:19). But it is an awesome thing to be given the power of understanding [TEBUNAH] to establish His Truth, for when the time comes for His Truth to be established, woe to the proud liars who sought to obstruct it, for they and their lies shall be crushed by His great understanding [TEBUNAH]. For "in the Mysteries of His understanding and in His glorious wisdom, God has ordained an end for falsehood, and in the time of His Visitation, He will destroy it forever. Then the Truth of the world, which during the dominion of falsehood has been sullied in the ways of wickedness until the appointed time of judgment, shall appear in triumph forever. God will then purify every deed of man with His Truth" (1QS 4:18-20, Dead Sea Scrolls). On that day "there shall be no more lies, and all the works of falsehood shall be put to shame" (1QS 4:23, Dead Sea Scrolls) by His great understanding [TEBUNAH] which the Lord shall entrust to the meek and humble. "This honor have all His godly ones" (Psalm 149:9).

"Happy the man who finds Wisdom, and the man who draws out great understanding [TEBUNAH]" (Proverbs 3:13) from the heart of Wisdom. For he shall have "the waters of great understanding [TEBUNAH] to drink" (Sirach 15:3, Hebrew Text) and having been filled he shall be able: "out of his heart" to "pour forth great understanding [TEBUNAH]" (Sirach 50:27, Hebrew Text), and give others to drink. Moreover, he who has TEBUNAH in his heart shall be able to draw out deep things from the hearts of others. For "counsel in the heart of man is like deep water, but a man of great understanding [TEBUNAH] will draw it out" (Proverbs 20:5). Having drawn out secret counsel, men who have TEBUNAH shall be able to go about "giving counsel by their great understanding [TEBUNAH]" (Sirach 44:3, Hebrew Text). And what they will counsel us is to hold on to TEBUNAH once we possess it, for "he who keeps great understanding [TEBUNAH] will find good" (Proverbs 19:8).

> If you hold on to TEBUNAH, happy are you!
> Because "Great Understanding [TEBUNAH] shall
> keep you" too (Proverbs 2:11).

THE SIXTH RUNG

D A A T H

[KNOWLEDGE]

When we have ascended to the sixth rung of the ladder, and are able to find, and truly perceive, that which is good, we shall know that we have received from the Lord: the gift of "Knowledge" [DAATH]. This great gift is given to us after we have climbed the rungs of Wisdom and full understanding, for "when the wise understands [SAKAL], he receives knowledge [DAATH]" (Proverbs 21.11). The Jewish scribes who translated that text into the Greek language understood this, and rendered it: "a wise man understanding [SUNION] will receive knowledge [GNŌSIN]." Let us know that just as "wisdom brings forth understanding for a man" (Proverbs 10:23, Greek Text), "understanding throws open the way to knowledge" (Corpus Hermeticum, *Libellus* IV.6a). For "if there be no understanding, there is no knowledge [DAATH]" (Pirke Aboth 3:21), and also "where there is no knowledge [DAATH], wisdom is lacking" (Sirach 3:25, Hebrew Text). It is written that "the ear of the wise seeks knowledge" (Proverbs 18:15b). But how shall the wise obtain knowledge unless they first understand? O Lord, "give me understanding that I may learn" (Psalm 119:73) for "understanding loves to learn and advance to knowledge" (Philo, *Decal.* 1). O Lord, "give me understanding that I may know" (Psalm 119:125), for "knowledge [DAATH] is easy to him who understands" (Proverbs 14:6); thus, "the heart of the understanding [BIN] gets knowledge" (Proverbs 18:15a), because the Lord "gives wisdom to the wise, and knowledge to those who know understanding" (Daniel 2:21). "You will know for you have understanding," said the ancient Christian Fathers (*Didache* 2:21). Let us then be wise and understanding, that we may obtain the great gift of knowledge from the Lord, because with "knowledge" [DAATH], we shall be able to do wonderful things for the glory of God. But let us first be aware that there is no knowledge for us unless we are ready to labour and suffer for the sake of the Lord, and be willing to die rather than disobey Him.

All the trials and sufferings we receive from the hands of God serve to prove and perfect us, so that we may be worthy to receive His "holy knowledge" — "the knowledge [DAATH] of the holy ones" (2 Maccabees 6:30; 1QSb 1:5 [Dead Sea Scrolls]), and "may be able to comprehend with all the saints" (Ephesians 3:18). For only "the upright will understand the knowledge [DAATH] of the Most High" (1QS 4:22, Dead Sea Scrolls). When "Enoch was found perfect," he "was taken as a sign of knowledge [DAATH] to all generations" (Sirach 44:16, Hebrew Text); a sign that we must strive to be perfect if we hope to receive knowledge from God. We are made "perfect through sufferings" (Hebrews 2:10), and He set an example for us: "through what He suffered . . . being made perfect" (Hebrews 5:8,9), and sanctifying Himself for our sakes, that we "might also be sanctified" (St. John 17:19). All suffering is "for the perfecting of the holy ones

. . . until we all attain to the unity of the faith, and of the knowledge of the Son of God, to a perfect [TELEIOS] man" (Ephesians 4:12,13), "perfect in knowledge" (Job 36:4) through Him; having "put on the nature which is renewed in full knowledge according to the image of its Creator" (Colossians 3:10). But the price of that renewal and knowledge, is perfect obedience to His will, and acceptance of our lot of suffering. Thus, St. Paul said: "for the excellency of the knowledge of Christ Jesus my Lord . . . I have suffered the loss of all things . . . that I may know Him" (Philippians 3:8,10). For "what does he know, who has not been tried?" (Sirach 34:9, Latin Vulgate), "he who has not been tried knows little" (Sirach 34:10, Greek Sinaiticus Text). "Now brethren, we make known to you . . . that in a great trial of affliction . . . you abound in everything, in faith, in utterance, and in knowledge" (2 Corinthians 8:1,2,7). Through the trials and afflictions that are sent to us, we are purified to receive His holy knowledge. When the pious Essenes prayed for constancy and knowledge, they first asked to be forgiven and purified: "forgive my sin, O Lord, and purify me from my iniquity, and graciously grant me a spirit of constancy and knowledge" (11QPs^a Col. XIX. ll. 13-15 [Plea for Deliverance, Dead Sea Scrolls]). As fire purges the dross and makes the refined silver shine; so does suffering purify us, enabling us to reflect "the light of knowledge" (Hosea 10:12, Greek and Syriac Texts; Testament of Levi 18:3) to His glory. Long ago, it dawned on man that "suffering leads to knowledge" (Herodotus 1.207; Aeschylus, *Ag.* 176f,249f.; Sophocles, *Oed. Col.* 7ff; Corpus Hermeticum 1.4ff.,482; Irenaeus I.4.5; Plotinus, *Enn.* IV.8,7), and "pain brings forth perception" (Philo, *L.A.* III.216). Thus, "the godly man . . . makes his sufferings contribute to the increase of his knowledge" (Corpus Hermeticum, *Libellus* IX.4b). The learned Jewish scribes who translated the Hebrew Holy Scriptures into Greek, had the same insight for they rendered "the *misery* of man is great to him" (Ecclesiastes 8:6, Hebrew Text), into "the *knowledge* [GNOSIS] of man is great to him" (Ecclesiastes 8:6, Greek Text). If we search through the Holy Bible we shall find a close relationship between discipline and knowledge: "Reprove one who has understanding [BIN], and he will understand [BIN] knowledge [DAATH]" (Proverbs 19:25), and become prudent. For "he who takes a reproof to heart, is prudent" (Proverbs 15:5), and "every prudent man acts with knowledge [DAATH]" (Proverbs 13:16). "A threat breaks down the heart of one who understands [PHRONIMOU], but a fool though scourged knows not" (Proverbs 17:10, Greek Text), that the rebuke which breaks down the heart of one who understands releases knowledge from it, as a broken kernel releases the seed. Truly "he who pricks the heart makes it to show her knowledge" (Sirach 22:19). Therefore, "whoever loves discipline, loves knowledge [DAATH], but he who hates reproofs is brutish" (Proverbs 12:1), he is "brutish in his knowledge" (Jeremiah 10:14; 51:17), "altogether brutish and foolish" (Jeremiah 10:8). But "he who has knowledge will not complain when he is disciplined," (Sirach 10:25, Greek Text, Cursives 248,70,106,307), for he knows all about "the disciplines [YASAR] of knowledge [DAATH]" (1QS 3:1, Dead Sea Scrolls; see also Philo, *Q.Gen.* IV. 14).

"Behold, happy the man whom God corrects, therefore do not despise the punishment of the Almighty for . . . you shall know . . . you shall know . . . know that it is for your good" (Job 5:17,24,25,27) that He has disciplined you, so that you may be worthy to receive His holy knowledge. "It is good for me that I have been afflicted that I may learn" (Psalm 119:71); "I know [now] that Your judgments are right and justly have You afflicted me" (Psalm 119:75) that I may learn and know. For "you have disciplined [YASAR] me and I was disciplined [YASAR] . . . surely after that, I turned back, I repented; and after that I was made to know [YADA']" (Jeremiah 31:18,19). Just as Gideon taught the men of Succoth a lesson when "he took the elders of the city, and thorns of the wilderness and briers, and with them [the painful thorns and briers] he made to know [YADA', i.e., "taught"] the men of Succoth" (Judges 8:16). Did not the Wisdom of Solomon reminisce how: "ungodly men denying the knowledge of Thee were scourged by the strength of Thine arm . . . that they might see and know"? (Wisdom 16:16,18). They were "brought to know [COGNOSCERE] . . . by torments" (2 Esdras 9:12), just as Antiochus towards the end of his life: "in sorrow and in pain . . . by these means being brought down from his great pride he began to come to full knowledge [EPIGNOSIS] by the scourge of God" (2 Maccabees 9:9,11). All these men "through the sufferings . . . knowing Him whom before they refused to know, they fully knew [EPEGNOSAN, i.e., "acknowledged"] the true God" (Wisdom 12:27). Also His own people "when they were tried, though they were being disciplined in mercy, they knew [EGNOSAN]" (Wisdom 11:9), they came to knowledge through the disciplines of the Lord. "Blessed is the man You discipline, O Lord, the man whom You teach from Your Law" (Psalm 94:12), because through Your discipline, O Lord, he is now ready to learn and know: "all that is revealed from the Law for knowledge" (Zadokite Fragment [CD] 15:13, A. Dupont-Sommer trans.; XIX.13-14 MS. A, C. Rabin).

Step by step, "in wisdom, and in great understanding [TEBUNAH], and in knowledge" (Exodus 31:3; 35:31) we climb the ladder towards the Truth, being "filled with wisdom, and great understanding [TEBUNAH], and knowledge" (1 Kings 7:14) by the Lord successively in the proper rungs. All "wisdom, and understanding, and knowledge of the Law are from the Lord" (Sirach 11:15, Greek Cursives 248,23,106,253), and He grants us these blessings, when we are ready for them. Among the Essenes, when the Teacher of righteousness taught the knowledge of God to his disciples, he did so only to those who "understood," for he knew that he himself was first given understanding before he was given knowledge: "these things I have knowledge of because of Your understanding" (1QH 1:21). And he praised the Lord saying: "You have given me understanding of Your Truth and have made known to me Your marvelous Mysteries" (1QH 7:26,27) after he received understanding. "What is man . . . that You should give him understanding [SAKAL] of such marvels and make known to him [after], the secret of Your Truth?" (1QH 10:3,4) Again, "I, gifted with understanding

[SAKAL], I have known You, O my God" (1QH 12:11), for "by Your understanding [BINAH] I know" (1QH 14:12), indeed, he knew that men "know You according to the measure of their understanding [SAKAL]" (1QH 1:31, Dead Sea Scrolls). "Blessed are You, O God of knowledge [DAATH], who have given to Your servant understanding [SEKEL] of knowledge [DEAH], to understand [BIN] Your marvels, and Your works without number" (1QH 11:27,28). O Lord, "open the fountain of knowledge [DAATH] to all who understand [BIN]" (1QH 2:18, Dead Sea Scrolls).

If we want to "improve understanding by knowledge" (Proverbs 9.6, Greek Text), we must strive to be good and "depart from evil" (Job 28:28), that we may have the understanding we need to be able to "know." Because "none of the wicked will understand" (Daniel 12:10), and none of the wicked will "know," for "they have no understanding to know" (Isaiah 44:18, Greek Text) that "the wicked do not understand knowledge" (Proverbs 29:7, Literal Translation). "Have all the workers of iniquity no knowledge?" (Psalm 14:4; 53:4). Yes, for "their wickedness blinded them, they know not the Mysteries of God" (Wisdom 2:21,22), they are "ever learning and never able to come to the knowledge of the Truth" (2 Timothy 3:7); "the way of the wicked is darkness, they know not" (Proverbs 4:19). "The works of the ungodly are far from knowledge" (Proverbs 13:19, Greek Text), and "to do good they have no knowledge" (Jeremiah 4:22), because they are "disabled from knowing [GNŌNAI] the things that are good" (Wisdom 10:8). "Miserable indeed, are all men by nature in whom there is no knowledge [AGNŌSIA] of God" (Wisdom 13:1). And happy indeed are all those who strive for perfection, for they have as their reward the greatest happiness: the joy of knowing God. Truly, O Lord, "to know You is perfect righteousness" (Wisdom 15:3), and perfect happiness for us. "All His sons of Truth shall rejoice in eternal knowledge [DAATH]" (1QM 17:8, Dead Sea Scrolls).

What shall we be able to do after we have received "knowledge [DAATH]" from God?

We shall be able to "act ['ASAH] with knowledge" (Proverbs 13:16), and have the "knowledge to work ['ASAH]" (1 Kings 7:14), and to "labour in wisdom and in knowledge" (Ecclesiastes 2:21) for the glory of the Lord.

We "know not the works of God who made all things" (Ecclesiastes 11:5), for "He does great things which we cannot know" (Job 37:5) unless he gives us the great gift of knowledge. The Lord gives us knowledge so that we may know that what we see around us are the works of His hands. Foolish are they "who from the good things that are seen are unable to know Him who exists, nor in paying attention to His works recognize the Artisan" (Wisdom 13:1). Those who are given knowledge to know His works "make known His deeds among the people" (Psalm 105:1; Isaiah 12:4), for to have knowledge of His works is to rejoice and sing forth His praises, making known to others the Author of those marvelous works.

With the gift of knowledge we shall be able to declare the works of the Lord, thereby enabling others to know His greatness and acknowledge Him. The Hebrew word NAGAD often rendered "to declare" in English, means to "put forth clearly," i.e., "to demonstrate well." Analogous to it, is another Hebrew word: SAPHAR, which means "to recount" in a convincing manner. Both of these words in their roots signify "to draw a line," and "to mark out" clearly. To be able through knowledge, "to declare" [NAGAD] or "to recount" [SAPHAR], is to be able to "make known" [YADA'] to others. Thus Elihu tells Job: "Declare [NAGAD] if you know [YADA'] it all" (Job 38:18). In turn, we read in the book of Isaiah: "who has declared [NAGAD] from the beginning that we may know?" (Isaiah 41:26). Elsewhere, "sing praises to the Lord . . . declare [NAGAD] among the peoples His doings" (Psalm 9:11), becomes: "praise the Lord . . . make known [YADA'] His doings among the peoples" (Isaiah 12:4). Again, the exhortation: "make known [YADA'] His works among the peoples" (1 Chronicles 16:8), may find a response in the prayers: "O Lord that I may . . . recount [SAPHAR] all Your wondrous works" (Psalm 26:6,7). For if we are able "to recount" well, through His knowledge, we are able to make it "known." Therefore, it is written: "that which we have heard and known [YADA'] because our fathers have recounted [SAPHAR] to us, we will not hide from their [grand] children but [also] recount [SAPHAR] to the generation to come the praises of the Lord, and His strength and His wonderful works that He has done . . . that the generation to come might know [YADA'] them . . . and recount [SAPHAR] them to their children" (Psalm 78:3,4,6), thereby making it also "known" to them.

A good way to give someone knowledge of a thing is to make the matter clear by putting it down in writing. For when we have before us the written explanation of a thing, it is easier for us to study it closely and refer to it whenever we need to. In the book of Ecclesiastes, we can see how "the Preacher sought to find delightful words and to write words of Truth correctly" (Ecclesiastes 12:10), so that we may be able to learn about them through his writings. "Have 'we' not written to you excellent things in counsels and knowledge [DAATH] that 'we' might make you know the certainty of the words of Truth?" (Proverbs 22:20-21). We write all these things down "to the intent that we might give knowledge to you by writing" (1 Esdras 6:12), for "in them [the writings, see vv. 42-46] is . . . the stream of knowledge" (2 Esdras 14:47). "Write the vision and make it clear [BA'AR = "to explain distinctly"] upon the tablets" (Habacuc 2:2) said the Lord to the prophet Habacuc. And Moses said to the elders: "Write upon the stones all the words of this Law very clearly" (Deuteronomy 27:8), so that the people would have it plainly written before their eyes and be able to learn and know all about the commandments found in the Law. But let us not forget that it requires knowledge to be able to write a clear explanation of a thing, to have it well understood by others. Thus, St. Paul wrote to the Ephesians: "Through revelation He made known to me the Mystery . . . I wrote . . . so that when you read you may understand my insight in the Mystery of Christ" (Ephesians 3:3,4). In an old apocryphal work called *The Secrets of Enoch*, God says to Enoch: "Give them the works written out by you, and they shall read them and know Me to be the Creator of all; and they shall understand that there is no other God but Me" (2 Enoch 33:8, Slavonic [A Text]). It was because he was taught by the Lord that Enoch knew all things, and wrote them down: "I know all things and have written down all things" (2 Enoch 40:2 [A Text]) so that his children would read and thereby also come to know them. Again, in the aforementioned work, Enoch says to his children: "take these books of the handwritings of your father and read them, for in them you shall learn all the works of the Lord . . . nothing shall make things known to you like my handwritings" (2 Enoch 47:2 [A Text]). Later on he tells them: "Give these [books] to all desiring them . . . that they may know the works of the Lord" (2 Enoch 54:1 [A Text]); "I have put all this down in writing that you may read and understand" (2 Enoch 66:8 [A Text]) through the books that Enoch wrote after he was given knowledge by God.

There is a very close relationship between the knowledge [DAATH] of God and the Truth:

> "You have made them to have knowledge [DAATH] of Your secret of Truth" (1QH 11:9, Dead Sea Scrolls).

> "You have made me have knowledge [DAATH] of Your secret of Truth" (1QH 11:16, Dead Sea Scrolls).

> "I have knowledge [DAATH] that Truth is in Your mouth and righteousness in Your hand, and in Your thought is all knowledge [DEAH]" (1QH 11:7,8, Dead Sea Scrolls).

> "Yours, Yours O God of knowledge [DAATH], are all the works of righteousness and the secret of Truth" (1QH 1:26,27).

> "What is man . . . that You should give him understanding of such marvels, and make known to him the secret of Your Truth?" (1QH 10:3,4).

> "Unto the son of man You have given an abundant portion of the knowledge [DAATH] of Your Truth" (1QH 10:28,29).

"All the nations shall know Your Truth" (1QH 6:12).

They shall "come to the knowledge of the Truth" (1 Timothy 2:4) when they shall read "the writing of Truth" (Daniel 10:21), "written . . . [to] make you know the certainty of the words of Truth" (Proverbs 22:20,21).

"Knowledge [DAATH] of the Truth" (1QS 9:17, Dead Sea Scrolls) gives us knowledge of His ways, and knowledge of what is well pleasing to the Lord. Taking the path of knowing His ways, we come to knowing Him. Thus "Moses said to the Lord . . . I pray You, if I have found favor in Your sight, please let me know Your ways, that I may know You" (Exodus 33:12,13). "God loves knowledge" (Zadokite Fragment (CD) 2:3 [MS.A]), and He created man "with a love of knowledge" (Book of Adam and Eve 27:3) because knowledge of God leads us to the love of God. As St. Bernard said: "the more we know God, the more we shall love Him," for "love is inseparable from knowledge" (St. Macarius), and "from knowledge comes love" of God (Shepherd of Hermas, *Vision* III.8.16:7), and zeal for Him.

What is it to have zeal for God? It is to be zealous that His will be done, and His Truth be upheld by all. For just as the knowledge of God leads us to the love of God and zeal for Him; so does knowledge of the Truth lead us to "the love of the Truth" (2 Thessalonians 2:10), and zeal for it. They who are zealous for "the Truth of God" (Romans 3:7) shall receive from the Lord that special knowledge which shall enable them to know and choose what is good and true; and perceive and reject that which is false and evil. "God loves knowledge" (Zadokite Fragment 2:3), and He desires us to have it (Hosea 6:6), because "the Lord loves judgment" (Psalm 37:28; Isaiah 61:8), and He knows that we need knowledge "to bring forth judgment for the sake of Truth" (Isaiah 42:3), in order to establish it. There is nothing better than the knowledge of God for bringing to light all that was hidden in the darkness. "That which is far off, and exceedingly deep, who can find it out?" (Ecclesiastes 7:24). The Lord with His knowledge, He can find it out, for "by His knowledge the depths are broken up" (Proverbs 3:20). "The heart of man is deep beyond all things" (Jeremiah 17:9, Greek Text), and "the works of Truth and the works of deceit are done in the hearts of men, and each of them the Lord knows, and there is no time at which the works of men can be hid from Him" (Testament of Judah 20:3,4). "Woe to them who hide deep from the Lord their counsel, and whose deeds are in the dark, and they say, 'Who sees us? Who knows us' " (Isaiah 29:15). Woe to them "for from Your knowledge no one who does unjustly is hidden . . . where then can a man hide himself from Your knowledge, O God?" (Psalms of Solomon 9:5,6). "God . . . knows the secrets of the heart" (Psalm 44:21), and "He reveals the deep and secret things for He knows what is in the darkness, and the light dwells with Him" (Daniel 2:22). "God . . . searches out the deep and the heart, and He surveys all their secrets for the Most High possesses knowledge . . . He declares . . . and reveals the deepest secrets" (Sirach 42:17,18,19, Hebrew Text [Masada Scroll]) to help those who are zealous for His Truth.

With "the light of knowledge" (Testament of Levi 4:3; 18:3; Testament of Benjamin 11:2, B Text; Hosea 10:12, Greek and Syriac Texts and Targum; see also pp. 37-38) given to us for the sake of His Truth and justice, we shall be able to reveal hidden things. With the same "light of knowledge" we shall be able to disperse the darkness of ignorance, and clarify things never before understood. We shall have the power to do so in the day "He shall make the teaching of knowledge appear as the light" (Sirach 24:27, Greek MS. 248), and "send knowledge as the light" (Sirach 24:37, Latin Vulgate) to us. Then, "as light disperses darkness, His knowledge will disperse . . . ignorance" (Philo, *Jos.* 106), for "God illuminates man with that knowledge whereby the darkness of error is dispelled from the soul, and Truth is seen in all its brightness" (Corpus Hermeticum, *Asclepius* III.29). Long ago "the day of the knowledge of the Truth dawned like the sun upon those who were lying in the darkness of ignorance" (Clement of Alexandria, *Stromata* VII.107.43) but many did not open their eyes. Therefore, they did not see "the light of the knowledge of the glory of God in the face of Jesus Christ" (2 Corinthians 4:6) His Son. But let us give "thanks to the Father who has enabled us to be partakers of the inheritance of the saints in light" (Colossians 1:12), for "He has poured forth, from the fountain of His knowledge the light that enlightens" us (1QS 11:3,4, Dead Sea Scrolls). "Let the rays of knowledge rise revealing and illuminating the hidden" (Clement of Alexandria, *Exh.* XI.15.4) for when the hidden is revealed, all shall return to Him. "May He make of you an example of holiness in the midst of His people, and a torch to shine upon the world in knowledge and to enlighten the face of many" (1QSb 4:27 [Book of Blessings], Dead Sea Scrolls) so that the world may bask in the light of His knowledge and acknowledge Him.

"The Lord is a God of knowledge, and by Him, actions are weighed" (1 Samuel 2:3). "For every purpose there is time and judgment [MISHPAT], therefore the misery of man is great upon him" (Ecclesiastes 8:6), inasmuch as he knows that for every action he will be judged some day by the Lord. "Wise men who know the times" (Esther 1:13) ask "the God of knowledge" (1QH 12:10, Dead Sea Scrolls), for that very important gift of knowledge which shall enable us to know both time and judgment. "A wise man's heart knows both time and judgment" (Ecclesiastes 8:5), therefore, he fears God and keeps His commandments for he knows that "God will bring every action to judgment along with every secret thing whether it is good or evil" (Ecclesiastes 12:14). Hence, those who are wise and understanding pray:

> "O Lord, make me to know my end and the number
> of my days, that I may know how frail I am" (Psalm
> 39:4).

> O God, "make us to know [YADA'] how to number
> our days that we may bring to You a heart of wis-
> dom" (Psalm 90:12).

"For man does not know his time" (Ecclesiastes 9:12) of judgment: the most important time of his life. All who are wise and understanding remember the lament of the Lord:

> "The stork in the heavens knows her appointed times;
> and the turtle dove and the swift and the thrush
> watch the time of their migration; but My people do
> not know the judgment of the Lord" (Jeremiah 8:7).

It is good knowledge to know that the Lord God is very merciful, but let us not forget that He is also very just:

> "The Lord God is merciful and gracious, longsuffer-
> ing, and abounding in lovingkindness and Truth; who
> keeps lovingkindness for thousands, who forgives
> iniquity, transgression, and sin; yet He will by no
> means leave the guilty unpunished" (Exodus 34:6,7).

If we keep in heart the holy knowledge that "we shall all stand before the judgment seat of God" (Romans 14:10), we shall not lose sight of the foundation upon which the ladder stands: the fear of the Lord. We shall then remember that "the fear of the Lord is the beginning of knowledge" (Proverbs 1:7).

> "This I pray: that your love may abound yet more and
> more in full knowledge" (Philippians 1:9).

THE SEVENTH RUNG

DEAH

[THE LORD'S KNOWLEDGE]

On the day we shall have attained full knowledge we shall be ready to ascend to the seventh rung of the ladder and receive from the Lord a most precious gift called DEAH: the very knowledge of God. "The Lord is a God of knowledge [DEAH]" (1 Samuel 2:3). We know that it is a great thing for man to receive from God the gift of "knowledge" [DAATH], but it is an even greater thing to receive from Him the superlative gift of His own "knowledge" [DEAH]. In comparison with God's DEAH, "man is brutish in his knowledge [DAATH]" (Jeremiah 10:14; 51:17).

"To whom shall He teach knowledge [DEAH]?" (Isaiah 28:9). Is it possible for us to learn knowledge [DEAH]? No. We can be informed about it and understand it, but we cannot acquire DEAH unless God gives it to us little by little, as one would feed a child. The Lord promised that He will give us: "Shepherds after My own heart, who will feed you with knowledge [DEAH] and understanding" (Jeremiah 3:15). And on that day — may the Lord hasten it — there shall be great peace: "the peace of God which surpasses all understanding" (Philippians 4:7). For "the end of knowledge is peace" (Clement of Alexandria, *Paed.* I.6.29:3). When "all your children shall be taught by the Lord, great shall be the peace of your children" (Isaiah 54:13). His people knew that "through his [the Messiah's] teaching, peace shall be greatly increased upon us" (Targum on Isaiah 53:5). And when He came and they did not accept His teaching, He wept and said of them: "If only you, even you, had known in this day the things that are hidden from your eyes" (St. Luke 19:42), they would have received both His knowledge and His peace. For through the knowledge of God we come to the love of God, and love for one another. Where there is no knowledge of God, there is no loving kindness (Hosea 4:1), and no peace. "There is no peace for the wicked, says the Lord" (Isaiah 48:22; 57:21), because "the wicked . . . do not know" (Psalm 82:4,5); "the wicked do not understand knowledge" (Proverbs 29:7b). But there is peace for the righteous because "the righteous know [YADA']" (Proverbs 29:7a) and "the upright shall understand the knowledge of the Most High" (1QS 4:22, Dead Sea Scrolls), therefore: "behold the upright, for the end of that man is peace" (Psalm 37:37, Literal Translation). "Righteousness and peace" (Psalm 85:10) go together for "the work of righteousness is peace, and the effect of righteousness is quietness and assurance forever" — "the peace of righteousness" (Isaiah 32:17; Baruch 5:4). Thus, the Lord cried out to His errant people: "O, that you had paid attention to My commandments! Then your *peace* would have been like a river, and your *righteousness* like the waves of the sea" (Isaiah 48:18). We should know that there is no peace for the cruel:

"O ye hardhearted, ye shall find no peace" (Enoch 5:4).

And no peace for the proud who:
"Spoke proud and insolent words against His righteousness . . . you shall have no peace" (Enoch 101:3).

Neither shall there be peace for covetous oppressors, liars, and sinners:

> "Woe to those who build unrighteousness and
> oppression, and lay deceit as a foundation . . . they
> shall have no peace" (Enoch 94:6).

> "Woe to you who build your houses through the
> grievous toil of others, and all their building materials
> are the bricks and stones of sin; I tell you, you shall
> have no peace" (Enoch 99:13).

> "Woe to you who write down lying and godless
> words; for they write down their lies that men may
> follow them and act godlessly toward their neighbor.
> Therefore they shall have no peace" (Enoch 98:15,16).

> "Woe to you obstinate of heart who work wickedness
> . . . you shall have no peace" (Enoch 98:11).

> "Woe to you, you sinners when you die, if you die in
> the greatness of your sins . . . woe to you for you shall
> have no peace" (Enoch 103:5,8).

> "You sinners shall be accursed forever, and you shall
> have no peace" (Enoch 102:3).

And they shall have no knowledge either, because the knowledge [DEAH] of
God is "holy knowledge" (2 Maccabees 6:30) which is given only to those who
are good and holy. They are the ones who shall die in the peace of the Lord:
"behold the upright, for the end of that man is peace" (Psalm 37:37).

The great day shall come when:

> "The wolf shall dwell with the lamb, and the leopard
> lie down with the kid and the calf and the lion and
> the yearling together, and a little child shall lead
> them. The cow and the bear shall feed: their young
> shall lie down together; and the lion shall eat straw
> like the ox. The nursing child shall play over the hole
> of the asp, and the weaned child shall put his hand on
> the viper's den. They shall not hurt or destroy in all
> My holy mountain; because the earth will be full of
> the knowledge [DEAH] of the Lord, as the waters
> cover the sea" (Isaiah 11:6-9).

We shall have great peace on the day the knowledge [DEAH] of the Lord shall fill the face of the whole earth.

If we desire to see the coming of that great day, let us call upon the name of the Lord for "He is our peace" — "in whom are hidden all the treasures of wisdom and knowledge" (Ephesians 2:14; Colossians 2:3), for "to the Lord belongs all holy knowledge" (2 Maccabees 6:30) that shall bring our peace.

> "May grace and peace be yours in fullest measure
> through the knowledge of God and of Jesus our Lord"
> (2 Peter 1:2).

THE EIGHTH RUNG

'ETSAH

[COUNSEL]

The wisdom, understanding, and knowledge we receive as we ascend towards the Truth aid us to understand the ways of the Lord, and come to know Him better. They also prepare us for the climb to the eighth rung of the ladder where we shall receive the unique gift of His good "counsel" ['ETSAH]. With 'ETSAH we obtain excellent guidance and protection from the Lord along with the ability to give others good advice using the wisdom, understanding and knowledge we have received from Him. Thus, by listening to our good counsel, others may be made wise and understanding, and find salvation through the knowledge of our Lord:

> "Hear counsel ['ETSAH] . . . that you may be wise" (Proverbs 19:20).

> "He who listens to counsel ['ETSAH] is wise" (Proverbs 12:15).

> "With the well counselled ['ETSAH] is wisdom" (Proverbs 13:10).

> "Wise in the counsel of understanding" (Psalms of Solomon 17:42).

We cannot give good counsel unless we first understand. Only then shall we be able to give "the counsel of understanding" (Psalms of Solomon 17:42), and become "an understanding [SEKEL] counsellor" (1 Chronicles 26:14). "For what can counsel do by itself without the understanding?" (Philo, *Q.Gen.* IV.56). In Holy Scripture, "counsel ['ETSAH] and understanding" (Job 12:13) often go together. "Ask counsel from all those who are understanding [PHRONIMOU]" (Tobit 4:18). And "say to Understanding: 'you are my counsellor'" (Proverbs 7:4, Syriac Text). "A man of counsel will not neglect understanding" (Sirach 32:22, Latin Vulgate), for he knows how much his counsel depends on his understanding. And he also knows that he must not neglect to keep the commandments and be good, for that is what gives him understanding (Job 28:28; Psalm 111:10). "At no time is the counsel of sinners understanding" (Sirach 19:22). But good counsel from the good is understanding, because it can make us understand. Thus, the Alexandrian Jewish Scribes who translated the Hebrew Bible into Greek rendered: "I will bless the Lord who has given me counsel" (Psalm 16:7, Hebrew Text) into: "I will praise the Lord who has made me understand" (Psalm 16:7, Greek Text). Let us not forget: "the counsel of the holy ones is understanding" (Proverbs 9:10, Greek Text), but not the counsel of sinners.

Because there is good and evil in this world we also need to have knowledge of good and awareness of evil before we can give good advice. "Good counsel shall guard you" (Proverbs 2:11, Greek Text) because good counsel knows what it is you have to be guarded from, and that takes knowledge. Evil counsel seeks to entrap but "woe to them who hide deep from the Lord their counsel, whose deeds are in the dark" (Isaiah 29:15) "for from Your knowledge no one who does unjustly is hidden" (Psalms of Solomon 9:5), and neither is his "deep and sinful counsel" (Isaiah 31:6, Greek Text), concealed from the knowledge of the Lord. If it is said that "the Most High . . . shall try your works and search out your deep counsels" (Wisdom 6:3), it is because "the Most High possesses knowledge" (Sirach 42:18, Hebrew Text [Masada Scroll]), and from "the knowledge of the Most High" (Numbers 24:16) nothing can be hidden. "The Lord comes who will both bring to light the hidden things of the darkness, and will make manifest the [hidden] counsels [BOULAS] of the hearts" (1 Corinthians 4:5).

"Counsel in the heart of man is like deep water" (Proverbs 20:5), and "Wisdom's counsels are profounder than the great deep" (Sirach 24:29), but far more profound are "the deep things of God" (1 Corinthians 2:10). "For what man can know the counsel [BOULĒN] of God? Or who can conceive what the Lord wills?" (Wisdom 9:13). "Who has known Your counsel [BOULĒN], unless You have given Wisdom and sent Your Holy Spirit from on high?" (Wisdom 9:17). "For the Spirit searches all things, yes, even the deep things of God" (1 Corinthians 2:10). We shall learn from the Holy Spirit that the Lord hides His counsel in our hearts as a seed: a living seed that shall transform us if we obey the directives of His good counsel. They who act upon the seed of His good counsel ['ETSAH] shall see it flourish from the ground of their hearts as "a great [MEGA] tree" (St. Luke 13:19), full of the fruits of His good counsel, to share with those in need. When the angel Uriel told Ezra that "the trees took counsel" (2 Esdras 4:13), it is because there is a close relationship between the Hebrew word for "tree" ['ETS], and 'ETSAH: the word for "counsel." In later Hebrew, 'ETSAH, has come to mean both "counsel" and "trees" [see Jerusalem Talmud: Erubin VIII. 25b; Shabbath III. 6a; Sukkah I.52c, Babylonian Talmud: Erubin 67b. See also Jeremiah 6:6.]. Rightly may good counsel be compared to a fruitful tree, since the ability to give good counsel is the fruition of all the wisdom, understanding, and knowledge that the righteous receive from the Lord. Thus, the righteous who possess the faculty of giving good counsel, may be referred to as: "trees of righteousness, the planting of the Lord, that He might be glorified" (Isaiah 61:3). Again, "the Paradise of the Lord, the trees of life, these are His holy ones, their planting is rooted forever, they shall not be uprooted" (Psalms of Solomon 14:2,3). "What blessing God bestows on those who love Him as they should. Since they become a paradise of delights, they rear in themselves a fruitful tree in fullest bloom, and are adorned with a variety of fruit" (*Epistle to Diognetus* 12:1). In that variety of fruit, we find "the peaceable fruit of righteousness" (Hebrews 12:11; St. James 3:18), the fruits of Wisdom [Sirach 24:19; 6:19], "the fruits of understanding" (Sirach 37:22), and "the fruit of . . . knowledge" (Sirach 37:22, Hebrew Text). All these fruits are delectable and gladden the heart, for they contain within them the seeds of Truth, and "sweet counsel" (Psalm 55:14; Proverbs 27:9). "The fruit of the righteous is a tree of life" (Proverbs 11:30) to those who accept the sweet counsel and the seeds of Truth within it. But "the fruit of the wicked" (Proverbs 10:16) is death to those who devour their "fruit of lies" (Hosea 10:13), and "evil counsel" (Isaiah 7:5). Let us remember the remonstration of Wisdom against the foolish who did not accept her advice: "they would have none of my counsel [as seed], they despised all my reproof [as cultivation]. Therefore, they shall eat the fruit of their own way and be filled with their own devices" which "shall destroy them" (Proverbs 1:30-31,32). We should beware of "the counsel of the wicked" (Job 10:3; 21:16; 22:18; Psalm 1:1) and "the counsels of the ungodly" (Wisdom 1:9), and have nothing to do with "the fruit of their thoughts" (Jeremiah 6:19), and "the fruit of their doings" (Micah 7:13), for the Lord said:

> "I will punish you according to the fruit of your doings" (Jeremiah 21:14).

> "For I, the Lord, search the heart, and examine the deepest motives, to give to each man according to his ways, and according to the fruit [PERI] of his doings" (Jeremiah 17:10).

The Lord "works all things after the counsel of His will" (Ephesians 1:11). And He makes known to us His will, and His ways through His good counsel. To know God's counsel is to know His ways, and vice versa. Thus, the Jewish Alexandrian scribes translated: "We do not desire the knowledge of Your ways" (Job 21:14, Hebrew Text) into "I desire not to know Your counsel" (Job 21:14, Greek Text). Inasmuch as there is such a close relationship between what God counsels and what He wills, the Greek word for "counsel" [BOULĒ, BOULĒMA, BOULOMAI], and the word for "will" [THELĒMA, THELŌ], are sometimes used interchangeably in both the Greek Old Testament, and in the New. For example the best Greek Codices render 1 Peter 4:3: "the will [THELĒMA] of the Gentiles" (Codices: Vaticanus, Sinaiticus, Alexandrinus, etc.); but there are variants which read: "the counsel [BOULĒMA] of the Gentiles" (Codex Petersburg and Uncials 915-917; 1838r; 1831-216; 1518s; 385rel). The Lord wills to guide us with His good counsel, consequently, the Psalmist says: "O Lord . . . You shall guide me with Your counsel" (Psalm 73:20,24). In turn, those who have listened to, and obeyed the counsel of the Lord, may become "leaders [ĒGOUMENOI, literally "guides"] of the people by their counsels" (Sirach 44:4). We can easily get lost without good counsel:

> "They are a nation lost ['ABAD] of counsel, neither is there any understanding in them" (Deuteronomy 32:28).
>
> "Is counsel lost ['ABAD] from the understanding? (Jeremiah 49:7).
>
> "Is your counselor lost ['ABAD]?" (Micah 4:9).
>
> "The Law [TORAH = "teaching"] shall be lost ['ABAD] from the priest, and counsel from the ancients" (Ezekiel 7:26).

Therefore, "keep my counsel and understanding that your soul may live, and . . . that you may go confidently in peace in all your ways, and that your foot may not stumble" (Proverbs 3:21,23, Greek Text).

Throughout the Holy Scriptures, God gives us "counsels . . . without ceasing for our admonishing and chastening, and the reformation of our whole life" (Philo, *Deus.* 182). And these good counsels are plain before our eyes in His commandments and precepts; and in the exhortations of His prophets and wise men. Nevertheless, all throughout the Holy Scriptures, God hides His marvelous counsel so that we may search for it as for the hidden treasures of His wisdom [W/U:1-46]. We see a beautiful instance of this in the theme of the search for God. The Holy Scriptures tell us to seek the Lord:

> "You shall seek the Lord your God" (Deuteronomy 4:29a).
>
> "Seek the Lord while He may be found" (Isaiah 55:6).
>
> "Seek ye My face" (Psalm 27:8).
>
> "Seek the Lord and His strength, seek His face continually" (1 Chronicles 16:11; Psalm 105:4).

And we are given the assurance that: "If you seek Him, He will be found by you" (1 Chronicles 28:9). We may sometimes feel like Job who cried out: "O, that I knew where to find Him!" (Job 23:3), and David, who said: "O when shall I come and see the face of God?" (Psalm 42:2, Literal Translation). Nevertheless, we are given the further promise that: "you shall find Him, if you seek Him with all your heart and with all your soul" (Deuteronomy 4:29b). To realize the significance of that good counsel is to "set your heart and your soul to seek the Lord your God" (1 Chronicles 22:19). It is to prepare ourselves to seek the Lord with the same intensity we are commanded to love Him: "with all our heart, and with all our soul, and with all our strength" (Deuteronomy 6:5). To seek Him with all our heart and with all our soul is to ardently search for Him with a longing that passionately cries out to Him:

"As a deer longs for running streams, so does my soul yearn for You, O God. My soul thirsts for God, for the living God; O when shall I come and see the face of God?" (Psalm 42:1-2).

"My soul yearns for You in the night, my spirit within me eagerly seeks You at dawn" (Isaiah 26:9).

"O God . . . my God, early will I seek You; my soul thirsts for You, my flesh longs for You" (Psalm 63:1).

Have we ever sought the Lord that way, or longed for Him with the same intensity? If not, how can we hope to find Him? For the Lord is not discovered unless He first shows Himself to us. And He is not seen unless He reveals Himself, drawn to us by that special ingredient which should be in every heart pursuing Him. By searching the Holy Scriptures for His hidden counsel, we shall find that crucial element we need to give us success in our venture. We shall discover that precious information in the seldom read Second book of Chronicles. There, we are told about a group of people who went to seek the Lord, and how they actually found Him because:

"They entered into a covenant to seek the Lord God of their fathers with all their heart and with all their soul . . . they . . . sought Him with their whole desire and He was found by them" (2 Chronicles 15:12,15).

They found the Lord because they sought Him with all desire, with all eagerness and wholehearted willingness to do everything required of them in the search of the Lord. We may be sure that before searching: "everyone . . . prepared his heart to seek God" (2 Chronicles 30:18,19) because only "the pure in heart . . . shall see God" (St. Matthew 5:8). And only those who desire Him with all their heart and with all their soul shall find Him by their side. For the Lord our God is drawn to us by our desire for Him, just as Wisdom herself is responsive towards those who yearn for her:

"Wisdom is near to those who seek her, and he that gives his desire to her shall find her" (Sirach 51:26, Hebrew Text).

"For "Wisdom hastens to make herself known to those who desire her" (Wisdom 6:13, RSV).

And Wisdom's invitation is to them" "Come to me, all you who desire me" (Sirach 24:19). Did not the Lord say: "If any man thirst, let him come to Me and drink?" (St. John 7:37). Let us with all desire hunger and thirst for Him who is our food and drink.

"The heart that is established by well advised counsel shall not fear at any time" (Sirach 22:16). For we know that "counsel and strength" (2 Kings 18:20; Isaiah 36:5) go together, and nothing can prevail over "the immutability of His counsel" (Hebrews 6:17). "For who has resisted His counsel [BOULĒMA]?" (Romans 9:19). "There are many plans in a man's heart; nevertheless, the counsel of the Lord shall stand" (Proverbs 19:21), because "the counsel of the Lord stands forever" (Psalm 33:11). Therefore, "every plan is established [KUN] by counsel" (Proverbs 20:18), and "without counsel, plans are frustrated; but with many counselors, they are confirmed [QUM]" (Proverbs 15:22), because good counselors possess "the counsel of God" (Acts 20:27), and "God brings to successful completion [SHALEM] the counsel of His messengers" (Isaiah 44:26). "Do nothing without counsel" (Sirach 32:19), and "let counsel go before every action" (Sirach 37:16), but make certain that the counsel you receive is from someone who is good. And may "the Lord . . . grant you your heart's desire, and fulfill all your counsel ['ETSAH]" (Psalm 20:1,4).

The Lord's good counsels are openly found in His commandments and precepts. And because these serve to check our wild impulses and rein us back into His ways, they may be referred to as "bonds," for we are in a positive way "bound" by His commandments, and "bound by the Law" (Romans 7:2; 1 Corinthians 7:39). And as a sign, we are told by the Lord to bind His commandments before us:

> "These words which I command you this day shall be in your heart . . . and you shall bind them for a sign in your hand" (Deuteronomy 6:6,8; 11:18).

> "Let your heart keep my commandments . . . bind them around your neck" (Proverbs 3:1,3).

> "Keep, my son, the command of your father, and do not forsake the law of your mother. Bind them upon your heart always, and tie them around your neck" (Proverbs 6:20,21).

> "Keep my commandments and live . . . bind them upon your fingers" (Proverbs 7:2,3).

Elsewhere, the Lord also refers to the covenant as a bond: "I will bring you into the bond of the covenant" (Ezekiel 20:37). "Wisdom's laws" (Wisdom 6:18) too, contain her good counsels, and since they bind us to His will, her counsels are likewise described as bonds. Thus, "be not grieved with her counsels" (Sirach 6:25, Hebrew Text), was rendered" "be not grieved with her bonds" (Sirach 6:25, Greek Text). There is much wisdom in that passage of the book of Sirach:

> "My son . . . put your feet into Wisdom's fetters, and your neck into her chain. Bow down your shoulder and bear her [as a yoke] and be not grieved with her bonds" (Sirach 6:23-25, Greek Text).

> "For in the end, her bonds shall become your robe of glory, and her chain an ornament of gold" (Sirach 6:29, Syriac Text).

In that text, the transformation of Wisdom's "bonds" or "counsels" into a robe of glory and an ornament of gold is reminiscent of the bondage, persecution, and tribulations that Joseph (Genesis 39:1- 41:57) and Daniel (1:5-10; 2:27-49; 5:1-6:28) both underwent for their steadfastness in the Lord's will. Coincidentally, in the end, they were both exalted and received a robe of glory and a chain of gold (Genesis 41:42; Daniel 5:29) saved by the wisdom, understanding, and knowledge they received from the Lord, by being subject to the bonds of His commandments [W/D:19-33]. For "Wisdom exalts to glory they who hold her fast" (Sirach 1:19), and who let themselves be held by the bonds of her good counsels.

The counsel of God contains wisdom, understanding, and knowledge. And through His good counsel we receive "the instruction of wisdom, justice, judgment [MISHPAT] and equity" (Proverbs 1:3). Thus, good counsel is excellent for doing judgment, and for works of justice; because in His counsel is "the wisdom of God . . . to do judgment [MISHPAT]" (1 Kings 3:28), and the "understanding to hear [SHAMA'] judgment" (1 Kings 3:11), and also the knowledge we need to know good from evil, and the Truth from the lies that sought to confound it. "Take counsel ['ETSAH] and do judgment" (Isaiah 16:3). "O how comely a thing is judgment in the gray-haired, and for the aged to fully know [EPIGNOSIS] counsel" (Sirach 25:4), for they who fully know counsel know how to judge well. But let us remember that we must first ascend the rungs of His wisdom, understanding, and knowledge before we can set foot on the eighth rung to receive the gift of His good counsel ['ETSAH]. For how shall we, in turn, be able to give others good counsel if we do not have wisdom, understanding, and knowledge? For "where there is no knowledge there is no persuasive counsel" (Sirach 3:25, Syriac Text).

"Lay up His words in your heart" (Job 22:22) and "submit yourself then to Him, and be at peace, for thereby you shall have the best fruits" (Job 22:21, Latin Vulgate), and everyone shall enjoy your "sweet counsel" (Psalm 55:14).

Believe in Him, for He said that "he who believes in Me . . . from his innermost being shall flow streams of living water" (St. John 7:38). Have faith in Him, and "you shall be like a watered garden, like a spring of water, whose waters never fail" (Isaiah 58:11). "Come all you who thirst, come to the water" (Isaiah 55:1) and live! Drink deeply, because "counsel is like a fountain of life" (Sirach 21:13).

THE NINTH RUNG

TACHBULOTH

[POWERFUL COUNSEL]

When we have attained to the ninth rung of the ladder, we shall receive from the Lord the great gift of TACHBULOTH [literally "powerful counsels"]. What in comparison TEBUNAH is to BIN, and DEAH is to DAATH; TACHBULOTH is to 'ETSAH. TACHBULOTH is a great and powerful gift because it enables us to marshal all His gifts of wisdom, understanding, knowledge, and counsel, for the sake of the Truth. "Every plan is established by counsel ['ETSAH], and with powerful counsel [TACHBULOTH] make war" (Proverbs 20:18). For with His "powerful counsel" [TACHBULOTH] we can set in array armies of reasonings, evidences, vindications, logical arguments and summations in defense of the Truth. And with all the power of His TACHBULOTH advance against, and put to rout all lies. "With whom shall you find the fight for the Law? With him who has in hand powerful counsels [TACHBULOTH]" (Sanhedrin 42a, Babylonian Talmud [MS. Munich]). "Where there is no vision the people are made naked" (Proverbs 29:18, Literal Translation) before their enemies. And "where there is no powerful counsel [TACHBULOTH] the people fall; but there is deliverance [TESHUAH] in a great [RAB] counselor" (Proverbs 11:14, Literal Translation), because in that "counselor" [singular in the text of Proverbs 11:14] is the powerful counsel [TACHBULOTH] of the Lord which makes him "great," for the "Lord of Hosts is . . . great in counsel and great in deed" (Jeremiah 32:18,19).

In the book of Job, we are told that through His TACHBULOTH, God is able to steer and turn all the clouds around make them do His will either for our benefit [favorable rains] or punishment [flood rains and lightnings]. "God . . . gives the clouds their load of moisture, He disperses the cloud of His lightning. By His powerful counsel [TACHBULOTH] they are turned around, that they may do whatever He commands them on the face of the inhabited earth. He brings His clouds for punishment [of man], or for His earth, or for lovingkindness, He causes it to happen" (Job 37:10, 11-13) by means of His TACHBULOTH. Because the Jewish scribes who translated the Hebrew Old Testament into Greek knew that His powerful counsel [TACHBULOTH] gives us the ability to steer things unerringly towards a goal, they rendered TACHBULOTH into KUBERNĒSIS: the Greek word for "governance," "generalship" or "good steering" at the helm. From that Greek word came the Latin word GUBERNATOR from which the English word "governor" is derived. A good governor or leader is in a way a great helmsman in that he skillfully steers the ship of state through troubled waters. In an old rabbinic work called the Pesikta Rabbati, Rabbi Tanchuma bar Abba [4th Century A.D.] commented on this aspect of TACHBULOTH when he said that "TACHBULOTH is not wise counsels" [a common rendering in English Texts], but "the art of steering." And he went on to say that "the art of steering refers to Moses in his generation, Joshua in his generation, and Samuel in his generation" (Pesikta Rabbati, Piska 47, Sect. 4). They were good leaders because all of them were righteous men, and being righteous they were all endowed by the Lord with TACHBULOTH to enable them to govern His people well. Furthermore, just as "there is a wisdom that abounds in evil" (Sirach 21:15, Latin Vulgate), a "wisdom . . . earthly, sensual and devilish" (St. James 3:15); so is there "evil counsel" (Isaiah 7:5), and "sinful counsel" (Isaiah 31:6, Greek Text), for such is "the counsel of the wicked" — "the men who devise iniquity and give evil counsel" (Job 21:16; Ezekiel 11:2) to drag others to perdition. And just as the Lord's powerful counsel [TACHBULOTH] enables one to marshal His gifts of wisdom, understanding, knowledge, and counsel for a good cause, so do the wicked in their craftiness muster up their guile, subterfuge and perversity into devising malicious stratagems for evil purposes. Thus, we are warned that "the advice [TACHBULOTH] of the wicked is deceit" (Proverbs 12:5), and his intent: the downfall of the unwary. "O Lord . . . let destruction come upon him unawares, and let his own net that he hid catch himself, into that very destruction let him fall" (Psalm 35:1,8). And let us place our trust in the Lord, for with the help of His powerful counsel, "the advice of the perverse is quickly brought to confusion" (Job 5:13), and "the wicked one is snared in the work of his own hands" (Psalm 9:16), for "his own counsel shall cast the wicked man down" (Job 18:7), but "the counsel of the Lord stands forever" (Psalm 33:11).

"A wise man will hear and increase in learning and a man of understanding will obtain powerful counsel [TACHBULOTH] to [be able to] understand a proverb, and its interpretation, the words of the wise and their riddles" (Proverbs 1:5,6). In addition to enabling us to direct things aright, TACHBULOTH also gives us the power to understand the hidden meaning of a proverb or parable and bring it to light. With TACHBULOTH we can solve intricate problems and provide the correct answer to the challenging riddles of the wise. Because by means of His "powerful counsel" [TACHBULOTH] we can draw again upon the previous gifts of His wisdom, understanding, knowledge, and counsel to give us insight into His hidden truths and counsels. Through the right explanation of His mysteries, TACHBULOTH enables us to bring His deep things to light. In this regard, His powerful counsel renders us an inestimable service because it is through the right interpretation of an enigmatic saying or a celestial vision that we obtain knowledge of the great truths found in them. Thus, after seeing a mysterious vision, Daniel was troubled because he could not understand it. Consequently, he asked one of the angels standing by "the true meaning [YETSAB]" of the vision, and Daniel relates that the angel "answered ['AMAR] me, and made me know the interpretation of the things" (Daniel 7:16) thereby bringing to light the prophetic truths found in the symbolic vision.

"Wisdom's counsels are profounder than the great deep" (Sirach 24:29), and "counsel ['ETSAH] in the heart of man is like deep water, but a man of understanding will draw it out" (Proverbs 20:5). Because "a man of understanding will obtain powerful counsel [TACHBULOTH]" (Proverbs 1:5), and with it bring to light all that is hidden in the darkness. Let us always remember that a man of understanding is able to climb the ladder to the rung of TACHBULOTH because he commenced his ascent from the base of that ladder which is: the fear of the Lord. If "evil men do not understand judgment" (Proverbs 28:5), it is because evil men do not have the fear of the Lord [FL/E:37-45]. But "they who fear the Lord understand judgment and shall bring forth powerful counsel [TACHBULOTH] out of the gloom" (Sirach 32:16, Hebrew Text, MS. E; see Greek and Latin Vulgate Texts ad loc.). And with His powerful counsel they shall enlighten us and direct us towards the Lord; for where the Lord is — there we shall find all Truth and salvation.

> "O Lord . . . Your counsels ['ETSAH] of old are
> faithful and true" — Isaiah 25:1.

179

THE TENTH RUNG

TUSHIYYAH

[DELIVERANCE THROUGH THE ABILITY TO SEE BRING FORTH, AND GRASP THE TRUTH]

Great rejoicing of heart awaits us in the tenth rung of the ladder, for in that last rung we shall fully possess TUSHIYYAH. Outside the Hebrew language, no words can adequately convey what His wonderful gift of TUSHIYYAH actually means. The Jewish scribes who translated the Hebrew Holy Scriptures into Greek [Septuagint] variously rendered it: "salvation," "deliverance," "safety," "power," "Truth" and "peace." Our own English versions of the Bible have a wide diversity of renderings for TUSHIYYAH, translating it: "ability," "achievements," "advice," "good advice," "sound advice," "counsel," "deeds," "deliverance," "efficiency," "enterprise," "equity," "guidance," "health," "help," "helpful insight," "intrigues," "sound judgment," "wise judgment," "justice," "sound knowledge," "persistence," "plans," "sound policy," "power," "power to aid myself," "prudence," "great prudence," "resource," "resourcefulness," "salvation," "substance," "substantial," "success," "that which is," "the thing as it is," "manifold understanding," "victory," "wisdom," "sound wisdom" and "true wisdom" [the various renderings for TUSHIYYAH in the DV, JB, JPSV, KJV, NAB, NAS, NEB, NIV, NJB, NKJV, NRSV, REB, RSV, RV versions of the Bible]. But what is the real meaning of TUSHIYYAH? If we compare two similar texts found in Isaiah and Jeremiah, we shall have an inkling of its significance:

> "The Lord of Hosts, He is wonderful in counsel, and great in TUSHIYYAH" (Isaiah 28:29).

> "The Lord of Hosts is great in counsel, and mighty in excellent deeds ['ALILIYYAH]" (Jeremiah 32:19).

The word 'ALILIYYAH is unique in the Hebrew language and is found nowhere else in the Old Testament or in ancient Rabbinic writings. It is derived from 'ALILAH, the Hebrew word used in 1 Chronicles 16:8; Psalms 9:11; 66:5; 77:12; 78:11; 103:7; 105:1 and Isaiah 12:4, for the marvelous deeds of God. From the alternate use of 'ALILIYYAH in the text of Jeremiah 32:19, we can see that TUSHIYYAH primarily denotes capability to do an effective action, a successful feat or act of deliverance. The special saving action made possible by the gift of TUSHIYYAH is reserved for the upright: "the Lord . . . treasures up [TSAPHAN] TUSHIYYAH for the upright" (Proverbs 2:6,7). It is for them alone and not for the wicked or deceitful, for "He frustrates the plans of the crafty so that their hands cannot perform TUSHIYYAH" (Job 5:12). The Lord takes the deceitful "in their own craftiness, and the counsel of the perverse is quickly overthrown. They meet with darkness in the daytime and grope at noon as in the night" (Job 5:13,14). "But He saves the poor from the sword . . . He saves them from the clutches of the mighty" (Job 5:15) through His TUSHIYYAH.

If we search the Holy Scriptures and seek the wisdom of the ancients, we shall discover the wonderful Truth that God sows in us His good gifts as seeds. For we are truly earthpeople, therefore God relates to us as Gardener to garden; Farmer to field; and Seed to ground. His first command to us was to "be fruitful and increase" (Genesis 1:28). It was an order given, as it were, to a plot of living ground, thereby implanting it with the seed of His command. "For the Word of God is alive and active" (Hebrews 4:12, Literal Translation), and it is given to us as a living seed: "as seed to the sower . . . so shall My word be that goes forth from My mouth" (Isaiah 55:10,11). Thus in our Lord's Parable of the Sower: "the word that was sown in them" (St. Mark 4:15) was sown as a seed by the Sower, for "the Seed is the Word of God" (St. Luke 8:11) and "the Sower sows the Word" (St. Mark 4:14) as a seed. The fruits that the Sower expects from "His Seed" (St. Luke 8:5) are "the fruits of understanding" (Sirach 37:22) it. This we know, because in the same Parable we are told that "he who hears the Word and understands it; he indeed bears fruit and brings forth . . . a hundredfold" (St. Matthew 13:23) from that Seed. But we must not forget that he who brings forth fruit from the Seed of His Word is he who hears, accepts, and keeps the Word as a seed in the ground of his "honest and good heart" (St. Luke 8:15, Literal Translation), for there is no bearing of fruit without keeping the seed. As the fruit is in a certain way hidden within the kernel of a seed, so is the great wisdom, understanding, and knowledge of God hidden within the Seed of His Word, waiting to be brought forth to His glory as fruit, from the hearts of all who keep His Seed.

"God is light" (1 John 1:5), and we shall become "children of light" (St. John 12:36) and true sons of "the Father of lights" (St. James 1:17) on the day we shall bring forth "the fruit of light which is in all goodness and righteousness and Truth" (Ephesians 5:9). We shall then know that "the fruit of light" is brought forth by those who keep the seed of light: the Word of God. Truly did the Psalmist say that like a seed, "light is sown [ZARA'] for the righteous" (Psalm 97:11), for it is they who keep His Word as a seed in their hearts. A seed breaks open in the good ground that holds it fast. Therefore, when the light-bearing seeds of His Word open up in the hearts of those who hold them fast, they shall receive light and understanding from them. For "the unfolding of Your words gives light and understanding to the simple" (Psalm 119:130) because like the righteous, "the simple believe every word" of God (Proverbs 14:15, Literal Translation), and they hold fast to what they believe. The keeping of the seeds of His word shall transform the hearts of the righteous, making them "upright [YASHAR] in heart." And it is the upright in heart who shall rejoice over the light and understanding received from the seeds of His Word. For "light is sown for the righteous, and joy for the upright [YASHAR] in heart" (Psalm 97:11), because "for the upright [YASHAR] light arises in the darkness" (Psalm 112:4, Literal Translation) as fruit from the seed of light that was sown.

By the same token, if the living testimonies of the Lord are kept like precious seeds, they will transform the hearts of those who hold them fast. For "Your testimonies which You have commanded [to be kept (see Deut. 6:17)] are righteousness and faithfulness" (Psalm 119:138, Literal Translation) for those who keep them. And they are also wisdom and understanding for those who hold them fast, for they shall receive instruction and counsel from His testimonies. For it is written: "Your testimonies . . . are my counsellors" (Psalm 119:24), and "with the well counseled is wisdom" (Proverbs 13:10). "Blessed are they who keep His testimonies [EDAH]" (Psalm 119:2), for "the testimony [EDUTH] of the Lord is sure, making wise the simple" (Psalm 19:7) who are well counseled by the testimonies of the Lord, which they keep in their hearts. Truly, those who have "kept Your testimonies," and "cleave to Your testimonies," shall become wise and "will speak of Your testimonies before kings, and not be ashamed" (Psalm 119:22,31,46).

Let us recall to mind that "the Seed is the Word of God" (St. Luke 8:11) which is sown in the ground of our hearts. "Receive with meekness the implanted Word which is able to save your souls" (St. James 1:21) because it is "the Word of life" (Philippians 2:16; 1 John 1:1). Whoever keeps His Words keeps "the words of eternal life" (St. John 6:68) and "brings forth fruit to God" — "fruit [KARPON] towards holiness and . . . eternal life" (Romans 7:4; 6:22). We shall understand all things if we do not forget that we are truly earthpeople, and our hearts are the ground upon which God sows the seeds of His Word, wisdom, understanding, and knowledge. "The invisible seminal artificer: the divine Word" (Philo, *Her.* 119) is sown as a seed, and so are "the seeds of wisdom" (Philo, *Q.Gen.* III.32). "Come to Wisdom as one who plows and sows and wait for her good fruit, for in tilling around her you will labor for a little while, but soon you will eat of her fruits": "the fruits of wisdom" (Sirach 6:19; Philo, *Ebr.* 212; Sirach 24:19). Likewise, "God sowed in the earthborn man: understanding" (Philo, *L.A.* I.79) and "understanding grows with us" (2 Esdras 7:64, Syriac Text) if we keep what God has sown: "the seeds . . . of understanding" (Philo, *Cong.* 123) "O Lord . . . cultivate our understanding whereby fruit may come" (2 Esdras 8:6) that we may rejoice in "the fruits of understanding" (Sirach 37:22) from the seeds You sowed. Remember, that we need to till the ground of our hearts to keep it good or else our "understanding is unfruitful" (1 Corinthians 14:14) and "not a germ is left of what might grow into understanding" (Philo, *Deus.* 130) in our hearts. As it was said poetically by William Wordsworth that "the Child is father of the Man," so "the Word of knowledge [as seed] is the Father of knowledge [as fruit]" (Odes of Solomon 7:7). If we "keep knowledge" (Proverbs 5:2; 10:14; Malachi 2:7) as seed, "knowledge shall be increased" (Daniel 12:4) in us, and we shall be "fruitful in every good work, and increase in the full knowledge of God" (Colossians 1:10). Then, after "the fruit of knowledge [DAATH] is upon his body" (Sirach 37:22, Hebrew Text), "the lips of the wise disperse [ZARAH] knowledge" (Proverbs

15:7) like seed to those who are ready to understand. Long ago, His people understood, that "the Law of righteousness" (Romans 9:31) was sown in their hearts to transform and enable them to bring forth "fruits of righteousness" (Philippians 1:11) for God:

> "I will put My Law in their inward parts" (Jeremiah 31:33).

> "Behold, I sow My Law in you, and it shall bring forth fruit in you" (2 Esdras 9:31)

> "Hear Me, you who know righteousness, the people in whose heart is My Law" (Isaiah 51:7).

The Lord sows His "Law for righteousness" (Romans 10:4) so that "the righteousness which is in the Law" (Philippians 3:6) may bear fruit in us. For within "the fruit of righteousness" (St. James 3:18) are seeds of praise to His glory, and seeds of peace for us to share with others. "Praise to God . . . is the fruit" (Hebrews 13:15), "praise: the first fruit of the lips from a holy and righteous heart" (Psalms of Solomon 15:5). "Honor the Lord with your just labors, and give Him the first of your fruits of righteousness" (Proverbs 3:9, Greek Text). The fruit of righteousness is also called "the peaceful fruit of righteousness" (Hebrews 12:11) for within it are seeds of peace for us to sow in others as "children of God" [St. Matthew 5:9]. Thus, "the fruit of righteousness is sown in peace by those who make peace" (St. James 3:18; see also Zechariah 8:12, RSV). God sows the seed in our hearts, and when we bring forth fruit from it, He allows us to share in the joy of giving His seed to others and also sowing to ourselves for a further increase:

> "Break up your fallow ground" (Jeremiah 4:3).

> "Prepare your hearts, so as to sow in them the fruits of the Law, it shall protect you in that time in which the Mighty One is to shake the whole creation" (2 Baruch 32:1).

> "Sow to yourselves in righteousness, reap lovingkindness" as fruit (Hosea 10:12).

> "Sow then for yourselves good things in your souls, that you may find them in your life" (Testament of Levi 13:6).

> "I sowed my fruits in hearts" (Odes of Solomon 17:14, Syriac Text).

We shall rejoice on the day we shall have brought forth "the fruit of righteousness" to His praise, for on that day we shall have become "trees of righteousness, the planting of the Lord, that He may be glorified" (Isaiah 61:3) by our fruits.

186

Throughout the Holy Scriptures and ancient writings we have seen that the Lord sows His Word, Law, wisdom, understanding and knowledge in our hearts, and waits for us to bring forth fruit from those wonderful seeds. With the same intention, "He treasures up [TSAPHAN = to hide as treasure] TUSHIYYAH for the upright" (Proverbs 2:7) as a precious seed to be kept by them, and brought forth as fruits of deliverance: "fruits . . . full of Your salvation" (Odes of Solomon 1:5, Syriac Text). That is why the Jewish scribes who translated the Hebrew Old Testament into Greek rendered "He treasures up TUSHIYYAH for the upright," into: "He treasures up [THĒSAURIZEI] salvation [SŌTĒRIAN] for those who walk uprightly" (Proverbs 2:7, Greek Text). For just as "Wisdom is a tree of life [in the end] to those who take hold of her [as seed in the beginning]" (Proverbs 3:18), so is TUSHIYYAH life and safety for those who "keep TUSHIYYAH":

> "Keep TUSHIYYAH and discretion, and they shall be
> life to your soul and adornment around your neck.
> Then you shall walk safely in your way, and your feet
> shall not stumble" (Proverbs 3:21-23).

For where there is TUSHIYYAH, there is TESHUAH ["salvation," "safety," "deliverance," "help," "victory"]. Thus, in translating the Hebrew Text of Proverbs 8:14, which reads: "Counsel is mine and TUSHIYYAH; I am Understanding, I have strength," the Jewish scribes rendered it in Greek: "Counsel and safety [ASPHALEIA] are mine. . . ." Furthermore, in the eighth and ninth rungs of the ladder, we learn that "there is deliverance [TESHUAH] in great counsel [or "a great counselor"]" (Proverbs 11:14), and if "good counsel shall guard you" (Proverbs 2:11, Greek Text), there is safety as well. Therefore, we may expect to find good counsel in company with TUSHIYYAH:

> "Counsel is mine and TUSHIYYAH" (Proverbs 8:14).

> "The Lord of Hosts is wonderful in counsel and great
> in TUSHIYYAH" (Isaiah 28:29).

> Strength, salvation, and safety oftentimes go together
> in the Holy Scriptures:

> "In God is my salvation . . . my strength" (Psalm 62:7).

> "Salvation and strength" (Revelation 12:10).

> "Saving strength" (Psalm 20:6).

> "O Lord . . . give Your strength . . . and save" (Psalm
> 86:15,16).

> "Stir up Your strength and come and save us" (Psalm
> 80:2).

"O God, the Lord, the strength of my salvation" (Psalm 140:7).

"The Lord is my strength and my shield" (Psalm 28:7)

"How have you helped without power? How are you able to save if the arm has no strength?" (Job 26:2, Literal Translation).

Therefore, we may also expect to find TUSHIYYAH associated with strength. We read that "with Him is strength and TUSHIYYAH" (Job 12:16) because in TUSHIYYAH is latent strength, safety, and salvation, just as within the tiny seed is the potential great tree that shall spring forth from it, if the seed is held fast.

The hope of salvation, is within the seed of TUSHIYYAH, because within that seed is the potential "tree of life" (Genesis 2:9; 3:22; Proverbs 3:18; 11:30; 13:12; 15:4; 4 Maccabees 18:16; Revelation 22:14) that shall bring forth "the fruit of life" (Hosea 10:12, Greek Text) for those who hold fast the seed. "The hope that is in you" (1 Peter 3:15) is like a dormant tree of life, for we know from the book of Proverbs that "hope deferred makes the heart sick, but desire [i.e., hope] fulfilled is a tree of life" (Proverbs 13:12). Thus, in his affliction, Job remonstrated against God in these words: "as the waters wear away the stones, You wash away the things which grow out of the dust of the earth; You destroy the hope of man" [as a washed away plant or tree] (Job 14:19). Again, he said that: "He [God] has removed my hope like a tree" (Job 19:10). Bildad used the same symbolism when he said that "the hope of the ungodly shall perish and his expectation shall be cut off" (Job 8:13,14), and "his hope shall be uprooted" (Job 18:14) when the time comes that "wickedness shall be broken like a tree" (Job 24:20). Job knew that he had TUSHIYYAH in him, for he was utterly confident in his own innocence that entitled him (Proverbs 2:7) to it: "Till I die I will not renounce my integrity, I hold fast my righteousness and will not let it go" (Job 27:5,6; see also 2:3,9; 31:6]). Nevertheless, he expressed doubt that he still retained TUSHIYYAH for he lost the hope of being delivered from his woes:

"Is TUSHIYYAH driven from me?" [as Adam in Genesis 3:22,24, was driven from the tree of life] (Job 6:13).

"You . . . dissolve my TUSHIYYAH" [As Adam's progeny and all that was planted in the earth were swept away by the flood] (Job 30:22).

But Job should have been more confident for he himself said that "there is hope for a tree when it is cut down, that it will sprout again and its tender shoots will not cease. Though its roots grow old in the earth, and its stump lay dying in the ground, yet at the scent of water it will flourish and bring forth boughs, as when it was first planted" (Job 14:7-9). For out of a stump, the Lord can germinate a tree, and from a dying root bring forth the branch that yields the fruit of salvation [Isaiah 11:1].

"The labors [ERGA] of the righteous produce life" — "the bread of life" (Proverbs 10:16, Greek and Latin Vulgate Texts; St. John 6:35,48) for "bread . . . is . . . life" (Sirach 34:21) to man. Indeed, "the vital things for life are water and bread" (Sirach 29:21). Just as a woman's labor brings new life into this world, so does the travail of man provide life giving bread for the hungry. But bringing forth "the fruit of the womb" (Psalm 127:3; Genesis 30:2; Deuteronomy 7:13; St. Luke 1:42), and that of "the earth whose fruits are raised by labor" (Testament of Issachar 5:5), is not an easy task but requires great effort. If there is no bread without labor, neither shall there be "bread of understanding" (Sirach 15:3) unless "understanding works" (Wisdom 8:6; see also Testament of Simeon 4:8, Greek B, Slavonic and Armenian Texts). "The Law [TORAH] of life and good understanding" (Sirach 45:5, Hebrew Text) is sown in us [2 Esdras 9:31-33] that we may work to bring forth from it: "fruit of life" — "bread of life" (Hosea 10:12, Greek Text; St. John 6:48), and "bread of understanding [SEKEL]" (Sirach 15:3, Hebrew Text). The early Jewish fathers knew that the study of the TORAH ["Law"] entails labor, and an ascetic life to make it yield for us the fruit of understanding:

> "This is the way that is right for the study of the TORAH: a morsel of bread with salt you must eat, and water by measure you must drink; you must sleep upon the ground, and live a life of hardship while you toil in the TORAH. If you do this, happy shall you be, and it shall be well with you" (Pirke Aboth 6:4).

For "O the happiness of the man . . . who brings forth understanding!" (Proverbs 3:13).

To bring forth understanding, we should take pains to till the ground where the seed was sown, and prune the branches that shall bear fruit from the seed. In other words, we should "cultivate our understanding" (2 Esdras 8:6) so that we may bring forth fruit in abundance to His glory [St. John 15:2,5,8]. Truly, "he who tills his own ground ['ADAMAH] shall be filled with bread [of understanding]. But he who pursues empty things [REIQIM], lacks understanding" (Proverbs 12:11), and will not be fed its "bread." "Man is land suffering" (*Epistle of Barnabas* 6:9), for "is not the life of man upon the earth a state of trial?" (Job 7:1, Greek Text), "all his days are sufferings, and his labor grief" (Ecclesiastes 2:23) until the day he shall rejoice in the fruits of his labor [Psalm 126:6; Ecclesiastes 2:10]. The Rabbis knew that understanding of the Torah may not be had without suffering [Midrash R. on Psalm 1 sect. 20], for the price of the bread of understanding is paid by hard labor in the field of His Word.

> "To seek and to search out by wisdom all that is done
> under heaven, is a grievous task God has given to the
> sons of man to be exercised by it" (Ecclesiastes 1:13;
> 7:25a),

for we are to "labor in wisdom, and knowledge, and beneficial things" (Ecclesiastes 2:21). And if it is said that "in much wisdom is much grief, and he who increases knowledge increases sorrow" (Ecclesiastes 1:18), it is because the bringing forth of fruit from His Word is no easy task. We are "taught by suffering" (Clement of Alexandria, *Exh.* III.43.4), and where there is no "discipline" [MUSAR], there is no "instruction" [MUSAR] and no understanding. Even the pagans knew that "all the undisciplined people [are] void of understanding" (Sibylline Oracles III.670). For "to depart from evil is understanding" (Job 28:28), and the undisciplined have not mortified in themselves:

> "all evil thoughts, adulteries, fornications, murders,
> thefts, covetousness, wickedness, deceit, sensuality,
> envy, slander, pride, and foolishness; for all these
> things proceed from within" (St. Mark 7:21-23).

To till the ground of our hearts is to pluck out and "put to death what is earthly in us: immorality, impurity, passion, evil desire, and greed which is idolatry" and "also put off all anger, wrath, malice, blasphemy and foul speech" (Colossians 3:5,8) for all these things prevent the growth of His seeds within us and keep us from bringing forth the fruits of wisdom, and understanding, and knowledge for Him. And because "to depart from evil is understanding" (Job 28:28), they who greatly desire to understand and become wise, separate themselves from lands, peoples, and things which keep them from following the commandments of the Lord which are the source of all understanding (Psalm 111:10; 119:100,104; Deuteronomy 4:5-6; 29:9; Joshua 1:7-8; 1 Kings 2:3; Proverbs 3:1,4; Sirach 1:25; 21:11; Zadokite Fragment (CD) 3:12-16; St. Matthew 7:24). That is why it is written:

> "All they who had separated themselves from the
> people of the lands to [follow] the Law of God . . .
> every one [of them] had knowledge and understand-
> ing" (Nehemiah 10:28).

> "The highway of the upright is to depart from evil"
> (Proverbs 16:17).

> "A wise man fears and departs from evil" (Proverbs
> 14:16).

> "Be not wise in your own eyes, fear the Lord and
> depart from evil" (Proverbs 3:7).

> For "Behold, the fear of the Lord, that is wisdom; and
> to depart from evil is understanding" (Job 28:28).

When the Lord desires to speak to our hearts, He draws us aside to a place apart as He did to His bride Israel: "Behold, I will allure her, and bring her into the wilderness and [there] I shall speak to her heart" (Hosea 2:14). Narrating in the singular, Moses sang of the people of God: "In the howling wilderness He led him about, He made him understand [BIN], He kept him as the apple of His eye" (Deuteronomy 32:10). Away from the attractions of the cities, "the people . . . found grace in the wilderness" (Jeremiah 31.2), and there they were taught by the Lord, and made to understand. Separated from all other peoples, the latter years spent sojourning through the desert were Israel's years of greatest fidelity to the Lord, a time of espousals. The Lord Himself recalled those years in endearing terms:

> "I remember the devotion of your youth, your love as
> a bride, how you went after Me in the wilderness, in a
> land not sown. Israel was holy to the Lord, the first
> fruits of His harvest" (Jeremiah 2:2,3).

In those days, to be separate in the wilderness became a proverbial term of fidelity to the Lord: "he who fulfills the Law makes himself like unto an empty wilderness, and disregards all other influences" (Midrash Rabbah on Numbers, Hukkat 19.26). In the history of Israel, a faithful remnant always held on to the desert ideal, separating themselves to observe the Law of the Lord more faithfully (1 Kings 19:18; Jeremiah 35:2-19; 1QS 8:13, Dead Sea Scrolls). We find nostalgia for the desert ideal breaking forth in the anguished cries of King David and Jeremiah: "O that I had the wings of a dove! I would fly away and be at rest, I would wander far away, I would lodge in the wilderness" (Psalm 55:6-7);

> "O, that I had in the wilderness, a lodging place for
> travelers, that I might leave my people, and go away
> from them. For they are all adulterers, a company of
> treacherous men" (Jeremiah 9:2).

Understanding the motives behind the separation of the just from the multitude, the Jewish philosopher Philo [c. 23 B.C.-A.D. 51] wrote:

> "The man of worth . . . having acquired a desire for a
> quiet life, withdraws from the public and loves soli-
> tude, his desire is to go unnoticed by the many not
> because he is misanthropical, for he is eminently a
> philanthropist, but because he has rejected vice which
> is welcomed by the multitude . . . therefore he secludes
> himself . . . and passes from ignorance to instruction,
> from folly to sound sense, from cowardice to courage,

from impiety to piety, from voluptuousness to self-control, from vaingloriousness to simplicity" (Philo, *Abr.* 22-24).

When the wise seek to understand a "hard" or enigmatic saying, they invariably seclude themselves to facilitate pondering over the problem within their hearts. For "who is able to understand such matters except he who has not his dwelling among men?" (2 Esdras 5:38). If we want to know "where is the place of understanding [BINAH], seeing that it is hidden from the eyes of all living, and kept hidden [SATHAR] from the birds of heaven" (Job 28:20,21), or if we wonder "where has the multitude of understanding hidden itself?" (2 Baruch 48:36); let us go to the wilderness or to a place apart, because "good insight shall hide itself and Understanding shall withdraw himself into his secret chamber" (2 Esdras 5:9) when he desires to resolve a problem. "The finding out of parables is a wearisome labor of the mind" (Sirach 13:26, Greek Text) and we have to "withdraw [SUG] and meditate" for that "laborious pondering" (Sirach 13:26, Hebrew Text). For "meditation takes place where there is no man present, but one is in undisturbed peacefulness" (Philo, *Q.Gen.* IV.140; Ḥagigah II.77b, Tanchuma Vaëra 5 [Jerusalem Talmud]), in a place apart from the crowd. In explaining why Moses led the people away from populous Egypt into the desert of Sinai, Philo said that "he who is about to receive the holy Laws must first cleanse his soul and purge away the deep-set stains which it has contracted with the motley promiscuous horde of men in cities. And to this he cannot attain except by dwelling apart" (Philo, *Decal.* 10,11), so Moses "first led them away from the highly mischievous associations of cities into the desert, to clear the sins of their souls and then began to set the nourishment before their understanding — and what should this nourishment be but Laws and Words of God?" (Philo, *Decal.* 13). Again, "the soul which is thirsty for understanding" goes to "the wilderness, for the perturbation and anxiety which come upon the various senses, and the floods of the various passions oppress the soul and do not permit it to drink pure waters" from "the springs of understanding" (Philo, *Q.Gen.* II.27; *Fug.* 187). As in the days of old "whenever we wish to get an accurate understanding of a subject, we hurry off to a solitary [EREMIAN] place; we close our eyes, we stop our ears; we say 'goodby' to our perceptive [via the senses] faculties" (Philo, *L.A.* II.25) in order to be able to concentrate better. Similarly, a wise man who desires to understand, secludes himself to wrestle with the problem he seeks to solve; and here is where TUSHIYYAH comes into play, for with the help of the Lord's TUSHIYYAH within him, he shall be able to reason and argue the Truth of the matter out, bringing it to light, to the joy of his understanding. Thus it is written in the book of Proverbs that:

"Through desire [LE-THA'AVAH], he who has separated [NIPHRAD] himself, seeks [YEBAQQESH] and with all [BECHOL] TUSHIYYAH shall argue out into the open [YITHGALA]. A fool has no delight in understanding, but — in uncovering [GALAH] his heart" (Proverbs 18:1,2 [For closest English rendering see KJV.]).

A man does not separate himself from others just for the sake of separation, for that would not be "good" (Genesis 2:18); but he may depart from evil and seclude himself by virtue of his desire to learn. Those who have a "desire for instruction" (Wisdom 6:17) and "hear Wisdom with all desire" (Sirach 3.31, Latin Vulgate), know that the Lord wants us to "desire Wisdom" (Sirach 1:25), and for that reason, God presents Wisdom to us as a desirable treasure (Job 28:12,15-18; Proverbs 3:15-16; 8:11,18-19,21; Wisdom 7:8-9,11,14; 8:5; Sirach 1:24; ibid. 15:6, Latin Vulgate; idem 41:12, Hebrew Text; Testament of Levi 13:7-8; 2 Baruch 44:14; 54:13; Romans 11:33; Colossians 2:3), and as a desirable beautiful woman (Proverbs 8:12,17; Wisdom 6:12,14,16; 8:2, etc.). Truly, "Wisdom is better than jewels, and all things that you can desire cannot be compared to her" (Proverbs 8:11), therefore, "my soul longed with desire for Wisdom" (Sirach 51:19, Hebrew Text); "my inmost being yearned for Wisdom, to look upon her" (Sirach 51:21, Hebrew Text). It is "through desire" (Proverbs 18:1) that we are motivated to "seek" (ibid.) but we may have to separate ourselves from all things to be able to seek and find desirable Wisdom, because "Wisdom . . . is not manifest to many" (Sirach 6:22), "the hidden Wisdom" (1 Corinthians 2:7) of God is "hidden" (Job 28:20,21). If we desire to understand wisdom, we separate ourselves, for "the understanding is bogged down by useless and irrelevant distractions" (Philo, *Q.Gen.* IV.193), and "the understanding . . . while it is cooped up in the city . . . is cabinned and cribbed like a prisoner in jail . . . but when it is gone out of the city, its thoughts and reflections are at liberty" (Philo, *Ebr.* 101) to "pursue holy Wisdom" (Clement of Alexandria, *Paed.* I.5.16:3), away from all distractions. We should know that the "divine Wisdom is a lover of solitudes" (Philo, *Her.* 127), and "the Word of God is a lover of wild and solitary places" (ibid. 243) where it can be heard in profound quietness. But let us not forget that it is "through desire" that we are moved to seek and find Wisdom, for "Wisdom is easily seen by those who love her and found by those who seek her" (Wisdom 6:12) "with their whole desire" (2 Chronicles 15:15). Indeed, "Wisdom is near to those who seek her, and he who gives his desire to her shall find her" (Sirach 51:26, Hebrew Text). "Desire accomplished is sweet to the soul, but to depart from evil is an abomination to fools" (Proverbs 13:19). Because "to depart from evil is understanding" (Job 28:28), and "a fool has no delight in understanding" (Proverbs 18:2a), therefore "do not speak in the ears of a fool for he will despise the understanding [SEKEL] of your words" (Proverbs 23:9). A fool has no desire for wisdom either, for "fools despise wisdom and instruction" (Proverbs 1:7). "He speaks as to one who is asleep, who utters wisdom to a fool" (Sirach 22:9, Latin

Vulgate), because "wisdom is too high for a fool" (Proverbs 24:7), and "when a fool hears a wise word, he laughs and casts it aside" (Sirach 21:15, Syriac Text). Moreover, "a fool . . . cannot keep counsel" (Sirach 8:17), and "a fool . . . will not hold knowledge" (Sirach 21:14), much less will he keep in himself to ponder: a wise word that he does not understand, so how can a fool delight in understanding? "Men of understanding find delight in their understandings, but fools delight in their folly" (Rabbi Joseph Kimchi in his *Shekel Hakodesh,* 18). Only "folly is joy to him who is void of understanding" (Proverbs 15:21). But a man of understanding knows that "to ponder upon wisdom is perfect understanding" (Wisdom 6:15), and also perfect joy, for to have "wisdom of heart" (Sirach 50:23, Hebrew Text) is to have "joyfulness of heart" (Sirach 50:23, Greek Text). "There is no joy above the joy of the heart" (Sirach 30:16) that understands wisdom.

"To withdraw and meditate is laborious pondering" (Sirach 13:26, Hebrew Text), but let us take heart because "to ponder upon wisdom is perfect understanding" (Wisdom 6:15). "If you hear a word [that you do not understand], let it remain with you, for so it is that a man should strive [AGONIZESTHAI] when he has heard it [the word that he does not understand] with endurance, and God will give him a blessing in that which he has sought" (Testament of Isaac l.164, Codex Vat. 61) to understand. What you do not understand, keep in your heart and ponder over it, as the blessed Virgin did [St. Luke 2:19,50-51]. "Meditate continually and He shall make your heart to understand and make you wise in that which you desire" (Sirach 6:37, Hebrew Text). If I do not understand a wise saying, a proverb or a parable: "I deliberate [LOGISAMENOS] these things within myself, and pondering in my heart" (Wisdom 8:17) I get to understand them, with the help of God and my companion. "My soul wrestled with Wisdom" (Sirach 51:19), for "in common exercise with Wisdom is understanding" (Wisdom 8:18). "Take hold of Wisdom and do not let her go" (Sirach 6:27), for "happy are all those who hold Wisdom fast" (Proverbs 3:18), because they shall understand and know her.

From the book of Proverbs (18:1) we learn that with the help of "all TUSHIYYAH" we shall be able to "fully argue out into the open" (YITHGALA' as in BT, Sanhedrin 6b; ibid. JT I.18b; Tanchuma Mishpatim 6; Yalkut to Proverbs 956), that which we struggled in our hearts to understand. And we shall rejoice in having understood it, as a woman rejoices over the child she brought forth with much labor from her womb. But let us not forget that we must *keep,* and ponder in our heart that which we hope to understand, so that we may some day rejoice in the Truth (1 Corinthians 13:6) we shall bring forth from it. In Proverbs 18:2: the "fool has no delight in understanding," because "a fool . . . cannot keep" (Sirach 8:17), and he cannot ponder because he is always "uncovering his heart" (Proverbs 18:2b) and "laying open his foolishness" (Proverbs 13:16b). "Weep for the fool because he lacks understanding" (Sirach 22:11). But "happy is the man who meditates in Wisdom and reasons holy things by his understanding" (Sirach 14:20, Greek MSS. 248,23,253). And happy are those who see and hear Wisdom brought to light, through the Lord's TUSHIYYAH.

In the Manual of Discipline of the Dead Sea Scrolls we find a wise saying that gives us insight concerning TUSHIYYAH:

> "In the everlasting Being has my eye beheld TUSHIYYAH" (1QS 11:5,6, A.Dupont-Sommer Translation).

For when "the Lord . . . lays up TUSHIYYAH for the upright" (Proverbs 2:6,7), He not only lays up "life" [CHAYYIM] and "salvation" [TESHU'AH] within them, but His very "Being" [YESH] as well, because He is the source of all life and salvation. He treasures up TUSHIYYAH in the heart of the upright as a pledge of security, provided they hold on to it until the very end. The Lord's intent in placing TUSHIYYAH as a seed within their hearts is that they should bring forth children seeds in abundance from it — to His glory and their salvation. And this they shall do on the day they shall bring forth from the seed of TUSHIYYAH: a tree of life, bearing the fruit of life full of the seeds of salvation: TUSHIYYAH. For "the garden of the Lord, the trees of life, are His holy ones; their planting is rooted forever, they shall not be uprooted" (Psalms of Solomon 14:2,3). Yes, they shall not be uprooted because from the very beginning they held fast in their hearts: the seed that was sown in them.

"With the counsel ['ETSAH] of TUSHIYYAH" (1QS 10:24, Dead Sea Scrolls), we shall learn a very important thing: it is through a seed that matter enters into life. For what comes to pass is that the lifeless elements of the ground which hold fast the seed are taken up to form part of the living tree. Thus, it was wisely said in the Psalms of Solomon [14:2,3] that the Lord's holy ones are both the garden ground and the trees of life sprung forth from it. But let us remember that only by keeping a living seed in the heart of the ground, may the earth aspire to life in the tree that shall rise from it. "If you wish to enter into life, keep the commandments" (St. Matthew 19:17) for "His commandment is life everlasting" (St. John 12:50). "Blessed are they who [keep and] do His commandments so that they may have a right to the tree of life" (Revelation 22:14, KJV), because "the tree of life is for all those who do His will" (4 Maccabees 18:16). And inasmuch as they who keep His commandments and do His will, please the Lord (St. John 14:15; 15:14; 8:28-29), they are the ones who shall have immortal life, for "they who do the things that please Him shall receive the fruit of the tree of immortality" which is "the tree of life" (Sirach 19:19, Greek Cursive 248; Genesis 3:22).

We "are God's tilled field [GEORGION]" (1 Corinthians 3:9), and we know that "the Seed is the Word of God" (St. Luke 8:11). The Lord sows His Word in the ground of our hearts so that it may bear fruit and bring forth an abundance of children seeds from the Seed that He sowed:

> "O that God would speak and open His lips before you, and that He would declare to you the secrets of wisdom: that TUSHIYYAH is double" (Job 11:5,6, Literal Translation).

TUSHIYYAH is accomplished when we have brought forth for the Lord, seed truly identical to the seed that He sowed; but in great abundance, to His glory. For it takes a hundred children words of God to give perfect praise to the One Word that was sown. For the Lord said: "In this is My Father glorified, that you bear much fruit" (St. John 15:8), full of children seeds in perfect array to his glory. "Praise to God . . . is the fruit" (Hebrews 13:15); "praise: the firstfruits of the lips from a holy and righteous heart" (Psalms of Solomon 15:5). The Lord sows His wisdom, understanding, and knowledge in our hearts because we need these gifts to be able to glorify and praise Him well and abundantly:

> "For to make known the glory of the Lord is wisdom given, and for the recounting of His many deeds is wisdom revealed to man: to make known to the simple His might, and to make the senseless understand [SAKAL] His greatness" (11QPS^a Col. XVIII.3-5 [Psalm 154:5-7], Dead Sea Scrolls; see also Sirach 15:9-10; Philo, *Q.Gen.* I.6).

> "He has given men understanding that He may be glorified in His marvelous works" (Sirach 38:6).

> "Grant me understanding, O Lord, in Thy Law, and teach me Thine ordinances, that many may hear of Thy deeds and peoples may honor Thy glory" (11QPs^a Col. XXIV.8-9 [Psalm 155:9-10], Dead Sea Scrolls).

> "I will sing with the understanding" (1 Corinthians 14:15).

> "Sing praises with understanding [SAKAL]" (Psalm 47:7).

> "He filled them with the knowledge of understanding . . . that they might declare His works with understanding" (Sirach 17:7-8, Greek MMS. 248,55, 106,254).

> "A fruit of praise and the offering of my lips I will sing with knowledge [DAATH] and all my lyre shall throb to the glory of God, and my lute and harp to the holy order which He has made" (1QS 10:8-9, Dead Sea Scrolls).

Let us keep the "Word [Seed] of life" (Philippians 2:16; 1 John 1:1; St. John 6:63) that we may "have life . . . more abundantly" (St. John 10:10) in "the fruit of life" (Hosea 10:12, Greek Text) we shall bring forth for Him.

Let us keep "the seeds of Wisdom" (Philo, *Q.Gen.* III.32) that we may bring forth "the fruits of wisdom" (Philo, *Ebr.* 212; Sirach 6:19) to His praise. For "without wisdom it is not possible to praise the Creator of all things" (Philo, *Q.Gen.* I.6) in the great day that "praise shall be uttered in wisdom and the Lord will prosper it" (Sirach 15:10).

Let us keep and cultivate "the seeds and plants of understanding" (Philo, *Cong.* 123) that we may bring forth "the fruits of understanding" (Sirach 37:22) to His glory.

Let us "keep knowledge" (Proverbs 5:2; Malachi 2:7) for "wise men lay up knowledge" (Proverbs 10:14) in their hearts as a seed so that "knowledge shall be increased" (Daniel 12:4) and keep on "increasing in the full knowledge of God" (Colossians 1:10) brought forth to His praise and glory in "the fruit of knowledge" (Sirach 37:22, Hebrew Text). Then, shall "the lips of the wise disperse [ZARAH] knowledge" (Proverbs 15:7) as "seed" [ZERA'], "sowing" [ZARA'] knowledge "so that all may know His glory and awesome might" (1QH 15:20,21). For they shall have "knowledge to recount His mighty deeds to all flesh" (1QH 18:23, Dead Sea Scrolls) because they kept the "Word [Seed] of knowledge" (Odes of Solomon 7:7).

Let us keep "the seeds of Truth" (Justin Martyr, *Apol.* I.44.29; Clement of Alexandria, *Strom.* I.c.1; Jeremiah 2:21) that we may become true and bring forth "the fruit of Truth" (Shepherd of Hermas, *Sim.* IX.19.96:2).

And let us "keep TUSHIYYAH" (Proverbs 3:21) that "we may bear fruit for God" (Romans 7:4). Because God sows His Word in us that we may bring forth fruit from it, and "God's Truth" may "abound . . . to His glory" (Romans 3:7). The Lord's TUSHIYYAH works in us to bring forth the Truth of His Word, and the first thing that it does in us is to "rub off" [GALA as in Proverbs 18:1a] the husk of the Seed-Word in our hearts, "to lay bare" [GALA] the kernel of Truth found within that Seed: "the essence of Your Word is Truth" (Psalm 119:160; St. John 17:17). But though we know that the Truth is in our hearts, it shall remain there dormant unless we awaken it by our great desire to bring it to fruit for the glory of God. Then TUSHIYYAH shall make "the plant of righteousness and Truth appear" (Enoch 10:16) from the Seed that God sowed, so that "Truth shall spring out of the earth" (Psalm 85:11) of our hearts to His praise. "For as the earth brings forth its buds, and as a garden causes the things that are sown in it to spring forth, so the Lord God will cause righteousness and praise to spring forth before all the nations" (Isaiah 61:11), when the time comes that He "shall reveal to them the abundance of peace and Truth" (Jeremiah 33:6): the peace found in "the peaceful fruit of righteousness" (Hebrews 12:11) full of the seeds of Truth. And in that day we shall be able to "abundantly [ROB] make known [YADA] TUSHIYYAH" (Job 26:3) because the Lord's TUSHIYYAH shall also be increased in us.

We receive TUSHIYYAH in the last and topmost rung of the ladder because our goal in climbing the ladder of understanding is to see and grasp the Truth. We learn from the prophet Micah that the Lord's TUSHIYYAH shall enable us to do so:

> "The voice [QOL] of the Lord cries [QARA] out to the
> city — and the one with TUSHIYYAH shall see
> [RAAH] Your name [SHEM]" (Micah 6:9).

To be able to see the name of the Lord is to be able to see the Truth, because "Truth ['EMETH] is the name of God" (Sanhedrin I.18, JT), "the Holy One is called Truth" (*Alphabet de Rabbi Akiba*, Prologue), for "The Lord God is Truth ['EMETH]" (Jeremiah 10:10; Zohar I.26-36). And because we place our name on our personal seal, it is also said that "the seal of the Holy One, blessed be He, is Truth" (Midrash Rabbah on Canticles 1.9, Para. 1; see also Shabbath 55a, BT), indeed, "Truth is the seal of God" (Midrash Rabbah on Genesis 8.5; see also Zohar II.89a-89b). With TUSHIYYAH, we shall see the wisdom behind the text of Micah 6:9 which brings out the relationship between hearing the voice of the Lord, and at the same time, seeing the Truth in "the voice of the words of the Lord" (1 Samuel 15:1). We find an example of this phenomenon in the book of Exodus 20:18 where it is written that "all the people *saw* [RAAH] the thunderings" [QOL, literally "voice"] instead of saying: "all the people *heard* the thunderings." Thus, the Septuagint [Greek Translation] rendered it verbatim: "all the people saw [ORAO] the voice [PHŌNEN]." In one of the oldest rabbinic commentaries on the book of Exodus: the *Mekilta de Rabbi Ishmael* (Tractate, *Bechodesh* IX.1-15), it is explained regarding this text that in the days of the revelation at Mount Sinai, the people were so "excellent" that "they interpreted the divine Word as soon as they heard it." That is to say they immediately saw and knew what God said. As Moses reminded the people later on in the book of Deuteronomy: "the Lord spoke to you from the midst of the fire . . . you saw no form [but "saw"] only a voice" (Deuteronomy 4:12). For when "God thunders [RAAM] with His voice [QOL] marvelously" — "the voice of the Lord hews out flames of fire" (Job 37:5; Psalm 29:7, Literal Translation) at the same time, so that His voice is both seen and heard. After all, when the Lord spoke at Mount Sinai it was to give the people His Law and His commandments. The people saw what the voice of the Lord said, because "the Law is light" (Proverbs 6:23), and "the commandment of the Lord is clear, giving light to the eyes" (Psalm 19:8). Thus, in Micah 6:9: "when the voice of the Lord cries out to the city — the one with TUSHIYYAH shall see Your name [i.e., "Truth"]", because with the help of the

Lord's TUSHIYYAH, that person shall immediately be able to see the Truth of what is said. There will come a time when the Lord shall inspire us to sing a new song so lucidly composed that many shall instantly see the Truth of His Word while hearing it sung. And many shall fear and trust in the Lord because they shall realize that He had a hand in its making:

> "He has put a new song in my mouth: Praise unto our
> God. Many shall *see* and fear, and put their trust in the
> Lord" (Psalm 40:3, Literal Translation).

In the end, we shall not only be able to see the Truth but we shall also be able to grasp it; because through the Lord's TUSHIYYAH the Truth shall arise in us from the Word that was sown in our hearts as a seed. And just as a sown and hidden grain of wheat reaches completion in the evident golden ear of grain sprung forth from it; so shall the sown Word be made resplendently manifest, in the Truth brought forth from it to His glory. Because "the perfection [TELOS] of the Word is Truth" (Philo, *L.A.* III.45).

> Blessed be the Lord God who through His wonderful
> TUSHIYYAH has "raised our understanding to the
> height of Truth" (Odes of Solomon 17:8).

> And "blessed are they who by means of Him have
> understood everything and have known the Lord in
> His Truth" (Odes of Solomon 12:13).

> For "the Lord is the Truth, and Wisdom, and Power of
> God" (Clement of Alexandria, *Strom.* II.c.11; ibid.
> IV.c.7; see also St. John 14:6; 1 Corinthians 1:24).

T H E   S U M M I T

'E M E T H

[TRUTH]

Thousands of years ago the Egyptians had insight to a very important truth:
"The man of understanding . . . Truth rises to him from his heart fully matured" (Instruction of King Meri-Ka-Re, Leningrad Papyrus 1116A).

"How good it is when a son accepts what his father says, for thereby fullness [of Truth] comes to him" (Instruction of Ptah-Hotep, l. 542, Prisse Papyrus, National Library, Paris).

They knew that he who becomes true to himself by leading a good life, shall bring forth truths from his heart. As the Jewish Essenes, later on, were to say concerning their Teacher of Righteousness: "He . . . causes the sprout of holiness to grow into the plant of Truth ['EMETH]" (1QH 8:10, Dead Sea Scrolls). Philo, the Jewish philosopher plainly stated that "the offspring of a perfected soul are perfect words and deeds" (*Q.Gen.* III.32) for "words are the offspring of the soul" (Clement of Alexandria, *Stromata* I.c.1). Long ago our ancestors knew that "he who speaks the Truth ['EMETH] shows [NAGAD] forth righteousness" (Proverbs 12:17), for it takes a life of righteousness to bring forth the Truth from our hearts. "He who walks uprightly and works righteousness . . . speaks the truth ['EMETH] from his heart" (Psalm 15:2). Thus, St. James said: "If anyone makes no mistake in what he says, he is a perfect man" (St. James 3:2). Those who are true bring forth Truths because they have believed, accepted and kept the Word of God in their hearts. The "Father" of the offspring Truths brought forth from the hearts of the righteous is "the Word of Truth" (Ephesians 1:13; St. James 1:18), "the implanted Word" (St. James 1:21) which they kept in their hearts. "The Word that is sown is hidden in the soul of the learner as in the earth . . . through time and labor, Truth will shine forth" from it (Clement of Alexandria, *Stromata* I.c.1.) "And the Truth which has been so long without fruit, shall be made manifest" (2 Esdras 6:28). "The Truth ['EMETH] of the world . . . shall appear in triumph forever" (1QS 4:19, Dead Sea Scrolls), because "Truth ['EMETH] shall spring up from the earth" (Psalm 85:11) and "the plant of righteousness and Truth shall appear" (Enoch 10:16) from the hearts of those who have held fast the Seed of His Word. For it is written that the Lord shall come to "judge the world with righteousness, and the people with His Truth" (Psalm 96:13). "You have hidden the Truth ['EMETH] until the time of judgment but then You will reveal it" (1QH 9:24, Dead Sea Scrolls), "and all the nations shall know Your Truth ['EMETH], and all the peoples Your glory" (1QH 6:12, Dead Sea Scrolls). O "may Your Truth ['EMETH] shine forth into everlasting glory and peace without end!" (1QH 11:26,27, Dead Sea Scrolls)

Just as "the thresher threshes in hope of a share in the crop" (1 Corinthians 9:10), so do the laborers in the field of His word hope for, and are rewarded by a share in the Truth brought forth from it. Because the Lord promised in Isaiah: "I will give them their wages [PE'ULLAH] in Truth ['EMETH]" (Isaiah 61:8). Again, "to him who sows righteousness: a reward of Truth ['EMETH]" (Proverbs 11:18). "You will reward the righteous with lovingkindness and Truth ['EMETH]" (Targum of the Amidah or Eighteen Benedictions). "My Word [of Truth] shall be your reward" (Targum Jerusalem on Genesis 15:1). Even the ancient Egyptians knew that Truth is the reward and inheritance of the just: "Truth, the great reward of god" (Instruction of Amen-Em-Opet XXI.1.5). "The strength of Truth is that it endures and a man may say that it is an inheritance" (Instruction Ptah-Hotep, 1.95, Prisse Papyrus; see also Carnarvon Tablet I., Cairo Museum). Conversely, the Babylonians knew that if Truth is the reward of the good, then the gods "with lies and not Truth they endowed them [the wicked] forever" (Babylonian Tablet 34773, British Museum). As Jeremiah said: "O Lord, my strength and my fortress . . . the nations [pagan] shall come to You from the ends of the earth and shall say, 'our fathers have inherited nothing but lies, emptiness, and the things of no profit'" (Jeremiah 16:19). But let us "gain the most profitable of all blessings: Truth" (Philo, *Ebr.* 39), "buy the Truth and do not sell it" (Proverbs 23:23). "I will not exchange Your Truth for riches" (1QH 14:29); "I know no riches equal to Your Truth" (1QH 15:22, 23, Dead Sea Scrolls), because "Truth ['EMETH] is to us like a friend dearer than anything else" (Rabbi Joseph Kimchi's *Shekel Hakodesh* 254).

Since Truth is the reward of the righteous, it is they who are given "an abundant portion of the knowledge of Your Truth ['EMETH]" (1QH 10:28,29, Dead Sea Scrolls). This was known as "man's inheritance in Truth ['EMETH] and righteousness" (1QS 4:24, Dead Sea Scrolls) since the greatness of his portion in the Truth depended on his righteousness. For to "the sons of Your good pleasure . . . You have made known to them Your secret of Truth ['EMETH] and given them understanding of all Your marvelous mysteries" (1QH 11:9,10, Dead Sea Scrolls). "You have cleansed man of sin for the sake of Your glory that he might be made holy for You and that he may be joined with Your sons of Truth ['EMETH] and . . . may be raised from the dust to [the knowledge of] Your secret of Truth" (1QH 11:10b,11,12, Dead Sea Scrolls). We can see from these texts that there is no inheritance for us in the Truth unless we first repent and lead a life of righteousness, for "to the penitent He has given the way of justice and He has strengthened them who were fainting in their endurance and has appointed to them the lot of Truth" (Sirach 17:20, Latin Vulgate). "When they are converted . . . knowledge will be revealed to them" (1QpHab. 10:17-11:1, Dead Sea Scrolls): knowledge of the Truth. Thus Daniel prayed "that we might turn away from our iniquities and understand Your Truth" (Daniel 9:13). St. Paul knew that we must have "repentance toward the full knowledge [EPIGNŌSIN] of the Truth" (2 Timothy 2:25), because "the full knowledge [EPIGNŌSIN] of the Truth is according to godliness" (Titus 1:1). And "God our Saviour . . . will have all men to be saved and to come to the full knowledge [EPIGNŌSIN] of the Truth" (1 Timothy 2:3,4). Thus, "in His love for man, the Lord invites all men to the full knowledge of the Truth" (Clement of Alexandria, *Exh.* IX.85.3). In the end, if we are good, we shall be crowned with the Truth: "an everlasting crown is Truth . . . righteousness has taken it and given it to you" (Odes of Solomon 9:8,10).

The end of considering spiritual things is Truth. When we climb the ladder of understanding we go "up into the light of Truth" (Odes of Solomon 38:1), for "the origin of Truth is in a habitation of light" (1QS 3:19, Dead Sea Scrolls). "Life has no clearer light than the Truth . . . which casts a beam more far reaching than the light" (Philo, *L.A.* III.45). Thus, "real Truth is like the sun" (Clement of Alexandria, *Strom.* VI.c.10), and "with a ray of Truth" (Philo, *Praem.* 25) the Lord shall illumine our hearts when the time comes for His Truth to be made manifest.

There is a close relationship between light and Truth. The "light [OR] . . . sown for the righteous" (Psalm 97:11) remains hidden like a seed in the ground of their hearts until "light [OR] arises unto the upright" (Psalm 112:4) from that seed they have kept and obeyed. Then, just as the righteous who bring forth Truth from the Seed of His word, are rewarded with a share in the Truth they brought forth for Him; His holy ones shall receive "an inheritance of light for the sake of . . . Truth" (1QM 13:9,10, Dead Sea Scrolls). Thus it is written that "for Your holy ones there was a very great light" (Wisdom 18:1; see also Enoch 5:6-8). "Walk in a manner worthy of the Lord, fully pleasing to Him, bearing fruit in every good work and increasing in the knowledge of God . . . giving thanks to the Father who has made us worthy to share in the inheritance of the holy ones in light" (Colossians 1:10,12). For "the fruit of light [from the seed of "light" that was "sown"], is found in all goodness and righteousness and Truth" (Ephesians 5:9). "O God . . . send forth Your light and Your Truth" (Psalm 43:1,3), for "God is Light" (1 John 1:5) and "God is Truth" (Horeb, *Mitzvoth* V.482).

"God is Light" (1 John 1:5), and "God Himself, who is Almighty, the Creator of all things . . . is the Truth" (*Epistle to Diognetus* 7:4,5; Odes of Solomon 38:4). And they who become "children of light" (St. John 12:36; St. Luke 16:8; 1 Thessalonians 5:5; 1QS 1:9; 2:16; 3:13,24,25; 1QM 1:9,11,13, Dead Sea Scrolls) and "children of Truth" (1QS 4:5,6; 1QM 17:8; 1QH 6:29; 7:29,30; 9:35; 10:27; 11:11, Dead Sea Scrolls), are they who have believed and held fast in their hearts: the Word of Truth. For they have been "born again, not of corruptible seed, but of incorruptible; by the Word of God, which lives and abides forever" (1 Peter 1:23). "Of His own will he brought us forth by the word of Truth, so that we might be, as it were, the first fruits" (St. James 1:18) of His Word of Truth. "For the Word of God is living and active" (Hebrews 4:12), and "the Word of God is at work in you" (1 Thessalonians 2:13) to bring forth from you: the fruit of light and Truth. "The Word of Truth . . . is . . . bringing forth fruit in you" (Colossians 1:5,6) that you "may be sanctified through the Truth" (St. John 17:19) which you labor to bring forth from it — through the Holy Spirit. "Because the Spirit is Truth" (1 John 5:6), and "He shall guide you into all the Truth" (St. John 16:13) and help you to obey the Truth (1 Peter 1:22) so that you may become a child of God. For "all who are led by the Spirit of God, these are the children of God" (Romans 8:14), and as such, they are also "children of Light" and "children of Truth." It is "through the sanctifying work of the Spirit" (1 Peter 1:2) that we are made true, because only the true shall be able to really bring forth the Truth to His glory.

> "All Your chosen ones are Truth ['EMETH]" (1QH 14:15, Dead Sea Scrolls).

> "The old man is falsehood, and the new man is Truth" (Abba Epiphanius, Bishop of Salamis c. A.D. 350, in *The Paradise of the Fathers*, Vol. II. Sect. 442, p. 245 [Syriac Text translated by A. W. Budge, London 1907]).

Let us "be converted to the Truth and turn away from all deceit" (1QS 6:15, Dead Sea Scrolls). And let us know that just as there are "men of Truth" (Exodus 18:21; 1QH 14:2; 1QpHab. 7:10, Dead Sea Scrolls), there are also "men of lies" (1QH 14:14; 1QpHab. 2:1,2; 5:9; Proverbs 19:22), and "men of deceit" (1QS 9:8,9,17; 10:20; 1QH 2:16; 4:20; Psalms 5:6; 43:1; 55:23; Proverbs 29:13) led by the "spirit of deceit" (1QS 4:9; 1QH 11:12) and "the spirit of wickedness" (1QS 5:20; 10:18,19). And let us understand that just as there are "children of light" (1QS 1:9; 2:16; 3:13,24,25,etc.), heirs of "the inheritance of light" (1QS 3:19), and "the lot of Truth" (Sirach 17:20, Latin Vulgate); there are also "children of darkness" (1QS 1:10; 1QM 1:1,10,14; 13:16; 1QH 6:18) recipients of "the inheritance of darkness" (1QM 1:11) and "the lot of deceit" (1QS 4:24). "All dominion over the children of deceit is in the hand of the angel of darkness" (1QS 3:20,21) and "all their works are in darkness" (1QM 15:9) because "the spirit of deceit . . . causes a man to walk in all the ways of darkness" (1QS 4:9,11) so that he may do in the darkness his "works of deceit" (1QH Fragment 3:10). As those who are true, labor to bring forth Truth from their hearts, so do the wicked "travail with iniquity, and conceive mischief, and bring forth lies" — "conceiving and uttering from the heart words of falsehood" (Psalm 7:14; Isaiah 59:13). But their days are numbered because God "hates perversity forever" (1QH 14:25), and "an abomination to Truth are the works of deceit" (1QS 4:17). "According to each man's share of Truth and righteousness does one hate deceit" (1QS 4:24), because one knows that "to the spirit of deceit belong cupidity and slackness in the service of righteousness, impiety and falsehood, pride and haughtiness, falsity and deception, cruelty and abundant wickedness, impatience and much folly, burning insolence and abominable deeds committed in the spirit of lust" (1QS 4:9,10) at the urging of the "father of lies" — "the devil" (St. John 8:44). There has always been an enduring struggle between "the Spirits of Truth and deceit" (1QH 4:23), but let us rejoice, because "perversity will no longer exist and shame will come upon all the works of deceit" (1QS 4:23). For "the Lord is the God of Truth" (Jeremiah 10:10, Literal Translation), and "in His mysteries of understanding and in His glorious wisdom, God has set an end for the existence of deceit; and at the time of His Visitation, He will destroy it forever. Then Truth ['EMETH] shall arise in the world forever . . . and God will cleanse by His Truth ['EMETH] all the works of every man, and will purify for Himself the bodily fabric of every man to banish all spirit of deceit from his members" (1QS 4:18,19,20,21); provided he has called upon the name of God: Truth. For we are all sanctified by the Truth of God (St. John 17:17,19). "All perfection rests in the Truth" (St. Ambrose, *De Officiis* I.248).

The ancients knew the value of Truth, and they held fast what they deemed to be true: "grasp hold of Truth" (Instruction of Ptah-Hotep l.150, Prisse Papyrus). "Take hold of Truth in your hands" (Ashurbanipal Tablet K 13770, Pl.27, l.81) for "he whose hand lays hold to the Truth" (R.J. Kimchi, *Shekel Hakodesh* 5) takes a hold on life and salvation:

> "Truth . . . is as necessary for life as bread" (Clement of Alexandria *Strom.* I.c.20).
>
> "He shall cause souls to live forever by the Truth of His name" (Odes of Solomon 41:15).
>
> "Let your life be the true Word inwardly received" (*Epistle to Diognetus* 12:7).
>
> "The Truth led me . . . and saved me . . . and became for me a haven of salvation" (Odes of Solomon 38:1,2,3; see Psalm 40:11).

"Love Truth" (Zechariah 8:19; 1QH 14:25) for "God Himself is a lover of Truth" (Letter of Aristeas 206). "Love the Lord God in Truth" (Tobit 14:7; Psalms of Solomon 10:4; 14:1), and "embrace the Truth in all its purity" (Philo, *Spec.* I.41). "Cleave to the Truth" (1QH 16:7) with all your strength as you would cleave to Him, for "the Lord is the Truth" (Clement of Alexandria, *Strom.* II.c.11).

Be "valiant for the Truth" (Jeremiah 9:3) and "strive for the Truth unto death and the Lord shall fight for you" (Sirach 4:28). "Truth is fallen in the street" and "Truth is lacking" (Isaiah 59:14,15) when there is no one to uphold it. Yet, "great is the Truth, and stronger than all things" (1 Esdras 4:35). "Truth . . . endures and is always strong, it lives and conquers forevermore . . . great is Truth and mighty above all things" (1 Esdras 4:38,41). "Great is Truth . . . never has it been overthrown . . . the strength of Truth is that it endures" (Instruction of Ptah-Hotep ll.5,95). Yes, "the Truth of the Lord endures forever" (Psalm 117:2; 100:5). And "we can do nothing against the Truth, but for the Truth" (2 Corinthians 13:8). Keep the Truth so that you may "become mighty in the Truth" (Odes of Solomon 25:10) and invincible, because "the Lord . . . keeps Truth forever" (Psalm 146:5,6).

"Rejoice in the Lord always" (Philippians 4:4). "Rejoice in Christ Jesus" (Philippians 3:3) "for the Law was given to us through Moses, but grace and Truth came through Jesus Christ" (St. John 1:17). Rejoice in Jesus, for He is the Truth (St. John 14:6), and "the Truth is in Jesus" (Ephesians 4:21). "Rejoice in the Truth" (1 Corinthians 13:6), exult in the Lord and cry out with all your heart:

> O Lord, "You are Truth ['EMETH] and all Your works
> are righteousness!" (1QH 4:40, Dead Sea Scrolls).

UNDERSTANDING

UNDERSTANDING AND ANSWERING

We need Understanding to be able to give a good answer,
and it is by the grace of a good reply that
Understanding is made known.

"How shall I be able to answer unless You make me to understand [SAKAL]?" (1QH 10:7, Dead Sea Scrolls).

"What wisdom or understanding have I that I should judge or answer by word in the House of the Lord?" (Assumption of Moses 11:15).

"Wisdom shall be made known by the speech, and understanding by the reply of the tongue" (Sirach 4:24, Hebrew Text).

"The Lord gave me enough understanding to answer" (Pesikta Rabbati, Piska 33.3).

"Because of the spirits [of understanding, etc., see Isaiah 11:2] which You have put in me I will utter a reply of the tongue to recount Your righteousness" (1QH 17:17, Dead Sea Scrolls).

"The spirit of my understanding [BINAH] makes me answer" (Job 20:3).

"Will a wise man give for answer a spirit of understanding?" (Job 15:2, Greek Text, Literal Translation).

"Daniel answered with counsel and understanding" (Daniel 2:14).

"For there is an excellent spirit in him [Daniel], and prudence and understanding are in him for interpreting dreams and answering hard questions and solving difficulties" (Daniel 5:12, Greek Text).

"Let men of understanding answer me" (Job 34:34, KJV).

"If you have understanding, answer your neighbor" (Sirach 5:12).

"Learn before you speak" (Sirach 18:19).

"Understand first, and then rebuke" (Sirach 11:7).

"Understand [BIN], and afterwards we will speak" (Job 18:2).

"They who have learned holy things shall find what to answer" (Wisdom 6:10).

Because "the knowledge of the holy is understanding" (Proverbs 9:10).

"Blessed is the man . . . who shall discourse holy things by his understanding" (Sirach 14:20, Greek Cursives 23,248,253).

"Blessed is the man who meditates on wisdom and speaks out in accordance with his understanding" (Sirach 14:20).

"Hear . . . understand what I say to you, and answer me" (Apocalypse of Abraham 26:2).

"Be meek to hear the Word so that you may understand and return a true answer" (Sirach 5:13, Latin Vulgate).

"Miss not the discourse of the elders, for they themselves learned from their fathers; because from them you will learn understanding to be able to give an answer in time of need" (Sirach 8:9).

"As long as I live I will speak, and as long as I have understanding I will answer" (2 Esdras 8:25).

"There is no just man beside You to understand Your Mysteries and to answer a word" (1QH 12:19,20, Dead Sea Scrolls).

"All who heard Him were astonished at His understanding and His answers" (St. Luke 2:47).

"And when Jesus saw that he answered with understanding [NOUNECHŌS], He said to him, 'you are not far from the Kingdom of God'" (St. Mark 12:34).

"Oh, that I knew where I might find Him, that I might come to His seat! . . . I would know the words which He would cry out to me, and understand what He would answer [AMAR] me" (Job 23:3,5).

"How . . . shall he answer his Maker and how shall he understand His works?" (1QH 12:27,28, Dead Sea Scrolls).

"Though he understands he will not answer" (Proverbs 29:19).

"The heart [seat of understanding] of the righteous ponders how to answer" (Proverbs 15:28).

"The heart [see 'Heart and Understanding'] of the wise gives understanding to his mouth and adds persuasiveness [LEQACH = learning and ability to elucidate] to his lips" (Proverbs 16:23).

Conversely

"They do not know nor do they understand, for He has smeared over their eyes so that they cannot see and their hearts so that they cannot understand. No one ponders in his heart, nor is there knowledge or understanding to answer [AMAR]" (Isaiah 44:18,19).

BELIEF AND UNDERSTANDING – FAITH AND UNDERSTANDING

Hearing the Word of the Lord and understanding it, leads to conviction,
belief in the Truth, and faith in Him. In turn, faith in the Lord
gives us greater understanding.

"Faith comes by hearing, and hearing by the word of Christ" (Romans 10:17).

"Instruction leads to faith" (Clement of Alexandria, *Paed.* Book I.6.30:2).

"By means of the rational faculties He has Himself endowed us with, He persuades us and leads us to faith" (Justin Martyr, *Apol.* I.10.18).

"How shall they believe in Him of whom they have not heard?" (Romans 10:14).

"I pray . . . for those also who shall believe in Me through their word" (St. John 17:20).

"He has circumcised our ears, so that when we hear the Word, we might believe" (*Epistle of Barnabas* 9:4).

"The gates of the Word are . . . opened by the key of faith" (Clement of Alexandria, *Exh.* I.10.3).

"Through faith we understand" (Hebrews 11:3).

"Before all, faith and the fear of God must take the lead in your heart, then you will understand these things" (Theophilus, *Ad Autolycum* I.7).

"The Holy Scriptures . . . are able to make you wise unto salvation through faith which is in Christ Jesus" (2 Timothy 3:15).

"The secrets of righteousness: the inheritance of faith" (Enoch 58:5).

"It is to men of faith that the heavenly secrets are revealed" (3 Enoch 48D10).

"You reveal what is hidden to the pure who in faith have submitted themselves to You and Your Law" (2 Baruch 54:5).

"To them alone has the Almighty God given . . . faith and excellent understanding in their hearts" (Sibylline Oracles III.584-85).

"Let us hold fast the profession of our faith without wavering . . . and let us thoroughly understand [KATANOEO]" (Hebrews 10:23,24).

"Keep My faith . . . and understand My knowledge" (Odes of Solomon 8:10,11).

"He who believes, sees intelligible and future things with the understanding" (Clement of Alexandria, *Strom.* V.c.3).

"What ignorance has bound, is by knowledge well loosened, and these bonds are as quickly as possible slackened by human faith and divine grace" (Clement of Alexandria, *Paed.* I.6.29:5).

"Teach me good understanding and knowledge for I have believed Your commandments" (Psalm 119:66).

"Your hand has levelled the way for those who believe in You" (Odes of Solomon 22:7).

"You have given Your understanding, O Lord, to Your believers" (Odes of Solomon 4:5).

"They who put their trust in Him shall understand Truth" (Wisdom 3:9).

"I am . . . the Truth" (St. John 14:6).

"He shows Himself to those who have faith in Him" (Wisdom 1:2, Latin Vulgate).

"He has revealed Himself and He has manifested Himself through faith, to which alone it is given to behold God" (*Epistle to Diognetus* 8:10-11).

With "the eyes of faith" (First Clement 3:4).

"For we walk by faith not by sight" (2 Corinthians 5:7).

"*Faith* to do His good pleasure" (Sirach 15:16, Greek Text).

"*Understanding* to do His good pleasure" (Sirach 15:15, Hebrew Text).

"*Faith and understanding*" (Clement of Alexandria, *Strom.* II.c.4).

"Faith . . . contributes to the process of learning" (Clement of Alexandria, *Strom.* II.c.6).

"No one shall learn anything without faith, since no one learns without preconception" (Clement of Alexandria, *Strom.* II.c.4).

"Preconception is grasping at something evident and the clear understanding of the thing" (ibid.).

"Faith is a preconception of the understanding" (ibid.).

"It is by understanding that faith is made perfect" (Clement of Alexandria, *Strom.* VII.c.10).

Faith not only gives us understanding,
but also leads us to the knowledge of God.

"Faith shall lead you . . . from faith to knowledge" (Clement of Alexandria, *Exh.* IX.88.1; *Strom.* VII.c.10).

"Believing . . . is the foundation of knowledge" (Clement of Alexandria, *Strom.* VII.c.10).

"Faith . . . is characterized by knowledge" (Clement of Alexandria, *Strom.* VI.c.8).

"Those who believe and fully know the Truth" (1 Timothy 4:3).

"We believe and have come to know" (St. John 6:69).

"Believe . . . that you may know and continue to know" (St. John 10:38, Vaticanus, Regius and Chester Beatty Texts).

"Forgive me my sin, O Lord, and purify me from my iniquity. Grant me a spirit of faith and knowledge" (11QPs^a XIX.13-15 [Plea for Deliverance], Dead Sea Scrolls).

"Blessed are those who serve Him in righteousness and know Him by faith" (1QM 13:2,3, Dead Sea Scrolls).

"Knowledge is the perfection of faith" (Clement of Alexandria, *Strom.* VI.c.18).

Conversely

"The violent . . . will not believe when they hear" (1QpHab. 2:6,7, Dead Sea Scrolls).

"The Word which they heard did not benefit them because it did not meet with faith in the hearers" (Hebrews 4:2).

"If you do not believe neither will you at all understand" (Isaiah 7:9, Greek, Syriac, and Old Latin Texts).

"The Word . . . is not understood by the unbelieving" (*Epistle to Diognetus* 11:7,8).

"He [Jesus: the Word of God] was not understood by unbelievers" (ibid. 11:2).

"They do not believe God nor understand His Power" (Clement of Alexandria, *Exh.* X.104.3).

"The god of this world has blinded the understanding of the unbelievers to keep them from seeing the light of the Gospel" (2 Corinthians 4:4).

"They have lost the clear vision which faith affords" (First Clement, *Epistle to the Corinthians* 3:4).

"Light has vanished from before us and darkness is our dwelling place forever because we have not believed in Him" (Enoch 63:6,7).

"Man believes with his heart" (Romans 10:10).

"O senseless ones and slow of heart to believe" (St. Luke 24:25).

"Do you not yet perceive or understand? Are your hearts hardened?" (St. Mark 8:17).

"They are darkened in their understanding . . . due to their hardness of heart" (Ephesians 4:18).

"How long will you people be without understanding? Your double-mindedness [i.e. doubts] makes you unable to understand" (Shepherd of Hermas, *Vision* III.10.18:9).

"There is no knowledge without faith" (Clement of Alexandria, *Stromata* V.c.1).

* *

"Believe in order that you may understand the Word of God" (St. Augustine, *Sermon XLIII*.vii.9).

"Understanding is the reward of faith. Therefore seek not to understand that you may believe, but believe that you may understand" (St. Augustine, *Homily on St. John's Gospel* XXIX.6).

THE BREADTH AND DEPTH OF UNDERSTANDING

We understand with the heart.

"God made . . . the heart for understanding" (Testament of Naphtali 2:8).

"The heart is deep beyond all things" (Jeremiah 17:9, Greek Text).

"You cannot find the depths of the heart of man" (Judith 8:14).

"Hide it in Your heart seven fathoms deep" (Story of Ahikar 2:56, Armenian Text).

"God gave Solomon Wisdom and Understanding exceedingly much, and largeness of heart" (1 Kings 4:29).

The measure of understanding.

"To His understanding there is no measurement" (Psalm 147:5).

"Wisdom's understanding is more full than the sea" (Sirach 24:29, Greek Vaticanus Text and Cursives 248,254 and Syriac Text).

"O Solomon, how wise you were in your youth and as a flood full of understanding . . . covering the whole earth" (Sirach 47:13,14,15).

We need understanding to appreciate the breadth of things

"Is there anyone who can understand the breadth of the heavens?" (Enoch 93:14).

"Have you understood the breadth of the earth?" (Job 38:18).

"It is He who made the earth broad and placed the waters in the sea" (Odes of Solomon 16:10).

"I bow my knees before the Father . . . that He would grant you according to the riches of His glory . . . that Christ may dwell in your hearts through faith; so that you, being rooted and grounded in love may be able to understand with all the saints what is the breadth and length and height and depth [of His understanding and knowledge]" (Ephesians 3:14,15,16,17).

O Lord "when You shall enlarge my heart" [i.e., Understanding], I shall understand that "Your commandment is exceedingly broad" (Psalm 119:32,96).

"Our heart is enlarged to teach you all things" (Clement of Alexandria, *Ante-Nicene Fathers* [Fragment IV, *Hypotyposes*], p. 578.)

217

"Not only is that which pertains to sensual pleasure or anger to be removed or destroyed but also the entire place of desire and anger where they lurk, in order that the understanding may have paths that are broad and free" (Philo, *Q.Gen.* IV.42).

"Understanding . . . has wide scope and grasps the ends of the universe" (Philo, *Agr.* 53).

*   *

Ancient non-Scriptural Texts on the breadth of Understanding.

"Unsearchable is his [the god's] heart; wide is his understanding" (Enuma Elish, Tablet VII. l.157).

"Powerful one, of wide understanding, director of gods and of men" (Hymn to Marduk, No. 9).

"Lugalluga who dragged off all of them into the sea, he who possesses all wisdom and who has a broad understanding" (Enuma Elish, Tablet VII. l.103).

"Your understanding is like a river whose spring never fails and [broad] as an immense sea which knows no decrease" (Babylonian Tablet 34505 ll. 23-24, British Museum).

"Of wide heart and deep understanding" (Hymn to Asshur).

"Gibil . . . who has broad understanding and is accomplished in insight and whose understanding is so deep that the gods, all of them, cannot fathom it" (Enuma Elish, Tablet VII.100.46).

"You surpass in understanding even Apsu [the great deep]" (Letter of Marduk Shumusur to Ashurbanipal, text found in R.F. Harper's *Assyrian and Babylonian Letters,* Vol. IX. No. 923).

"Who can understand the counsel of the gods in the midst of the heavens? The plan of a god is deep waters; who can know it?" (Sippar Text of Nippur, H.C. Rawlinson Translation).

"He sent a messenger with a broad understanding knowing the heart of the gods" (Myth of Adapa III. ll.9-10; see also *Keilinschriftliche Bibliothek* VI, p. xviif., and *Proceedings of the Society of Biblical Archeologists,* Vol. XVI, 1894, p. 274f).

"With a wide understanding Ea had perfected him" (Myth of Adapa, Fragment I. Col. 3).

"Ea gave him a broad heart to understand the formation of the country" (ibid.; for similar texts see Böllenrucher's *Gebete und Hymnen an Mergal, Hymnen und Gebete an Sin* [Leipzig, *Sem. Studien,* 1907] and Craig's *Assyrian and Babylonian Religious Texts,* Vol. I).

"Bel . . . the wide heavens are thy heart [i.e., 'understanding']" (*The Cuneiform Inscriptions of Western Asia*, IV. R.40, No.I).

CHILDREN AND UNDERSTANDING

"After him [King David] arose a son, a man of understanding [EPISTĒMŌN-SAKAL]" (Sirach 47:12, Greek and Hebrew Texts).

"An understanding [PHRONIMĒ] daughter shall bring an inheritance to her husband" (Sirach 22:4, Greek and Latin Vulgate Texts).

"An understanding [PHRONIMOS] son gladdens his mother" (Proverbs 17:21, Greek Text).

"He who keeps the Law is an understanding [BIN] son" (Proverbs 28:7).

"He who gathers in the summer is an understanding [SAKAL] son" (Proverbs 10:5).

"Behold, My son will understand" (Ascension of Isaiah 4:21).

"Understand, O son of man" (Daniel 8:17).

"Blessed is the man who finds wisdom and the son of man who draws out understanding" (Proverbs 3:13, Syriac Text).

"The sons [UIOI] of Agar who seek understanding [SUNESIN] upon earth" (Baruch 3:23).

"The sons of man according to their understanding [SEKEL]" (1QH Fragment 11:4, Dead Sea Scrolls; ibid. 10:4).

"The Lord looked down from heaven upon the sons of man, to see if there were any who understand [SAKAL] and seek God" (Psalm 14:2; 53:2).

"He is your understanding [PHRONIMOS] son" (Hosea 13:13, Greek Text).

"The Great One has given to the sons of men . . . to understand in their heart . . . God has decreed and created the sons of men to understand words of knowledge" (4QEnᶜ XIII.2-3 [Cave 4, Aramaic Fragments of Enoch], Dead Sea Scrolls).

"They brought us a man of understanding [SEKEL] of the sons of Mahli" (Ezra 8:18).

"David, the son of Jesse was wise and a light . . . and understanding and perfect in all his ways before God and men. And the Lord gave him an understanding [BINAH] and enlightened spirit" (11QPsᵃ XXVII.2-4, Dead Sea Scrolls).

"Wise in *heart*" (Exodus 28:3, Hebrew Text; Job 9:4, Hebrew Text).

"wise in *understanding*" (Exodus 28:3, Greek Text; Job 9:4, Greek Text).

"Every *wise-hearted* man" (Exodus 36:1, Hebrew Text; ibid. 28:3).

"Every one *wise in understanding*" (Exodus 36:1, Greek Text; ibid. 28:3).

"My *son*, if your heart is wise, my heart shall rejoice" (Proverbs 23:15).

"God, the Father of reasonable understanding" (Philo, *De Providentia*, Fragment 2,6; see also Tikkunei ha-Zohar, Tikkun 56.89b-90b).

The Ancient Egyptians and Babylonians also extolled the understanding of the "sons."

"There is no one else who knows thee [the god Aton] except thy son whom thou causest to understand thy plans and thy power" (Hymn to Aton, l. 12).

"O [Ninib] strong son, firstborn of Bel, great perfect son of Isara . . . warlike art thou, perfect in understanding" (Ninib Texts 1 and 4, Texts found in M. Jastrow's *Die Religion Babyloniens und Assyriens* and F. Hrozny's *Mythen von dem Gotte Ninrag* [Ninib]).

It is the children who are taught; therefore they are expected to understand. It is also to them that secret things are revealed.

"Come, O children, listen to me, I will teach you" (Psalm 34:11).

"The Spirit of the Lord . . . teaches the sons of men to know His ways" (Odes of Solomon 3:12).

"Wisdom teaches her children" (Sirach 4:11, Hebrew and Syriac Texts).

"My son . . . incline your ear to wisdom, and apply your heart to understanding" (Proverbs 2:1,2).

"My son, pay attention to my wisdom, and bow down your ear to my understanding" (Proverbs 5:1).

Wisdom says: "Now therefore, hear me, O you children, for happy are they who keep my ways" (Proverbs 8:32).

Wisdom says: "I am the mother of fair love, and fear, and knowledge and holy hope; I therefore, being eternal, am given to all my children who are named by Him" (Sirach 24:18).

"Give ear, my son, receive my advice, and do not refuse my counsel" (Sirach 6:23).

"If you desire, my son, you shall be wise, and if you apply your heart you shall be prudent, if you are willing to hear and incline your ear, you shall be instructed" (Sirach 6:31-32, Hebrew Text).

"My son, listen to me and learn understanding [EPISTĒMĒN] and mark my words with your heart" (Sirach 16:24; see also Ezekiel 3:10).

221

"Hear me, my son, and accept my instruction and do not despise me, and in the end you shall understand my choice words [EMER pl.]" (Sirach 31:22, Hebrew Text).

"O children hear me, and pay attention to the choice words [EMER pl.] of my mouth" (Proverbs 7:24).

"My son, pay attention to my words [DABAR pl.], and incline your ears to my choice words [EMER pl.]" (Proverbs 4:20).

So that you may "understand the choice words [EMER pl.] of understanding [BINAH]" (Proverbs 1:2).

And "the parables of understanding" (Sirach 6:35).

"My son . . . incline your ear to wisdom, and apply your heart to great understanding" (Proverbs 2:1,2).

"Hear me, my son, and be wise, and make your heart happy in the way" (Proverbs 23:19).

"Do you have children? Instruct them" (Sirach 7:23).

"Even as the Father taught Me" (St. John 8:28)

"He who teaches his son will make his enemies envious, and will glory in him, in the presence of friends" (Sirach 30:3).

*Having been taught, a son of man can put forth riddles
and parables. And he can make known hidden
things and mysteries to others.*

"Unto the son of man You have given an abundant portion of the knowledge of Your Truth" (1QH 10:28,29, Dead Sea Scrolls [A. Dupont-Sommer Transl.]).

"Hear my son of the marvelous gifts entrusted to a son of man, a light of the captivity . . . a holy light, a saintly man . . . verily this man stands alone in his generation by reason of his knowledge of holy mysteries" (Letter of Sussman Shesnowski to his son in Poland re Hayyin Samuel Jacob Falk, the Baal Shem of London [c. 1780]. see *Transactions of the Jewish Historical Society* Vol. V. p. 148 and Rainsford MSS. at the British Museum).

"Son of man, put forth a riddle and propound a parable to the house of Israel" (Ezekiel 17:2).

"Son of man . . . utter a parable to the rebellious house" (Ezekiel 24:2,3).

Jesus, the Son of Man, "spoke many things to them in parables" (St. Matthew 13:3).

"He [Jesus] taught them many things by parables" (St. Mark 4:2)

"All these things Jesus spoke to the multitudes in parables, and He did not speak to them without a parable so that what was spoken through the prophet might be fulfilled saying: 'I will open My mouth in parables; I will utter things hidden since the foundation of the world'" (St. Matthew 13:34-35; Psalm 78:2).

"Son of man, make Jerusalem know her abomination" (Ezekiel 16:2; 22:2).

Jesus said: "O Jerusalem, Jerusalem, you who kill the prophets and stone those who are sent to you" (St. Luke 13:34).

"Son of man . . . make them know the abominations of their fathers" (Ezekiel 20:4).

Jesus said to them: "Woe to you for you build the tombs of the prophets whom your fathers killed" (St. Luke 11:47).

"You are sons of those who murdered the prophets" (St. Matthew 23:31).

"Son of man . . . when I speak with you, I will open your mouth, and you will say to them, 'Thus says the Lord God: he who has ears to hear, let him hear!'" (Ezekiel 3:25,27).

Jesus the Son of Man and the Son of God, said to them: "He who has ears to hear, let him hear!" (St. Matthew 11:15; 13:9,43; St. Mark 4:9,23; 7:16; St. Luke 8:8; 14:35).

"The secret things belong to the Lord our God; but the things that are revealed belong to us and to our children forever" (Deuteronomy 29:29).

"That which we have heard and known because our fathers have recounted [SAPHAR] to us, we will not hide from their [grand] children but [also] recount [SAPHAR] to the generation to come the praises of the Lord, and His strength and His wonderful works that He has done . . . that the generation to come might know them . . . and recount [SAPHAR] them to their children" (Psalm 78:3,4,6).

"Wisdom said: 'To you, O men, I call, and my voice is to the children of men'" (Proverbs 8:4).

"Jesus declared, 'I thank You, Father, Lord of Heaven and earth, that You have hidden these things from the wise and understanding and revealed them to babes'" (St. Matthew 11:25; St. Luke 10:21).

"No one knows the Father except the Son, and anyone to whom the Son wills to reveal Him" (St. Matthew 11:27).

Conversely

"By revelation He made known to me the mystery as I have written briefly. So that when you read this, you may understand my insight in the Mystery of Christ which in other generations was not made known to the sons of men" (Ephesians 3:3,4,5).

"Jesus said: 'I stood in the midst of the world, and in flesh I was seen by them, and I found all men drunk, and none did I find thirsty among them, and my soul grieved over the sons of men because they are blind in the heart [i.e., understanding]'" (*Oxyrrynchus Agrapha*, Logion 3, ll. 11-21; *Gospel of Thomas*, Logion 28, Pl.86[21-26]).

"Being deceived as children [NĒPIŌN literally, "babes"] without understanding [APHRONŌN]" (Wisdom 12:24).

"They are foolish children without understanding [BIN]" (Jeremiah 4:22).

"Among the sons [of men], a young man, void of understanding" (Proverbs 7:7).

*   *

"I [Wisdom] was beside Him as a master workman: and I was daily His delight, rejoicing before Him always, rejoicing in the habitable world: His earth; and my delights were the sons of men" (Proverbs 8:30-31).

[Wisdom delights in the good sons of men because they understand her.]

Truly, "Wisdom rests in the heart of him who has understanding" (Proverbs 14:33).

*   *

"Praise the Lord . . . who created the sons of men from out of the womb of their mother and . . . gives unto them wisdom of heart [i.e., "understanding"]" (Sirach 50:20,23, Syriac Text; see also "The Heart and Understanding").

UNDERSTANDING COMFORTS, ENLIVENS AND STRENGTHENS US. IT CONVERTS US AND PERSUADES US TO BE GOOD.

Gracious words comfort the sorrowful, and they who understand know how to speak words of comfort to enliven and strengthen others.

"A word spoken in due season, how good it is!" (Proverbs 15:23).

"Grief in the heart of man shall bring him low but a good word shall make him glad" (Proverbs 12:25).

"The King . . . comforted her with loving words" (Esther 15:8).

"The words of a wise man's mouth are gracious" (Ecclesiastes 10:12).

"Good understanding gives grace" (Proverbs 13:15).

"Grace shall be found in the lips of one who understands" (Sirach 21:16).

"Are you proficient in speaking? Then go and comfort and endeavor to save an afflicted soul" (*Epistle of Barnabas* 19:10).

"Job answered and said . . . 'I have understanding . . . hear diligently my speech and let this be your consolations'" (Job 12:1,3; 21:2).

"All who heard Him were astonished at His understanding . . . all spoke well of Him and marvelled at the gracious words which proceeded out of His mouth" (St. Luke 2:47; 4:22).

"The Lord . . . talked with me with good and comforting words" (Zechariah 1:13).

"The Lord God has given me the tongue of those who are taught [and understand], that I may know how to uphold by a word him who is weary" (Isaiah 50:4).

"You have instructed me . . . and my tongue has been as the tongue of Your taught ones" (1QH 7:10, Dead Sea Scrolls).

"The tongue of those who are taught was given to me to restore the spirit of those who stagger, and to sustain the weary with the Word" (1QH 8:36, Dead Sea Scrolls).

"Behold, you have instructed many, and you have strengthened the weak . . . your words have upheld him who was falling" (Job 4:3,4).

When the Lord desires to comfort us, He gives us understanding of His Words, and reveals to us His hidden things for our consolation.

225

"Blessed is the man whom You shall instruct, O Lord, and shall teach him out of Your Law; that You may give him relief from the days of tribulation" (Psalm 94:12,13).

"That all may learn, and all may be comforted" (1 Corinthians 14:31).

"If Your teaching [TORAH] had not been my delight, I should have perished in my affliction" (Psalm 119:92).

"Your Law is my delight" (Psalm 119:77).

"Your testimonies are my delight" (Psalm 119:24).

"The statutes of the Lord are right, rejoicing the heart" (Psalm 19:8).

"According to the greatness of His compassion, the Most High . . . revealed to me the Word, that I might receive consolation" (2 Baruch 81:4).

"Do you, Baruch, direct your heart to that which has been said to you, and understand those things which have been shown to you, for there are in them many consolations for you" (2 Baruch 43:1).

"O Lord . . . comfort me then, and show Your servant the interpretation and meaning of this fearful vision, that You may perfectly comfort my soul . . . and he said to me, 'this is the interpretation of the vision. . . .'" (2 Esdras 12:7,8,10).

"The Lord revealed to you the revelation, for He had compassion on you and thereby renewed your spirit, and put aside your weakness, and strength came to you, and you were made powerful in the faith" (Shepherd of Hermas, *Vision* III.12.20:2,3).

"You reveal to those who fear You what is prepared for them, that henceforth they may be comforted" (2 Baruch 54:4).

"By Your secrets You have strengthened his heart" (1QH 17:22, Dead Sea Scrolls).

"He [Isaiah] saw by an excellent spirit what would come to pass in the last days, and he comforted those who mourned in Zion by revealing what was to occur to the end of time, and the hidden things before they came to pass" (Sirach 48:24-25)

"He has sent me to show you all these things and to say to you: 'be of good comfort'" (2 Esdras 6:33).

"I . . . leave you the words of this letter . . . that you may be comforted [by the "revelations" therein]" (2 Baruch 78:5).

"Therefore, my brothers, I have written to you that you may comfort yourselves" (2 Baruch 82:1).

And "comfort them [who mourn] with knowledge" (1QS 9:18, Dead Sea Scrolls).

We are comforted and strengthened by understanding the Truths found in the Holy Scriptures and other Sacred Writings.

"Gladden the soul of Your servant by Your Truth" (1QH 11:30, Dead Sea Scrolls).

"My soul rejoiced in Your covenant and Your Truth" (ibid. 10:30,31).

"May Your Truth shine forth unto everlasting glory and happiness without end" (ibid. 11:26,27).

"He has strengthened them . . . He has apportioned to them the lot of Truth" (Sirach 17:20, Latin Vulgate).

"You shall be comforted in Jerusalem" — "The city of Truth" (Isaiah 66:13; Zechariah 8:3).

"We have the holy books of Scripture in our hands to comfort us" (1 Maccabees 12:9).

"Whatever was written in former days was written for our instruction, that by the steadfastness and the comfort of the Scriptures we might have hope" (Romans 15:4).

"Judas Maccabeus . . . exhorted his people . . . comforting them from the Law and the Prophets . . . and he made them more cheerful" (2 Maccabees 15:1,8,9).

"The Lord said . . . 'bring out the books from My storehouses . . . the choice and comforting books'" (2 Enoch 22:12, Slavonic A Text).

"I know another mystery, books shall be given to the righteous and the wise to become a cause of joy and uprightness and much wisdom . . . and they shall believe in them and rejoice over them" (Enoch 104:12,13).

It is with the heart that we understand; therefore, we comfort one another by speaking to the heart.

"Comfort ye My people . . . speak to the heart" (Isaiah 40:1,2).

"He comforted them and spoke to their hearts" (Genesis 50:21).

"You have comforted me, you have spoken to my heart" (Ruth 2:13, Literal Translation).

"Comfort your heart with a morsel of bread" — "the bread of understanding" (Judges 19:5; Sirach 15:3).

"That you may know . . . and . . . comfort your hearts" (Ephesians 6:22).

"And let it feed on what it understands" (2 Esdras 8:4, Latin Text).

Understanding enlivens and strengthens us.

"The words that I have spoken to you, they are spirit, and they are life" (St. John 6:63).

"This is my comfort in my affliction, that Your Word has given me life" (Psalm 119:50, Literal Translation).

"The teaching of the Lord is perfect, restoring the soul" (Psalm 19:7).

"Your teaching is life" (2 Baruch 38:2).

"I will never forget Your precepts for through them You give me life" (Psalm 119:93).

"Through Your precepts I get understanding" (Psalm 119:104).

"Give me understanding, and I shall live" (Psalm 119:144).

"May He enlighten your heart with life-giving understanding" (1QS 2:3, Dead Sea Scrolls).

"Instruct the people . . . if you teach them, you will give them life" (2 Baruch 45:1,2).

"You . . . are strengthened [ESTERIGMĒNOUS] in the Truth that you have" (2 Peter 1:12).

"To Him who is able to strengthen you according to my gospel and the preaching of Jesus Christ" (Romans 16:25).

"You have instructed . . . you have strengthened the weak . . . your words have upheld him who was falling" (Job 4:3,4).

"Be strengthened [ESTERIGMĒNOS] in your understanding" (Sirach 5:10).

"I long to see you that I may impart to you some spiritual gift to strengthen you" (Romans 1:11).

We receive strength from the Truth, Wisdom, and Understanding found in His Holy Words which are the food of our souls.

"Man does not live by bread alone, but by every Word that proceeds out of the mouth of the Lord" (Deuteronomy 8:3).

"Out of His mouth comes knowledge and understanding" (Proverbs 2:6).

"I will give you shepherds after My own heart, who will feed you with knowledge and understanding" (Jeremiah 3:15).

"Feed My lambs . . . feed My sheep" (St. John 21:15,17).

"Strengthen your brothers" (St. Luke 22:32).

With "the bread of understanding and . . . the water of wisdom" (Sirach 15:3).

"Come . . . why do you spend your money for that which is not bread, and your labor for that which does not satisfy? Hear Me with attention, and eat what is good and delight yourselves in fatness. Incline your ear, and come to Me, hear and your soul shall live" (Isaiah 55:1,2,3).

Understanding turns us away from evil and persuades us to be good.

"Give me understanding, and I shall keep Your Law, yes, I shall observe it with all my heart" (Psalm 119:34).

"I will run the way of Your commandments when You shall enlarge my understanding" (Psalm 119:32).

"Through Your precepts I get understanding: therefore I hate every false way" (Psalm 119:104).

"Give to Your people a heart of wisdom and an understanding of prudence and . . . they shall not sin" (Ps. Philo, *Biblical Antiquities* XXI.2).

"You have taught him understanding of Your Mysteries that he may not sin against You" (1QH 17:21,22, Dead Sea Scrolls).

"Teaching understanding to those whose spirit has gone astray and instructing in doctrine those who murmur" (1QS 10:26-11:1, Dead Sea Scrolls).

"He opens the understanding of men . . . to turn a man from unrighteousness" (Job 33:16,17, Greek Text).

"I have knowledge [DAATH] through the abundance of Your goodness . . . I have bound myself not to sin against You, and not to do anything of all that is evil in Your eyes" (1QH 14:17,18, Dead Sea Scrolls).

"Desire that you may be filled with the knowledge of His will in all wisdom and spiritual understanding so that you may walk worthy of the Lord, fully pleasing to Him, bearing fruit in every good work and increasing in the knowledge of God" (Colossians 1:9,10).

"O Lord, You have put understanding in the heart of Your servant that he may do what is good and right before You and restrain himself against deeds of wickedness" (1QH 14:8-9, Dead Sea Scrolls).

"The affections of our appetites are resisted by the temperate understanding, and bent back again, and all the impulses of the body are reined in by reasoning" (4 Maccabees 1:35).

"The understanding has skill to direct the irrational powers within us like a pilot or a charioteer" (Philo, *Det.* 54).

"The temperate understanding has power to conquer the pressure of the passions" (4 Maccabees 3:17).

"The temperate understanding repels all these malignant passions" (4 Maccabees 2:16).

"The temperate understanding is able to be superior to the passions and to transform some and destroy others" (4 Maccabees 2:18).

Hence, it is called "the holy leader: Understanding" (4 Maccabees 2:22).

Thus "While the soul is illumined by the bright and pure rays of wisdom, through which the soul sees God and His potencies, none of the messengers of falsehood has access to the reason, but all are barred from passing the bounds . . . but when the light of understanding is dimmed and clouded, they who are of the fellowship of darkness win the day" (Philo, *Deus.* 3).

"If a man understands the design of God by which all things are ordained, he will despise all material things and his vices will be healed" (Corpus Hermeticum, *Asclepius* III.22a).

"Be ye wise in God and prudent; understanding the order of His commandments and the laws governing every word, so that the Lord may love you" (Testament of Naphtali 8:10).

"All men shall fear and shall declare the work of God for they shall understand [SAKAL] what He has done" (Psalm 64:9).

"Will you not understand so as to fear Him who created the foundations of the earth?" (Targum on Isaiah 40:21).

"When I understand [BIN], I am afraid of Him" (Job 23:15).

"My friends . . . I will warn you whom to fear: fear Him who, after He has killed, has power to cast into hell; yes, I tell you, fear Him!" (St. Luke 12:4,5).

"The Law of the Lord is perfect, converting the soul; the testimony of the Lord is sure, making wise the simple" (Psalm 19:7).

"The Divine Word disciplines and admonishes the soul . . . and turns it back to sovereign Wisdom" (Philo, *Q.Gen.* III.30).

"The Levites caused the people to understand the teaching . . . they read in the book of the Law of God distinctly and gave the explanation and caused them to understand [BIN] the reading and . . . all the people wept when they heard [and understood] the words of the Law" (Nehemiah 8:7,8,9).

"The Levites taught the Law of the Lord making all of them understand it . . . the Levites taught the multitude . . . they all wept when they heard [and understood] the Law" (1 Esdras 9:48,49,50).

"And all the people went their way to eat and to drink and to send presents to one another and to make great rejoicing, because they had understood the words that were declared to them" (Nehemiah 8:12).

"He shall instruct them [to make them understand] in all that has been found . . . so that they may separate themselves from all those who have not departed from all perversity" (1QS 9:20, Dead Sea Scrolls).

"I will lead the blind in a way they do not know, and in paths they have not known I will guide them. I will turn the darkness before them into light, and make crooked things straight. These things will I do for them, and will not forsake them. They shall be turned back, they shall be greatly ashamed. . . ." (Isaiah 42:16,17).

"I send you to open their eyes, and turn them from darkness to light and from the power of Satan to God, that they may receive forgiveness of sins" (Acts 26:17,18).

"The teaching of Truth was in his mouth . . . and he did turn many away from iniquity" (Malachi 2:6).

"They shall be converted by Your glorious mouth" (1QH 6:14, Dead Sea Scrolls).

For "out of His mouth comes knowledge and understanding" (Proverbs 2:6).

"By his knowledge shall My righteous servant make the many to be righteous" (Isaiah 53:11).

"I will teach transgressors Your ways and sinners shall be converted to You" (Psalm 51:13).

"They who are understanding [SAKAL] . . . turn many to righteousness" (Daniel 12:3).

"Instructing his opponents that God may perhaps give them repentance towards the full knowledge [EPIGNŌSIN] of the Truth" (2 Timothy 2:25).

"Do teach me what I do not see [and know]; if I have done iniquity, I will do it no more" (Job 34:32).

"The Lord has directed my mouth by His Word, and He has opened up my understanding by His light . . . and gave me the ability that I might speak the fruit of His peace to convert the souls of those who are willing to come to Him" (Odes of Solomon 10:1-3).

"If men saw this, not with bodily eyes, but rather with the eyes of the understanding [NOUS]; they would certainly be converted to virtue" (Philo, *Q.Gen.* IV.51).

"The Lord give you understanding [SEKEL] and insight [BINAH], . . . that you may keep the Law of the Lord your God" (1 Chronicles 22:12).

"I am the one who reveals Your Mysteries to the children of men . . . I did it for Your sake that strife may not abound in Israel" (Megillah 3a, BT).

But that "the peace of God which surpasses all understanding" (Philippians 4:7) may flourish.

"If therefore you also have good understanding, then will both wicked men be at peace with you, and the profligate will reverence you, and turn towards good" (Testament of Benjamin 5:1).

"Prophets were inspired and taught by God Himself" (Theophilus, *Ad Autolycum* II.9) therefore they understood.

"God . . . sent prophets to them from among their brothers to teach and remind them of the content of the Law, to convert them to repentance so that they would no longer sin" (ibid. III.11).

"He shall go before them in the spirit and power of Elijah, to turn the hearts of the fathers to the children, and the disobedient to the understanding [PHRONĒSEI] of the righteous" (St. Luke 1:17).

"The Lord . . . rebukes, and trains, and teaches them, and turns them back to Him as a shepherd does to his flock" (Sirach 18:13).

"Wisdom" says "be converted at my reproof" (Proverbs 1:21,23).

For "he who hears reproof gets understanding" (Proverbs 15:32).

"A wise heart that has understanding will abstain from sins, and have success in the works of justice" (Sirach 3:32, Latin Vulgate).

"Reproof gives wisdom" (Proverbs 29:15).

"He who wins souls is wise" (Proverbs 11:30).

"A man who is accustomed to disgraceful talk *will not be instructed in wisdom* all the days of his life" (Sirach 23:15, Syriac Text).

"A man who is accustomed to disgraceful talk *will never be reformed* all the days of his life" (ibid., Greek Text).

"A new heart [i.e., understanding] will I give you and a new spirit will I put within you . . . and cause you to walk in My statutes and you shall keep My judgments and do them" (Ezekiel 36:26,27; Ibid. 11:19,20).

"Be transformed by the renewing of your understanding" (Romans 12:2).

"Be renewed in the spirit of your understanding [NOUS], and put on the new man, created after the likeness of God in righteousness and holiness of the Truth, therefore, putting away all falsehood" (Ephesians 4:23,24,25).

Conversely

"There remained not in her [Israel] prophets to prophecy and cause her to [understand and] turn to Him by repentance" (Targum on Lamentations 4:6).

"The sons of men having no understanding of these things, sin and provoke the Most High" (Testament of Levi 3:10).

The persuasive words of wisdom, of those who understand, induce
others to repent if they are willing to listen;
but not if they are obdurate.

"The understanding sows worthy, fitting and persuasive things in those who are not discordant in aiming at the Truth" (Philo, *Q.Gen.* IV.56)

"As God's steward . . . holding fast the faithful word as taught, so that he may be able by sound doctrine both to exhort and convince those who contradict" (Titus 1:7,9).

"Apollos . . . an eloquent man . . . mighty in the Scriptures . . . he powerfully convinced the Jews in public, showing by the Scriptures that Jesus was the Christ" (Acts 18:24,28).

"Christ . . . whom we preach, warning every man and teaching every man in all wisdom, that we may present every man perfect in Christ Jesus" (Colossians 1:27,28).

"Who shall know Your thought, unless You give Wisdom, and send Your Holy Spirit from above so that the ways of men may be corrected, and men may learn the things that please You?" (Wisdom 9:17,18, Latin Vulgate).

"Never did a man speak the way this man [Jesus] speaks" (St. John 7:46).

"Behold, the world has gone after Him" (St. John 12:19).

"All who heard Him were astonished at His understanding" (St. Luke 2:47).

"Where there is no knowledge, there is no persuasive counsel" (Sirach 3:25, Syriac Text).

"Hear and understand" (St. Matthew 15:10).

"Hear Me, all of you, and understand" (St. Mark 7:14).

"The understanding [BIN] charmer" (Isaiah 3:3).

"The wicked . . . they are like the deaf adder that stops her ear, so that she will not hear the voice of charmers, charming never so wisely" (Psalm 58:3,4,5).

"They [the wicked] have scorned the Law of the Most High . . . they are now unable to make a good repentance for life [and understand]" (2 Esdras 7:81,82, Syriac Text).

"His soul has abhorred instructions of knowledge . . . he is unable to repent [and understand]" (1QS 2:26-3:1, Dead Sea Scrolls).

"Ye wicked . . . ye have rejected the knowledge of the Most High, for His works have not taught you. Nor has the understanding of His creation which is before you at all times persuaded you" (2 Baruch 54:17,18).

"My tabernacle is destroyed, and all My cords are broken, My children have departed from Me and they are gone . . . because the shepherds have become brutish, and have not sought the Lord" (Proverbs 28:5), therefore, "they shall not understand [SAKAL], and all their flocks shall be scattered" (Jeremiah 10:20,21).

"My people have been lost sheep, their shepherds have caused them to go astray" (Jeremiah 50:6).

For "they are shepherds who cannot understand" (Isaiah 56:11).

"Jesus . . . saw a great multitude, and He was moved with compassion towards them, because they were like sheep without a shepherd; and [so] He began to teach them many things" (St. Mark 6:34).

Jesus "Christ, in whom are hidden all the treasures of wisdom and knowledge" (Colossians 2:2,3).

THE COMING AGE OF UNDERSTANDING

"The angels showed me, and from them I heard everything, and from them I understood what I saw, but not for this generation, but for a remote one which is yet to come" (Enoch 1:2).

"To whom the Law has now been a hope, and understanding an expectation . . . shall wonders appear in their time for they shall behold the world which is now invisible to them" (2 Baruch 51:7,8).

"Then, indeed, He will raise up a kingdom for all ages . . . to godly men, to all of whom He promised to open out the earth and the world, and the portals of the blessed, and all joys, and everlasting understanding and eternal gladness" (Sibylline Oracles III.767-777).

"In those days . . . the children of the earth shall see . . . and shall understand all the words of this book" (Enoch 100:1,6).

"Books will be given to the righteous and the wise to become a cause of joy and uprightness and much wisdom" (Enoch 104:12).

"In the end . . . the holy people shall be given the delights of Paradise . . . and there shall be given to them a heart that understands the good" (Apocalypse of Moses 13:3,4,5).

"In the final end, the time of renewal" — "the just will understand the knowledge of the Most High, and the perfect of way will have understanding of the wisdom of the sons of Heaven" (1QS 4:25,22, Dead Sea Scrolls).

"The Most High will visit the world which was made by Him . . . then you shall understand" (2 Esdras 9:2,4).

"In the time of His visitation . . . the Truth of the world, which during the dominion of falsehood has been sullied in the ways of wickedness until the appointed time of judgment, shall appear in triumph forever" (1QS 4:18,19,20, Dead Sea Scrolls).

"Sorrow and sighing shall be no more, and wrong-doing shall be at an end and Your Truth shall break forth as the dawn in never ending glory" (1QH 11:26,27, Dead Sea Scrolls).

"Then they will see My salvation and the end of My world . . . the heart of the inhabitants of the earth will be converted to a different understanding, for evil will be destroyed and deceit will be blotted out and faith will flourish and corruption shall be overcome and Truth which has been fruitless for so long shall be declared" (2 Esdras 6:25,26,27-28).

"Truths which in this world are taught, will in the world to come be known without teacher" (Pirke Aboth 4:31).

"All the Teaching [TORAH] which you learn in this world is vanity compared with the Teaching which will be learned in the world to come" (Midrash Rabbah on Ecclesiastes 2:1).

"For the days are coming, says the Lord, when . . . I will put My Teaching [TORAH] within them, and I will write it upon their hearts . . . and no longer shall each man teach his neighbor and each one his brother, saying: 'know the Lord,' for they shall know Me, from the least of them to the greatest" (Jeremiah 31:31,33-34).

"The age which is not yet awake shall be roused . . . and the reward shall be made manifest" (2 Esdras 7:31,35).

"At its [the present age's] close . . . the chosen righteous of the eternal plants of righteousness shall receive sevenfold instruction concerning all His creation" (Enoch 93:10).

"Then shall the Lord disclose these things, and the glory of the Lord shall be seen" (2 Maccabees 2:8).

"For His righteousness' sake He will magnify the Law, and make it honorable" (Isaiah 42:21).

"The Law shall be found perfect, without lies" (Sirach 34:8).

"In the end you shall understand my words" (Sirach 31:22, Hebrew Text).

"In the time of the end . . . knowledge shall increase" (Daniel 12:4).

"The vision . . . in the end, shall speak and not lie . . . for the earth shall be filled with the knowledge of the glory of the Lord, as the waters cover the sea" (Habacuc 2:3,14).

"The earth shall be full of the knowledge of the Lord as the waters cover the sea" (Isaiah 11:9).

"Just as one can neither see nor seek out or know the depths of the sea, even so, no man upon earth can know or understand the secrets of the Most High except in the time when He shall appear in His glory" (2 Esdras 13:52, Armenian Text).

"The holy Lord will come forth with wrath and chastisement to execute judgment on earth. In those days violence shall be cut off from its roots, and the roots of unrighteousness together with deceit, and they shall be destroyed . . . and the righteous shall arise from their sleep, and Wisdom shall arise and be given to them" (Enoch 91:7,8,10).

"When the congregation of the righteous shall appear, sinners shall be judged for their sins . . . and light shall appear to the righteous and elect . . . when the secrets of the righteous shall be revealed" (Enoch 38:1,2,3).

"Now we see in a mirror dimly, but then face to face. Now I know in part, then I shall fully know [EPIGNŌSOMAI]" (1 Corinthians 13:12).

"For nothing is hidden, except to be revealed; nor is anything secret, except to come to light" (St. Mark 4:22).

"Towards [future] all the riches of the full assurance of understanding and the knowledge of God's Mystery" (Colossians 2:2).

"Who among you will give ear to this and will listen attentively and hear [and understand it] for the time to come?" (Isaiah 42:23).

"In that day the deaf shall hear the words of a book, and out of their gloom and darkness the eyes of the blind shall see. The meek shall again increase their joy in the Lord, and the poor among men shall exult in the Holy One of Israel" (Isaiah 29:18-19).

"For that which has not been told them they shall see, and that which they have not heard they shall understand" (Isaiah 52:15).

"As regards the latter day things, God has put them all in my understanding" (Sibylline Oracles III.821).

"In the latter days you shall understand it" (Jeremiah 30:24).

"In the latter days you shall understand it with understanding [BINAH]" (Jeremiah 23:20).

"During the whole epoch of wickedness . . . they will not grasp instruction until there shall arise he who teaches righteousness in the end of days" (Zadokite Fragment [CD] 6:10,11).

COMPASSION AND UNDERSTANDING

"The way of compassionate understanding" (2 Baruch 3:20, Syriac Text).

"Let not kindness and fidelity leave you; bind them around your neck, write them on the tablet of thine heart. So shalt you find favor and good understanding [SAKAL] in the sight of God and man" (Proverbs 3:3,4)

"The wicked err when they devise . . . but kind and righteous men do all kinds of good. The workers of iniquity do not understand Truth and kindness, but kindness and Truth are with the workers of good things [and they understand]" (Proverbs 14:22, Syriac Text).

"The righteous one perishes and no one lays it to heart [see "Pondering and Understanding"]; kind men are taken away and no one understands" [because along with the kind men understanding is taken away] (Isaiah 57:1).

"The righteous one gives and does not hold back" (Proverbs 21:26).

"The righteous one is generously merciful and compassionate" (ibid., Greek Text).

"Righteous men pity and are kind" (Proverbs 13:9b, Greek Text).

"These [righteous] men excel in virtue and possess full understanding" (Letter of Aristeas v. 200).

"A righteous man understands [SAKAL]" (Proverbs 21:12).

Because he has "the understanding [PHRONĒSEI] of the righteous" (St. Luke 1:17).

And "the wisdom of his righteousness" (Psalms of Solomon 17:31)

"Blessed are you righteous ones, for to you are revealed the deepest secrets of the Law" (Zohar, *Idra R.* II.26).

"The righteous always have light" (Proverbs 13:9a, Greek Text).

For "unto the upright there arises light in the darkness because he [the upright] is gracious and full of compassion and righteous" (Psalm 112:4).

"Loose the bands of wickedness, undo the heavy burdens, let the oppressed go free . . . break every yoke . . . deal your bread to the hungry, bring the poor that are cast out, into your house . . . cover the naked . . . help those in need. Then shall your light break forth as the morning" (Isaiah 58:6-8).

"If you draw out your soul to the hungry, and satisfy the afflicted soul, then shall your light arise" (Isaiah 58:10).

"Light . . . imparts understanding" (Psalm 119:130).

"Strengthen the weak hands, and support the feeble knees. Say to the fainthearted, 'take courage, and do not fear! Behold, your God will come with vengeance; the recompense of God will come, He will come and save you.' Then the eyes of the blind will be opened, and the ears of the deaf will be unstopped" (Isaiah 35:3-5).

Conversely

"Great in folly and lacking in understanding was he [merciless Rehoboam]" (Sirach 47:23, Hebrew Text).

"A ruler who is a great oppressor lacks understanding" (Proverbs 28:16).

"A man of violence does not receive understanding" (Sirach 32:18, Hebrew MS. E, Geniza Fragment).

"The spirit of hatred darkened my understanding" (Testament of Gad 6:2).

"They are darkened in their understanding . . . due to their hardness of heart, they have become callous" (Ephesians 4:18,19).

"Evil men do not understand" (Proverbs 28:5).

"None of the wicked shall understand" (Daniel 12:10).

"The wicked do not understand knowledge" (Proverbs 29:7).

"The wicked; their light is withheld" (Job 38:15).

"The light of the wicked shall be put out" (Job 18:5).

Because "the heart of the wicked is without pity" (Proverbs 12:10, Greek Text).

Thus, Job in his trials, protesting his innocence cries out:

"Did I not weep for him who was in trouble? Was not my soul grieved [compassionately] for the poor? Yet, when I looked for good, evil came; and when I waited for light, there came darkness" (Job 30:25-26).

*   *

"Jesus . . . went about doing good and healing all who were oppressed by the devil" (Acts 10:38).

239

"Jesus . . . had compassion on them, and healed their sick" (St. Matthew 14:13,14).

"Jesus went about all the cities and villages . . . He saw the crowds, He had compassion for them, because they were harassed and helpless" (St. Matthew 9:35,36; St. Mark 6:34).

"Jesus called His disciples to Him and said, 'I have compassion on the crowd, because they have been with Me now three days, and have nothing to eat; and I am unwilling to send them away hungry, lest they faint on the way'" (St. Matthew 15:32).

"Jesus had compassion on them, and touched their eyes, and immediately their eyes received sight" (St. Matthew 20:34).

"Jesus, moved with compassion, put forth His hand and touched him" [the leper] (St. Mark 1:41).

"When the Lord [Jesus] saw her [the widow of Nain], He had compassion on her and said to her, 'do not weep'" (St. Luke 7:13).

"Jesus spoke to them saying: 'I am the light of the world; he who follows Me will not walk in the darkness, but will have the light of life'" (St. John 8:12).

Jesus "Christ, the Power [see "The Power and Strength of Understanding"] of God and the wisdom of God" (1 Corinthians 1:24).

Jesus "Christ, in whom are hidden all the treasures of wisdom and knowledge" (Colossians 2:2,3).

For "the Son [Jesus Christ] is the Understanding [NOUS], Word, and Wisdom of the Father" (Athenagoras, *Emb.* XXIV).

UNDERSTANDING AND COUNSELLING

"Hear me, my son, and accept the counsel of understanding [CONSILIUM INTELLECTUS]" (Sirach 6:24, Latin Vulgate).

"Seek counsel always from the understanding [PHRONIMOU]" (Tobit 4:18, Greek Vaticanus B Text).

"Counsel from the understanding [SUNETOU]" (Jeremiah 18:18, Greek Text).

"The heart is established by the counsel of good understanding" (Sirach 22:16).

"Say . . . to understanding, 'you are my counsellor'" (Proverbs 7:4, Syriac Text).

"God will make him mighty by means of His holy Spirit, and wise by means of the counsel [BOULE] of understanding" (Psalms of Solomon 17:42).

"Men renowned for their power, giving counsel by their understanding" (Sirach 44:3).

"From their understanding the godly have devised good counsel" (Isaiah 32:8, Greek Text, Literal Translation).

"Powerful counsel [TACHBULOTH] is rooted in understanding" (Sirach 37:17, Hebrew Text).

"A man of understanding will obtain powerful counsel [TACHBULOTH]" (Proverbs 1:5).

"They who fear the Lord understand . . . and shall bring forth powerful counsel [TACHBULOTH] out of the gloom" (Sirach 32:16, Hebrew Text, MS. E).

"As the water jar contains water, understanding contains . . . counsel" (Philo, *Q.Gen.* IV.98).

"The understanding has two connatural daughters: counsel and consent" (Philo, *Q.Gen.* IV.55).

"That which reflects is called understanding and its counsel is directed towards the good" (Philo, *Q.Gen.* IV.58).

"Whatever man meditates in his heart, his understanding counsels" (2 Enoch 66:3).

"Speech is the expounder of the plans which understanding has formed in its own counsel chamber [BOULEUTERIO]" (Philo, *Det.* 40).

"The counselling understanding" (Philo, *Q.Exod.* II.13).

"Counsellors by their understanding" (Sirach 44:3, Hebrew Text).

"Jonathan, David's uncle, was a counsellor, a man of understanding" (1 Chronicles 27:32).

"Zechariah, his son, was an understanding [SEKEL] counsellor" (1 Chronicles 26:14).

Pentephres "was a counsellor of Pharaoh because he was understanding beyond all the princes of Pharaoh" (Joseph and Asenath 1:3(5)).

"They inquire [for counsel] at the mouth of the one who understands [PHRONI-MOU]" (Sirach 21:17).

"The counsel [BOULĒ] of the holy is understanding" (Proverbs 9:10, Greek Text).

"A man of counsel will not neglect understanding" (Sirach 32:22, Latin Vulgate).

"What can counsel do by itself without the understanding?" (Philo, *Q.Gen.* IV.56).

Conversely, where there is no understanding, there is a lack of good counsel.

"Is counsel perished from the understanding?" (Jeremiah 49:7, Literal Translation).

"They are a nation void of counsel because there is no understanding in them" (Deuteronomy 32:28; Zadokite Fragment [CD] 5:17, MS.A).

"They were destroyed because they had no understanding and perished through their lack of counsel [ABOULIAN]" (Baruch 3:28).

"The counsel of sinners is not understanding [PHRONESIS]" (Sirach 19:22).

"Great in folly and lacking in understanding [BINAH] was he [Rehoboam] who by his [bad] counsel made the people revolt" (Sirach 47:23, Hebrew Text).

Such is the close relationship between understanding and counselling, that we find them used interchangeably.

"I will praise the Lord who has given me *counsel*" (Psalm 16:7, Hebrew Text).

"I will praise the Lord who has made me *understand*" (Psalm 16:7, Greek Text).

"I will praise the Lord who has given me *understanding*" (Psalm 16:7, Latin Vulgate).

"*Understanding* is a wellspring of life" (Proverbs 16:22).

"*Counsel* is a wellspring of life" (Sirach 21:13).

"O how beautiful it is . . . for ancient men to know *counsel*" (Sirach 25:4, Greek Text).

"O how beautiful it is . . . for ancient men to know *understanding*" (Sirach 25:4, Syriac Text).

"With whom did He take *counsel*, and who made Him *understand* [BIN]?" (Isaiah 40:14, Hebrew Text).

"Who has known the *understanding* [NOUS] of the Lord? And who has been His *counsellor?*" (Isaiah 40:13, Greek Text).

"He has no need of anyone who *understands* [BIN]" (Sirach 42:21, Hebrew Text).

"He has no need of any *counsellor*" (Sirach 42:21, Greek Text).

*   *

"The more counsel, the more understanding" (Pirke Aboth 2:8).

We understand with the heart,
therefore our heart counsels us.

"Do you also understand the counsel of your heart, for you have no one more faithful to you" (Sirach 37:13, Hebrew Text).

"The heart that is established by its well advised [DIANOĒMATOS] counsel shall not fear at any time" (Sirach 22:16).

Counsel and Understanding are paired.

"Good counsel shall guard you, and holy understanding shall keep you" (Proverbs 2:11, Greek Text).

"My son, keep my counsel and understanding, do not let them flow by thee" (Proverbs 3:21, Greek Text).

Even the Pagans knew the relationship
between Understanding and good Counsel

"Hear the counsel of Shumbeawelum whose understanding is like Enlilbanda, the experienced counsel of Shumbeawelum whom Enlilbanda gave understanding to" (Ras Shamra Tablet 22.439, ll. 1-4, C.H. Gordon's *Ugaritic Texts*, Vol. V).

UNDERSTANDING "DAWNS" AND IS SEEN BY THE EYES OF OUR UNDERSTANDING.

The light of understanding shall rise in our hearts when we shall begin to understand the wisdom and Truth of His Word.

"Understanding [PHRONĒSIS] is truly a thing of the dawn, all radiancy and brightness" (Philo, *Plant.* 40).

"Understanding" is "like one enlightened by the flash of the sun's beam after night" (Philo, *Cher.* 62).

"If the sun shall have risen, that is, the Understanding that shines so brilliantly in us" (Philo, *L.A.* III.35).

"We have erred from the way of Truth, and the light of justice has not shined unto us, and the sun of understanding has not risen upon us" (Wisdom 5:6, Latin Vulgate).

"If you do not adapt yourself to the vision of holiness, you will end your life in blindness, unable to see the sun of understanding" (Philo, *Q.Exod.* II.51).

For "The sun of understanding sends out its incorporeal rays most luminously and splendidly upon pure souls" it "wishes to illuminate the understanding of the wise man" (Philo, *Q.Gen.* IV.1).

"Sun in a figurative sense is used of the human understanding . . . for the understanding is like a sun" (Philo, *Som.* I.77).

"Understanding is the great sunlight of the soul" (Philo, *Cong.* 47)

"The soul is illumined by the bright and pure rays of understanding [PHRONĒSIS], through which the wise man sees God and His powers, none of the messengers of falsehood had access to . . . the light of understanding" (Philo, *Deus.* 3).

"The understanding is the sight of the soul illuminated by rays peculiar to itself, whereby the vast and profound darkness of ignorance is dispelled" (ibid. 46).

"I will light the lamp of understanding in your heart; it will not be extinguished until what you are to write is finished" (2 Esdras 14:25).

"And we have the prophetic Word made more sure. You will do well to pay attention to this as to a lamp shining in a dark place, until the day dawns and the morning star [understanding] rises in your heart" (2 Peter 1:19).

"Words of the man of understanding addressed by him to all the sons of the dawn" [i.e., those who understand] (Cave IV Fragment, Dead Sea Scrolls).

"I understood [BIN] it in the early morning" (1 Kings 3:21).

Because "the rising sun reveals all things" (Sirach 42:16, Hebrew Text).

"Who has given understanding to the cock [that crows at dawn]?" (Job 38:36).

"Blessed is He who has given the rooster understanding" (Berakoth 60b, BT).

"Learn where there is insight [PHRONĒSIS], where is strength, where is understanding [SUNESIS], that you may know also where is length of days, and life where there is the light of the eyes, and peace" (Baruch 3:14).

"May He enlighten your heart with life-giving understanding" (1QS 2:3, Dead Sea Scrolls).

Wisdom and Truth provide light for the understanding.

"The light of the understanding is wisdom" (Philo, *Spec.* I.288).

"As our eyes are illuminated by the sun's rays, so is the understanding by wisdom" (ibid.).

"The end of the word is Truth, which casts a beam more far reaching than light" (Philo, *L.A.* III.45).

"Life has no clearer light than Truth" (ibid.).

"The rising of the dawn is the brightness of inward Truth . . . holy men long to see the true dawn . . . that deep innermost light" (St. Gregory the Great, *Morals on the Book of Job*, Book IV.46).

"Your Truth shall break forth as the dawn in never ending glory" (1QH 11:26, Dead Sea Scrolls).

Those who are good shall behold the wonderful wisdom and Truth of His Word, with the eyes of their understanding.

"The understanding sees, the understanding hears" (Epicharmus, quoted by Clement of Alexandria, *Strom.* Book II.c.5; also Tertullian in *De Anima*).

"The eyes of the body do not see [spiritual things], but the clear and pure understanding is taught to see" (Philo, *Q.Gen.* IV.152).

"Not the eyes of the body but those of the understanding" (Philo, *Q.Gen.* IV.141).

"Come and contemplate, not with your eyes only, but with your understanding" (*Epistle to Diognetus* 2:1, Literal Translation).

"If men saw this, not with bodily eyes, but rather with the eyes of the understanding, they would certainly be converted to virtue" (Philo, *Q.Gen.* IV.51).

"Understanding is the eye of the soul" (Clement of Alexandria, *Paed.* I.9.77:2).

"What the eye is to the body, understanding and wisdom are to the soul" (Philo, *Q.Gen.* I.11).

"The sight of the understanding, the dominant elements of the soul, surpasses all the other faculties of the mind" (Philo, *Abr.* 57).

"Let us contemplate Him with the understanding" (First Clement 19:3).

"O Understanding, with the spiritual eyes opened, behold Him who is within you" (Philo, *Q.Gen.* IV.138).

"Open the eyes of the heart [understanding] that we may know You" (First Clement 59:3).

"Through Him [Jesus Christ] the eyes of our heart have been opened" (First Clement 36:2; 1 John 5:20; St. Luke 24:45).

"Blessed are the pure in heart for they shall see God" (St. Matthew 5:8).

"I [God] . . . am discerned by the understanding and not by sight" (Philo, *Spec.* I.46).

"He who sees God is he who understands God" (Clement of Alexandria, *Paed.* I.9.77:2).

The wicked are blind in understanding.

"The understanding of the pleasure-loving man is blind" (Philo, *Q.Gen.* IV.245).

"Our understanding is darkened by vain desires" (Second Clement 19:2).

"Walk not as other Gentiles walk in the vanity of their mind, having the understanding darkened" (Ephesians 4:17,18).

"Our foolish and darkened understanding" (First Clement 36:2).

"The god of this world has blinded the understanding of those who do not believe" (2 Corinthians 4:4).

"Blind in understanding" (Philo, *Fug.* 144).

"Blind men whose understanding, through covetousness, has lost the power to see" (Philo, *De Providentia.* Fragment 2,12).

"Folly has shed profound darkness over their understanding" (ibid. 2,20).

"Hatred darkened my understanding" (Testament of Gad 6:2).

"Jealousy blinded my understanding" (Testament of Simeon 2:7).

"Anger . . . lying, darkens his understanding" (Testament of Dan 2:4).

"Sodomites . . . blind in the understanding" (Philo, *Conf.* 27).

"Fornication . . . insatiableness . . . fighting . . . obsequiousness and chicanery . . . lying . . . injustice . . . darkens a young man's understanding" (Testament of Reuben 3:3-8).

*   *

"What is man . . . that You should visit him in the early morning?" (Job 7:17,18).

"What is man . . . that You should give him understanding? . . . " (1QH 10:3,4, Dead Sea Scrolls).

THE DELIGHTS AND JOYS OF UNDERSTANDING

"Happy is he who dwells with a wife who understands" (Sirach 25:8).

"The eyes for sight . . . the understanding for joy" (2 Enoch 30:9).

"In length of days: understanding" (Job 12:12).

"The joy of a man is length of days" (Sirach 30:22).

"Happy is he who keeps the Law" (Proverbs 29:18).

Because "he who keeps the Law of the Lord gets the understanding thereof" (Sirach 21:11).

"The Law of life and understanding" (Sirach 45:5, Hebrew Text).

"Happy is he who has found understanding [PHRONĒSIN]" (Sirach 25:9).

"O the happiness of a man who finds wisdom and who brings forth understanding!" (Proverbs 3:13).

"O how abundant is Your goodness which You have laid up for them who fear You" (Psalm 31:19).

"Eye has not seen, nor ear heard, neither has it entered the heart [i.e., understanding] of man the things which God has prepared for those who love Him" (1 Corinthians 2:9).

God "has prepared goodness for him in the place of understanding" (Testament of Naphtali 10:8, Hebrew Text).

"I have understanding through the abundance of Your goodness" (1QH 14:17, Dead Sea Scrolls).

"May He grant you *wisdom* of heart" (Sirach 50:23, Hebrew Text).

"May He grant us *joyfulness* of heart" (ibid., Greek Text).

"All the people went their way to eat and drink and to send gifts and to make great rejoicing, because they had understood the words [of the Law] which were declared to them" (Nehemiah 8:12).

"They went their way, everyone to eat and drink, and make merry, and give portions to those who had nothing, and to make great cheer; because they understood the words wherein they were instructed" (1 Esdras 9:54-55).

"To the man who is good in His sight, He has given wisdom, and knowledge, and joy" (Ecclesiastes 2:26)

"There is no joy above the joy of the heart" (Sirach 30:16).

"God made . . . the heart for understanding" (Testament of Naphtali 2:8).

"In the love of wisdom is good delight" (Wisdom 8:18, Literal Translation).

"My heart [i.e., understanding] delighted in wisdom" (Sirach 51:20, Latin Vulgate).

But "a fool has no delight in understanding" (Proverbs 18:2).

Because "fools despise wisdom" (Proverbs 1:7).

And "wisdom is too high for a fool" (Proverbs 24:7).

"The heart of those who seek the Lord rejoices" (Psalm 105:3).

Because "they who seek the Lord understand all things" (Proverbs 28:5).

"All those who put their trust in You rejoice" (Psalm 5:11).

For "they who put their trust in Him shall understand the Truth" (Wisdom 3:9).

"Happy is the man who fears the Lord, who greatly delights in His commandments" (Psalm 112:1).

"I will delight myself in Your commandments, which I have loved" (Psalm 119:47).

"I love Your commandments above gold, yes, above fine gold" (Psalm 119:127).

For "a good understanding have all those who do His commandments" (Psalm 111:10).

"Joshua took the garments of wisdom and put them on, and girded his loins with the girdle of understanding. And it came to pass that his heart was kindled and his spirit stirred up" (Ps. Philo, *Biblical Antiquities* XX.3).

"And beginning with Moses and all the prophets, He interpreted to them in all the Scriptures the things concerning Himself . . . they said to each other, 'Did not our hearts burn within us while He talked to us on the road, and while He opened to us the Scriptures?'" (St. Luke 24:27,32).

"Light . . . and joy" (Psalm 97:11).

"Light and understanding" (Psalm 119:130).

"Behold, I long for Your precepts" (Psalm 119:40)

"Behold, how I love Your precepts" (Psalm 119:159).

"I have sought Your precepts" (Psalm 119:94,45).

"I will meditate on Your precepts" (Psalm 119:15,78).

"I esteem right all Your precepts concerning everything" (Psalm 119:128).

"The precepts [PIQQUDIM] of the Lord are right, rejoicing the heart" (Psalm 19:8).

Because "through Your precepts [PIQQUDIM] I get understanding" (Psalm 119:104, see v. 100).

"The fruit of understanding is the life of contemplation, winning for us unmixed gladness as from wine" (Philo, *Fug.* 176).

"A wise man's understanding is at his right hand" (Ecclesiastes 10:2).

"At Your right hand are pleasures forevermore" (Psalm 16:11).

"Men of understanding find delight in their understanding" (Rabbi Joseph Kimchi's *Shekel Hakodesh* 18).

THE DESIRE FOR WISDOM AND UNDERSTANDING

First of all we should love God
and desire Him above all things.

"You shall love the Lord your God with all your heart, and with all your soul, and with all your strength" (Deuteronomy 6:5).

"He who loves father and mother more than Me is not worthy of Me; and he who loves son or daughter more than Me is not worthy of Me" (St. Matthew 10:37).

"To love Him with all the heart, and with all the understanding and with all the soul, and with all the strength . . . is much more than all whole burnt offerings and sacrifices" (St. Mark 12:33).

"Your name, even the remembrance of You is the desire of our souls. With my soul I have desired You in the night, my spirit within me diligently seeks You" (Isaiah 26:8,9).

"My soul longs . . . my heart and my flesh cry out for the living God" (Psalm 84:2).

"As the deer longs for the water brooks, so my soul longs for You O God. My soul thirsts for God, for the living God; when shall I come and behold the face of God?" (Psalm 42:1-2).

"I stretch out my hands to You; my soul thirsts for You like a parched land" (Psalm 143:6).

"If anyone thirsts, let him come to Me and drink" (St. John 7:37).

"Seek ye My face" (Psalm 27:8).

"Seek the Lord and His strength, seek His face continually" (1 Chronicles 16:11).

"If you seek Him, He will be found by you" (1 Chronicles 28:9).

"You shall find Him, if you seek Him with all your heart and with all your soul" (Deuteronomy 4:29).

"They entered into a covenant to seek the Lord, the God of their fathers, with all their heart and with all their soul . . . they . . . sought Him with their whole desire and He was found by them" (2 Chronicles 15:12,15).

"God goes out to meet us . . . and to show Himself to those who desire to see Him" (Philo, *Fug.* 141).

251

We see God in the Truth of His Word, and we should love
and desire His Words, for they are the food and drink
of our souls. And in them is found all our Wisdom,
Understanding and Knowledge.

"His image is the most holy Word" (Philo, *Conf.* 97; St. John 1:1).

"The face of God is the Word by whom God is manifested and made known" (Clement of Alexandria, *Paed.* I.7.57:2).

"Let us contemplate Him with the understanding" (First Clement 19:3).

"Envisioning God with the keen sighted eyes of the understanding" (Philo, *Exod.* II.39).

"For . . . the most pure understanding is wholly filled to overflowing with the appearance of God." (Philo, *Q.Gen.* IV.8).

"From my youth You have appeared to me in the understanding of Your judgment" (1QH 9:31, Dead Sea Scrolls).

"Open the eyes of our heart that we may know You" (First Clement 59:3).

"Reveal Yourself to me that I may see You with knowledge [GNOSTOS]" (Exodus 33:13, Greek Text).

"Where there is no open vision [of the Lord], the Word of the Lord is precious" (1 Samuel 3:1).

"The words of the Torah direct a man's understanding to the knowledge of the All Present One" (Midrash Rabbah on Numbers 14.4).

"Make me to know Your way that I may know You" (Exodus 33:13).

"Learning . . . when pursued with the right course of conduct leads us through wisdom, the artificer of all things, to the Ruler of All" (St. Ignatius, *Epistle to the Ephesians* 20:1).

"With them to whom Wisdom is known, she continues even to the sight of God" (Sirach 6:23b, Latin Vulgate).

"Men who speak the Truth shall be found with wisdom, and shall advance, even till they come to the sight of God" (Sirach 15:8, Latin Vulgate).

*   *

"Man does not live by bread alone, but by every Word that proceeds out of the mouth of the Lord" (Deuteronomy 8:3).

"Your words were found, and I ate them, and Your Word became to me a joy and the delight of my heart" (Jeremiah 15:16).

"The soul is not fed with the things of the earth that decay, but with such words as God shall have poured like rain out of that lofty and pure region of life to which the prophet has given the title of 'heaven'" (Philo, *L.A.* III.162).

"The food of the soul is not earthly but heavenly" (ibid.).

"The Word of God: the heavenly incorruptible food of the soul" (Philo, *Her.* 79).

"Do not labor for the food which perishes, but for the food which endures to eternal life . . . Jesus then said to them, 'truly, truly, I say to you, it was not Moses who gave you the bread from heaven; My Father gives you the true bread from heaven . . . I have come down from heaven'" (St. John 6:27,32,38).

"Jesus said to them, 'I am the bread of life; he who comes to Me shall never hunger, and he who believes in Me shall never thirst . . . I am the bread which came down from heaven'" (St. John 6:35,41).

"That Your sons whom You love might learn, O Lord, that it is not the production of crops that feeds man, but that Your Word preserves those who trust in You" (Wisdom 16:26).

"The soul . . . is fed by knowledge in its various forms and not by food and drink of which the body stands in need" (Philo, *L.A.* III.161).

"When they sought to know what is it that nourished the soul, they became learners and found it to be a saying of God, that it is the Divine Word, from which all kinds of instruction and wisdom flow in a perpetual stream" (Philo, *Fug.* 137).

"The righteous . . . desire instruction even as one who hungers desires bread" (Targum on Isaiah 32:6).

"The bread of understanding" (Sirach 15:3).

"Desire the sincere milk of His Word that you may grow thereby" (1 Peter 2:2).

"My soul longs with desire for the Law" (Yebamoth 63b, BT).

"He who seeks the Law [with hunger and desire] shall be filled thereby" (Sirach 32:15).

"A man can learn well only that part of the Torah which is his heart's desire" (Abodah Zarah 19a, BT).

"I have treasured the words of His mouth more than my necessary food" (Job 23:12).

"The sovereign understanding is nourished with those things that are seen through wisdom" (Philo, *Q.Gen.* IV.98).

"The source of wisdom is the Word of God on high" (Sirach 1:5, Greek Cursives 243,23,55,70,106,253, and Latin Vulgate, Syro-Hexaplar and Sahidic Texts).

Because they are the nourishment of our souls,
we should desire, love, and delight in His Words,
and His Wisdom, Understanding, and Knowledge.

"The very true beginning of Wisdom is the desire for instruction" (Wisdom 6:17).

"Desire my words and you shall be instructed" (Wisdom 6:11).

"How sweet are Your Words to my taste! Yes, sweeter than honey to my mouth" (Psalm 119:103).

"Your Word is very pure, therefore Your servant loves it" (Psalm 119:140).

"I rejoice at Your Word, as one who finds great spoil" (Psalm 119:162).

"Behold, I long for Your precepts" (Psalm 119:40).

"I esteem right all Your precepts concerning everything" (Psalm 119:128).

"Behold, how I love Your precepts" (Psalm 119:159).

"The precepts of the Lord are right, rejoicing the heart" (Psalm 19:8).

"My soul has kept Your testimonies, and I love them exceedingly" (Psalm 119:167).

"I have rejoiced in the way of Your testimonies, as much as in all riches" (Psalm 119:14).

"Your testimonies . . . are the rejoicing of my heart" (Psalm 119:111).

"Your testimonies are my delight" (Psalm 119:24).

"O that my ways were directed to keep Your statutes!" (Psalm 119:5).

"Your statutes have been my songs" (Psalm 119:54).

"I will delight myself in Your statutes" (Psalm 119:16).

"I will lift up my hands [with longing] towards Your commandments" (Psalm 119:48).

"Make me walk in the paths of Your commandments, for therein do I delight" (Psalm 119:35).

"I love Your commandments above gold, yes, above fine gold" (Psalm 119:127).

"I shall delight in Your commandments, which I love" (Psalm 119:47).

"My soul breaks with longing for Your judgments [MISHPATIM] at all times" (Psalm 119:20).

"The judgments of the Lord are true and righteous altogether; they are more desirable than gold, yes, even much fine gold; sweeter also than honey and drippings of the honeycomb" (Psalm 19:9,10).

"O how I love Your Law! It is my meditation all the day" (Psalm 119:97; Yebamoth 63b, BT).

"Happy is the man" whose "delight is in the Law of the Lord, and on His Law he meditates day and night" (Psalm 1:1,2).

"Your Law do I love" (Psalm 119:113).

"O Lord . . . Your Law is my delight" (Psalm 119:174,22,70,77,92).

"Meditate in the fear of the Most High and think upon His commandments continually. Then He will instruct your heart and make you wise in that which you desire" (Sirach 6:37, Hebrew Text).

"If you desire Wisdom, keep the commandments and the Lord shall freely give her to you" (Sirach 1:25).

"Desire for wisdom" (Wisdom 6:20).

"All the things that may be desired cannot compare with wisdom" (Proverbs 8:11).

"Wisdom is more precious than rubies, and nothing of all you may desire can compare with her" (Proverbs 3:15).

"A good ear will hear Wisdom with all desire" (Sirach 3:31, Latin Vulgate).

"My soul longed with desire for Wisdom" (Sirach 51:19, Hebrew Text).

"My inmost being burned with desire for Wisdom" (Sirach 51:21, Hebrew Text).

"Wisdom hastens to make herself known to those who desire her" (Wisdom 6:13, RSV).

"Come to me [Wisdom] all you who desire me, and be filled with my fruits" (Sirach 24:19).

"I loved Wisdom above health and beauty" (Wisdom 7:10).

"I loved Wisdom and sought her out from my youth" (Wisdom 8:2).

"Love Wisdom and she shall keep you" (Proverbs 4:6).

"I [Wisdom] love those who love me" (Proverbs 8:17).

"In the love of Wisdom is good delight" (Wisdom 8:18, Literal Translation).

"Sight . . . results in desire" (Wisdom 15:5).

"The woman saw that the tree was good for food, and that it was a delight to the eyes, and that the tree was to be desired [CHAMAD] to make one understand [SAKAL], she took from its fruit and ate" (Genesis 3:6).

"My soul longed to understand in my heart" (Apocalypse of Abraham, 30:1).

"Daniel, you man of desires [CHAMUDOTH], understand the words that I speak to you" (Daniel 10:11).

"I am come to show it to you, because you are a man of desires [CHAMUDOTH]" (Daniel 9:23).

"Gabriel . . . made me to understand and talked with me and said, 'O Daniel, I am now come forth to give you understanding and insight'" (Daniel 9:21,22).

"Desire that you may be filled with the knowledge of His will in all wisdom and spiritual understanding" (Colossians 1:9).

"My food is to do the will of Him who sent Me, and to accomplish His work" (St. John 4:34).

"Happy is he who has found understanding" (Sirach 25:9).

"What your heart desires I will tell you because you have sought to know" (Apocalypse of Abraham 30:2).

"Wise men treasure up knowledge" (Proverbs 10:14).

"By knowledge shall the storehouses be filled" (Proverbs 24:4).

"I will give you shepherds after My own heart, who will feed you with knowledge and understanding" (Jeremiah 3:15).

"The lips of the wise disperse knowledge" (Proverbs 15:7).

"Since you were fashioned you have been created with a love of knowledge" (The Book of Adam and Eve, 27:3).

"Knowledge is pleasant to your soul" (Proverbs 2:10).

"The words of the pure are pleasant" (Proverbs 15:26).

"Pleasant words are as a honeycomb, sweet to the soul and healing to the bones" (Proverbs 16:24).

"Come . . . why do you spend your money for that which is not bread, and your labor for that which does not satisfy? Hear Me with attention, and eat what is good, and delight yourselves in abundance. Incline your ear, and come to Me, hear, and your soul shall live" (Isaiah 55:1,2,3).

Wisdom cried out: "Come eat of my bread and drink of the wine I have mingled" (Proverbs 9:5).

Jesus: the Word of God [St. John 1:1,14; 1 John 1:1,3; 5:7; Revelation 19:13] said: "I am the bread of life" (St. John 6:48).

"I am the living bread that came down out of heaven; if anyone eats of this bread, he shall live forever" (St. John 6:51).

"Christ, in whom are hid all the treasures of wisdom and knowledge" (Colossians 2:2,3).

"Come, Lord Jesus" (Revelation 22:20).

UNDERSTANDING KNOWS HOW TO DIVIDE

"By the knowledge [GNŌSEI] of the Lord the days were distinguished and . . . in the fullness of His understanding [EPISTĒMĒS] the Lord has divided them [mankind] and made their ways diverse" (Sirach 36[33]:8,11).

"You have divided all these things in the Mysteries of Your understanding [SEKEL] to make Your glory known" (1QH 13:13, Dead Sea Scrolls).

"By His power [see "Understanding and Power"] dividing holy things among them from the profane" (Sirach 18:3, Greek Cursives 106, 248).

"God has deprived the ostrich of wisdom, neither has He divided [CHALAQ, i.e., "apportioned"] understanding unto her" (Job 39:17).

"An understanding [NOĒMŌN] servant shall have rule over foolish masters and shall divide portions among brothers" (Proverbs 17:2, Greek Text).

DONKEYS AND UNDERSTANDING

"The ox *knows* his owner,
and the ass [*understands* what is in] his master's manger;
but Israel does not *know,*
My people do not *understand*" (Isaiah 1:3).*

> *In Isaiah 1:3 the imagery of the *ox* who *knows* and the *ass* who *understands* is very apt because bulls and oxen (both are called SHOR in Hebrew) are all eyes [through its large eyes, a bull scans and determines the exact borders of a field or a meadow that it considers its own territory; and woe to anyone trespassing those borders]. In the Holy Scriptures, there is a close relationship between seeing and knowing, we "see and know" (*Vide* Jeremiah 5:1; 12:3; Exodus 2:25; Deuteronomy 4:35; Isaiah 6:9; 44:9; Judith 14:5; 2 Esdras 7:37, Syriac Text). Thus, being always on the lookout, bulls and oxen are good models for "seeing and knowing." In turn we "hear and understand" (see pp. 282-290). And who has not heard about the long ears of a donkey?

"Be not like a horse or a mule, without understanding" (Psalm 32:9; see also Tobit 6:17 Latin Vulgate and Vetus Latina); rather be like a donkey that understands or an ox that knows.

"A stupid man will get understanding, when a wild ass's colt is born a man" (Job 11:12, RSV) having "a man's understanding" (Midrash Rabbah to Numbers 14.4) and able to speak and reprove (Numbers 22:21-32) that stupid man.

The expression "the ass [KHAMOR] of the Torah" is one thought to be a wonderful sage and supreme master of the Torah. This adage derives KHAMOR or CHAMOR from c̲hakam m̲ufla ve-rav r̲abbanan, the Hebrew words for "wise sage and supreme master" (Tikkunei ha-Zohar, Tikkunim nosoferim, 10,147b).

UNDERSTANDING ENCOMPASSES AND APPREHENDS

"He encompassed [SABAB] him about, He made him understand [BIN]" (Deuteronomy 32:10).

"I encompassed [SABAB] with my understanding to know and to search and to seek out wisdom" (Ecclesiastes 7:25).

"Blessed are they who have encompassed the understanding of Jesus Christ, for they shall be in light" (Acts of Paul and Thecla 6).

"When I sought to know this, it was too difficult for me, until I went into the Sanctuary of God; then I understood [BIN]" (Psalm 73:16,17).

"I will encompass [SABAB] Your altar [in the Sanctuary], O Lord, so that I may [understand and] proclaim with the voice of thanksgiving, and declare all Your wonderful works" (Psalm 26:6,7).

For "He has given men understanding [BINAH] that He may be glorified in His wonderful works" (Sirach 38:6, Hebrew and Greek Texts).

"All . . . who have understanding in the works of God" (Zadokite Fragment 1:1,2, MS.A) shall glorify Him.

"Blessed is he who understands the Lord's works and glorifies the Lord God" (2 Enoch 42:14, B Text).

The Pagans knew that good Understanding
encompasses and embraces all Wisdom.

"You embrace the totality of wisdom, you counsel the people" (Sumerian Tablet, Nippur N/K 1743+10858, University of Pennsylvania Museum, Philadelphia).

Our Lord's understanding is far greater than the wisdom of
Solomon, since it encompasses and embraces all Wisdom.

Jesus "Christ, in whom are hidden all the treasures of wisdom and knowledge" (Colossians 2:2,3).

Because He himself "is the Understanding of the Father" (St. Ignatius, *Epistle to the Ephesians* 3:2; see also Athenagoras, *Emb.* XXIV).

And "the understanding is a vast and receptive storehouse" (Philo, *Deus,* 42).

Jesus is the infinite "storehouse of understanding" (2 Baruch 44:14) in whom all wisdom and knowledge are stored.

"The queen of the South will arise at the judgment with this generation and condemn it; for she came from the ends of the earth to hear the *wisdom* of Solomon, and behold, a greater *thing* [PLEION] than Solomon [i.e., Solomon's wisdom] is here" (St. Matthew 12:42; St. Luke 11:31).

"His (the Lord's) understanding is superior to all wisdom" (Odes of Solomon 28:20).

Good Understanding is able to apprehend and master Wisdom.

"Your understanding should be able to apprehend" (Philo, *Deus.* 78).

"The understanding stretches out to seize" (Philo, *Q.Gen.* II.34).

"The understanding grasps before the senses" (Philo, *Q.Gen.* IV.32).

"Things unseen by sense but seized by the understanding" (Philo, *Spec.* IV.192).

"If these other powers could be apprehended it would not be by sense but by the understanding at its purest" (Philo, *Spec.* I.46).

"The immaterial, the invisible, the apprehended by the understanding alone" (Philo, *Spec.* I.20).

"Understanding . . . has wide scope and grasps the ends of the universe" (Philo, *Agr.* 53).

"It is the attribute of understanding to apprehend" (Philo, *Mig.* 78).

"Apprehend by means of the understanding" (Philo, *Abr.* 58).

"Spoken words contain symbols of things apprehended only by the understanding" (Philo, *Abr.* 119).

"One who receives these things not with his eyes alone but with his understanding will be able to grasp the greatest causes" (Philo, *Q.Gen.* IV.163).

"Understanding [EPISTĒMĒ] is a sure grasp leading up through true and sure reason to the knowledge [GNŌSIS] of the cause" (Clement of Alexandria, *Strom.* VI.c.18).

"Understanding throws open the way to knowledge of things divine, and enables us to apprehend God" (Corpus Hermeticum, *Libellus* IV.6a).

"Our God, the only true God, is not an object of sense, made out of matter: He is apprehended by the understanding alone" (Clement of Alexandria, *Exh.* IV.51.6).

*   *

"Pursue Wisdom like a hunter, and lie in wait in her ways" (Sirach 14:22).

"They who watch for Wisdom shall embrace her" (Sirach 4:13, Latin Vulgate).

"Seize [KATALĒPSETAI] Wisdom" (Sirach 15:1).

"Take firm hold [EGKRATĒS] of Wisdom, and do not let her go" (Sirach 6:27).

"Draw near to Wisdom . . . and when you draw close to her do it as a hero and as a mighty one" (Sirach 1:22, Greek Sinaiticus Text).

"Come unto Wisdom with all your might" (Sirach 6:26).

Conversely

"Men without understanding will not be able to seize [KATALĒPSONTAI] Wisdom" (Sirach 15:7, Literal Translation).

*   *

"I bow to you my comrade, I grasp your wisdom" (Babylonian Theodicy V.45, Babylonian Tablet 34633, British Museum).

"My reliable fellow-holder of knowledge" (Ashurbanipal Tablet K 8491+13929, l. 78, British Museum).

*   *

"The noble understanding is a fighter and a contestant [AGONISTES] and is by nature good in struggle" (Philo, *Q.Gen.* IV.163).

"The understanding seizes its adversary in its hand and holds him" (ibid.).

"The understanding which has come down from heaven, though it be fast bound to the constraints of the body nevertheless . . . holding to its own nature of true manhood has the strength to be victor instead of victim in the wrestling bout" (Philo, *Her.* 274).

262

"My soul wrestled with Wisdom" (Sirach 51:19).

"In common exercise with Wisdom is Understanding [PHRONĒSIS]" (Wisdom 8:18).

"Every hour I suffer agonies of heart striving to understand the way of the Most High" (2 Esdras 5:34).

"Azazel revealed the eternal secrets which were preserved in heaven and which the sons of men were striving to understand" (Enoch 9:6, Syncellus Greek Fragment).

"Who has gone up into heaven and taken her [Knowledge] and brought her down from the clouds?" (Baruch 3:29).

"The Kingdom of Heaven suffereth violence, and the violent bear it away by force" (St. Matthew 11:12).

Meaning of the term "Kingdom of Heaven."

"Woe to you, scribes and Pharisees, hypocrites! because you shut the *Kingdom of Heaven* from men; for you do not enter in yourselves, nor do you allow those who would enter to go in" (St. Matthew 23:13).

"Woe to you lawyers! for you have taken away the key of *knowledge;* you did not enter in yourselves, and you hindered those who were entering" (St. Luke 11:52).

"The Pharisees and Scribes have received the keys of *knowledge,* they have hidden them. They did not enter and they did not let those enter who wished to do so" (Gospel of Thomas, Logion 39).

"Your glorious Kingship is great together with Your marvelous Mysteries in the heights of heaven" (1QM 14:14, Dead Sea Scrolls).

"He [Solomon, in his youth] was perfect and true, shunned evil and understood the mysteries of heaven" (Second Targum [Sheni] to Esther c.2).

"To him [Solomon] was given a large key to open the gates of wisdom and understanding" [i.e., "the key of knowledge" to "the mysteries of Heaven" (ibid.).

God made Solomon so wise that He told him that "there was none like you before you and none like you shall arise after you" (1 Kings 3:12). Nevertheless, ancient Scriptural and Jewish tradition prophecied that the Messiah would come as the greatest of teachers and the Revealer of all hidden things for he was to be fully endowed with the seven gifts of the Holy Spirit (Isaiah 11:2-3; Targum Isaiah 11:2; Midrash Numbers Rabbah 13.11; Midrash Ruth Rabbah 3.14; Targum Ruth 3:15, Sanhedrin 93b, B.T.). It was also said that he would have perfect knowledge of God directly acquired by himself (Midrash Numbers Rabbah 14.2). Moreover, being seated at the right hand of God, the Holy One reveals all the secret meanings of the Torah to him (Pesikta Hadta p. 47 [in Jellinek's *Beth ha Midrash*, vol. VI, pp. 36-70]). Thus, the Messiah will teach a new Torah (Alphabet de Rabbi Akiba 27-28 [op. cit., Vol. III, pp. 12-64]). "The Holy One will give the new Torah through the Messiah. The 'New Torah' means the secrets and mysteries of the Torah which have remained hidden until now" (Midrash Talpiyot 58a; see also Yemenite Midrash, pp. 349-350 found in Yehuda Ibn Shemuel's, *Midrash Geulah*). "The Torah which a man learnt in this world is vanity compared with the Torah of the Messiah" (Midrash Ecclesiastes Rabbah 11.1). "In the days of the Messiah, the Torah will return to its renewal" (Pesikta Rabbati fol. 75a) because "the Messiah will make clear for them the words of the Torah" (Midrash Genesis Rabbah 98.9; Sanhedrin 97a, B.T.). Thus, "the Messianic time will be an era of purity and perfect knowledge" (Zohar, *Mathnitim* [found in the section Toldoth following *Midrash Haneelam*]) for "the Messiah . . . will give light to the eyes of Israel" (Pesikta Rabbati, Piska 36.1) because when he comes "the things which are concealed from you, you will see" (Midrash Numbers Rabbah 19.6). Yes, "when the Righteous Messiah comes we shall also understand the blank spaces of the Torah" for "he will reveal to us even the meaning of the blank spaces in the Torah" (Levi Yitzchak's, *Imre* Tzaddikim, p. 10 [5b]).

The Messiah would be able to do all this because as the Son of Man he *understands* and *encompasses* all the hidden things of wisdom and knowledge by his great understanding. For he "is the Son of Man who has righteousness and with whom dwells righteousness, and who reveals all the treasures of that which is hidden" (Enoch 46:3; see also ibid. 49:1-3; 51:3) because he is the "Messiah, in whom are hid *all* the treasures of wisdom and knowledge" (Colossians 2:2,3). "His understanding is superior to all wisdom" (Odes of Solomon 28:20) even the great wisdom of Solomon, because He is "Messiah, the Power [see "The Power and Strength of Understanding"] of God and the Wisdom of God" (1 Corinthians 1:24).

UNDERSTANDING ESTABLISHES AND EXALTS, AND IS EXALTED IN THOSE WHO UNDERSTAND.

It is through Understanding that things are established.

"Lord . . . You are wise in creating . . . and [You are] understanding in establishing what exists" (First Clement 60:1).

"The Lord by wisdom has founded the earth, and by great understanding [TEBUNAH] He has established the heavens" (Proverbs 3:19).

"By the knowledge of His heart [i.e., understanding] He established the dawn" (11QPs XXVI.4 [Hymn to the Creator], Dead Sea Scrolls]).

"The world . . . was established according to the abundance of the understanding of Him who sent it" (2 Baruch 56:4).

"Through wisdom is a house built, and by understanding it is established" (Proverbs 24:3).

"A multitude of wise men is salvation to the world, and a King who understands [PHRONIMOS] establishes his people" (Wisdom 6:24).

"An unconstrained King will destroy his city, but through the understanding [SAKAL] of its princes it becomes inhabited [and established again]" Sirach 10:3, Hebrew Text).

"Through one man of understanding, a city will be filled with people" (Sirach 16:4).

"Understanding . . . has a stability which no argument can shake . . . Understanding . . . is defined as a sure and certain apprehension which cannot be shaken by argument" (Philo, *Cong.* 140,141).

"He enthroned above all, the holy leader Understanding" (4 Maccabees 2:22).

*　　　*

"Understanding shall establish him" (Instruction of Ptah-Hotep, Line 58, Prisse Papyrus, National Library, Paris).

"I am Sia [Egyptian god of understanding] at the right hand of Re, who establishes the heart of him who stands before the Tephet of Nu" (Book of the Dead 174,18.19 [see E. Naville's Das *Agyptische Todtenbuch der XVIII bis XX Dynastie*, 2 Vol., Berlin, 1886]).

*　　*

A heart that is "established," is a heart that understands.

"He shall *establish your heart*" (Sirach 6:37, Greek Text).

"He shall *make your heart to understand*" (ibid., Hebrew Text).

"The heart that is *established* by its well advised [DIANOĒMATOS] counsel shall not fear at any time" (Sirach 22:16, Greek Text).

"The heart that *understands* through its own counsel shall not fear at any time" (ibid., Syriac Text).

Conversely

"If you will not believe, surely you shall not be *established*" (Isaiah 7:9, Hebrew Text).

"If you will not believe, neither will you at all *understand*" (ibid., Greek, Syriac, and Old Latin Texts).

Understanding exalts.

"If a man of understanding hears a wise word, he will give praise to it and add to it" (Sirach 21:15).

"Every man of understanding knows Wisdom and will give praise to him who finds her" (Sirach 18:28).

"Praise God with understanding, ye who fear the Lord" (Psalms of Solomon 2:37).

"God is King of all the earth, sing praises with understanding [SAKAL]" (Psalm 47:7, Hebrew and Greek Texts).

"I will sing [praises] with the understanding" (1 Corinthians 14:15).

"They shall lay it to heart, and know that I am the Lord their God, for I will give them a heart and ears to hear [and understand] and they shall praise Me" (Baruch 2:30-32).

"He has given men understanding so that He may be glorified in His marvelous works" (Sirach 38:6).

"He gave them to glory in His marvelous works forever so that they may declare His works with understanding" (Sirach 17:9, Greek Cursives 55,106,248,254).

"I will exalt You, O my Rock, and because Your works are marvelous I will praise You . . . for You have made me to know the secret of Truth, and have revealed Your wonders to me" (1QH 11:15,16,17, Dead Sea Scrolls).

"I will sing . . . praise to You without ceasing . . . Blessed are You O God of knowledge, who have given to Your servant understanding of knowledge to comprehend Your marvelous and Your wonderful works without number" (1QH 11:23,24,27,28).

"Sing a new song to God who is worthy to be praised. Sing, yes, shout to Him with joyful clamor, for it is good to sing praises to God with the whole heart [i.e., understanding]" (Psalms of Solomon 3:2).

"The stars of heaven praise Him with understanding" (Teezala Sanbat [Ethiopic Jews' liturgical work: *"The Commandments of the Sabbath"*, p. 25, *Falasha Anthology*, Trans. by Wolf Leslau, Vol. VI, Yale Judaica Series]).

"Make me understand the way of Your precepts, then shall I speak [SIACH] of Your wonderful works [exaltingly]" (Psalm 119:27, see v. 104a).

"Grant me understanding, O Lord, in Your Law, and teach me Your ordinances, so that many may hear of Your deeds and peoples may honor Your glory" (11QPsᵃ Col. XXIV.9-10 [Psalm 155], Dead Sea Scrolls).

"He granted as their portion a heart to understand, and He set His eye upon their hearts to show them the greatness of His works so that they might praise His holy name" (Sirach 17:6-7, Latin Vulgate).

"All men shall fear [God] and shall declare the work of God [to His exaltation], for they shall understand [SAKAL] His deed" (Psalm 64:9).

"And because I contemplate Your glory I will recount Your marvels because I have understood all things" (1QH 10:20,21, Dead Sea Scrolls).

"A man of understanding is the crown of the wise" [for he knows how to exalt them, see Sirach 21:15] (Proverbs 14:24, Greek Text).

Those who understand shall be exalted through their understanding.

"Do not despise a poor man who has understanding [SAKAL]" (Sirach 10:22, Hebrew Text).

For "a man shall be praised according to his understanding [SAKAL]" (Proverbs 12:8).

Because "good understanding [SAKAL] wins favor" (Proverbs 13:15).

"There is a poor man who is honored for his understanding [SEKEL]" (Sirach 10:29, Hebrew Text).

"A servant who has understanding [SAKAL] is exalted" (Sirach 10:24, Hebrew Text).

"His understanding [SEKEL] is extolled to the clouds" (Sirach 13:22, Hebrew Text).

"An understanding [SAKAL] servant shall have rule over a son who causes shame" (Proverbs 17:2).

"An understanding servant shall have rule over his masters" (Sirach 20:27, Syriac and Arabic Texts).

"Nobles shall serve a servant who has understanding" (Sirach 10:25, Greek Sinaiticus Text and Cursives 248,23,106,307).

"Wisdom rests in the heart of him who has understanding" (Proverbs 14:33).

Therefore "everyone who has understanding knows Wisdom" (Sirach 18:28).

"And Wisdom shall exalt him" (Sirach 15:5).

"Wisdom exalts to honor those who hold her fast" (Sirach 1:19).

"Exalt Wisdom and she shall exalt you" (Proverbs 4:8).

"With the humble is Wisdom" (Proverbs 11:2).

"The wisdom of the humble shall exalt his head, and make him sit in the midst of great men" (Sirach 11:1, Greek, Hebrew, and Latin Vulgate Texts).

For "he who has understanding will please great men" (Sirach 20:27, Greek Text).

"He shall show forth the instruction of Wisdom which he has been taught and shall glory in the Law of the covenant of the Lord. Many shall praise his understanding" (Sirach 39:8,9, Syriac Text).

"Behold My Servant shall understand [SAKAL], he shall be exalted and extolled, and be very high . . . kings shall shut their mouths because of him, for that which has not been told them they shall see, and that which they have not heard they shall understand" (Isaiah 52:13,15).

"A patient man will endure until the right moment, and then joy shall spring up to him . . . and the lips of many shall declare his understanding" (Sirach 1:23-24).

"Now will I arise says the Lord, now will I be glorified, now will I be exalted [because] now you shall see, and now you shall understand" (Isaiah 33:10-11, Greek Text).

Conversely

"You have hidden their heart from understanding [SEKEL], therefore You will not exalt them" (Job 17:4, Literal Translation).

THE FACE AND UNDERSTANDING

"A man may be known by his look and an understanding man may be known by his face when you meet him" (Sirach 19:29).

"Woe to those who are wise in their own eyes, and understanding [BIN] in their own face [PANIM]" (Isaiah 5:21).

"The Lord gives Wisdom and from His face [PROSŌPON] comes knowledge and understanding" (Proverbs 2:6, Greek Text).

"The knowledge of the glory of God in the face of Jesus Christ" (2 Corinthians 4:6).

"Make Your face shine upon Your servant and teach me" (Psalm 119:135).

"Through me You have enlightened the face of many [i.e., made them understand]" (1QH 4:27, Dead Sea Scrolls).

"May He make of you a torch to shine upon the world in knowledge to enlighten the face [i.e., understanding] of many" (1QSb 4:27 [Book of Blessings], Dead Sea Scrolls).

*   *

"Happy is the man who *finds understanding* [PHRONĒSIN]" (Sirach 25:9, Greek Text).

"Happy is the man who *finds a true friend*" (ibid., Latin Vulgate and Syriac Text).

"Iron sharpens iron so does a man sharpen the face [i.e., understanding] of his friend" (Proverbs 27:17).

"So that they may see and know and consider and understand [SAKAL] *together*" [as good friends] (Isaiah 41:20).

"Be perfectly joined [KATARTIZO] together in the same understanding [NOUS] and in the same counsel [GNŌMĒ]" (1 Corinthians 1:10).

"As in water face answers to face, so the understanding of man to man" (Proverbs 27:19).

*   *

The word "Spirit" is oftentimes synonymous with Understanding [see "Spirit and Understanding"] hence:

"The face manifests the spirit" (Testament of Simeon 5:1).

"The spirit of my understanding" (Job 20:3).

"My soul recovered the spirit of understanding" (2 Esdras 5:22).

"Spirit of . . . understanding" (Isaiah 11:2).

"An understanding spirit" (Wisdom 7:22).

"The spirit of understanding" (Testament of Judah 20:2; Testament of Levi 18:7).

"He who keeps the Law becomes master of *the spirit thereof*" (Sirach 21:11, Syriac Text).

"He who keeps the Law gets the *understanding thereof*" (ibid., Greek Text).

To see the "face" of something is to "understand" that thing.

"There is blindness in anger, my children, and no angry man sees the face of Truth" (Testament of Dan 2:2 [B,A, and S Texts, Literal Translation]).

Because "the spirit of anger blinds his eyes . . . and darkens his understanding" (idem 2:4).

So that he cannot "understand the Truth" (Wisdom 3:9).

Pray "before the Lord our God, that we might turn from our iniquities and understand Your Truth" (Daniel 9:13).

"The Lord . . . understands in the darkness: the face" (Sirach 23:19, Syriac Text).

FAITHFULNESS AND UNDERSTANDING

"Behold, I have taught you statutes and judgments . . . keep, therefore, and do them, for this is your wisdom and understanding in the sight of the nations" (Deuteronomy 4:5,6).

"Keep therefore, the words of this covenant and do them so that you may understand [SAKAL]" (Deuteronomy 29:9).

"Be careful to do according to all the Law which Moses My servant commanded you, turn not from it to the right hand or to the left, so that you may understand [SAKAL]" (Joshua 1:7).

"Keep the charge of the Lord your God, to walk in His ways, to keep His statutes, His commandments, His ordinances, and His testimonies, as it is written in the Law of Moses, that you may understand [SAKAL] in all that you do and wherever you turn" (1 Kings 2:3).

"Hezekiah . . . trusted in the Lord God of Israel . . . he held fast to the Lord; he did not depart from following Him, but kept the commandments which the Lord commanded Moses. And the Lord was with him, and he understood [SAKAL]" (2 Kings, 18:1,5,6,7).

"A good understanding [SEKEL] have all those who do His commandments" (Psalm 111:10).

"My son, do not forget my Law, but let your heart keep my commandments . . . so shall you find favor and good understanding [SEKEL] in the sight of God and man" (Proverbs 3:1,4).

"Everyone who hears these words of Mine, and does them, shall be likened to a man of understanding [PHRONIMŌ] " (St. Matthew 7:24).

"I have more understanding [SAKAL] than all my teachers, for Your testimonies are my meditation" (Psalm 119:99).

"I understand more than the aged, because I have kept Your precepts" (Psalm 119:100).

"Through Your precepts I get understanding" (Psalm 119:104).

"Whosoever teaches noble things and does them, shall be enthroned with Kings as Joseph was" (Testament of Levi 13:9).

"Pharaoh said to Joseph . . . 'there is no one so understanding [BIN] and wise as you'" (Genesis 41:39).

The "faithful and understanding [PHRONIMOS] servant" (St. Matthew 24:45; St. Luke 12:42).

"It is only by doing God's will that man can attain to the understanding of those things which he desires to know" (St. Augustine, *Homily on Psalms* 119:104).

"Jesus said to them . . . 'I always do the things that are pleasing to Him'" (St. John 8:25,29).

"My food is to do the will of Him who sent Me, and to accomplish His work" (St. John 4:34). "I do not seek My own will, but the will of Him who sent Me" (St. John 5:30).

"For I have come down from heaven, not to do My own will, but the will of Him who sent Me" (St. John 6:38).

"Let not My will, but Yours, be done" (St. Luke 22:42).

"Jesus . . . began teaching them in their synagogue, so that they became astonished and said, 'where did this man get this wisdom and these miraculous powers?'" (St. Matthew 13:54).

"The multitudes were amazed at His teaching" (St. Matthew 7:28).

"What is this wisdom given to Him?" (St. Mark 6:2).

"All who heard him were amazed at His understanding and His answers" (St. Luke 2:47).

"Jesus . . . said to them, 'hear and understand!'" (St. Matthew 15:1,10).

"Hear Me, all of you, and understand!" (St. Mark 7:14).

"He [Jesus] opened up their understanding that they might understand the Scriptures" (St. Luke 24:45).

"We know that the Son of God has come and has given us understanding, to know Him who is true" (1 John 5:20).

"We have the understanding [NOUS] of Christ" (1 Corinthians 2:16).

"Christ, in whom are hidden all the treasures of wisdom and knowledge" (Colossians 2:2,3; see also St. Luke 2:40).

"Christ, the power of God, and the wisdom of God" (1 Corinthians 1:24).

"They have kept Your Word, now they have come to know" (St. John 17:6,7).

"If any man does His will, he shall know concerning the teaching" (St. John 7:17).

*   *

"Blessed is he who meditates on these things, and he who lays them to heart will become wise. For if he does them, he will be strong for all things, for the light of the Lord is his path" (Sirach 50:28-29).

"He who keeps the Law will be able to seize Wisdom" (Sirach 15:1).

"If you desire Wisdom, keep the commandments and the Lord shall give her to you" (Sirach 1:25).

"Through Your commandments You have made me wiser than my enemies" (Psalm 119:98).

When Wisdom "has proved him by her Laws, then she will return the straight way to him and comfort him and reveal to him her secrets" (Sirach 4:17,18).

"Fear of sin and good works are the foundation of Wisdom" (Pirke Aboth 3:9,10).

"Let the Word of Christ dwell in you richly in all wisdom, teaching and admonishing one another" (Colossians 3:16).

*   *

"Jesus began to do and teach" (Acts 1:1).

"To one who learns for the sake of doing, God grants the gift of teaching" (Pirke Aboth 4:6).

"It is better to keep silence and be something than to talk and be nothing. Teaching is an excellent thing, provided the teacher practices what he teaches" (St. Ignatius, *Epistle to the Ephesians* 20:1).

"Understanding is not seen in speech but in action and in earnest doings" (Philo, *L.A.* I.75).

"I [Ezra] understood [BIN]" (Ezra 8:15).

Because: "Ezra . . . prepared his heart to seek the Law of the Lord, and to do it, and to teach" (Ezra 7:10).

*   *

"It is great glory to follow the Lord, for length of days shall be received from Him" (Sirach 23:28, Greek Cursive 248; ibid. 23:38, Latin Vulgate).

"In length of days: understanding" (Job 12:12).

"Jesus said to him . . . 'Come and follow Me'" (St. Matthew 4:19; 8:22; 9:9; 16:24; 19:21; St. Mark 2:14; 8:34; 10:21; St. Luke 5:27; 9:23,59; 18:22; St. John 1:43; 21:19,22).

"I am the light of the world; he who follows Me shall not walk in the darkness, but shall have the light of life" (St. John 8:12).

UNDERSTANDING AND FLYING

"Does the hawk fly by your understanding [BINAH]?" (Job 39:26).

The ostrich cannot fly because "God has not divided [i.e., "apportioned"] understanding [BINAH] to her" (Job 39:17).

"Man, his flesh is from the earth . . . his understanding is from the swiftness of angels" (2 Enoch 30:8).

THE FORMING OF UNDERSTANDING

"By what means can I obtain understanding [SEKEL] unless You form [YATSAR] it for me?" (1QH 10:6, Dead Sea Scrolls).

"I [the Lord] . . . formed the understanding and heart" (Odes of Solomon 8:18).

"The Lord is also pleased to take away from the travail of his soul, to show him light, and to form [PLASAI] him with understanding" (Isaiah 53:11, Greek Text).

"He [God] sought to form [in us] an understanding conscious of righteousness" (*Epistle to Diognetus* 9:6,7).

"He formed in His understanding a great and indescribable conception" (*Epistle to Diognetus* 8:17,18).

"He who formed their hearts [understanding] alike, He understands [BIN]" (Psalm 33:15).

"Shall the work say of Him who made it, 'He made me not?' or shall the thing formed [YATSAR] by Him say of Him who formed it, 'He does not understand [BIN]'?" (Isaiah 29:16).

"He who formed the eye shall He not thoroughly understand [KATANOEI]?" (Psalm 94:9, Greek Text).

"What answer shall clay give? And that which is formed by hand [and should understand] what counsel can it understand [BIN]?" (1QS 11:22, Dead Sea Scrolls).

"All the people have known of your understanding [SUNESIN] because the formation [PLASMA] of your heart is good" (Judith 8:29).

"When God formed the first Understanding He called it: Man" (Philo, *Q.Gen.* I.53).

"Set in motion and formed and quickened by the understanding" (Philo, *Op.* 9.)

"Speech is the expounder of the plans which understanding has formed in its own counsel chambers" (Philo, *Det.* 40; see also Philo, *Spec.* II.207).

"They form his understanding" (Philo, *Q.Exod.* II.13).

"When it is said in the book of Genesis that 'the Lord God formed [VAYYITZER] the Man' [Genesis 2:7], the word "formed" [VAYYITZER], is written uniquely with a double yod ['y'] instead of the usual single yod ["formed" = VAYITZER]; because only Man did God endow with superior excellencies and penetrating understanding" (Midrash Haneelam, Bereshith 17, *Torah Shelemah* 2.126).

"Let them understand from them [His beautiful creation] how much more powerful is He who formed them" (Wisdom 13:3).

"The Lord . . . forms [YATSAR] the spirit of man within him" (Zechariah 12:1)

"The spirit which God forms for him" is "the spirit which gives understanding" (1QH 4:31, Dead Sea Scrolls; Enoch 49:3).

*   *

"Understand first, and then rebuke" (Sirach 11:7).

"You . . . have reproved [CORRIPIO] them with Your understanding [INTEL-LECTUS]" (2 Esdras 8:10,12, Latin Vulgate).

"He has formed me [with understanding] to rebuke them with His instruction" (Habacuc 1:12, Greek Text).

*   *

"Homage to thee O Ra! Supreme Power . . . who forms the earth by his under-standing" (The Litany of Ra, l. 66 [Egyptian Hieroglyph at Thebes, Biban El-Markud], Transl. by E. Naville).

*   *

Only the faithful and righteous have true understanding.
Thus, when an idolater forms an idol he does it
without any understanding.

"A castoff piece [of wood] from among them, useful for nothing, a stick crooked and full of knots, he takes and diligently carves when he has nothing else to do, and forms it by the skill of his licentiousness [ANESEŌS = "a letting go of the passions"], and fashions it to the image of a man" (Wisdom 13:13, Greek Codices Vaticanus, Sinaiticus, Alexandrinus, Venetus Marcianus, also Cursives 23,68,157,253, 296 and Aldine Septuagint).

THE FRUITS OF UNDERSTANDING

"God sowed understanding in the earthborn Man" (Philo, *L.A.* I.79).

"O Lord . . . cultivate our understanding whereby fruit may come" (2 Esdras 8:6).

"Profitable fruitage . . . yielded by the understanding" (Philo, *Som.* II.22).

"Only the wise man knows whose fruit is the fruit of understanding" (Philo, *Plant.* 138).

"A wise man instructs his own people, and the fruits of his understanding are faithful" (Sirach 37:26, Latin Vulgate).

"The fruits of understanding are commendable in his mouth" (Sirach 37:22).

"The fruits of his understanding do not fail" (Sirach 37:23).

"He who hears the Word and understands it; he indeed bears fruit [of understanding], and yields, in one case a hundredfold, in another sixty, and in another thirty" (St. Matthew 13:23).

Conversely

"If I pray in a tongue, my spirit prays but my understanding [NOUS] is unfruitful" (1 Corinthians 14:14).

*   *

Since the fruits are found in the branches,
Understanding is symbolically found in the branch of a tree.

"The branches of trees exalt my words" [see "Understanding Establishes and Exalts"] (11QPs Col. XXVIII, l. 3 [Psalm 151:3], Dead Sea Scrolls).

"In length of days: understanding" (Job 12:12).

"Wisdom's branches are length of days" [i.e., they bear the fruits of understanding] (Sirach 1:20).

Conversely

"When its branches are withered [unproductive of fruit], they are broken off; women come and make a fire of them. For it is a people of no understanding [i.e., they have no fruits of understanding in their branches]" (Isaiah 27:11).

*   *

"Re gives to thee Hu [god of utterance] and Sia [god of understanding] sweetness" (Ritual of Amon, Berlin Papyrus G II.52 [Publ. by A. Moret, Paris 1902 in *Annales du Musée Guimet*, 14).

"Hu is in it with abundance of food and Sia brings to it good things to eat" [i.e., fruits of understanding] (Abydos Hieroglyphs I, Plate 50a Line 16 [see A. Moret's *Abydos*, 2 Vols. Paris, 1869-80]).

GRACE AND UNDERSTANDING

"Grace which confers understanding, makes Mysteries plain, announces seasons, and rejoices over the faithful" (*Epistle to Diognetus* 11:6,7).

"The Psalmist accordingly considers understanding as the greatest grace" (Clement of Alexandria, *Strom.* VI.c.8).

"Unless a man by God's great grace receives the power to understand what has been said and done by the prophets . . . he cannot explain the meaning of them" (Justin Martyr, *Dial.* 92.1).

"According to the richness of His grace which He has caused to abound in us in all wisdom and understanding" (Ephesians 1:7,8).

"He [Moses] grew in grace, first of understanding, then of body" (Philo, *Mos.* II.69).

"And the Child grew and became strong, being filled with wisdom, and the grace of God was upon Him . . . and all who heard Him were amazed at His understanding" (St. Luke 2:40,47).

"His son Jesus Christ our Lord . . . through whom we have received grace" (Romans 1:3,5).

"The grace of God which is given to you by Jesus Christ so that in everything you are enriched by Him, in all speech and in all knowledge" (1 Corinthians 1:4,5).

"We know that the Son of God has come and has given us understanding, in order that we might know Him who is true" (1 John 5:20).

"Grace and Truth came through Jesus Christ" (St. John 1:17).

"Grace and Truth surround His Presence" (11QPs[a] XXVI. 3 [Hymn to the Creator], Dead Sea Scrolls).

"The Spirit of *grace*" (Hebrews 10:29; Zechariah 12:10).

"The Spirit of *understanding*" (Testament of Levi 18:7; Testament of Judah 20:2).

"The heart that is *established*" (Sirach 22:16, Greek Text).

"The heart that *understands*" (ibid., Syriac Text).

"He shall *establish* your heart" (Sirach 6:37, Greek Text).

"He shall make your heart to *understand*" (ibid., Syriac Text).

"It is a good thing that the heart be *established by grace* [i.e., understanding]" (Hebrews 13:9).

"God bestowed on man two graces which are more than mortal animals possess, understanding and speech" (Corpus Hermeticum XII.2).

"O Most High . . . by Your grace alone have we received this light of knowledge . . . gracing [XARISAMENO] on us understanding [NOUS]" (Corpus Hermeticum, *Asclepius* III).

"Grace and good understanding" (Proverbs 3:4) go together.

"Blessed are You, O God of knowledge, who have given to Your servant understanding of knowledge to understand Your marvels and Your works without number because of the abundance of Your grace" (1QH 11:27-28, Dead Sea Scrolls).

"You have opened knowledge in the midst of me concerning the Mysteries of Your understanding . . . You have revealed it to me according to the abundance of grace" (1QH 12:13,14, Dead Sea Scrolls).

"Let that which is good for edifying, as fits the occasion, come forth from your mouth that it may impart grace [i.e., give understanding] to those who hear" (Ephesians 4:29).

Joseph: "a man mighty in wisdom and knowledge, the Spirit of God is upon him and the grace [of understanding] is in him" (Joseph and Asenath, 4:8(10)).

"Good understanding gives grace" (Proverbs 13:15).

"Grace shall be found in the lips of one who understands [SUNETOU]" (Sirach 21:16).

"Let your speech always be with grace [i.e., understanding], seasoned as it were with salt" (Colossians 4:6).

"He shall put a taste [referring to "salt"] into it as does understanding into a man" (Sifre Vayikra N'dab. Par. 12, Chapter 14 [re. Leviticus 2:13]; see also Yalkut Leviticus 454, Arukh [Complete ed. Kohut, 1878]).

UNDERSTANDING GROWS

"You have said that the understanding grows with us" (2 Esdras 7:71, Syriac Text).

"The seeds and plants of understanding [EPISTĒMĒS]" (Philo, *Cong.* 123).

"Gather a crop of understanding" (Pirke Derek Eretz, S, p.7).

Conversely

"Not a germ is left of what might grow into understanding" (Philo, *Deus.* 130).

HEARING AND UNDERSTANDING

"Do not say that a thing which cannot be heard will be understood" (Pirke Aboth 2:5).

"He who has ears to hear let him hear!" (St. Matthew 13:9; St. Mark 4:9, etc.).

"Hear Me, all of you, and understand" (St. Mark 7:14).

"Hear and understand" (St. Matthew 15:10).

"Hear my voice, and understand my words" (2 Esdras 8:19).

"He said to me: 'Hear Abraham, and understand what I say to you' " (Apocalypse of Abraham 26:2).

"Hear now these things, and understand them" (2 Esdras 16:35).

"Hear this, all you peoples; give ear, all you inhabitants of the world, both low and high, rich and poor together. My mouth will speak wisdom, and the meditation of my heart [will speak] of understanding" (Psalm 49:1-3).

"It is through hearing that the flow of words comes into the understanding and soul" (Philo, *Q.Gen.* IV.107).

"To [really] hear is to understand" (Clement of Alexandria, *Strom.* II.c.4).

"He who listens only with the tips of his ears gets only a vague perception of what is said, while to him who listens carefully, the words enter more clearly and the things heard travel on all the paths, so that they form his understanding with deep impressions as if it were wax" (Philo, *Q.Exod.* II.13).

"Thus we may say quite properly that the understanding is the hearing's hearing" (Philo, *Cong.* 143).

"For the ears hear but the understanding through the ears hears better than the ears" (ibid.).

"Ears . . . not those which are external, but those of the understanding: . . . inward ears" (St. Chrysostom, *Homily* II in 2 Corinthians, par. 7).

"The understanding [SUNETON] hearer" (Isaiah 3:3, Greek Text).

"All who could hear with understanding" (Nehemiah 8:2).

"Moses, when he heard, was filled with understanding" (Ps. Philo, *Biblical Antiquities.* XIX.4)

"Hear me, you men of understanding" (Job 34:10).

"If you now have understanding, hear this: give ear to the voice of my words" (Job 34:16).

"Hear me, O you wise men, and give ear to me, you who have understanding [EPISTAMENOI]" (Job 34:2, Greek Text).

"O you nations that hear and understand" (2 Esdras 2:34).

"Hear me all you who know righteousness and have understanding in the works of God" (Zadokite Fragment [CD] 1:1,2, MS. A).

"If you love to hear, you shall receive understanding, and if you incline your ear, you shall be wise" (Sirach 6:33, Greek Cursives 248,253, Aldine Septuagint, Syriac and Old Latin Texts).

"Be willing to hear every divine discourse and do not let the parables of understanding [SUNESIS] escape you" (Sirach 6:35).

"Hear me, my son, and learn understanding, and pay attention to my words with your heart; I will show forth instruction by weight, and will declare knowledge exactly" (Sirach 16:24-25).

"Hear, my son, and be wise, and make your heart happy in the way" (Proverbs 23:19).

"Behold, my eye has seen all this, and my ear has heard and understood it" (Job 13:1).

"Give, therefore, Your servant a heart that hears [SHAMA']. . . so that I may understand [BIN]" (1 Kings 3:9).

"Behold, I have done according to your words. Behold, I have given you a wise and understanding [BIN] heart" (1 Kings 3:12).

"Does not the ear try words as the mouth tastes food?" (Job 12:11).

"For the ear tries words as the mouth tastes food" (Job 34:3).

"As the palate tastes different kinds of venison, so does an understanding [SUNETĒ] heart [KARDIA] detect false words" (Sirach 36:19).

"Does not the *ear* try words?" (Job 12:11; 34:3, Hebrew Text).

"Does not the *understanding* [NOUS] try words?" (Job 12:11; 34:3, Greek, Symmachus Version).

"Give ear to my choice words [EMER] O Lord, and understand [BIN] my meditation" (Psalm 5:1).

"Happy is he . . . who discourses in the ears of those who listen" (Sirach 25:9).

"An attentive ear is the desire of a wise man" (Sirach 3:29).

"A good ear will hear wisdom with all desire" (Sirach 3:31, Latin Vulgate).

"Hear my teaching . . . and come to my understanding" (Story of Ahikar 2:1, Syriac B Text).

"Hear wisdom . . . and receive understanding" (2 Baruch 51:4).

"Hear my voice, and understand my discourse" (2 Esdras 8.19).

"Hear me, my son . . . and do not despise me, and in the end you shall understand my choice words" (Sirach 31:22, Hebrew Text).

"How can I see unless You uncover my eyes, and how can I hear unless You uncover my ears?" (1QH 18:19,20, Dead Sea Scrolls).

"The eyes of those who see shall not be closed, and the ears of those who hear shall listen attentively, and the heart of the quick [see "The Quickness of Understanding"] shall understand [BIN] to know [YADA'], and the tongue of the stammerers shall be ready to speak plainly" (Isaiah 32:3-4).

"He has given me an ear to hear" (Isaiah 50:4, Greek Text).

"You, O my God, have uncovered my ear to the teaching" (1QH 6:3,4, Dead Sea Scrolls).

"You have uncovered my ears to wonderful Mysteries" (1QH 1:21).

"You have uncovered my ear . . . You have opened my heart to Your understanding [BINAH]" (1QH Fragment 4:7,12, Dead Sea Scrolls).

"He circumcised our ears and our hearts, so that we might understand" (*Epistle of Barnabas* 10:12).

"He circumcised our ear so that when we hear the Word we might believe" (*Epistle of Barnabas* 9:4).

"Hear the Word of the Gospel and believe" (Acts 15:7).

For "faith comes from hearing, and hearing by the word of Christ" (Romans 10:17).

"And they brought to Him a man who was deaf and had an impediment in his speech; and they entreated Him to lay His hand upon him. And He took him aside from the multitude by himself, and put His fingers into his ears, and after spitting, He touched his tongue; and looking up to heaven He sighed, and said to him, 'Ephphatha!' that is 'Be opened!' and his ears were opened, and the impediment of his tongue was released, and he spoke plainly" (St. Mark 7:32-35; see also Isaiah 32:3-4).

"Hear me and I will instruct you" (2 Esdras 7:49).

"Instruction leads to faith" (Clement of Alexandria, *Paed.* I.6.30:2).

And "through faith we understand" (Hebrews 11:3).

May "the will of God . . . be done always upon him who hears not only with the outward ear but in the depths of the heart [i.e., understanding] and remains in faith without doubting" (Testament of Isaac I:3,6).

> *Conversely, those who are unable to hear, or who*
> *refuse to hear, will not receive any understanding.*

"Why do you not understand My speech? Because you cannot hear My word" (St. John 8:43).

"Hear O foolish people and without understanding, who have eyes, but see not, who have ears, but hear not" (Jeremiah 5:21).

They "have eyes to see, but see not, they have ears to hear, but hear not, for they are a rebellious house" (Ezekiel 12:2).

"He sees many things, but does not observe them, his ears are open but he does not hear" (Isaiah 42:20).

"There is no understanding to him who hears" [without really paying attention] (Isaiah 33:19, Greek Text).

"You hear indeed, but do not understand [BIN], and you see indeed, but do not know [YADA]" (Isaiah 6:9).

"Blind in knowledge, and deaf in understanding" (Clement of Alexandria, *Exh.* X.105.1).

*   *

"I have seen what I did not know, and heard what I did not understand" (2 Esdras 10:35).

> *To really be able to hear is to understand. Thus, the*
> *Hebrew word "to hear" [SHAMA'] is often rendered "understand" in our Bibles.*

"Confound their language so that they may not understand [SHAMA', literally "hear"]" (Genesis 11:7).

"They did not know that Joseph understood [SHAMA'] them" (Genesis 42:23).

"Whose language you shall not understand [SHAMA']" (Deuteronomy 28:49).

"Of deeper speech than you can understand [SHAMA']" (Isaiah 33:19).

"An ancient nation whose language you do not know, neither understand [SHAMA'] what they speak" (Jeremiah 5:15; Ezekiel 3:6).

"Please speak to your servants in the Aramaic language for we understand [SHAMA'] it" (2 Kings 18:26; Isaiah 36:11).

"I have heard [SHAMA'] said of you [Joseph] that you can understand [SHAMA'] a dream to interpret it" (Genesis 41:15).

"As an angel of God is my lord the King, able to *hear* [SHAMA'] between good and evil" (2 Samuel 14:17).

"Give therefore, Your servant a heart that hears to judge Your people, that I may *understand* [BIN] between good and evil" (1 Kings 3:9).

Other ancient peoples also knew about the relationship between "Hearing" and "Understanding."

"Hear ye Rephaim and understand!" (Rephaim Text III.1.13).

"Hear O victorious Baal, understand O rider of the clouds" (CTA 4[II AB], V.122, Ugaritic Texts).

"Give ear, my friend, understand my thoughts, heed the choice expression of my words" (Assur Tablet VAT 10567 Lines 265-266 [Vorderasiatisches Museum, Berlin]).

"Pay attention, my friend and understand my ideas, heed the choice expression of my words" (Babylonian Tablet 34773 Lines 265-66, British Museum).

"To pay attention is an advantage for a son who hears, for if hearing enters into one who listens, the listener becomes a hearer" [i.e., a "judge" who is capable of hearing cases and adjudicating] (Instruction of Ptah-Hotep l. 235).

Because through hearing he will acquire "understanding [BIN] to hear [SHAMA'] judgment" (1 Kings 3:11).

In the ancient Sumerian language GISHTU means both "to hear" and "to understand" (A. Deimel's *Sumerian Lexicon* 449,66). UZNU, the Akkadian word for "ear" also means "understanding." The usage of the Egyptian word SDM: "to hear" for "to understand" is found in the Egyptian Texts Sin 31+ and Wen-Amon 77.

*   *

To be able to really understand deep things,
We must not only hear, but pay very close attention.

"Hear, O children, the instruction of a father, and pay attention to know understanding [BINAH]" (Proverbs 4:1).

"My son, pay attention to my words [DABAR pl.], incline your ear unto my choice words [EMER pl.]" (Proverbs 4:20).

Thereby you shall "understand [BIN] the choice words [EMER pl.] of understanding [BINAH]" (Proverbs 1:2).

"Give ear, O my people, to my teachings; incline your ears to the choice words [EMER pl.] of my mouth" (Psalm 78:1).

"Give ear and hear My voice [QOL], pay attention and hear My choice words [IMRAH]" (Isaiah 28:23; 32:9).

"Hear, and I will speak to you, and pay attention and I will enable you to hear My words" (2 Baruch 15:4).

"Hear O Israel, and I will speak to you, and pay attention, O seed of Jacob, and I will instruct you" (2 Baruch 31:3).

"Hear me, and I will instruct you, pay attention to me, and I will tell you more" (2 Esdras 5:32).

"Hear, O Israel, the commandments of life, give ear to know understanding [PHRONĒSIN]" (Baruch 3:9).

"My son . . . incline your ear to wisdom, and apply your heart to great understanding [TEBUNAH]" (Proverbs 2:1,2).

"My son, pay attention to my wisdom, and incline your ear to my great understanding [TEBUNAH]" (Proverbs 5:1).

"I gave ear intently to your great understandings [TEBUNAH pl.]" (Job 32:11).

"All the words that I shall speak to you receive in your heart, and hear with your ears" (Ezekiel 3:10).

"Then you shall hear as much as your ears are able to understand" (2 Esdras 10:56).

"I bowed down my ear a little and received Wisdom" (Sirach 51:21, Latin Vulgate).

"I inclined my ear but a little and received Wisdom, and great was the instruction I found" (Sirach 51:16).

"Hear the Word of Truth, and receive the knowledge of the Most High" (Odes of Solomon 8:8).

"Hear me and I will instruct you, and [hear me again] a second time, and I will admonish you" (2 Esdras 7:49, Latin Codex Sangermanensis).

"He who hears admonition gets understanding" (Proverbs 15:32).

"Admonition is the censure of protective care, and produces understanding" (Clement of Alexandria, *Paed.* I.9.76:1).

"Who among you will give ear to this? Who will pay attention and understand for the time to come?" (Isaiah 42:23).

"Hear my words, O you wise men, and give ear to me you who have understanding [EPISTAMENOI]" (Job 34:2, Greek Text).

The first requisite towards really being able to hear is silence.

"Be silent and hear, O Israel" (Deuteronomy 27:9).

"Be silent and I will speak" (Job 33:31).

"There was silence and I heard a voice" (Job 4:16).

"Be silent, and I shall teach you wisdom" (Job 33:33).

"Hearken unto this, O Job, stand still and understand the works of God" (Job 37:14).

"Be still and know that I am God" (Psalm 46:10; see also 1 Kings 19:12,13).

When something that is heard is well understood it is said to be "seen."

"The Lord . . . has put a new song in my mouth: praise to our God, many shall see [RAAH] it" (Psalm 40:3).

"Who has stood in the council of the Lord, and has seen [RAAH] and heard His Word?" (Jeremiah 23:18).

"All the people saw [RAAH] . . . the voice [QOL]" (Exodus 20:18).

"You have seen [RAAH] . . . what I have spoken" (Exodus 20:22).

"Behold, my eye has seen all this, my ear has heard and understood it" (Job 13:1).

"Now, children, hear me, and I will open your eyes to see and understand the works of God" (Zadokite Fragment [CD] 2:14,15, MS. A).

"Though I . . . understand [EIDO = "to see"] all mysteries and all knowledge . . . and have not love, I am nothing" (1 Corinthians 13:2).

*　　*

The Hebrew word AMAR: "to answer" or "to say," is derived from the Akkadian word AMAR which means "to see":

"Who thought he would see [AMAR] his sun" (SU Text, The Archeological Museum, Ankara, Turkey).

"In the gates of splendid wonderment my omens were very clearly seen [AMAR]" (Ludlul Bel Nemeq VAT Tablet 9303 in the Vorderasiatische Museum, Berlin. see also *Journal of the American Oriental Society,* Vol. 74 [1954] p. 229, n. 47).

A clear "answer" [AMAR] makes one "see" [AMAR].

*　　*

We listen to ordinary "words" [DABAR], but we pay close attention to "choice words" [EMER, IMRAH].

"Pleasant choice words [EMER pl.] are pure" (Proverbs 15:26).

"The choice words [IMRAH pl.] of the Lord are pure words [IMRAH pl.]; as silver refined in a furnace on the earth, purified seven times" (Psalm 12:6).

"The choice word [IMRAH] of the Lord is tried" (Psalm 18:30).

"Every choice word [IMRAH] of God is pure" (Proverbs 30:5).

"Hear My voice [QOL], give ear to My choice word [IMRAH]" Isaiah 32:9; see also Genesis 4:23).

"O children, hear me, and pay attention to the choice words [EMER pl.] of my mouth" (Proverbs 7:24).

"My son, pay attention to my words [DABAR pl.], and incline your ears [pay close attention] to my choice words [EMER pl]" (Proverbs 4:20).

291

So that you may "understand [BIN] the choice words [EMER pl.] of understanding [BINAH]" (Proverbs 1:2).

For "by the choice word [EMER] is wisdom made known" (Sirach 4:24, Hebrew Text).

"Pay attention and hear My choice words [IMRAH pl.]" (Isaiah 28:23).

"Hear me, my son. . . . and do not despise me, and in the end you will understand my choice words [EMER pl.]" (Sirach 31:22, Hebrew Text).

*   *

"The angels showed me, and from them I heard everything, and from them I understood" (Enoch 1:2).

*   *

"They who give heed unto Him are the poor of the flock" (Zadokite Fragment 1:9, MS. B1).

Thus, "the poor of the flock . . . knew that it was the Word of the Lord" (Zechariah 11:11).

"A poor wise man" (Ecclesiastes 9:15).

"The poor man who has understanding" (Proverbs 28:11).

"The poor man who knows" (Ecclesiastes 6:8).

All of these 'poor' ones know that their wisdom, understanding, and knowledge come from hearing and paying close attention to the Word of the Lord.

THE HEART AND UNDERSTANDING

"God made . . . the heart for understanding" (Testament of Naphtali 2:8).

"The heart is the seat of understanding" (Midrash Rabbah on Psalm 103.3; see also Berakoth 61a, BT).

"Understanding [BINAH] is in the heart" (Zohar III.28b-29a, Raya Mehemna).

"He gave them a heart to understand" (Sirach 17:6).

"The Great One has given to men to . . . understand with the heart" (Enoch 14:2).

"I will give them a heart, and they shall understand" (Baruch 2:31, Latin Vulgate).

"The Word of the Lord has given you a heart not to forget but to understand" (Jerusalem Targum on Deuteronomy 29:4).

"An understanding heart" (Sirach 36:19; ibid. 26:24, Hebrew Text).

"To whom God gave understanding [EPISTĒMĒN] in their heart" (Exodus 36:2, Greek Text).

"The Great One has given to the sons of men . . . to understand in their heart" (4Q En^c XIII.2 [Cave 4 Aramaic Fragments of Enoch], Dead Sea Scrolls).

"What is man that You should . . . set Your *heart* upon him?" (Job 7:17, Hebrew Text).

"What is man that You should . . . set Your *understanding* [NOUS] upon him?" (ibid., Greek Text).

"Wisdom will enter your *heart*" (Proverbs 2:10, Hebrew Text).

"Wisdom will enter your *understanding*" (ibid., Greek Text).

"He who gets *heart* [LEB] loves his own soul" (Proverbs 19:8, Hebrew Text).

"He who obtains *understanding* [PHRONĒSIN] loves himself" (ibid., Greek Text).

"You shall love the Lord your God with all your *heart*" (Deuteronomy 6:5, Hebrew Text).

"You shall love the Lord your God with all your *understanding*" (ibid., Greek Text; St. Mark 12:33).

"Within whose heart You have set understanding [BINAH]" (1QH 2:18, Dead Sea Scrolls).

"Understanding [BINAH] is the heart of which it is said: 'the heart understands'" (Tikkunei ha-Zohar, Second Preface 17a-17b).

The ancient Egyptians and Babylonians also knew that the heart was for understanding.

"Amon . . . his heart is Sia [Egyptian god of understanding]" (Hymn to Amon, Papyrus Leiden [344] l.350, Recto 5,15).

"Sia [god of understanding] is the heart of Re" (Dendara Temple Hieroglyph Vol. III p. 139 in E. Chassinat's *Le Temple de Dendara*, 4 Vols. Cairo, 1934-35).

"Hu [god of the utterance] is in his mouth, Sia [god of understanding] is in his heart" (Stele of Kuban I.18).

"Hu is in your mouth, Sia is in your heart, and your tongue is the shrine of Maat [goddess of Truth]" (ibid. XVIII.12).

"Sia is understanding which is in your heart" (Sehetepibre Papyrus).

"Understanding is that which is in your heart" (Koptos XII.3,4 [Petrie]).

"My heart is understanding, my reins are counsel" (Babylonian Tablet VAT 10251, ll.13-18 [Voderasiatisches Museum, Berlin]).

*   *

Conversely

"He who is *void of heart* [LEB]" (Proverbs 11:12, Hebrew Text) is "a man *void of understanding* [PHRONIMOS HESUCHIAN]" (ibid., Greek Text).

"They have no heart to understand" (Book of Jubilees 22:18).

"He has daubed over their eyes so that they cannot see, and their hearts so that they cannot understand" (Isaiah 44:18).

"Do you not yet perceive or understand? Are your hearts hardened?" (St. Mark 8:17).

"They did not understand . . . because their hearts were hardened" (St. Mark 6:52).

"Make the heart of this people fat . . . lest they . . . understand with their heart" (Isaiah 6:10).

"You have kept their heart from understanding" (Job 17:4).

"Having the understanding darkened . . . because of their hardness of heart" (Ephesians 4:18).

*   *

To be wise in Heart is to be wise in Understanding.

"Wise in *heart*" (Exodus 28:3, Hebrew Text).

"Wise in *understanding*" (ibid., Greek Text).

"He is wise in *heart*" (Job 9:4, Hebrew Text).

"He is wise in *understanding*" (ibid., Greek Text).

"Every wise [CHAKAM] *hearted* [LEB] *man*" (Exodus 36:1, Hebrew Text).

"Everyone *wise in understanding*" (ibid., Greek Text).

"Speak unto all who are *wise-hearted*" (Exodus 28:3, Hebrew Text).

"Speak to all those who are *wise in understanding*" (ibid., Greek Text).

"The fool shall be a servant to the *wise in heart*" (Proverbs 11:29, Hebrew Text).

"A fool shall be a servant to the *man of understanding* [PHRONIMŌ]" (ibid., Greek Text).

Because "the wise in heart is a man of understanding" (Proverbs 16:21, Syriac Text).

"All who are *wise-hearted*" (Exodus 31:6, Hebrew Text).

"Everyone who is *understanding [SUNETO] in heart*" (ibid., Greek Text).

"Hear me, you *men* [ENOSH Pl.] *of heart* [LEBAB]" (Job 34:10, Hebrew Text).

"Hear me you who are *understanding* [SUNETOI] *in heart*" (ibid., Greek Text).

"The *heart* of the *wise* understands" (Sirach 3:27, Hebrew Text).

"The *heart* of the *understanding* [SUNETOU] will understand" (ibid., Greek Text).

*   *

The Hebrew word for "heart [LEB, LEBAB]" is synonymous with "understanding."

"He who commits adultery with a woman lacks understanding [literally *"lacks heart"* (LEB)]" (Proverbs 6:32).

"An old man who is an adulterer *lacking understanding* [SUNESEI]" (Sirach 25:2).

"A young man void of understanding [literally *"lacking heart"* (LEB)]" (Proverbs 7:7).

"A young man *void of understanding* [A-PHRŌN]" (ibid., Greek Text).

"To him who lacks understanding [literally *"lacks heart"* (LEB)]" (Proverbs 9:4, Hebrew Text; ibid. 9:16).

"To them who *lack understanding* [ENDEESI PHRENŌN]" Proverbs 9:4, Greek Text; ibid. 9:16).

"He who is void of understanding [literally *"lacks heart"* (LEB)] despises his neighbor, but a man of great understanding [TEBUNAH] holds his peace" (Proverbs 11:12).

"A man *void of understanding* [ENDEĒS PHRENŌN] sneers at his fellow citizens, but a man of understanding [PHRONIMOS] is quiet" (ibid., Greek Text).

"He who gets understanding [literally *"gets heart"* (LEB)] loves his own soul" (Proverbs 19:8, Hebrew Text; also compare Job 34:10 in the Hebrew and Greek Texts).

"He who *obtains understanding* [PHRONĒSIN] loves himself" (ibid., Greek Text).

"He who is without understanding [literally *"without heart"* (LEB)] will not abide [with] Wisdom" (Sirach 6:19, Hebrew Text).

But "Wisdom rests in the heart of him who has understanding [BIN]" (Proverbs 14:33).

Because "a man of understanding is faithful to the Law of God" (Sirach 33:3, Latin Vulgate).

"Every man of understanding knows wisdom" (Sirach 18:28).

UNDERSTANDING HIDES

"For the nature of understanding is to be very deep, not superficial, it does not display itself openly but loves to hide itself in secrecy; it is discovered not easily but with difficulty and much labor" (Philo, *Som.* I.6).

"Where is the place of understanding [BINAH]? Seeing that it is hidden ['ALAM] from the eyes of all living, and kept hidden [SATHAR] from the birds of the heavens" (Job 28:20,21).

"To whom have the roots of wisdom been revealed? Or who has known the hidden things of understanding?" (Sirach 1:6, Syriac Text).

"There is no searching of His great understanding [TEBUNAH]" (Isaiah 40:28).

"Good insight shall hide itself, and understanding shall withdraw himself into his secret chamber, and shall be sought by many, and yet not be found" (2 Esdras 5:9,10).

"Where has the multitude of understanding hidden itself?" (2 Baruch 48:36).

"You did hide the fountain of understanding [BINAH] and the secret of Truth" (1QH 5:26, Dead Sea Scrolls).

"You have kept hid [TSAPHAN] their heart from understanding [SEKEL]" (Job 17:4, Literal Translation).

"The understanding [BINAH] of their men of understanding [BIN] shall be hidden [SATHAR]" (Isaiah 29:14).

"Be unobtrusively modest [TSANA' = "concealed," "chaste," "shy"] in understanding [SAKAL]" (Sirach 32:3, Hebrew Text).

"He will hide his words until his time, and the lips of many shall declare his understanding [SUNESIN]" (Sirach 1:23).

*   *

"Jesus hid Himself" (St. John 8:59).

"Jesus . . . departed and did hide Himself from them" (St. John 12:36).

"He [Jesus Christ] secretly withdrew Himself into the wilderness" (St. Luke 5:16; Ibid., 9:10).

Jesus "Christ, in whom are hidden all the treasures of wisdom and knowledge" (Colossians 2:2,3).

Jesus "Christ, the Power [see "The Power and Strength of Understanding"] of God and the Wisdom of God" (1 Corinthians 1:24).

THE HUMBLE, THE MEEK, THE POOR, AND UNDERSTANDING

"And the Child [Jesus] grew and became strong in spirit, filled with wisdom" (St. Luke 2:40).

"And all who heard Him [Jesus Christ] were astonished at His understanding" (St. Luke 2:47).

"Learn from Me, for I am meek and humble of heart" (St. Matthew 11:29).

"A man of understanding is humble in spirit" (Targum on Proverbs 17:27).

"Humility discloses to us the light of understanding" (St. Gregory *Morals on the Book of Job* XXV.30)

"Let a man first grasp the way of humility and then ask God for understanding" (Tanna debe Eliyahu Rabba p. 31 [ed. Friedman]).

"The man who has both much understanding and humility is called blessed by all who look upon him" (Rabbi Joseph Kimchi's *Shekel Hakodesh* 67).

"To the way of humility I incline, and thus will my heart gain understanding" (ibid. 79).

"Therefore, as God's chosen ones, holy and beloved, put on tender compassion, kindness, humility of understanding [TAPEINOPHROSUNĒN], meekness, and patience" (Colossians 3:12).

"Be humble [TSANA'] in understanding" (Sirach 32:3, Hebrew Text).

"He who has a humble understanding" (Sotah 5b; Sanhedrin 43b, BT).

"With the humble is wisdom" (Proverbs 11:2).

"The humble . . . they are most pleasing in God's sight" (St. Chrysostom, *In Matthew Homily* 65.6 [PG vol.58 p.625]).

"God gives to a man who is good in His sight, wisdom and knowledge and joy" (Ecclesiastes 2:26).

"Humbly [TSANA'] will I declare my knowledge" (Sirach 16:23, Hebrew Text).

*   *

"Be meek to hear the Word, so that you may understand and return a true answer with wisdom" (Sirach 5:13, Latin Vulgate).

"The friendly and particularly meek understanding loves reproof and becomes familiar with those who discipline it" (Philo, *Q.Gen*. III.26).

"Many are exalted and esteemed but the Mysteries of God are revealed to the meek [PRAESIN]" (Sirach 3:19, Greek Sinaiticus Text and Cursives 248,106,253).

"Who is wise and understanding among you? Let him show by his good conduct his works in the meekness of wisdom" (St. James 3:13, Literal Translation).

"A man's modesty may be seen in the union of meekness and wisdom" (R. Joseph Kimchi's *Shekel Hakodesh* 120).

*   *

"Happy the man whom poverty has not broken nor yet destitution has shattered him, for there [in poverty] is wisdom and knowledge, and there [in want] is understanding" (Sirach 25:10, Syriac Text).

"Blessed are the poor in spirit, for theirs is the Kingdom of Heaven" [i.e., understanding and knowledge in "the Mysteries of the Kingdom of Heaven" [St. Matthew 13:11] (St. Matthew 5:3).

"The lovers and practisers of understanding [PHRONĒSIS] and every virtue are almost universally poor, obscure, of little repute and in a humble position" (Philo, *De Providentia*, Fragment 2,1, Quoted by Eusebius in *Praep. Evang.* VIII.14.386).

"The poor man who has understanding" (Proverbs 28:11).

"The poor man is honored for his understanding" (Sirach 10:29, Hebrew Text).

"More lordly is the poor man who understands than the rich man without understanding" (Philo, *Q.Gen*. III.22).

"These things are grievous to a man of understanding: the upbraiding of a houseroom [for he is poor and has no money to pay the rent], and the reproaching of the money lender [to whom the poor man is in debt]" (Sirach 29:28).

"Anxious care may befall a man of understanding [the worries of the poor]" (Proverbs 17:12, Greek text).

"The rich man speaks and his helpers are many, and though his words are ugly they are veneered over. The poor man stumbles and they jeer at him. He speaks with understanding [SAKAL] and there is no place for him [because he is poor]" (Sirach 13:21, Hebrew Text).

"My son . . . this is the way of the world: if a poor man speaks with understanding, he is not listened to, and he is called a fool" (Story of Ahikar v.112, Slavonic V Text).

"Men of understanding are counted as refuse" (Sirach 26:28, Literal Translation).

"The poor man's wisdom is despised, and his words are not heard" (Ecclesiastes 9:16).

"Do not despise the poor man who has understanding" (Sirach 10:22, Hebrew Text).

For "it is not right to despise the poor man who has understanding" (Sirach 10:23, Greek Text).

Because someday "the wisdom of the poor man shall lift up his head and make him sit in the midst of nobles" (Sirach 11:1, Hebrew and Greek Texts).

"Better is a poor and wise child, than an old and foolish King" (Ecclesiastes 4:13).

"A poor wise man . . . by his wisdom delivered the city" (Ecclesiastes 9:15).

"Understanding counsels" (2 Enoch 66:3).

"The counsel of the poor" (Psalm 14:6).

"A man of understanding [NOEMŌN] knows" (Sirach 21:7).

"The poor man who knows . . . ." (Ecclesiastes 6:8).

"Riches are not to men of understanding [for they are usually poor]" (Ecclesiastes 9:11).

Good slaves and servants possess the humility and meekness that gives them Understanding.

"Who then is the faithful and understanding [PHRONIMOS] slave whom his Master made ruler over his household, to give them food in due season?" (St. Matthew 24:45; St. Luke 12:42).

"Free men shall serve the servant who is understanding" (Sirach 10:25, Greek Sinaiticus Text and Cursives 248,23,106,307).

"Let your soul love an understanding [SAKAL-SUNETON] servant" (Sirach 7:21, Hebrew Text and Greek Sinaiticus, Alexandrinus Texts and Cursive 248).

"An understanding [PHRONIMOS] servant calms a man's anger" (Proverbs 18:14, Greek Text).

"The King's favor is toward an understanding [SAKAL] servant" (Proverbs 14:35).

"An understanding servant shall have rule over his masters" (Sirach 20:27, Syriac and Arabic Texts).

"A servant who has understanding [SAKAL] shall be exalted" (Sirach 10:24, Hebrew Text).

"Behold, My servant shall understand [SAKAL], he shall be exalted and extolled, and be very high" (Isaiah 52:13).

"I am Your servant, give me understanding" (Psalm 119:125).

"Blessed are You O God of knowledge, who have given to Your servant understanding" (1QH 11:27,28, Dead Sea Scrolls).

Needless to say, an understanding servant is also wise.

"A wise man by his words makes himself beloved" (Sirach 20:13).

"He who is wise in words will advance himself [to honor]" (Sirach 20:27).

"A wise servant shall have prosperous doings [because he is wise and understanding]" (Proverbs 13:13, Greek Text).

*   *

*Conversely, the proud, the covetous rich, the violent
and the scoffers, have neither knowledge nor understanding.*

"He who lifts himself up with pride . . . his wisdom will depart from him" (Pesachim, folio 66b, BT).

"Men of pride will not see wisdom" (Sirach 15:7, Hebrew Text).

Because "Wisdom is far from men of pride" (Sirach 15:8).

"They have not known My Law by reason of their pride" (2 Baruch 48:40).

"The proud . . . they knew Him not" (Psalms of Solomon 2:35).

"Neither shall he understand [BIN] . . . because he shall magnify himself above all" (Daniel 11:37).

"He is proud, understanding nothing" (1 Timothy 6:4).

"There is no understanding where there is bitterness of feeling" (Sirach 21:15, Latin Vulgate; see also St. James 3:14-15).

"They obeyed not, neither did they incline their ear, but made their neck stiff so that they might not hear, nor receive instruction [thus, they shall not understand]" (Jeremiah 17:23).

"He who strives to be rich . . . knows not" (Proverbs 28:22).

"The newly rich . . . know nothing, they have never dreamt of the true wealth which has eyes to see, whose substance is the perfect virtues and the actions which conform with them; it is a blind wealth against which they have struck, and taking it for their support they fail of necessity to see the road which is before them" (Philo, *Spec.* II.23).

"Because you say, 'I am rich, and have become wealthy, and have need of nothing,' you do not know that you are . . . blind" (Revelation 3:17).

"Like blind men whose understanding through covetousness has lost the power to see" (Philo, *De Providentia*, Fragment 2,12).

"Their riches concealed from them the Truth and darkened them" (Shepherd of Hermas, *Sim.* IX.30.107:4).

"Wealth has led astray the hearts [i.e., understanding] of princes" (Sirach 8:2, Hebrew Text).

"He who is grasping even though he possesses things is nevertheless dull of understanding" (Story of Ahikar 2:92, Armenian Text).

"See your kings and your great ones, those who are clothed in soft garments, they shall not be able to understand the Truth" (Gospel of Thomas, Logion 78).

"Man who is held in honor [for his riches] . . . understands not" (Psalm 49:20).

"One ought not to respect a rich man who is void of understanding" (Sirach 22:23, Greek Cursives 248,106).

"One who lives in luxury . . . does as he pleases . . . and does not understand [NOEI] what he is doing" (Shepherd of Hermas, *Sim.* VI.5.65:3).

"For men shall put on more adornments than a woman, and more coloured garments than a virgin, in royalty, grandeur, and in power and in silver and gold and purple and in splendor and in food they shall be poured out as water. Therefore they shall be wanting in doctrine and wisdom" (Enoch 98:2,3).

"They [the rich] became insolent in their prosperity and they were without understanding" (Psalms of Solomon 1:6 [Von Gebhardt Transl.])

"They are greedy dogs which do not know [YADA] satisfaction, they are shepherds who do not know [YADA] how to understand" (Isaiah 56:11).

"He who has much business does not become wise" (Pirke Aboth 2:6).

"Those . . . who are mixed up in affairs of business and in wealth and in heathen friendships and many other affairs of this age — those absorbed in these things do not understand parables about divinity. For they are darkened by these affairs" (Shepherd of Hermas, *Mand.* X.1.40:4).

"Just as fine vineyards, whenever they are neglected, are made barren by thorns and various weeds, so men who believe and engage in these many affairs, as mentioned before, stray from their purpose and understand nothing at all of righteousness, but when they hear about divinity and Truth, their mind is busy with their own affairs and they understand nothing at all" (Shepherd of Hermas, *Mand.* X.1.40:5; see also St. Matthew 13:22-23).

"Truly I say to you, that it is hard for a rich man to enter the Kingdom of Heaven" [and be able to understand "the Mysteries of the Kingdom of Heaven" (St. Matthew 13:11)] (St. Matthew 19:23).

However, "refrain from many affairs and you will in no wise sin, for those who engage in many affairs also sin much since they are overburdened by their affairs and do not serve the Lord . . . but if anyone is occupied with one concern, he is able to serve the Lord because his understanding is not corrupted away from the Lord but he will serve Him with a pure understanding" (Shepherd of Hermas, *Sim.* IV.53:5,7).

The rich man who "understands about his wealth and works for the poor man out of the gifts of the Lord, rightly fulfills his ministry" (Shepherd of Hermas, *Sim.* II.51:7).

"In very Truth the wealth which is not blind but keen of sight is abundance of virtues" (Philo, *Abr.* 25).

"The prince who lacks great understanding [TEBUNAH] is also a great oppressor" (Proverbs 28:16).

"Because he has oppressed and forsaken the poor, and because he has violently taken away a house which he did not build, surely he shall not know [YADA] . . . darkness shall be his treasure" (Job 20:19,20,26).

"A man of violence does not receive understanding" (Sirach 32:18, Hebrew Text, MS. E).

"A man of impatient spirit is very much without understanding [APHRŌN]" (Proverbs 14:29, Greek Text).

"A scoffer seeks wisdom and does not find it" (Proverbs 14:6).

"Wisdom is far from scoffers" (Sirach 15:8, Hebrew Text).

"The study of the Law is not found among merchants" (Pirke Aboth 2:6).

"The occupation with vain things in which Solomon engaged led him astray. For when a scholar engages in too many affairs, they confound him so that he loses his wisdom" (Ḥagigah II.77b [JT]; Tanchuma Vaëra 5).

"O Solomon, how wise you were in your *youth* and as a flood full of understanding . . . covering the whole earth" (Sirach 47:13,14,15).

But not in your old age when "you did stain your honor and pollute your seed" (Sirach 47:20).

"Wine and women make wise men fall off" (Sirach 19:2, Latin Vulgate; see also 1 Kings 11:1-9).

"We must watch with utmost care lest the wisdom we have received should take away the light of humility" (St. Gregory, *Morals on the Book of Job* XXVII.75).

UNDERSTANDING AND JUDGMENT

*Before we can make a right judgment, we must
know how to understand between good and evil.*

"Give Your servant a heart that hears [i.e., an understanding heart; see "Hearing and Understanding"] to judge Your people, that I may understand [BIN] between good and evil" (1 Kings 3:9).

"You . . . have asked for yourself understanding [BIN] to hear judgment" (1 Kings 3:11).

"I will raise up for David a righteous Branch, and a King shall reign and understand [SAKAL-SUNĒSEI], and shall execute judgment [MISHPAT-KRIMA] and righteousness on the earth" (Jeremiah 23:5, Hebrew and Greek Texts).

"The breastplate of *understanding* [SUNESEŌS]" (Testament of Levi 8:2).

"The breastplate of *judgment* [MISHPAT]" (Exodus 28:15,29,30).

"Speak, you who are the elder, for it is fitting that you should, but [speak] with judicious understanding [EPISTĒMĒ]" (Sirach 32:3, Greek Cursive 248).

UNDERSTANDING IS THE KEY TO KNOWLEDGE

"Understanding throws open the way to knowledge of things divine and enables us to apprehend God" (Corpus Hermeticum, *Libellus* IV.6a).

"God . . . gives wisdom to the wise, and knowledge to those who know [YADA] understanding [BINAH]" (Daniel 2:21).

"When the wise understands [SAKAL] he receives knowledge [DAATH]" (Proverbs 21:11, Hebrew Text).

"A wise man understanding [SUNION] will receive knowledge [GNŌSIN]" (ibid., Greek Text).

"If there be no understanding there is no knowledge" (Pirke Aboth 3:21).

"Understanding loves to learn and advance to knowledge" (Philo, *Decal.* 1).

"Understanding [EPISTĒMĒ] is a sure grasp leading up through true and sure reasons to the knowledge [GNŌSIN] of the cause" (Clement of Alexandria, *Strom.* VI.c.18).

"The heart of the understanding [BIN] gets knowledge" (Proverbs 18:15a).

"Give me understanding, that I may know" (Psalm 119:125).

For "knowledge is easy to him who understands" (Proverbs 14:6).

"You will know for you have understanding" (*Didache* 2:21).

"Within whose heart You have set understanding [BINAH] that he might open the fountain of knowledge to all who understand [BIN]" (1QH 2:18, Dead Sea Scrolls).

"What is man . . . that You should give him understanding [SAKAL] of such marvels and make known to him the secret of Your Truth?" (1QH 10:3,4, Dead Sea Scrolls).

"By Your understanding [BINAH] I know" (1QH 14:12, Dead Sea Scrolls).

"I, gifted with understanding, I have known You O my God" (1QH 12:11, Dead Sea Scrolls).

People "know You according to the measure of their understanding" (1QH 1:31, Dead Sea Scrolls).

"Blessed are You O God of knowledge who have given to Your servant under-standing of knowledge" (1QH 11:27,28, Dead Sea Scrolls).

"Who is wise, and he shall understand these things? [Who is] understanding [BIN] and he shall know them?" (Hosea 14:9).

*   *

THE LAW AND UNDERSTANDING

"He gave them understanding [EPISTĒMĒN] and the Law of life for a heritage" (Sirach 17:11).

"The Law of life and great understanding [TEBUNAH]" (Sirach 45:5, Hebrew Text).

"He who keeps the Law gets the understanding thereof" (Sirach 21:11).

"Man would not rightly have understood My judgment if he had not accepted the Law" (2 Baruch 15:5).

"To know the Law is the mark of a good understanding" (Proverbs 9:10, Greek Text).

"A man of understanding will put his trust in the Law, and the Law is faithful to him as when one inquires at the oracle" (Sirach 33:3, Greek Text).

"A man of understanding understands the Word [of the Lord] and His Law" (Sirach 33:3, Hebrew Text).

"Whoever occupies himself with the Law . . . to him are revealed the secrets of the Law" (Kallah Rabbathi 54a).

"All wisdom is in the doing of the Law" (Sirach 19:20).

Conversely

"He shall not become wise who hates the Law" (Sirach 33:2, Hebrew Text).

LENGTH OF DAYS AND UNDERSTANDING;
THE AGED AND UNDERSTANDING

"Wisdom is with the aged, and in length of days: understanding" (Job 12:12).

"Learn where insight [PHRONĒSIS] is . . . and where is understanding [SUNE-SIS] that you may be able to know where there is length of days and life" (Baruch 3:14).

"A ruler who is a great oppressor lacks understanding, but he who hates covetousness shall prolong his days [i.e., he shall live long and understand]" (Proverbs 28:16).

Because "in length of days: understanding" (Job 12:12).

"Days should speak and multitude of years should know wisdom [i.e., multitude of years should understand] (Job 32:7).

Because "understanding knows wisdom" (Sirach 18:28; see also Proverbs 14:33).

"Do you know it, because you were born then? Or [understand it] because the number of your days is great?" (Job 38:21).

"What do you know that we do not know? What do you understand [BIN] that is not in us? For with us are both the gray-headed and very aged men [who understand], much older than your father" (Job 15:9,10).

"Behold, God is great, and we know Him not, neither can the number of His years be searched out" (Job 36:26).

Because "there is no searching of His understanding" (Isaiah 40:28).

"My son, forget not my teaching, and let your heart keep my commandments, for length of days, and years of life, and peace shall they add to you" (Proverbs 3:1,2).

"Behold, I have taught you statutes and judgments, just as the Lord my God commanded me . . . keep therefore and do them, for this is your wisdom and your understanding in the sight of the nations" (Deuteronomy 4:5,6).

"Wisdom's branches are length of days [i.e., they bear the "fruits of understanding"]" (Sirach 1:20).

Because "in length of days: understanding" (Job 12:12).

"From the beginning of your days, all the people have known your understanding" (Judith 8:29).

"They who seek the Lord understand all things" (Proverbs 28:5).

"It is great glory to follow the Lord, for length of days shall be received from Him" (Sirach 23:38, Latin Vulgate).

"In length of days: understanding" (Job 12:12).

"Despise not the traditions of the aged, which they heard from their fathers; because from them you will obtain understanding so that you may be able to answer in time of need" (Sirach 8:9, Hebrew Text).

"It is not given to youth but to old age to discern things precious and worthy of reverence, particularly those which are judged not by the deceitful and unreasoning sense, but by the understanding [NOUS] when absolutely pure and unalloyed" (Philo, *Aet.* 77).

"O how beautiful a thing it is . . . for the aged to know understanding!" (Sirach 25:4, Syriac Text).

"He [God] knows the understanding of the aged" (Job 12:20, Greek Text).

"Speak, you who are the elder, for it is fitting that you should, but with judicious understanding [EN AKRIBEI EPISTĒMĒ]" (Sirach 32:3, Greek Cursive 248).

"Speak, O gray-headed one, for it is your privilege, but be humble in understanding" (Sirach 32:3, Hebrew Text).

"The prince of the people [shall be praised] for the wisdom of his speech, but the word of the ancients [shall be praised] for the understanding" (Sirach 9:24, Latin Vulgate).

"I understand more than the ancients [who understand]" (Psalm 119:100).

"Great men are not wise [per se], nor do the aged understand [per se] judgment" (Job 32:9, Latin Vulgate).

"For old age is not honored for length of days, nor measured by number of years; but understanding [PHRONĒSIS] is gray hairs for men, and blameless life is ripe old age" (Wisdom 4:8,9).

"No one is old but one who has acquired wisdom" (Kiddushin 32b, BT; see also 2 Baruch 17:1-3).

"He who is enamoured of understanding [PHRONĒSEŌS], and wisdom, and faith in God, may be justly called 'elder'" (Philo, *Abr.* 271).

"O how beautiful a thing it is . . . for the aged to thoroughly know good counsel [see "Understanding and Counselling"]. O how beautiful a thing is the wisdom of old men" (Sirach 25:4,5).

"They who are grey, not through time but in goodness of counsel" (Philo, *Plant.* 40).

"A goodly old age, not meaning the life of long duration but the life with understanding [PHRONĒSEŌS]" (Philo, *Her.* 290).

"As the clear light is upon the holy candlestick so is the beauty of the face in ripe old age" (Sirach 26:17).

For "a man's wisdom makes his face to shine" (Ecclesiastes 8:1).

Conversely

"A man weak and short-lived and of small power to understand" (Wisdom 9:5).

"Short-lived people, the frail ones whose very words were frail . . . without understanding" (Baba Bathra 137b, BT).

"I am indeed younger than my brothers, but in understanding I am as old" (4 Maccabees 11:14).

UNDERSTANDING AND LIFE

"Understanding is a wellspring of life to him who has it" (Proverbs 16:22).

"Give me understanding and I shall live" (Psalm 119:144).

"He made Man and bestowed upon him understanding, which is par excellence the life principle of the life principle itself" (Philo, *Op.* 66).

"May He enlighten your heart with life-giving understanding" (1QS 2:3, Dead Sea Scrolls).

"He made Man, and put his heart in the midst of the body, and gave him breath, life, and understanding" (2 Esdras 16:61).

"The breath of the Almighty has given me *life*" (Job 33:4).

"The breath of the Almighty, gives them *understanding*" (Job 32:8).

"Let us fast forty days, perhaps the Lord will have pity on us and will leave us understanding and life" (Book of Adam and Eve 35:2, Slavonic Text).

"Are they living and understanding?" (Philo, *Som.* I.22).

"Set in motion, formed and given life by the understanding" (Philo, *Op.* 9).

"Learn where insight is . . . and where is understanding that you may be able to know where there is length of days, and life" (Baruch 3:14).

"I understand more than the ancients, because I keep Your precepts" (Psalm 119:100).

"Through Your precepts I get understanding" (Psalm 119:104).

"I will never forget Your precepts, because through them You have given me life" (Psalm 119:93).

"See how I love Your precepts, give me life, O Lord" (Psalm 119:159).

"He gave in his [Moses'] hand precepts: the Law of life and understanding" (Sirach 45:5, Hebrew Text).

"He gave them understanding [EPISTĒMĒN] and the Law of life for a heritage" (Sirach 17:11).

"Hear, O Israel, the commandments of life, give ear to know understanding" (Baruch 3:9).

"Forsake the foolish, and live, and go in the way of understanding" (Proverbs 9:6).

"Hear, O Israel, the statutes and the judgments which I teach you, do them that you may live . . . keep them therefore and do them, for this is your wisdom and your understanding in the sight of the nations" (Deuteronomy 4:1,6).

"O Lord . . . give us the seed of a new heart and cultivation to our understanding that there may come fruit of it . . . whereby everyone shall live" (2 Esdras 8:6).

"The fruit of understanding [EPISTĒMĒS] is the life of contemplation" (Philo, *Fug.* 176).

"All the commandments which I am commanding this day you shall be careful to do, that you may live" (Deuteronomy 8:1).

"A good understanding have all those who do His commandments" (Psalm 111:10).

"The understanding [PHRONĒMA] of the Spirit is life and peace" (Romans 8:6).

"The thoughts of the understanding are ways of life that he may turn aside [from evil] and escape hell" (Proverbs 15:24, Greek Text).

"To depart from evil is understanding" (Job 28:28).

"Depart from evil, and it shall be health to your body and nourishment to your bones" (Proverbs 3:7,8).

*   *

"The life, prosperity, and health of a man is understanding" (Instruction of Ptah-Hotep, l. 545, Prisse Papyrus, National Library, Paris).

*   *

Conversely

"They were destroyed, because they had no understanding [PHRONĒSIN]" (Baruch 3:28).

"Fools die for lack of understanding" (Proverbs 10:21).

"The man void of understanding shall die by a snare" (Proverbs 13:14, Greek Text).

"They have fallen to their destruction for lack of understanding" (1QH 4:7, Dead Sea Scrolls).

"Man . . . without understanding is like the beasts that perish" (Psalm 49:20).

"Having the understanding darkened, being alienated from the life of God through ignorance that is in them, because of the blindness of their heart" (Ephesians 4:18).

"From morning till evening they shall be cut down, and because no one understands, they shall perish forever" (Job 4:20, Latin Vulgate).

"Because they do not understand [BIN] the deeds of the Lord nor the work of His hands, He shall destroy them" (Psalm 28:5).

*   *

"The truly existent One planted the tree of *life* by His lucid *understanding*" (Philo, *Q.Gen.* I.55).

MAN AND UNDERSTANDING

Babes and children are too young to understand.

"As babes without understanding [APHRONŌN]" (Wisdom 12:24).

"As to children without the use of reason" (Wisdom 12:25).

"Be not children in your understanding but in malice be babes, and in understanding be fully mature" (1 Corinthians 14:20).

"Have . . . the understanding of a man" (Proverbs 30:2).

"Those who did receive their share of knowledge and understanding became complete men" (Corpus Hermeticum, Book IV.4).

Understanding is the prerogative of Man.

"Understanding . . . is Mankind's peculiar property" (Philo, *Prob.* 12).

"Understanding is found in Man alone" (Sepher Ha-Tappuach).

"The understanding in each of us is in the true and full sense: the Man" (Philo, *Her.* 231).

"The understanding may be truly called the man within the man" (Philo, *Cong.* 97).

"Man, is the understanding within us" (Philo, *Q.Gen.* I.94).

"The understanding in us, call it: 'Man'" (Philo, *Cher.* 57).

"When God formed the first Understanding, He called it: 'Man'" (Philo, *Q.Gen.* I.53).

"Man is a symbol of understanding" (Philo, *Q.Gen.* I.25).

"Man: that is understanding" (Philo, *L.A.* I.92).

"Man: is the reasoning faculty in each of us" (Philo, *Agr.* 108).

"He set the understanding which is the real man in us" (Philo, *Plant.* 42).

"That which is, one might say, naturally male in us is the understanding" (Philo, *Q.Gen.* III.46).

"Man . . . his understanding, like his body, is masculine, capable of dissolving or destroying the designs of deceit" (Philo, *Q.Gen.* I.33).

"The understanding . . . holding to its own nature of true manhood has the strength to be victor" (Philo, *Her.* 274).

317

"If you have *understanding,* answer your neighbor" (Sirach 5:12, Greek Text).

"If you have *manhood* [ISH] with you, answer your neighbor" (ibid., Hebrew Text).

"There is no wisdom, nor *understanding,* nor counsel against the Lord" (Proverbs 21:30, Hebrew Text).

"There is no wisdom, nor *manliness* [ANDREIA] nor counsel. . . ." (ibid., Greek Text).

"Hear me, you *men* of heart" (Job 34:10, Hebrew Text, Literal Translation).

"Hear me, you who are *understanding* [SUNETOI] in heart" (ibid., Greek Text).

"Joshua . . . girded his loins with the girdle of understanding" (Ps. Philo, *Biblical Antiquities,* XX.3).

"Gird up the loins of your understanding [DIANOIA]" (1 Peter 1:13).

"According to his understanding [SEKEL] . . . he shall strengthen his loins" (1QSᵃ 1:17 [The Rule Annexé], Dead Sea Scrolls).

"Be strong and act manfully that you may be understanding [SUNĒS] in all that you do" (Joshua 1:7, Greek Text).

"Stand fast in the faith and show yourselves men [i.e., understand]" (1 Corinthians 16:13).

Because "through faith we understand" (Hebrews 11:3).

"All the works of the Lord are good . . . no one can say this is good or that is evil, for all show themselves men [i.e., they will be understood] in their time" (Sirach 39:16,17, Syriac Text).

"What do you know that we do not know? What do you understand that is not in us? [as men they claim to have "understanding *in* them" (Deuteronomy 32:28)]" (Job 15:9).

"The understanding that is *in* man" (Clement of Alexandria, *Exh.* X.98.4).

It is the prerogative of real men to have understanding: "Sung by all who are men [ANDRES] with no blindness of the understanding but with the keenest vision [of true men who understand]" (Philo, *Agr.* 81).

In contradistinction, the effeminate "men of Sodom" were "blind in understanding" (Philo, *Fug.* 144).

"The Sodomites . . . were barren of wisdom and blind in the understanding" (Philo, *Conf.* 27).

"We contribute to lack of understanding [APHROSUNĒ] by slackness, indolence, luxury, effeminacy, and by complete irregularity of life" (Philo, *Ebr.* 20,21).

"O my Understanding, never show weakness or slacken" (Philo, *Mig.* 222).

"Be firm [ESTĒRIGMENOS] in your understanding" (Sirach 5:10).

"Possess a piercing [OXUN = "piercing," "quick"] understanding [NOUN]" (Letter of Aristeas v. 276).

"And penetrating understanding" (Midrash Haneelam, Bereshith 17).

"Come to Wisdom with all your understanding" (Sirach 6:26, Syriac Text).

"Draw near to Wisdom . . . and when you draw close to her do it as a hero and a mighty one [with your understanding]" (Sirach 1:22, Greek Sinaiticus Text).

"I . . . pierced her [Wisdom's] unseen parts" (11QPsª Sirach Col. XXI. Line 17, Dead Sea Scrolls).

"I had my understanding joined with her [Wisdom] from the very beginning" (Sirach 51:20, Greek Text).

"Every man of understanding knows Wisdom" (Sirach 18:28).

In the book of Wisdom [3:14], the righteous eunuch is promised the gift of understanding which comes with faith: "to him [the righteous eunuch] shall be given faith's particular gift" [see "Belief and Understanding"]. Having been granted the power of understanding through his faith, the righteous eunuch shall no longer lament the weakness and sterility of his physical "root" because he now possesses "the root of understanding [PHRONĒSEŌS]" which "does not fail" (Wisdom 3:15; see also Isaiah 56:3-5).

"To become a eunuch would be a very good thing if so our soul would be able to escape wickedness and unclean passion" (Philo, *L.A.* III.237).

"Understanding is contrary to the flesh" (Corpus Hermeticum, *Libellus* X.10).

"The understanding becomes pure when it is not darkened by any object of sense" (Philo, *Som.* I.84).

"There are eunuchs [spiritual] who have made themselves eunuchs for the sake of the Kingdom of Heaven [i.e., to have understanding and knowledge in the "Mysteries of the Kingdom of Heaven"; see "Purity, Chastity, Celibacy and Understanding"]" (St. Matthew 19:12).

"The term 'eunuchs' are the companions who study the Torah and who abstain from sexual intercourse (literally "castrate themselves" [figuratively speaking]) during the six weeks that they labor at the Torah" (Zohar II.89a-89b).

*   *

"That which is excellent of the spirit of man is understanding" (Proverbs 17:27, Literal Translation).

"Beasts . . . understand nothing" (Book of Adam and Eve 18:1).

"Man . . . who does not understand is like the beasts that perish" (Psalm 49:20).

"A stupid man will get understanding, when a wild ass's colt is born a man" (Job 11:12, RSV).

Having "a man's understanding" (Midrash Rabbah to Numbers 14:4).

*   *

"Give thy daughter in marriage . . . to a mighty man [GEBER] of understanding" (Sirach 7:25, Hebrew Text).

For the Scriptural term: "a man of understanding," see Proverbs 10:23; 11:12; 12:8; 15:21; 17:27; 20:5; Ezra 8:18; Sirach 6:36; 7:25; 18:28; 19:2; 26:28; 27:12; 33:3 (Greek Text); ibid. 7:25; 33:3 (Hebrew Text); 2 Maccabees 11:13.

*   *

"I made a covenant with my eyes; why then should I understand [BIN] upon a virgin?" (Job 31:1).

"Be ashamed . . . to thoroughly understand [KATANOĒSEŌS] upon another man's wife" (Sirach 41:17,21).

"Do not understand [BIN] upon a virgin" (Sirach 9:5, Hebrew Text).

N.B   In the vivid imagery of the Holy Scriptures and other ancient writings, understanding is given masculine connotations not to delimit understanding exclusively to the male sex, but because what is desired to be understood and known is the beautiful and feminine Wisdom of God. [see W/V:1-34; W/K:1-5; and "Wife, Women, and Understanding."]

320

NEW THINGS AND UNDERSTANDING

"They shall recount Your glory in all Your dominion. For You have caused them to understand [SAKAL] what they had not known, by bringing to an end the former things and by creating things that are new" (1QH 13:11-12, Dead Sea Scrolls).

"Understand the new things [BERIAH pl.] of the Most High and meditate continually on His commandments, and He will make your heart to understand and make you wise in that which you desire" (Sirach 6:36, Hebrew Text).

"New things do I declare before they spring forth, I shall cause you to *hear* [and understand] them" (Isaiah 42:9; see "Hearing and Understanding").

"O Lord . . . give us the seed of a *new* heart and cultivation of our understanding so that there may come fruit from it whereby every-one shall live" (2 Esdras 8:6, Syriac Text).

"Be renewed in the spirit of your understanding" (Ephesians 4:23).

"The just will understand the knowledge of the Most High, and the perfect of way will have understanding of the wisdom of the sons of Heaven . . . in the final end, the time of renewal" (1QS 4:22,25; see "The Coming Age of Understanding").

"Be transformed by the renewing of your understanding" (Romans 12:2).

"In the time of the "new heavens" and the "new earth" (Isaiah 65:17; 66:22; Revelation 21:1) our understanding shall also be renewed.

New things cause us to know.

"Behold, I will do a new thing; now it shall spring forth, shall you not know it?" (Isaiah 43:19).

"If the Lord creates a new thing . . . then you shall know" (Numbers 16:30).

"The Lord will do a new thing on the earth . . . and make known to you" (Enoch 106:13).

"Enlightening with new knowledge all the Gentiles with the light of knowledge" (Testament of Benjamin 11:2 [B, S¹ Texts).

Thus, in Isaiah 48:6-8 the Lord remonstrates against His people that although He has shown them new things, they have not received knowledge from them because of their treachery and transgressions.

"I have shown you new things from this time forth, even hidden things, and you did not know them . . . yes, you did not hear [and understand], and you did not know . . . because I knew that you would deal treacherously, and from the womb you were called a transgressor" (Isaiah 48:6,8).

PARABLES, PROVERBS, AND UNDERSTANDING

"The parables of understanding [EPISTĒMĒS] are in the treasures of wisdom" (Sirach 1:24).

"My heart knew much wisdom and knowledge [GNŌSIN], parables and understanding [EPISTĒMĒN]" (Ecclesiastes 1:17, Greek Text).

"The proverbs of Solomon . . . to receive [from them] the instruction of understanding [SAKAL]" (Proverbs 1:1,3; see also 2 Chronicles 30:22 and Sirach 50:27, Hebrew Text).

"Hear me [my son] and *receive my proverbs*" (Sirach 16:24, Hebrew Text; see also Syriac Text).

"Hear me, my son, and *learn understanding* [EPISTĒMĒN]" (ibid., Greek Text).

"Let not the proverbs of understanding [SUNESEOS] escape you" (Sirach 6:35).

"Solomon . . . how wise you were in your youth! You overflowed like a river with understanding. Your soul covered the whole earth, and you filled it with enigmatic parables . . . for your songs and proverbs and parables, and for your interpretations the countries marvelled at you" (Sirach 47:13,14,17).

"They who had understanding in sayings became also wise themselves and poured forth fitting proverbs" (Sirach 18:29).

"The finding out of parables is a wearisome labor of the mind" (Sirach 13:26).

They who are not wise and understanding "shall not be found where parables are spoken" (Sirach 38:33).

"The parables of the wise they will not understand" (Sirach 38:33, Syriac Text).

On the other hand "he who devotes himself to the study of the Law of the Most High will seek out the wisdom of all the ancients . . . and penetrate the subtleties of parables; he will seek out the hidden meaning of proverbs and be at home with the enigmas of parables" (Sirach 39:1,2,3).

For "whoever occupies himself with the Law . . . to him are revealed the secrets of the Law [and the parables and proverbs found within it]" (Kallah Rabbathi 54a).

"Pay attention to know understanding [BINAH]" (Proverbs 4:1).

"Give ear to know [GNŌSIN] understanding [PHRONĒSIN]" (Baruch 3:9).

"Incline your ear to my great understanding [TEBUNAH]" (Proverbs 5:1).

"I gave ear to your great understandings [TEBUNAH pl.]" (Job 32:11).

Therefore "I will incline my ear to a parable" (Psalm 49:4) because only by paying close attention shall we discover the hidden wisdom, understanding, and knowledge found within the parables of those who understand.

Truly, "a parable shall be found in the lips of the understanding [SUNETOU]" (Sirach 21:16, Greek Sinaiticus Text).

*   *

"He [Jesus] taught them many things in parables" (St. Mark 4:2).

"With many such parables He [Jesus] was speaking the word to them as they were able to hear [and understand] it; and He did not speak to them without a parable, but privately He explained everything to His own disciples" (St. Mark 4:33-34).

"Then the disciples came and said to Him, 'why do You speak to them in parables?' And He answered and said to them, 'to you it has been given to know the mysteries of the Kingdom of heaven, but to them it has not been given . . . that is why I speak to them in parables'" (St. Matthew 13:10-11,13).

"All this Jesus said to the crowds in parables, and He did not speak to them without a parable. This was to fulfill what was spoken by the prophets: 'I will open my mouth in parables, I will utter what has been hidden since the foundation of the world'" (St. Matthew 13:34-35).

"Jesus Christ . . . is the understanding of the Father" (St. Ignatius, *Epistle to the Ephesians* 3:2).

"The Son [Jesus Christ] is the understanding [NOUS], Word and Wisdom of the Father" (Athenagoras, *Emb.* XXIV).

Jesus "Christ, the Power [see "The Power and Strength of Understanding"] of God and the Wisdom of God" (1 Corinthians 1:24).

"Christ, in whom are hidden all the treasures of wisdom and knowledge" (Colossians 2:2,3).

*   *

Conversely

"Like a lame man's legs, which hang useless, is a parable in the mouth of fools" (Proverbs 26:7).

"Like a thorn that goes up into the hand of a drunkard is a proverb in the mouth of fools" (Proverbs 26:9).

"Excellent speech is not fitting for a fool" (Proverbs 17:7).

"Weep for the fool, for he lacks understanding" (Sirach 22:11).

*　　*

THE PAST [WHAT IS BEHIND US] AND UNDERSTANDING

"Remember the days of old, understand [BIN] the years of many [past] generations" (Deuteronomy 32:7).

"Do not despise the traditions of the aged which they have heard from their fathers because from them [the past traditions of the aged] you will obtain understanding" (Sirach 8:9, Hebrew Text).

"Where were you when I laid the foundations [in past times] of the earth? declare if you know understanding" (Job 38:4).

"Have you not understood [BIN] from the foundations of the earth?" (Isaiah 40:21).

"Remember not the former things, neither understand [BIN] the [past] things of old" (Isaiah 43:18).

"They [the wicked] have not known the Mystery to come [future] and have not understood past things" (1QMyst. 1:3 [Book of Mysteries], Dead Sea Scrolls).

"Lo, He goes ['ABAR] by me [alongside], and I do not see [and know], He passes on [CHALAPH] also, and I do not understand [BIN] Him" (Job 9:11).

"Behold, I go forward but He is not there and backward [in the past], but I cannot understand [BIN] Him" (Job 23:8).

*　　*

"The gods partake of thy beauty, their hearts revive when they see Sia [god of understanding] following thee [i.e., behind thee] and Hu [god of utterance] in front of thee" (Egyptian Ritual of Amenophis I, Chester Beatty Papyrus IX.9, *Hieratic Papyri in the British Museum,* Vol. III Pl.54+p.92 [Ed. A. H. Gardiner, London, 1935].

PATIENCE AND UNDERSTANDING

"He who is slow to anger is of great understanding [TEBUNAH], but he who is quick-tempered exalts folly" (Proverbs 14:29).

"A quick-tempered man acts ill-advisedly, but a man of understanding endures many things" (Proverbs 14:17, Greek Text).

"He who is void of understanding despises his neighbor, but a man of great understanding [TEBUNAH] holds his peace" (Proverbs 11:12).

"The temperate understanding repels all these malignant passions ["violence, love of power, empty boasting, arrogance, loudness, and slander," v.15] as it also repels anger: for it masters even this" (4 Maccabees 2:16).

"The temperate understanding is able to be superior to the passions" (ibid. 2:18).

"Beware, that you be not greatly enraged and be like those who are wanting in understanding" (Sirach 13:8, Hebrew Text).

"My son, if fierce anger seizes you, do not say a word lest you be called one without understanding" (Story of Ahikar, 2:.26, Slavonic Text; ibid., 2:48, Armenian Text).

"He who forbears to utter a hard word has full knowledge [EPIGNŌMŌN], and a patient man is understanding [PHRONIMOS]" (Proverbs 17:27, Greek Text).

"Be patient and of good understanding" (Shepherd of Hermas, *Mand.* V.1.33:1).

Have "a spirit of humility and slowness to anger, and great compassion and eternal goodness, and understanding [SEKEL], and insight [BINAH], and mighty wisdom" (1QS 4:3,4, Dead Sea Scrolls).

"The understanding [SEKEL] of a man defers his anger, and it is his glory to pass over a transgression" (Proverbs 19:11).

"A patient man will bear for a time, and afterwards joy shall spring up to him. He will hide his words for a time and the lips of many shall declare his understanding" (Sirach 1:23-24).

"He who knows knowledge spares his choice words [EMER pl.] and a man of understanding is of a cool spirit" (Proverbs 17:27).

"He who restrains his lips is understanding [SAKAL]" (Proverbs 10:19).

"He who restrains his tongue shall be filled with understanding" (Proverbs 15:4, Greek Text).

"Even a fool, when he keeps his peace, is considered wise, and he who restrains his lips is esteemed a man of understanding [BIN]" (Proverbs 17:28).

"Someone keeps silence and he is understanding [PHRONIMOS]" (Sirach 20:1).

"The understanding [SAKAL] shall keep silence in that time, for it is an evil time" (Amos 5:13).

"An understanding [PHRONIMOS] servant calms a man's anger" (Proverbs 18:14, Greek Text).

Patiently accepting reproof gives Understanding.

"He who listens to a reproof gets understanding" (Proverbs 15:32).

"A reproof goes deeper into a man of understanding [BIN] than a hundred blows to a fool" (Proverbs 17:10).

"Reprove one who has understanding [BIN], and he will understand knowledge" (Proverbs 19:25).

*   *

"Jesus held His peace" (St. Matthew 26:63).

"He [Jesus] was silent and made no answer" (St. Mark 14:61).

"When He was accused by the chief priests and elders, He made no answer" (St. Matthew 27:12).

"He gave them no answer, not even to a single charge, so that the governor wondered greatly" (St. Matthew 27:14).

"All who heard Him were astonished at His understanding" (St. Luke 2:47).

"Christ, in whom are hidden all the treasures of wisdom and knowledge" (Colossians 2:2,3).

"We know that the Son of God has come, and has given us understanding" (1 John 5:20; see also St. Matthew 15:10; St. Mark 7:14; St. Luke 24:45).

*   *

"The Lord is slow to anger, and great in power [see "The Power and Strength of Understanding"]" (Nahum 1:3).

"For a long time I have held My peace, I have been silent and restrained Myself; now like a woman in labor I will cry out, I will gasp and pant. I will lay waste the mountains and hills, and dry up all their vegetation. I will turn the rivers into islands, and dry up the pools. And I will lead the blind by a way they do not know, in paths they have not known I will guide them. I will turn the darkness before them into light, and crooked things straight. These things I will do and not leave them undone" (Isaiah 42:14-16).

Note: Slowness to anger and holding one's peace give us "great understanding" [TEBUNAH, see Proverbs 14:29; 11:12, etc.]. God "by His understanding He smites the proud" (Job 26:12) and removes all obstacles, making straight what is crooked and enlightening those in the darkness as well.

*   *

"Be patient and of good understanding . . . for the Lord dwells in patience but the devil in anger" (Shepherd of Hermas, *Mand.* V.1.33:1,3).

Conversely

"A man of impatient spirit is very much without understanding [A-PHRŌN]" (Proverbs 14:29, Greek Text).

"Anger . . . leads the mind to frenzy and does not allow understanding to work in men" (Testament of Simeon 4:8).

"A man of violence does not receive understanding" (Sirach 32:18, Hebrew Text MS. E).

"The spirit of anger . . . blinds his eyes, and . . . darkens his understanding" (Testament of Dan 2:4).

"There is blindness in anger . . . no angry man sees the face [see "Face and Understanding"] in [EN] Truth" (Testament of Dan 2:2, B, A, and S Texts).

"Readiness to anger banishes understanding, the long suffering man procures it" (Evagrius Ponticus [A.D. 370]).

"Bad temper is first of all foolish, impetuous and without understanding [A-PHRŌN]" (Shepherd of Hermas, *Mand.* V.2.34:4).

The angry man: "vacillates in everything he does, being pulled here and there by the evil spirits, and totally blinded from a good understanding [DIANOIA]" (Shepherd of Hermas, *Mand.* V.2.34:7).

"The spirit of hatred darkened my understanding" (Testament of Gad 6:2).

"Who cannot control his temper is lacking in understanding" (Ibn Gabirol, *Mibhar Ha-Peninim* ["The Choice of Pearls"]).

329

UNDERSTANDING AND PEACE

"The understanding of the Spirit is life and peace" (Romans 8:6, Literal Translation).

"Learn where understanding [PHRONĒSIS] is . . . so that you may also know where is length of days, and life, and where is light of the eyes and peace" (Baruch 3:14).

"Be of one understanding [AUTO PHRONEITE], be at peace" (2 Corinthians 13:11).

"After him [David], rose up a son [Solomon], a man of understanding [EPISTĒ-MŌN] . . . and to him God gave peace" (Sirach 47:12,13).

"The Lord gave Solomon wisdom [and understanding; see 1 Kings 3:12; 4:29] . . . and there was peace" (1 Kings 5:11).

"It is great understanding [TEBUNAH] to do His good pleasure" (Sirach 15:15, Hebrew Text) [i.e., those who please the Lord receive the gift of great understanding; see also Psalm 111:10; Ecclesiastes 2:26, etc.]

"When a man's ways please the Lord, He makes even his enemies to be at peace with him" (Proverbs 16:7).

"If, therefore, you also have good understanding, then will both wicked men be at peace with you, and the profligate will reverence you" (Testament of Benjamin 5:1).

"You will keep him in perfect peace, whose mind is stayed on You, because he trusts in You" (Isaiah 26:3).

For "they who put their trust in Him shall understand Truth" (Wisdom 3:9).

"I will reveal to them the abundance of peace and Truth" (Jeremiah 33:6).

"When all your children shall be taught by the Lord [they shall understand and] abundant shall be the peace [SHALOM] of your children" (Isaiah 54:13).

"Through that stability and peace of understanding" (Philo, *Conf.* 132).

"Through the Messiah's teaching [which gives understanding], peace shall be increased upon us" (Targum on Isaiah 53:5; see St. Luke 19:42).

"Through faith we understand" (Hebrews 11:3).

"May the God of hope fill you with all joy and peace in believing" (Romans 15:13).

"O how I love Your Law! It is my meditation all the day" [see "Pondering, Meditating and Understanding"] (Psalm 119:97).

"Great peace have they who love Your Law" (Psalm 119:165).

"In those days the children shall begin to study the laws and to seek the commandments, and to return to the paths of righteousness [see "Righteousness and Understanding"] . . . and all their days they shall live in peace and joy" (Jubilees 23:26,29).

"God be gracious to you . . . and open your hearts [i.e., give understanding] in His Law and commandments, and send you peace" (2 Maccabees 1:2,4).

"The peace of God, which surpasses all understanding" (Philippians 4:7).

"For He is our peace" (Ephesians 2:14).

"Peace, and joy in the Holy Spirit" : "the Spirit of understanding" (Romans 14:17; Sirach 39:6; Testament of Levi 2:3; 18:7; Testament of Judah 20:2; Psalms of Solomon 17:42; Isaiah 11:2; Nehemiah 9:20).

"From peace, joy fills the understanding" (St. Isaac of Syria [Nineveh c. A.D. 560], *Mystic Treatise* c.45).

Conversely

"None of the wicked shall understand" (Daniel 12:10).

"Evil men do not understand" (Proverbs 28:5).

"The wicked do not understand" (Proverbs 29:7).

"The wicked . . . do not know, neither will they understand, they walk about in darkness" (Psalm 82:4,5).

Therefore, "'there is no peace for the wicked' says the Lord" (Isaiah 48:22; 57:21; 59:7-8).

"Their hearts failed, and their minds [DIANOIAI] melted [i.e., they were terror-stricken], and there was no understanding [PHRONĒSIS] in them" (Joshua 5:1, Greek Text).

"All the life of the ungodly is spent in anxiety" (Job 15:20, Greek Text).

PHYSICIANS AND UNDERSTANDING

"The understanding [EPISTĒMĒ] of the physician shall lift up his head, and in the sight of great men he shall be held in admiration" (Sirach 38:3; see "Understanding Establishes and Exalts, and is Exalted in those who Understand").

PLACE OF UNDERSTANDING

"Where shall Wisdom be found? And where is the place of Understanding?" (Job 28:12).

"Where then does Wisdom come from? And where is the place of Understanding?" (Job 28:20).

"Learn where Understanding [PHRONĒSIS] is . . . who has found out her place?" (Baruch 3:14,15).

"Young men have seen the light, and dwelt upon the earth, but the way of understanding they have not known, nor understood the paths thereof, nor laid hold of it" (Baruch 3:20,21, Literal Translation).

"Where is the place of Understanding [BINAH]? . . . God understands the way thereof, and He knows the place thereof [of Understanding]" (Job 28:20,23).

N.B. Understanding is *in* us if we are good, [see sections on "Heart," "Man," "Faithfulness," the "Righteous," and "Understanding"].

PONDERING, MEDITATING AND UNDERSTANDING

"Is not the ponderer of hearts He who understands [BIN]?" (Proverbs 24:12).

"Who has *pondered* the Spirit of the Lord?" (Isaiah 40:13, Hebrew Text).

"Who has *known* the understanding of the Lord?" (ibid., Greek Text).

"They did not understand the saying which He spoke to them . . . but His mother kept all these sayings in her heart" (St. Luke 2:50,51).

"Mary kept all these things and pondered them in her heart" (St. Luke 2:19).

"To ponder upon Wisdom is perfect understanding" (Wisdom 6:15).

"O how I love Your Law! it is my meditation all the day" (Psalm 119:97).

"The book of the Law shall not depart from your mouth, but you shall meditate on it day and night . . . then you shall have good understanding [SAKAL]" (Joshua 1:8).

"If your sons had been occupied in the meditation of the Law of the Lord, their understanding would not have been led astray" (Ps. Philo, *Biblical Antiquities* XXII.5).

"I have more understanding [SAKAL] than all my teachers, for Your testimonies are my meditation" (Psalm 119:99).

"Happy is the man who meditates on Wisdom and reasons holy things by his understanding" (Sirach 14:20, Greek Sinaiticus Text and Cursives 248,23,253).

"He who meditates Wisdom's ways in his heart shall also have understanding in her secrets" (Sirach 14:21).

"My mouth shall speak of Wisdom; and the meditation of my heart [shall speak] of great Understanding [TEBUNAH]" (Psalm 49:3).

"Give ear to my choice words [EMER], O Lord, understand [BIN] my meditation" (Psalm 5:1).

"They will inquire at the mouth of one who understands [PHRONIMOU] in the congregation, and they will ponder his words in their heart" (Sirach 21:17).

"The words of those who are understanding [PHRONIMŌN] are weighed in the balance [i.e., they are pondered]" (Sirach 21:25).

But "the [seeming] knowledge of those without understanding [ASUNETOU] are as words without sense" (Sirach 21:18).

"Make a balance and a weight for your words [i.e., understand first, and weigh your words well before you speak]" (Sirach 28:25).

"I will show forth instruction by weight [i.c., I will teach with words that shall be weighed* by those who understand], and [I shall] declare His understanding [EPISTĒMĒN] accurately" (Sirach 16:25 Greek Cursives 248, 106 and Alexandrinus Text)

   *"weighed": the Hebrew word for "to ponder" and "to weigh" is the same word: TAKAN.

UNDERSTANDING GIVES POWER
THE POWER AND STRENGTH OF UNDERSTANDING

"God is mighty . . . He is mighty in the power [KOACH] of understanding" (Job 36:5).

"He is wise in understanding, and great in power" (Job 9:4, Greek Text).

"Great is our Lord, and of great power: His great understanding [TEBUNAH] is infinite" (Psalm 147:5).

"Great power and understanding [SUNESIS] in the vision was given to him" (Daniel 10:1, Greek Text).

"Why is the power of understanding given to me?" (2 Esdras 4:22).

"Have you gained power for yourself by your insight and understanding?" (Ezekiel 28:4, Greek Text).

"By your abundant understanding [EPISTĒMĒ] . . . you have multiplied your power" (Ezekiel 28:5, Greek Text).

"Understanding has mighty power" (Corpus Hermeticum, *Libellus* IX. 10).

"Whoever is with understanding [PHRONĒSEI] is wholly lordly and independent and masterful" (Philo, *Q.Gen.* III.22, Greek Fragment).

"May the name of God be blessed from everlasting to everlasting, for wisdom and *understanding* are His" (Daniel 2:20, Greek Text).

Blessed be the name of God forever and ever, for wisdom and *power* are His" (Daniel 2:20, Hebrew Text).

"By His *great understanding* [TEBUNAH] He has stretched out the heavens" (Jeremiah 10:12; 51:15; see also Proverbs 3:19).

"By My *power* I have stretched out the heavens" (Targum on Isaiah 48:13; see also Targum [Sheni] to Esther c.13).

"In much *understanding* the Lord has divided them" (Sirach 33:11).

"You have divided these things in the Mysteries of Your *understanding* [SAKAL]" (1QH 13:13, Dead Sea Scrolls).

"By His *power* dividing holy things among them from the profane" (Sirach 18:3, Greek Cursive 248).

"The Lord . . . by [His] *great understanding* [TEBUNAH] He has established the heavens" (Proverbs 3:19).

"By His transcendent *power* He established the heavens" (First Clement, *Epistle to the Corinthians* 33:3).

"The God of powers who by His invisible and *mighty power* . . . and with the Word of His strength established the heavens" (Shepherd of Hermas, *Vision* I.3.3:4).

"I will give you shepherds after My own heart, who will feed you with knowledge and *understanding*" (Jeremiah 3:15).

"The Lord . . . shall feed His flock with *power*" (Micah 5:4, Greek Text).

"All [angelic] beings powerful in understanding" (4QSl 39.I.21 [Angelic Liturgy], Dead Sea Scrolls).

"The understanding in all its powers" (Philo, *Mut.* 34).

"The understanding [SUNESEI] of the powerful [DUNASTŌN]" (Sirach 10:3).

"You alone are . . . powerful [DUNATOS] in understanding [EPISTĒMĒ]" (Judith 11:8).

"The Holy Great One . . . has created and given to man the power of understanding" (Enoch 14:2,3).

"Endowed in the understanding, the divinest part of us, with power [DUNAMEI] such as athletes possess" (Philo, *Det.* 29).

"By the power [KOACH] of my hand I have done it . . . for I am understanding [BIN]" (Isaiah 10:13).

"Understanding [as power] has been granted to you over all the spirits of the air" (Testament of Solomon 22:1 [117]).

For "understanding has mighty power" (Corpus Hermeticum, *Libellus* IX.10).

"To whom has He given *power* to declare His works?" (Sirach 18:4, Greek Cursives 248,106).

"To declare His works with *understanding*" (Sirach 17:9, Greek Cursives 248,106,254,55).

For "He has given men *understanding* so that He might be honored in His marvelous works" (Sirach 38:6, Greek and Hebrew Texts).

"Glorifying Him where can we get *power* [i.e., understanding] sufficient for our task?" (Sirach 43:28).

"I am full of power [i.e., understanding] by the Spirit of the Lord" (Micah 3:8).

"The Spirit of understanding and of power" (Enoch 49:3).

"Seek not the things that are too hard for you, nor search the things that are beyond your power [to understand]" (Sirach 3:21, Greek Text).

"O Lord, my Lord, who is able to know such things? . . ." (2 Esdras 5:38).

"As for me I am unwise and powerless [to understand]" (2 Esdras 5:39, Syriac Text).

"I have no power [A-DUNATA] to understand [NOĒSAI]" (Proverbs 30:18, Greek Text).

"If he does them [the counsels and commandments], he shall be powerful [i.e., understanding] in all things" (Sirach 50:29).

Because "a good understanding have all those who do His commandments" (Psalm 111:10; see also Deuteronomy 4:6 [see "Faithfulness and Understanding"]).

"Bless the Lord, all you His angels, who are mighty in power [i.e., understanding], who do His commandments" (Psalm 103:20).

"All [angelic] beings powerful in understanding [SEKEL]" (4QSl 39.I.21 [Angelic Liturgy], Dead Sea Scrolls).

"An angel is an intellectual soul wholly understanding" (Philo, *Q.Exod.* II.13).

"Man . . . his flesh is from the earth . . . his understanding is from the swiftness of angels" (2 Enoch 30:8).

"Gabriel ["Powerful is God"], make this man [Daniel] to understand [BIN] the vision" (Daniel 8:16).

"To give to the simple understanding [BIN] into the power of Your strength [i.e., the Lord's understanding] . . . and to give man understanding into the Mystery" (1QH Fragment 15:4,5, Dead Sea Scrolls).

"Give us, Lord, wisdom and power of understanding" (Canon of the Ancient Liturgy of the Abyssinian Jacobites).

"Put power [i.e., understanding] into me that so having obtained this gift, I may enlighten those of my race who are in ignorance, my brothers" (Corpus Hermeticum, *Libellus* I.32).

"Eloquent . . . and powerful [i.e., understanding] in the Scriptures . . . he mightily convinced the Jews in public, showing by the Scriptures that the Christ was Jesus" (Acts 18:24,28; see also St. John 5:39; St. Luke 24:27,32,45-49; see also Acts 9:22).

"I do not know these parables, nor do I have the power to understand them" (Shepherd of Hermas, *Sim.* V.3.56:1).

"Unless a man by God's great grace receives the power to understand" (Justin Martyr, *Dial.* 92.1).

"The ram will I liken to wise men [who understand], which shall be born of you and shall enlighten your sons" (Ps. Philo, *Biblical Antiquities* XXIII.7).

"As long as the disciples are small [i.e., "of small power" to understand] cover up for them the words of the Torah [i.e., hide from them the secret meaning of the words] but when they are grown up and have become powerful as rams [i.e., when they have the power of understanding] then lay open to them the secrets of the Torah" (Rabbi Simeon ben Halafta in the name of Rabbi Samuel ben Nahman [see Abodah Zarah II.41c, JT; Ḥagigah 13a, BT; Yalkut to Proverbs 961; Dikduke Soferim re Proverbs 27:26.]).

"You have manifested Your power [i.e., understanding] unto me in Your marvelous counsel" (1QH 4:28, Dead Sea Scrolls).

"Your counsel of understanding" (Sirach 6:24, Latin Vulgate; see "Understanding and Counselling").

"Men renowned for their power [i.e., understanding] giving counsel by their understanding" (Sirach 44:3).

"Learn where understanding [PHRONĒSIS] is, where is strength" (Baruch 3:14).

"I am Understanding [BINAH], I have strength" (Proverbs 8:14).

"Shall mighty man [GEBER] born of mighty man [GEBER] have understanding [SAKAL]?" (1QH 9:15,16, Dead Sea Scrolls).

"A mighty man [GIBBOR] of understanding [SAKAL]" (Jeremiah 50:9).

"Understand mightily [ME'OD]" (Jeremiah 2:10).

"Give your daughter . . . to a mighty man [GEBER] of understanding" (Sirach 7:25, Hebrew Text).

In the book of Enoch, the Elect One "is mighty [i.e., understanding] in all the secrets of righteousness" because "in Him dwells the spirit of wisdom, and the spirit which gives insight and the spirit of understanding and power" (Enoch 49:2,3)

With the power of his understanding the Elect One "reveals all the treasures of that which is hidden" (Enoch 46:3).

He "had power to explain to others what he understood" (J. Stobaeus' *Hermetica, Exc. XXIII.5*).

"Gates of *understanding*" = "Gates of *strength*" (3 Enoch 1:11; 8:1).

"The *understanding* . . . has the *strength* to be victor" (Philo, *Her.* 274).

"The *Almighty* . . . will He not *understand* [BIN]?" (Job 11:7,11).

"It is the *understanding* of the *Almighty* that you are tempting and no one shall know it ever" (Judith 8:13, Greek Codex 58 and Old Latin and Syriac Texts).

"The *understanding* possessed by Bezaleel was from the *Almighty*" (Exodus Rabbah 48.4).

"The Lord, the Creator of the ends of the earth does not faint, nor does He get weary [because He is *Almighty: All Strong*] there is no searching of His *understanding*" (Isaiah 40:28; see also Job 37:23).

"The *Mighty One* His ways are past finding out" (2 Baruch 44:6).

"The *Almighty* Lord . . . He searches out the deep and the heart, and He has *understanding* of their devices" (Sirach 42:17,18, Greek Sinaiticus and Alexandrinus Texts).

"The breath of the *Almighty* gives them *understanding*" (Job 32:8).

"To them alone the *Mighty God* has given discreet counsel and faith and an excellent *understanding* in their hearts" (Sibylline Oracles III.584-85).

"*Mighty One* . . . You instruct created things in the *understanding* of You" (2 Baruch 48:1,9).

"The *Most Mighty* formed us" (Ps. Philo, *Biblical Antiquities* XVI.5; see "The Forming of Understanding").

"Shall the thing formed by Him say: 'He has no *understanding*'?" (Isaiah 29:16).

"The *Most Mighty* . . . He took His *power* [i.e., understanding] away from you" (Ps. Philo, *Biblical Antiquities* XX.4).

Since it is the Holy Spirit who gives us understanding [see "The Spirit and Understanding"], the gift of the Holy Spirit is also referred to as "Power": "I am full of power [i.e., understanding] by the Spirit of the Lord" (Micah 3:8; St. Luke 24:49; Acts 1:5,8; 10:38; Romans 15:19; 1 Corinthians 2:4; 1 Thessalonians 1:5).

"The Kingdom of God is not eating and drinking, but righteousness and peace and joy in the *Holy Spirit*" (Romans 14:17; see "The Delights and Joys of Understanding").

"The Kingdom of God does not consist in words but in *power*" (1 Corinthians 4:20).

"All who heard Him were amazed at His understanding and His answers" (St. Luke 2:47).

"They were amazed at His teaching, for His word was with power" (St. Luke 4:32).

"Jesus answered and said to them, 'you are mistaken, because you do not know the Scriptures nor the power [i.e., the understanding] of God'" (St. Matthew 22:29; St. Mark 12:24).

"Why do you not know My speech? Because you have no power [DUNASTHE, i.e., understanding] to hear My word" (St. John 8:43).

"I have yet many things to tell you, but you have no power [DUNASTHE, i.e., understanding] to bear them now" (St. John 16:12).

"The power of understanding" (2 Esdras 4:22; Enoch 14:3; St. Augustine *Commentary on Psalms* 119:66 etc.).

"The power to understand" (Ephesians 3:18; Philo, *Mig.* 55, etc.).

Conversely

"A man weak and shortlived and of small power to understand" (Wisdom 9:5).

"O my Understanding, never show weakness or slacken" (Philo, *Mig.* 222).

"Their understanding has fainted" (Ps. Philo, *Biblical Antiquities* XV.6).

"You lack power [i.e., understanding] because of your softness and doublemind-edness" (Shepherd of Hermas, *Vision* III.11.19:2).

"Your double-mindedness makes you unable to understand" (ibid., *Vision* III.10.18:9).

"I am completely without power [DUNAMAI] to understand" (Shepherd of Hermas, *Similitude* IX.14.91:4).

"We have not the power to understand its true interpretation" (Sifre to Deuteronomy, Sect. 306).

"They cannot gather strength to understand" (1QH Fragment 10:3, Dead Sea Scrolls).

"They have no power [DUNANTAI] to understand this themselves" (Epistle of Jeremy 42).

"I lay down on the ground as one dead, my understanding being collapsed" (2 Esdras 10:30).

"Do not be shaken in your understanding [NOUS]" (2 Thessalonians 2:2).

"Be steadfast in your understanding" (Sirach 5:10).

*   *

Just as "bread . . . strengthens the heart of man" (Psalm 104:15), so does "the bread of understanding" (Sirach 15:3) fortify us.

Let us eat "the bread [LECHEM] of the mighty [ABBIR] ones" (Psalm 78:25) so that we may have "the understanding of the powerful" (Sirach 10:3).

*   *

In the Akkadian language, the word for "understanding" and "strength" was the same word: UZNI. Another Akkadian word: EMER means both "to have understanding" and "to be strong."

Ancient Non-Scriptural Texts on the Power on Understanding.

"O Lord Bel, thou prince, who art mighty in understanding" (Hymn to Marduk No. 10).

"*Powerful* one of wide *understanding*, director of gods and men" (Hymn to Marduk No. 9).

Conversely: "Mot, son of El, lifted up his voice and cried: 'How shall Baal understand? For indeed, Hadad's [i.e., Baal, as god of thunder] strength shall be cut off" (Baal Text I*i,20,21,22).

*   *

"Jesus Christ . . . His role is the Understanding of the Father" (St. Ignatius, *Epistle to the Ephesians* 3:2).

"The Son of God: the Creative Understanding" (Synesius, *Hymn to Christ*).

"Where the Lord Jesus Christ dwells there is much understanding. Cleave to the Lord and you will perceive and understand all things" (Shepherd of Hermas, *Mand.* X.1.40:6).

"Christ . . . the door which we who desire to understand God must discover" (Clement of Alexandria, *Exh.* I.10.2).

"Christ, in whom are hidden all the treasures of wisdom and knowledge" (Colossians 2:2,3).

"The Son [Jesus Christ] is the *Understanding,* Word and Wisdom of the Father" (Athenagoras, *Emb.* c.XXIV, also X).

"Christ, the *Power* [i.e., Understanding] of God and the Wisdom of God" (1 Corinthians 1:24).

UNDERSTANDING AND PRAISE

"He has given men understanding [EPISTĒMĒN] so that He may be honoured [by their praises] in His mighty works" (Sirach 38:6).

"I will give them a heart and they shall understand, and ears, and they shall hear, and they shall praise Me" (Baruch 2:31,32, Latin Vulgate).

"He granted as their portion a heart to understand, and He set His eye upon their hearts to show them the greatness of His works so that they might praise His holy name" (Sirach 17:6-8, Latin Vulgate).

"He filled them with the insight of understanding . . . that they might declare His works with understanding" (Sirach 17:7,9, Greek Text, Cursives 248,254,106,55).

"Sing praises with understanding [SAKAL-SUNETŌS]" (Psalm 47:7, Hebrew and Greek Texts).

"I will sing [praises] with the Spirit, and I will sing with the understanding also" (1 Corinthians 14:15).

"Grant me understanding, O Lord, in Your Law, and teach me Your ordinances so that many may hear of Your deeds and people may honor Your glory" (11QPs^a XXIV.9-10 [Psalm 155:9-10], Dead Sea Scrolls).

"Through Your precepts I get understanding" (Psalm 119:104).

"Make me understand the way of Your precepts, then I shall tell of Your wondrous works" (Psalm 119:27).

"They shall praise the Lord who seek Him" (Psalm 22:26).

For "they who seek the Lord understand all things" (Proverbs 28:5).

"The stars of heaven praise Him with understanding" (Teezala Sanbat ["The Commandments of the Sabbath"] found in the *Falasha Anthology*, p. 25, Trans. by Wolf Leslou, Vol. VI. *Yale Judaica Series*).

"David, the son of Jesse, was wise, and light like the light of the sun, and literate, and understanding [BIN] and perfect in all his ways before God and men. And the Lord gave him an understanding [BINAH] and enlightened spirit. And he wrote three thousand six hundred psalms [of praise]; and songs to sing before the altar" (11QPs^a XXVII.2-5 [Psalm 151:2-5], Dead Sea Scrolls).

"All who could understand [BIN] instruments of music" (2 Chronicles 34:12).

344

"He instructed about the song [of praise] because he was understanding [BIN]" (1 Chronicles 15:22).

"They . . . who were instructed in the songs of the Lord, all they who were understanding [BIN]" (1 Chronicles 25:7).

"Praise [EULOGEITE] God, you who fear the Lord, with understanding [EPIS-TĒMĒ]" (Psalms of Solomon 2:37).

"Sing a new song to God who is worthy to be praised. Sing, raise a cry unto Him with joyful sound, for it is good to sing praise to God with the whole heart [i.e., with the whole understanding]" (Psalms of Solomon 3:2).

"The understanding [PHRONĒSEI] of the righteous" (St. Luke 1:17).

"The understanding of the virtuous" (Philo, *Q.Exod.* II.116).

"A righteous man understands" (Proverbs 21:12).

"Sing for joy in the Lord, O you righteous ones. Praise from the upright is beautiful [because they have understanding]" (Psalm 33:1).

Conversely: "A hymn of praise is not fitting in the mouth of a sinner, for it has not been sent from the Lord. Because a hymn of praise should be uttered in wisdom" (Sirach 15:9,10).

And "Wisdom will not enter a deceitful soul nor dwell in a body enslaved to sin" (Wisdom 1:4).

But "the mouth of the righteous utters wisdom" (Psalm 37:30).

"The mouth of the righteous flourishes with wisdom" : "the wisdom of his righteousness" (Proverbs 10:31; Psalms of Solomon 17:31).

"Without wisdom it is not possible to praise the Creator of all things" (Philo, *Q.Gen.* I.6).

Because "to make known the glory of the Lord is wisdom given, and for recounting His many deeds is wisdom revealed to man" (11QPs[a] XVIII.5-6 [Psalm 154.5,6], Dead Sea Scrolls).

"Declare His works with understanding" (Sirach 17:9, Greek Cursive 106).

"They who put their trust in Him shall understand Truth" (Wisdom 3:9).

"I have put my trust in the Lord God, that I may declare all Your works [with understanding]" (Psalm 73:28).

"Who is the wise man who can understand this? And to whom has the mouth of the Lord spoken, that he may declare it?" (Jeremiah 9:12).

"Out of His mouth comes knowledge and understanding" (Proverbs 2:6).

"Declare it if you know [YADA] understanding" (Job 38:4).

"All men shall fear, and shall declare the work of God, for they shall understand [SAKAL] His work. The righteous shall be glad in the Lord, and shall trust in Him, and all the upright in heart shall glory" (Psalm 64:9-10).

"All Your works shall praise You, O Lord, and Your holy ones shall bless You. They shall tell of the glory of Your kingdom and speak of Your power. To make known to the sons of man His mighty acts, and the glorious majesty of His kingdom" (Psalm 145:10-12).

"He has filled me with words of Truth that I may proclaim Him. And like the flowing water, Truth flows from my mouth. And my lips declare His fruits, for he has caused His knowledge to abound in me" (Odes of Solomon 12:1-3).

"I give You thanks, O Lord, who have put understanding [BINAH] into the heart of Your servant . . . that he may praise Your name" (1QH 14:8,9,10, Dead Sea Scrolls).

"They [Your holy ones] shall recount Your glory in all Your dominion. For You have caused them to understand what they had not known" (1QH 13:11, Dead Sea Scrolls).

"Has not the Lord made the holy ones to declare all His wonderful works which the Lord Almighty has firmly settled to be established for His glory?" (Sirach 42:17, Latin Vulgate).

Because "the knowledge of the holy ones is understanding [the understanding needed to declare His works to His praise]" (Proverbs 9:10).

"The Word rejoices in teaching the holy ones through whom the Father is glorified" (*Epistle to Diognetus* 12:26-28).

"I will praise the Lord, who has given me understanding" (Psalm 16:7, Latin Vulgate).

PRINCES AND UNDERSTANDING

"Prince of understanding" (3 Enoch 10:5; 48D,v.6).

"A king who is reckless destroys his city, but through the understanding [SEKEL] of its princes it becomes inhabited [again]" (Sirach 10:3, Hebrew Text).

"Leaders [Hebrew Text: "princes"] of the people by their counsel and by their understanding" (Sirach 44:4).

"He was understanding beyond all the princes of Pharaoh" (Joseph and Asenath 1:3(5)).

"Son of man, say to the prince of Tyre . . . 'behold, you are wiser than Daniel, there is no secret they can hide from you. With your wisdom and your understanding you have acquired riches for yourself'" (Ezekiel 28:2,3,4).

"Hear, O you Kings; give ear, O you princes!" (Judges 5:3).

"Give ear to know understanding" (Proverbs 4:1; see also Baruch 3:9).

"Incline your ear to my understanding" (Proverbs 5:1).

Conversely

"The prince who lacks great understanding [TEBUNAH] is also a great oppressor" (Proverbs 28:16).

"The Lord your God . . . cuts off the spirit [see "Spirit and Understanding"] of princes" (Psalm 76:11,12).

*   *

"O lord Bel, thou prince who art mighty in understanding" (Hymn to Marduk No. 10).

UNDERSTANDING AND PROPHECY

"The latter things, God has put them all in my understanding that I may proclaim the things that shall be, and that were before, and tell them to mortal men" (Sibylline Oracles III.821-823).

"A man of understanding is of an excellent spirit" (Proverbs 17:27).

"He [the prophet Isaiah] saw by an excellent spirit what would come to pass . . . he showed the things that will happen at the end of time, and the hidden things before they came" (Sirach 48:24,25).

PURITY, CHASTITY, CELIBACY AND UNDERSTANDING

"Create in me a clean heart [see "Heart and Understanding"], O God ["for who can say I have made my heart clean, I am pure from my sins"? (Proverbs 20:9)], and renew a right spirit within me . . . then I will teach transgressors Your ways, and sinners shall be converted to You" (Psalm 51:10,13).

Wisdom purifies the understanding
because the Wisdom of God is chaste.

"The wisdom from above is first of all chaste" (St. James 3:17).

"Wisdom . . . pervades and penetrates all things by reason of her pureness" (Wisdom 7:24).

"The understanding is cleansed by Wisdom and the Truths of Wisdom's teaching" (Philo, *Spec.* I.269).

"Vice shall not prevail against wisdom" (Wisdom 7:30).

We shall find Wisdom by leading pure lives,
and from her we shall obtain understanding.

"I found wisdom in purity [TAHOR], and through her guidance I obtained understanding" (Sirach 51:20, Hebrew Text).

"Who is to be considered the daughter of God but Wisdom who is the first-born mother of all things and most of all of those who are greatly purified in soul?" (Philo, *Q.Gen.* IV.97).

"It is Wisdom's name that the holy oracles proclaim by 'Bathuel,' a name meaning: 'Daughter of God'; yes, a true-born and ever-virgin daughter" (Philo, *Fug.* 50).

"Follow after and pursue the genuine and unmated virgin, the Wisdom of God" (Philo, *Q.Exod.* II.3).

"Draw near to Wisdom . . . and when you draw close to her do it as a hero and a mighty one" (Sirach 1:22, Greek Sinaiticus Text).

"When you have taken hold of Wisdom, do not let her go" (Sirach 6:27).

"Come unto her with all your soul" (Sirach 6:26).

"Wisdom shall bring you to honor when you shall embrace her" (Proverbs 4:8).

"It is as play to a fool to do mischief, but a man of understanding has Wisdom [he courts, sports with, and possesses Wisdom]" (Proverbs 10:23).

"Companionship with Wisdom has no bitterness, and cohabitation with her has no pain, but gladness and joy" (Wisdom 8:16).

"There is understanding in the experience of her company" (Wisdom 8:18c).

"In the kinship of Wisdom there is immortality, and in the love [PHILIA] of her is good delight" (Wisdom 8:17,18a).

"Those who woo her in guilelessness and sincerity secure the favors of Wisdom" (Philo, *Ebr.* 49).

"Those who love [ERŌSIN] Wisdom with a love that is guileless and pure and genuine [shall discern her]" (Philo, *Virt.* 62).

"God loves nothing so much as the man who cohabits [SUNOIKOUNTA] with Wisdom" (Wisdom 7:28).

"If you desire Wisdom, keep righteousness and the Lord shall give her to you" (Sirach 1:33, Latin Vulgate; ibid., 1:25, Greek Text).

"Meditate continually on His commandments and He will make your heart to understand and make you wise in that which you desire" (Sirach 6:37, Syriac Text).

"My soul has longed for Wisdom" (Sirach 51:19, Hebrew Text).

"Wisdom I loved and diligently sought her from my youth, and I desired to take her as my bride, and I became enamoured of her beauty" (Wisdom 8:2).

"I was determined to take Wisdom to live with me, knowing that she would be a counsellor of good things and a comfort in cares and grief" (Wisdom 8:9).

Yes, "when I was yet young . . . I desired Wisdom. My heart [i.e., understanding] delighted in her . . . from my youth up I sought after her . . . I determined to do her . . . my soul has wrestled with her and in my doings I was very capable . . . I directed my soul unto her and I found her in pureness" (Sirach 51:13,15,18,19,20, Greek Text).

"The plan which is not entertaining impure thought comes and is called Wisdom" (Midrash Genesis Rabbah 90.3).

"He who desires to possess Wisdom must give up the [erotic] love of women" (*Liber Scintillarum* 18:82 [PL 88 pp. 597-817], quotation of St. Augustine).

O Solomon "how wise you were in your *youth,* and as a flood full of understanding" (Sirach 47:13,14).

But not in your old age when "you laid your loins beside women [promiscuously] and through your body you were brought into subjection. You stained your honor, and defiled your posterity" (Sirach 47:19-20; 1 Kings 11:1-9).

"Whoever desires to become powerful in Wisdom, he must not let women rule over him" (Arabic Proverb in Erpenius' *Arabic Grammar* with notes by A. Schultens; see *A Century of Arabic Proverbs*).

"A wise man is not wise until he has conquered all his lusts" (ibid.).

"If all men should become wise, the world would be depopulated [because of sexual abstinence]" (ibid.).

"No Essene takes a wife, because a wife . . . cajoles the understanding" (Philo, *Apol. Pro. Jud.* 11:15 quoted in Eusebius' *Praep. Evang.* VIII.5.11).

*   *

"The understanding [NOUS] becomes pure [KATHAROS] when it is not darkened by any object of sense" (Philo, *Som.* I.84).

Thus, "it is not given to youth [with all its passions] but to old age to discern things precious and worthy of reverence, particularly those which are judged, not by unreasoning and deceitful sense, but by the understanding [NOUS] when absolutely pure and unalloyed" (Philo, *Aet.* 77)

"No one alone is held worthy of . . . inspiration from above, of a heavenly and divine portion" except "the wholly purified understanding which disregards not only the body, but that other section of the soul which is devoid of reason and steeped in blood, aflame with seething passions and burning lusts" (Philo, *Her.* 64).

"For the nature of flesh is alien to Wisdom so long as it is familiar with desire" (Philo, *Q.Gen.* I.90).

"This wisdom which consists of rectitude of soul and of reason, and purity of life" (Clement of Alexandria, *Strom.* VI.c.7).

"What must the lover of Wisdom be like? For you do yearn to see her, to embrace her in purest fashion, to see her stripped of all else, with no evil between yourself and her, so that you may take hold of her. Yet only to some few chosen souls does Wisdom thus present herself . . . if you would arrive at that union, I have but one piece of advice to give; I know of only one means: we have to shun the allurements of the senses . . . believe me; the moment you can truthfully say that earthly pleasures make no appeal to you, in that very instant you will see what you have been craving to see [i.e. Wisdom unveiled]" (St. Augustine, *Soliloquia* i,23).

"Nothing fights so hard against another thing as does Wisdom against sensual pleasure" (Philo, *Q.Gen.* IV.41).

For "pleasures . . . bewitch the understanding" (Philo, *Spec.* I.9).

351

And "there are no two things so utterly opposed as understanding [EPISTĒMĒ] and pleasures of the flesh" (Philo, *Deus.* 143).

"Understanding is contrary to the flesh" (Corpus Hermeticum, *Libellus* X.10).

"The delightful experience of abounding pleasure is the ruin of the understanding" (Philo, *Agr.* 108).

And since "understanding [EPISTĒMĒ] comes into being through estrangement from sensuality . . . it follows that the lovers of Wisdom reject rather than choose sensuality" (Philo, *Cher.* 41).

"Lack of understanding and lack of continence [go together]" (Philo, *Som.* II.181).

"If the understanding is safe and unimpaired, free from the oppression of the iniquities or passions . . . it will gaze clearly on all that is worthy of contemplation" (Philo, *Sob.* I.5).

"The understanding of the pleasure-loving man is blind and unable to see those things which are worth seeing . . . the sight of which is wonderful to behold and desirable" (Philo, *Q.Gen.* IV.245).

"O Understanding, if you do not prepare yourself, excising desires, pleasures, griefs, fears, follies, injustices and related evils, and if you do not change and adapt yourself to the vision of holiness, you will end your life in blindness unable to see the sun of understanding" (Philo, *Q.Exod.* II.51).

For "the sun of understanding sends out its incorporeal rays most luminously and splendidly upon pure souls which gaze directly into the rays and behold them" (Philo, *Q.Gen.* IV.1.) [Conversely, see Wisdom 5:6, Latin Vulgate.]

"You . . . reveal what is hidden to the pure who in faith have submitted themselves to You and Your Law" (2 Baruch 54:5).

"An understanding clean of every spot, this understanding is the initiate of the holy mysteries" (Philo, *Praem.* 120,121).

"Purify yourselves of uncleanness and I will tell you the hidden secrets, the concealed date of the end, the reward of the righteous and the punishment of the wicked and what the pleasures of Paradise will be" (Targum Ps. Jonathan on Genesis 49:1).

"When one has received the reasonings of Wisdom and has tasted marriage with her, he remains her mate and husband" (Phil, *Q.Gen.* III.21).

And becomes one of "those who have Wisdom for their life-mate" (Philo, *Som.* II.234).

Among women too there were "virgins who have kept their chastity not under compulsion, like some Greek priestesses, but of their own free will in their ardent yearning for Wisdom. Eager to have Wisdom for their life-mate they have spurned the pleasures of the body and desire no mortal offspring but those immortal children which only the soul that is dear to God can bring to birth" (Philo, Cont. 68; see also Philo, *Abr.* 100).

And what are these children but "the offspring of understanding [PHRONĒ-SEŌS] and righteousness and all excellence"? (Philo, *L.A.* III.150).

"Let there be the constant and profound longing for Wisdom which fills her scholars and disciples with Truths glorious in their exceeding loveliness" (Philo, *Spec.* I.50).

'The chaste are rewarded by receiving illumination from the concealed [heavenly] light' (Zohar II.229b-230a).

"Wisdom is the brightness of eternal light" (Wisdom 7:26).

And let us not forget that "Wisdom will never enter a deceitful soul nor dwell in a body enslaved to sin" (Wisdom 1:4).

"A wise man was asked, 'What is understanding?' and he answered, 'Modesty.' Again he was asked, 'What is modesty?' and he replied, 'Understanding'" (Ibn Gabirol, *Improvement of Moral Qualities*).

"If you wish to be pure in understanding, guard your senses" (Testament of Reuben 6:1).

"The man of integrity . . . does not look [lustfully] on the beauty of women lest he should pollute his understanding" (Testament of Issachar 4:2,4).

"For nothing else so constrains and oppresses the understanding as do desires for sensual pleasures" (Philo, *Q.Gen.* IV.177).

"Our understanding is darkened by vain desires" (Second Clement 19:2; Ephesians 4:17,18; Romans 1:21).

"The fascination of vice obscures the things that are good, and the wandering allurements of concupiscence [EPITHUMIA] perverts the innocent [AKAKOS] understanding [NOUN]" (Wisdom 4:12).

"The distraction of concupiscence undermines the clear understanding of the innocent" (St. Ephrem, *Ad. Init. Prov.* i.p.67 [Asemani]).

"One who is *wanton* [SPATALON = "dissolute," "living riotously"]" (Sirach 21:15).

"One who is *without understanding* [A-SUNETOS]" (ibid., Greek Cursives 106,248).

"Harlotry, and wine, and new wine, take away the understanding" (Hosea 4:11).

"Wine and women [i.e., harlotry] will make men of understanding to fall away" (Sirach 19:2).

"The spirit of fornication . . . darkens every young man's understanding from the Truth so that he is not able to understand the Law of God, nor the admonition of his fathers" (Testament of Reuben 3:3,8).

"Fornication . . . deceives the mind and understanding" (Testament of Reuben 4:6).

"In fornication there is neither understanding nor godliness" (Testament of Reuben 6:4).

"A man who is a fornicator . . . he does not understand . . . and he does not know" (Sirach 23:24,27,28, Latin Vulgate).

"He who commits adultery with a woman lacks understanding" (Proverbs 6:32).

"Spouses when they commit adultery . . . do not understand" (Hosea 4:14).

"An old man who is an adulterer lacking understanding" (Sirach 25:2, Greek Text, Literal Translation).

"They . . . who give themselves to their lusts [are] as the horse and mule, which do not have understanding" (Tobit 6:17, Latin Vulgate).

"Everyone neighed [like a horse] after his neighbor's wife . . . foolish people and without understanding" (Jeremiah 5:8,21).

"If fornication does not overcome your understanding, neither can Beliar [the Devil] overcome you" (Testament of Reuben 4:11).

"Joseph . . . guarded himself from a woman [the adulterous wife of Potiphar] and purged his thoughts from all fornication and found favor in the sight of God and men" (Testament of Reuben 4:8).

"To the man who is good in His sight God gives wisdom, knowledge and joy" (Ecclesiastes 2:26).

"God was with him [Joseph] . . . and gave him favor and wisdom in the sight of Pharaoh, King of Egypt" (Acts 7:9,10).

"Pharaoh said to Joseph . . . 'there is no one so understanding [BIN] and wise as you'" (Genesis 41:39).

*   *

"Put away from you all wicked desire and clothe yourself with good and chaste desire; for clothed with this desire you will hate wicked desire and you will rein yourself in, even as you wish. For wicked desire is wild and is with difficulty tamed. For it is terrible and consumes men exceedingly by its wildness. Especially is the servant of God terribly consumed with it, if he falls into it he is devoid of understanding" (Shepherd of Hermas, *Mand.* XII.1.44:1-2).

"Scripture prays that the understanding will see and be keen-sighted and avoid those who are licentious and foolish and atheistic, and, after leaving them behind will hasten with all its might toward continence and holiness" (Philo, *Q.Gen.* IV.45).

"When the understanding begins to take the higher road it becomes better and progresses, leaving behind earthbound and low things which men who are undisciplined pursue and admire" (Philo, *Q.Gen.* IV.46).

"When the progressive understanding becomes still purer, it removes still farther and separates itself from the guilty and unlivable way of life" (Philo, *Q.Gen.* IV.55).

"Know, that in the last days difficult times will come. For men will be lovers of self, lovers of money, proud, arrogant, blasphemous, disobedient to parents, ungrateful, unholy, inhuman, implacable, slanderers, without self control, brutal, haters of good, treacherous, reckless, swollen with conceit, lovers of pleasure rather than lovers of God . . . this sort are . . . ever learning, and never able to come to the knowledge of Truth [because they have no understanding]" (2 Timothy 3:1-4,6,7).

"Being filled with all unrighteousness, evil, covetousness, malice; full of envy, murder, strife, deceit, malice; they are gossips, slanderers, haters of God, insolent, arrogant, boastful, inventors of evil, disobedient to parents, without understanding" (Romans 1:29-30,31).

Also "the traits of the soul are blind and unproductive of wisdom in those ones which Scripture calls Sodomites" (Philo, *Q.Gen.* IV.36).

For "the Sodomites . . . were barren of wisdom and blind in the understanding" (Philo, *Conf.* 27; idem *Fug.* 144).

"Become not, my children, as Sodomites who did not know" [because they had no understanding] (Testament of Asher 7:1, Literal Translation).

All of them had "degrading passions, even their women changed the natural use [of sex] for that which is against nature, and in the same way also the men gave up natural relations with women and were consumed with passion for one another, men with men committing indecent acts . . . God gave them over to a faulty [ADOKIMON] understanding [NOUN]" (Romans 1:26,27,28).

355

Because of "lewdness and other insatiable lusts . . . that grossness of flesh which is the enemy of quickness of understanding" (Philo, *Mos.* II.185).

"Put off your old nature which belongs to your former manner of life and is corrupt through deceitful lusts, and be renewed in the spirit of your understanding" (Ephesians 4:22,23).

"Lust . . . is barren of excellent things and blinded to all that is worthy of the soul's contemplation" (Philo, *Ebr.* 223).

Those "who leave the paths of uprightness . . . walk in the ways of darkness" (Proverbs 2:13).

"Their own wickedness has blinded them" (Wisdom 2:21).

"The god of this world has blinded the understanding of those who do not believe" (2 Corinthians 4:4).

"In the lust of concupiscence . . . the gentiles do not know God" (1 Thessalonians 4:5).

"It is impossible for him who has a high and true knowledge of God to be a slave to pleasures that are contrary to Him" (Clement of Alexandria, *Strom.* VII.c.12).

"The most pure understanding . . . and perfection of virtue [go together]" (Philo, *Q.Gen.* IV.8).

"Beware of fornication . . . if you wish to be pure in understanding . . . women likewise should not associate with men [promiscuously], so that they also may be pure in understanding" (Testament of Reuben 6:1,2).

"If you keep silence in purity of heart, you shall understand" (Testament of Naphtali 3:1).

"Pure as regards corporeal lusts and pure in holy thoughts are those who attain to the knowledge of God" (Clement of Alexandria, *Strom.* IV.c.6).

"In Truth, the wise man's understanding [DIANOIA] is a palace and house of God" (Philo, *Praem.* 123).

"In the understandings of those who have been purified to the utmost, the Ruler of the universe walks" (Philo, *Som.* I.148).

"The man of self-control who by unwearied and unswerving labor has made the excellent virtues his own has for his crown the vision of God" (Philo, *Praem.* 27).

"For the beginning and end of happiness is to be able to see God" (Philo, *Q.Exod.* II.51; Psalm 16:11).

"If you wish to see God, take to yourself means of purification worthy of Him" (Clement of Alexandria, *Exh.* I.10.2).

"We shall see Him as He is, and every man who has this hope in him purifies himself, even as He is pure" (1 John 3:2,3).

"Being pure . . . you will then see" (Testament of Solomon, 6:10(31)).

"Blessed are the pure in heart, for they shall see God" (St. Matthew 5:8).

"Strive for peace with all men, and for the holiness without which no one will see the Lord" (Hebrews 12:14).

"Whosoever sins has not seen Him nor known Him" (1 John 3:6).

For "when there is sin in a man such a man cannot see God" (Theophilus, *Ad Autolycum* I.2).

"O man, your ungodliness brings darkness upon you and you cannot see God" (ibid., ending).

"Your iniquities have made separation between you and your God, and your sins have hidden His face from you" (Isaiah 59:2).

"I will behold Your face in righteousness" (Psalm 17:15).

"The most pure understanding is wholly filled to overflowing with the appearance of God" (Philo, *Q.Exod.* II.27).

*   *

We should pray to the Lord for the gift of Chastity so that we may truly understand.

"Wisdom and *understanding* and knowledge of the Law are from the Lord" (Sirach 11:15, Greek Text Cursives 248,23,106, and Old Latin Texts).

"Wisdom and *continence* and knowledge of the Law are from the Lord" (ibid., Syriac Text).

We also see that "lack of understanding and lack of continence [go together]" (Philo, *Som.* II.181).

"Wise souls pure as virgins . . . situated amidst the ignorance of the world, kindle the light and rouse the understanding and illumine the darkness, and dispel ignorance, and seek Truth, and await the appearance of the Teacher" (Clement of Alexandria, *Strom.* V.c.3).

"The adornment of the commandments is chastity" (Derek Eretz Zuta V.4).

"God loves nothing better than chastity" (Pesikta Rabbati, Piska 185b).

*   *

"Is it not my heart-felt prayer that my understanding should be a true and noble lady, eminent for chastity and modesty, and all other virtues?" (Philo, *Fug.* 154).

*   *

"And I heard a voice from heaven like the sound of many waters and like the sound of loud thunder; the voice I heard was like the sound of harpists playing on their harps. And they sang a new song before the throne and before the four living creatures and before the elders; and no one could learn that song except the hundred and forty four thousand who had been redeemed from the earth. It is these who have not defiled themselves . . . for they are virgins [and being chaste they had the understanding needed to "learn that song"]" (Revelation 14:2-3,4).

Thus the "virgin daughter" of Jephthah was "more wise than her father and a maiden of understanding more than all the wise who are here" (Ps. Philo, *Biblical Antiquities* XL.4).

*   *

"Good understanding gives grace" (Proverbs 13:15).

"Grace [CHARIS] shall be found in the lips of the understanding [SUNETOU]" (Sirach 21:16).

"He who loves purity of heart, because of the grace of his lips the King shall be his friend" (Proverbs 22:11).

"The sayings of the pure are held in honor" (Proverbs 15:26, Greek Text).

*   *

"Your prayer has indeed been heard before the Most High; for the Mighty One has seen your uprightness and has also observed the chastity [PUDICITIAM] which you have maintained from your youth. Therefore He has sent me to show you all these things" (2 Esdras 6:32,33).

*   *

"The Lord only is righteous" (Sirach 18:2).

"Which one of you convicts Me [Jesus Christ] of sin?" (St. John 8:46).

"The ruler [the devil] of this world . . . has no power over Me [Jesus]" (St. John 14:30).

"I have kept My Father's commandments and abide in His love" (St. John 15:10).

"Not that any man has seen the Father, except the One [Jesus] who is from God" (St. John 6:46).

"I [Jesus] speak the things which I have seen with My Father" (St. John 8:38).

"He who has seen Me [Jesus] has seen the Father" (St. John 14:9).

"I and the Father are One" (St. John 10:30).

"He [Jesus] committed no sin; no guile was found in His mouth" (1 Peter 2:22).

"We . . . have a High Priest [Jesus Christ], holy, blameless, unstained, separated from sinners, exalted above the heavens" (Hebrews 7:26).

"One [Jesus] who in every respect has been tempted as we are, yet without sinning" (Hebrews 4:15).

"Him [Jesus] . . . who knew no sin" (2 Corinthians 5:21).

For "Christ is the fulfillment of the Law for righteousness" (Romans 10:4).

"Jesus . . . the Holy and Righteous One" (Acts 3:13,14).

"Jesus Christ the Righteous" (1 John 2:1).

"He [Jesus] is pure . . . in Him there is no sin" (1 John 3:3,5).

Jesus "Christ, in whom are hidden all the treasures of wisdom and knowledge" (Colossians 2:2,3).

"Christ, the Power of God and the Wisdom of God" (1 Corinthians 1:24).

*　　*

"Evil desire is wild and hard to tame . . . if a servant of God falls into it he lacks understanding, and will be terribly destroyed by it" (Shepherd of Hermas, XII.1.44:2).

"The man of great understanding [TEBUNAH] who asks and seeks to remain firm [in his understanding], will not rest until he dismisses his [concupiscent] desire, and drives it wholly away from him" (R. Joseph Kimchi's *Shekel Hakodesh* v. 130).

"O man of understanding [BIN]! Be not confident until your understanding [SEKEL] has conquered your desire" (ibid. v. 131).

"Simplicity, innocence, purity, cheerfulness, Truth, understanding [SUNESIS] unanimity, and love [go together]" (Shepherd of Hermas, *Sim.* IX.15.92:2).

THE QUICKNESS OF UNDERSTANDING

"The understanding grasps before the senses" (Philo, *Q.Gen.* IV.32).

"The understanding . . . is not quiescent but unsleeping and constantly in motion" (Philo, *Abr.* 162).

"The eye of the understanding is quick to discern" and possesses "quickness to learn" (Philo, *Jos.* 106; idem *Agr.* 168).

"To possess a quick [OXUN] understanding [NOUN] and to be able to form a sound judgment in every case is one of the good gifts of God" (Letter of Aristeas v.276).

"He [Moses] was ever opening the Scroll . . . and digesting their contents inwardly with quick understanding" (Philo, *Mos.* I.48).

Moses "had passed on the lesson to those who were of quick understanding" (Philo, *Mos.* II.141).

"The ones who have the fear of God and seek after godliness and Truth, and whose hearts are turned to the Lord perceive and understand quickly everything that is said to them" (Shepherd of Hermas, *Mand.* X.1.40:6).

"The heart of the quick [MAHAR] shall understand to know [YADA]" (Isaiah 32:4).

"Set in motion and formed and quickened by Understanding" (Philo, *Op.* 9).

"Pervading all spirits that are quick of understanding . . . more mobile than any motion" (Wisdom 7:23,24).

"The operation and invisible movements of the understanding, the quickness of its particular actions and its discoveries . . . display an infinite resourcefulness" (Letter of Aristeas v.156).

"Moved by the understanding to their proper work and activities" (Philo, *Q.Gen.* IV.56).

"That grossness of flesh which is the enemy of quickness of understanding" (Philo, *Mos.* II.185).

"Even the swiftest understanding falls short of apprehending Him" (Philo, *Som.* I.184).

"The swiftness of the resurrection (1 Corinthians 15:52) will surpass the swiftness of understanding" (Syriac *Book of the Bee* c. 57, Trans. E.A. Wallis Budge).

An angel "flies swiftly" (Daniel 9:21).

"Man . . . his understanding is from the swiftness of angels" (2 Enoch 30:8).

Having a quick understanding we should be "swift to hear"
[see "Hearing and Understanding"], and be "eager" in our
understanding.

"Hear, O you wise men and you who are diligent in knowledge and you who are quick [MAHARAIM i.e., "quick in understanding"]" (1QH 1:34,35, Dead Sea Scrolls).

"Be swift to hear . . . if you have understanding, answer your neighbor" (Sirach 5:11,12).

"Let every man be swift to hear" (St. James 1:19).

"Be always ready to give an answer" (1 Peter 3:15).

"All who heard Him were amazed at His understanding and His answers" (St. Luke 2:47).

"They received the Word with all eagerness of understanding, examining the Scriptures daily, to see whether these things were so" (Acts 17:11).

Conversely

"The Lord looked down from heaven upon the sons of man to see if there were any who understand" (Psalm 14:2).

"O you sons of man, how long will you be slow of heart?" (Psalm 4:2, Greek Text).

"O foolish ones [A-NOETOI, literally "without understanding"], and slow [BRADEIS] of heart" (St. Luke 24:25).

"The mouth of one who understands is praised by a man; but he who is slow of heart is had in derision" (Proverbs 12:8, Greek Text).

*　　*

O "God of righteousness and understanding [SEKEL]" (1QH Fragment 7:8, Dead Sea Scrolls).

"Quicken me through Your righteousness" (Psalm 119:40).

For "by Your righteousness You do make them understand (SAKAL)" (11QPs[a] Col. XIX.3 [Plea for Deliverance], Dead Sea Scrolls).

"Through them [Your precepts] You have quickened me" (Psalm 119:93, KJV).

For "through Your precepts I get understanding" (Psalm 119:104).

UNDERSTANDING IS RECEIVED

"Hear wisdom . . . receive understanding" (2 Baruch 51:4).

"If you love to hear, you shall receive understanding" (Sirach 6:33, Greek Cursives 258,253; ibid., Aldine Text, Syriac and Old Latin Texts).

"Incline your ear, and receive the words of understanding" (Sirach 2:2, Latin Vulgate).

"Receive complete understanding" (Epistle of Barnabas 10:10).

"You will receive instruction" (Sirach 8:9, Hebrew Text).

"You will learn understanding" (ibid., Greek Text).

We must ask to be given Understanding.

"What is he that is flesh to understand Your works?" (1QH 15:15, Dead Sea Scrolls).

"How can I understand unless You give me understanding?" (1QH 12:33, Dead Sea Scrolls).

"O Lord . . . give me understanding" (Psalm 119:33,34,73,125,144,169).

"Give me understanding, O Lord, in Your Law" (11QPs^a XXIV.9 [Psalm Scroll 155:9], Dead Sea Scrolls).

"Give us out of Your godly treasure: understanding, knowledge, and wisdom" (Targum on the Amidah or Eighteen Benedictions).

"The Lord gives wisdom, out of His mouth comes knowledge and understanding" (Proverbs 2:6).

"I will praise the Lord, who has given me understanding" (Psalm 16:7, Greek and Latin Vulgate Texts).

"I give You thanks, O Adonai, who have put understanding in the heart of Your servant" (1QH 14:8, Dead Sea Scrolls).

"What then is man, he who is but earth and potter's clay and will return to dust, that You should give him understanding of such marvels and make known to him Your secret of Truth?" (1QH 10:3,4, Dead Sea Scrolls).

"What is he, the spirit of flesh, to understand all these things and to understand Your great secrets of Truth?" (1QH 13:13,14, Dead Sea Scrolls).

"What am I that You should teach me Your secret of Truth and give me understanding of Your marvelous deeds?" (1QH 11:3,4, Dead Sea Scrolls).

"The Lord gave him [David] an understanding and enlightened spirit" (11QPsᵃ XXVII.4 [Psalm Scroll 151:4], Dead Sea Scroll).

"The Lord gave me understanding and wisdom" (Testament of Zebulon 6:1).

Conversely

"A man of violence does not receive understanding" (Sirach 32:18, Hebrew Text, MS. E [5th Genizah Fragment]).

"The natural man [in contradistinction to the "spiritual" man] does not receive the things of the Spirit of God" (1 Corinthians 2:14).

The "vessel" of Understanding.

"By what means can I obtain understanding unless You form it [as a vessel] for me?" (1QH 10:6, Dead Sea Scrolls).

"Our understanding . . . is contained in the body as in a vessel" (Philo, *Mig.* 193; see also Zohar II.42b-43a, Raya Mehemna Section).

"How then shall your vessel be able to understand the way of the Most High?" (2 Esdras 4:11).

"For as the water jar contains water, . . . understanding [EPISTĒMĒ] contains Law, counsel, and contemplation of divine Truths" (Philo, *Q.Gen.* IV.98).

"The understanding is a vast and receptive storehouse in which all that comes through sight or hearing and the other organs of sense is placed and treasured" (Philo, *Deus.* 42).

"The storehouse of understanding" (2 Baruch 44:14).

"Learn this and store it in your understanding" (Sibylline Oracles III.562).

"He received in his understanding [SUNESIS] three doctrines" (Epistle of Barnabas 10:1).

"That they might know You according to the measure of their understanding" (1QH 1:31, Dead Sea Scrolls).

"The Creator freely gave man the Word, but the understanding He sent down to earth as waters in a great basin. He then appointed a herald angel to exhort men to dip their hearts into that basin. Those who did, received their share of knowledge and understanding and so became complete men" (Corpus Hermeticum Book IV.4).

"Out of his heart . . . poured forth understanding" (Sirach 50:27, Hebrew Text).

*   *

"Blessed be our Lord [Jesus] who has endowed us with wisdom and understanding of His secrets" (*Epistle of Barnabas* 6:10).

"Ask, and it will be given to you" (St. Matthew 7:7; St. Luke 11:9).

"If you are willing to receive it . . ." (St. Matthew 11:14).

"The Lord [Jesus Christ] will give you understanding in all things" (2 Timothy 2:7).

REPENTANCE AND UNDERSTANDING

"True repentance of a godly sort destroys ignorance, and drives away the darkness, and enlightens the eyes, and gives knowledge to the soul, and leads the mind to salvation. And those things which it has not learnt from men, it knows through repentance" (Testament of Gad 5:7-8).

"Repentance . . . this means passing from ignorance to understanding . . . from senselessness to prudence, from laxity to continence, from injustice to justice, from timidity to boldness" (Philo, *Virt.* 180).

"Repentance is understanding [BINAH]" (Zohar II.122a, Raya Mehemna; ibid. III.123a).

"Repentance is itself understanding . . . to repent is great understanding" (Shepherd of Hermas, *Mand.* IV.2.30:2).

"Understanding [BINAH] is called 'Repentance' [TESHUVAH]" (Zohar III.74a-75a; ibid. I.90a).

"I am the angel set over repentance, and I give understanding to all who repent" (Shepherd of Hermas, *Mand.* IV.2.30:2).

"Let us therefore repent and pass from ignorance to understanding, and from foolishness to insight" (Clement of Alexandria, *Exh.* X.93,1).

"That we may turn away from our iniquities and understand Your Truth" (Daniel 9:13).

"Repentance towards a full knowledge [EPIGNŌSIS] of the Truth" (2 Timothy 2:25).

"Repent, O backsliding children . . . and I will give you shepherds after My own heart, who will feed you with knowledge and understanding" (Jeremiah 3:14,15).

"If a man runs to the Lord, the evil spirit flees away from him, and his understanding is enlightened" (Testament of Simeon 3:5).

"Repentance on earth leads to reception of the highest secrets in heaven" (Midrash Talpiyot 166a).

"Repent and become wise" (Justin Martyr, *Apol.* II.12.37).

"I repented . . . and the angel of the Lord showed me" (Testament of Judah 15:4,5).

"I saw concerning the seven spirits of deceit, when I repented" (Testament of Reuben 2:1).

"With set purpose of my soul for seven years, I repented before the Lord and . . . I saw" (Testament of Reuben 1:9-2:1).

"Turn [i.e., repent] at my reproof and I will pour out my spirit unto you and will make my words known to you" (Proverbs 1:23).

"Repent . . . and you shall receive the gift of the Holy Spirit" (Acts 2:38).

"They will repent acknowledging that I am the Lord their God, and I shall give them a heart, and ears that hear [i.e., understand] and they will praise Me" (Baruch 2:30,31,32).

"I was converted, I repented, and after that I was made to know [YADA]" (Jeremiah 31:19).

"Ye who have repented, and who have recently returned to the Law know . . ." (Targum on Isaiah 33:13).

For "repentance and the knowledge of God [go together]" (Justin Martyr, *Dial.* XIV.1).

"Repent O Jacob . . . that you may be illuminated" (Baruch 4:2).

"Turn again to the Most High, and turn away from iniquity and He will lead you out of darkness into the light" (Sirach 17:26).

"To the penitent He has given the way of justice . . . and [He] has appointed unto them the lot of Truth" (Sirach 17:20, Latin Vulgate).

"The perfection of wisdom is repentance" (Berakoth 17a, BT).

UNDERSTANDING AND REPROVING

"You brought him up with Your righteousness, and nurtured him in Your Law, and reproved [CORRIPIA] him with Your understanding [INTELLECTU]" (2 Esdras 8:12, Latin Text).

"He had formed me [see "The Forming of Understanding"] to reprove with His instruction" (Habacuc 1:12, Greek Text).

"Understand first and then reprove" (Sirach 11:7).

"He who hears reproof gets understanding" (Proverbs 15:32).

"Reprove one who has understanding and he will understand [BIN] knowledge" (Proverbs 19:25).

"He who regards reproof is prudent" (Proverbs 15:5).

"But he who hates reproof is brutish" (Proverbs 12:1).

"The rod and reproof give wisdom" (Proverbs 29:15).

"The friendly and particularly meek understanding loves reproof" (Philo, *Q.Gen.* III.26).

For "he who regards reproofs shall be made wise" (Proverbs 16:17, Greek Text).

"Reprove a wise man and he will love you" (Proverbs 9:8b).

Conversely

"One who is insensitive to reproach will never be instructed in wisdom" (Sirach 23:15, Syriac Text).

"He who refuses reproof errs" (Proverbs 10:17b).

"Do not reprove a scoffer, lest he hate you" (Proverbs 9:8a).

"A scoffer does not love one who reproves him" (Proverbs 15:12).

"He who hates to be reproved is in the way of sinners" (Sirach 21:6).

THE RIGHT HAND AND UNDERSTANDING

"A wise man's understanding is at his right hand" (Ecclesiastes 10:2).

"In length of days: understanding" (Job 12:12).

"Length of days is in Wisdom's right hand" (Proverbs 3:16).

"My *right hand* has stretched out the heavens" (Isaiah 48:13).

"He has stretched out the heavens by His *understanding*" (Jeremiah 10:12, 51:15; see Proverbs 3:19).

"By his *understanding* He has stretched out the heavens" (11QPs^a Col. XXVI.8 [Hymn to the Creator], Dead Sea Scrolls).

"By the right hand of Your power [see "The Power and Strength of Understanding"]" (1QH 18:7, Dead Sea Scrolls).

"By My power I have stretched out the heavens" (Targum on Isaiah 48:13).

"Let us . . . draw down from heaven Truth, with her companion Prudence that, diffusing her light around, she may enlighten all who are involved in darkness and may free men from error, extending to them understanding [SUNESIN] as if it were a strong right hand for their salvation" (Clement of Alexandria, *Exh.* I.2.3).

"When he saw that I lay on the ground as one dead, my understanding being collapsed, he grasped my right hand and strengthened me" (2 Esdras 10:30).

"I am Understanding, I have strength" (Proverbs 8:14).

"To whom has the *arm* of the Lord been revealed?" (Isaiah 53:1).

"To whom has the *understanding* of wisdom been revealed?" (Sirach 1:7, Syriac and Sahidic Texts).

"Awake, awake, put on strength, O *arm* of the Lord . . . was it not You ["O *arm* of the Lord"] who did cut Rahab into pieces?" (Isaiah 51:9).

"By His *great understanding* [TEBUNAH] He smites through Rahab" (Job 26:12b, Literal Translation).

"By His glorious arm, dividing the water before them" (Isaiah 63:12; see "Understanding knows how to Divide").

"He divides the sea by His power" (Job 26:12a, Literal Translation).

"You did divide the sea by Your Power" (Psalm 74:13; see "The Power and Strength of Understanding").

"He is King of all things, by His power dividing" (Sirach 18:3, Greek Cursive 248).

"In much understanding [EPISTEMES] the Lord has divided them" (Sirach 33:11).

Note: In Jewish tradition the "arm of the Lord" (Isaiah 51:9) is identical to His right arm and hand. Thus in the Hebrew 3 Enoch 48:1,2,3,4 : the "right hand of the Most High" is "His great arm" (3 Enoch 48:6-10) glorified. In the same work "the arm of the Lord" (Isaiah 51:9) and "His glorious arm" (Isaiah 63:12) are referred to as "the great right hand of God".

"In that moment" that the Holy One will "reveal His great arm and show it to the nations of the world, the Messiah will appear unto them" (3 Enoch 48:9-10, A text).

"The Lord has sworn by His right hand and by the arm of His power" (Isaiah 62:8).

"By the right hand of Your power [or 'arm']" (1QH 18:7, Dead Sea Scrolls).

"The right hand of the power of God" (St. Luke 22:69).

"In His hand are both we and our words and also, all understanding [PHRONESIS] and insight [EPISTEME] of works" (Wisdom 7:16).

"He [King David] fed them according to the integrity of his heart and guided them by the great understanding [TEBUNAH] of his hands" (Psalm 78:72).

*   *

"Christ . . . the arm of the Lord" (Clement of Alexandria, *Exh.* XII. 120.4).

"Christ, the Power of God" (1 Corinthians 1:24).

"The Son [Jesus Christ] is the Understanding, Word and Wisdom of the Father" (Athenagoras [c. A.D. 177], *Emb.* c.XXIV; ibid. c.X).

"Christ, in whom are hidden all the treasures of wisdom and knowledge" (Colossians 2:2,3).

"The Lord said to my Lord, 'sit Thou at My right hand'" (Psalm 110:1; St. Matthew 22:44; St. Mark 12:35-37).

"The high priest said to Him: 'I adjure You by the living God, that You tell us if You are the Christ, the Son of God.' Jesus said, 'I am, and ye shall see the Son of Man sitting on the right hand of power, and coming with the clouds of heaven'" (St. Matthew 26:64; St. Mark 14:62).

"Christ Jesus . . . who is at the right hand of God" (Romans 8:34; see also Colossians 3:1).

"Christ . . . the door which we who desire to understand God must discover" (Clement of Alexandria, *Exh.* I.10.2; St. John 10:9).

"Where the Lord [Jesus Christ] dwells there is much understanding. Cleave then to the Lord and you will understand and perceive all things" (Shepherd of Hermas, *Mand.* X.1.40:6).

"The godly Christian alone is rich and wise . . . having become righteous, holy and understanding through Jesus Christ" (Clement of Alexandria, *Exh.* XII.122.4; St. Matthew 15:10; St. Luke 24:45; 1 John 5:20; 2 Corinthians 3:14-16).

*   *

The Ancient Egyptians also knew that Understanding sits at the right hand of the Deity.

"Sia [god of understanding] who is at the right hand of Re [the principal deity]" (*Ancient Egyptian Pyramid Texts,* Ed. R.O.Faulkner, Oxford 1969. Utterance No. 250).

"It is Sia who says what is in the heart of the great one at the feast of the red garment, for he is Sia [Understanding] at the right hand of Re" (ibid. Utterance No. 267-268).

"I am Sia [Understanding] at the right hand of Re, who establishes the heart of him who stands before the Tephet of Nu" (*Egyptian Book of the Dead* 174,18.19 [E. Naville's *Das Agyptische Todtenbuch der XVIII bis XX Dynastie,* 2 Vols).

RIGHTEOUSNESS AND UNDERSTANDING

O "God of righteousness and understanding [SEKEL]" (1QH Fragment 7:8, Dead Sea Scrolls).

"By Your righteousness You do make them understand [SAKAL]" (11QPs^a Col. XIX.3 [Plea for Deliverance], Dead Sea Scrolls).

"The understanding [PHRONĒSEI] of the righteous [DIKAION]" (St. Luke 1:17).

"Hold fast to the Lord and you will perceive and understand all things" (Shepherd of Hermas, *Mand.* X.1.40:3).

"For where the Lord dwells, there is also great understanding" (ibid.).

"A righteous man understands [SEKEL]" (Proverbs 21:12).

"The understanding of the virtuous" (Philo, *Q.Exod.* II.116).

"The righteous . . . Wisdom guided him in right paths, and showed him the kingdom of God, and gave him knowledge of holy things" (Wisdom 10:10).

"Blessed are you righteous ones, for to you are revealed the deepest secrets of the Law" (Zohar II.26a [*Idra R.*]; ibid. III.215a-215b).

"All His works and all that He has created He has revealed to the righteous" (Enoch 61:13).

"All ye who know righteousness, and have understanding in the works of God" (Zadokite Fragment [CD] 1:1,2, MS. A).

"We contribute towards understanding . . . by desire for virtue, by zeal for noble things, by continuous study therein, by persistent self training, by unwearied and unflagging labor" (Philo, *Ebr.* 20.21).

Hence it is called "holy understanding" and "godly [EUSEBĒS] understanding [EPISTĒMĒ]" (Proverbs 2:11, Greek Text; 4 Maccabees 11:21).

"The understanding of the holy ones" (Proverbs 2:11, Syriac Text).

"The imitation of those who have already been proved, and who have led correct lives is most excellent for the understanding" (Clement of Alexandria, *Strom.* I.c.1).

"Keep the charge of the Lord your God, to walk in His ways, to keep His statutes, His commandments, His ordinances and His testimonies, as it is written in the Law of Moses, that you may understand [SAKAL] in all that you do" (1 Kings 2:3).

Because "a good understanding have all those who do His commandments" (Psalm 111:10).

Thus "he who keeps the Law is an understanding [BIN] son" (Proverbs 28:7).

For "he who keeps the Law of the Lord gets the understanding thereof" (Sirach 21:11).

"Keep therefore the words of this covenant that you may understand [SAKAL]" (Deuteronomy 29:9; Ibid. 4:6).

"My son, do not forget my Law, but let your heart keep my commandments . . . so shall you find favor and good understanding [SAKAL] in the sight of God and man" (Proverbs 3:1,4).

"Do all that is written in the Law . . . then you shall have good understanding [SEKEL]" (Joshua 1:8).

"A man of understanding is faithful to the Law of God, and the Law is faithful to him" (Sirach 33:3, Latin Vulgate).

"The Law of life and great understanding [TEBUNAH]" (Sirach 45:5, Hebrew Text).

"Those who have been justified in My Law and have had understanding in their life" (2 Baruch 51:3).

"Hezekiah . . . trusted in the Lord God of Israel . . . he held fast to the Lord; he did not depart from following Him, but kept the commandments [of the Lord] which the Lord commanded Moses. And the Lord was with him and he understood [SAKAL]" (2 Kings 18:1,5,6,7; see "Faithfulness and Understanding").

"The heart of the *righteous*" (Proverbs 15:14, Syriac Text).

"The heart of him who has *understanding*" (ibid., Hebrew Text).

"Wisdom rests in the heart of the *righteous*" (Proverbs 14:33, Syriac Text).

"Wisdom rests in the heart of him who has *understanding*" (ibid., Hebrew Text).

"Breastplate of *righteousness*" (Ephesians 6:14).

"Breastplate of *understanding*" (Testament of Levi 8:2).

"Let thy soul love a *good* servant" (Sirach 7:21, Greek Vaticanus and Ephraemi Texts).

"Let thy soul love an *understanding* servant" (ibid., Hebrew Text and Greek Sinaiticus and Alexandrinus Texts and Cursive 248).

"One who *fears the Lord*" (Sirach 16:4, Syriac Text).

"One who has *understanding*" (ibid., Greek Text).

"They who fear the Lord shall understand His judgment" (Sirach 32:16, Hebrew Text).

"The fear of the Lord is the beginning of wisdom, and all those who practice it have good understanding" (Proverbs 1:7, Greek Text).

"They who in fear [of the Lord] are wise and understanding" (2 Baruch 46:5).

"There is wisdom in the heart of a good man" (Proverbs 14:33, Greek Text).

For "Wisdom . . . enlightens the heart of all who give heed to her" (Sirach 4:11, Syriac Text).

"Wisdom rains down understanding [EPISTĒMĒN] and knowledge of understanding and exalts to honor those who hold her fast" (Sirach 1:19, Greek Text Cursives 248,70,106).

"To the man who is good in His sight He has given wisdom and knowledge and joy" (Ecclesiastes 2:25).

"To the godly He has given wisdom" (Sirach 43:33; see also Enoch 5:8).

"He who keeps the Law will be able to seize Wisdom" (Sirach 15:1).

"If you desire Wisdom, keep the commandments and the Lord shall give her to you" (Sirach 1:25).

"This is the love of God: that we keep His commandments" (1 John 5:3).

"This is love: that we walk after His commandments" (2 John v.6).

"He who has My commandments and keeps them, he it is who loves Me" (St. John 14:21; 14:15; 15:10).

"He has given wisdom to those who love Him" (Sirach 1:10).

"From generation to generation wisdom passes into holy souls" (Wisdom 7:27).

"The righteous shall arise from their sleep, and wisdom . . . shall be given to them" (Enoch 91:10).

"Who is wise and will keep these things? They will understand" (Psalm 107:43).

"Because You are righteous You order all things righteously" (Wisdom 12:15).

"He who is noble devises noble things, and by noble things he stands" (Isaiah 32:8).

"The thoughts of the righteous are right" (Proverbs 12:5).

"For he who has good understanding sees all things rightly" (Testament of Benjamin 3:2).

"My words declare the uprightness of my heart, and my lips speak knowledge clearly" (Job 33:3).

"He who speaks Truth shows forth righteousness" (Proverbs 12:17).

"The mouth of the righteous utters wisdom" (Psalm 37:30).

"The mouth of the righteous flourishes with wisdom" (Proverbs 10:31).

"The discourse of a godly man is always with wisdom" (Sirach 27:11).

"The wisdom of his righteousness" (Psalms of Solomon 17:31).

"Without wisdom it is not possible to praise the Creator of all things" (Philo, *Q.Gen.* I.6).

"To make known the glory of the Lord is wisdom given, and for recounting His many deeds is wisdom revealed to man, so as to make known to the simple His might, and explain to the senseless His greatness" (11QPs^a XVIII.7-8 [Psalm Scroll 154:7], Dead Sea Scrolls).

"Praise shall be uttered in wisdom" (Sirach 15:10).

"The righteous and the pious . . . their meditation is on the Law of the Most High, and their words in making known His might" (11QPs^a XVIII.14 [Psalm 154:14], Dead Sea Scrolls).

"The congregation of Your holy ones . . . shall recount Your glory in all Your dominion. For You have caused them to see what they had not known" (1QH 13:8,11, Dead Sea Scrolls).

"Praise from the upright is beautiful" (Psalm 33:1).

"His ways are plain to the *holy*" (Sirach 39:24).

"They are all plain to *him who understands*" (Proverbs 8:9).

"A holy race of God-fearing men adhering to the counsels and the mind of the Most High . . . in righteousness possessing the Law of the Most High . . . to them alone the Mighty God has given discreet counsel and an excellent understanding in their hearts" (Sibylline Oracles III.573-574,580,584-585).

"The upright will understand the knowledge of the Most High and the perfect of way will have understanding of the wisdom of the sons of Heaven" (1QS 4:22, Dead Sea Scrolls).

"All these matters will be understood by everyone who seeks for the wisdom of God, and is pleasing to Him through faith and righteousness and good deeds" (Theophilus of Antioch, *Ad Autolycum* II.38).

"Good reasoning is the understanding accompanied by a life of rectitude, putting foremost the consideration of wisdom" (4 Maccabees 1:15).

"The auxiliaries of our faith are fear [of God] and patient endurance; our allies are long-suffering and patient endurance, as long as these remain intact in all that concerns the Lord, wisdom, understanding, insight and knowledge will be happy to join their company" (*Epistle of Barnabas* 2:2-3).

"Take righteousness as your guide with the help of the understanding which God bestowed upon you" (Letter of Aristeas v.267).

"A most excellent man . . . shall understand everything" (Sibylline Oracles V.47).

"These men excel in virtue and possess full understanding" (Letter of Aristeas v.200).

"The holy people shall be given the delights of Paradise . . . and there shall be given to them a heart understanding the good" (Apocalypse of Moses 13:4,5).

"I will understand [SAKAL] in a perfect way . . . I will walk within my house with integrity of heart" (Psalm 101:2).

"If you keep silence in purity of heart, you shall understand" (Testament of Naphtali 3:1).

"Through Your precepts I get understanding" (Psalm 119:104).

"I understand more than the ancients because I keep Your precepts" (Psalm 119:100).

"From the beginning of your days all the people have known of your understanding because the formation of your heart is good [AGATHON]" (Judith 8:29).

"There is wisdom in the heart of a *good* [AGATHĒ] man" (Proverbs 14:33, Greek Text).

For "Wisdom rests in the heart of *him who has understanding*" (ibid., Hebrew Text).

"The mouth of the *righteous* flourishes with wisdom" (Proverbs 10:31).

"In the lips of *him who has understanding* wisdom is found" (Proverbs 10:13).

"Your mercy is obtained by all the sons of Your good pleasure [i.e., those who do His will]; for You have made known to them Your secret of Truth and given them understanding of all Your marvelous Mysteries" (1QH 11:9,10, Dead Sea Scrolls).

"If any one is willing to do His will, he shall know" (St. John 7:17).

"To the righteous who do His command He has made known the words of His good pleasure" (Targum on Isaiah 40:13).

"They have kept Your word, now they have known" (St. John 17:6,7).

"Be able to comprehend with all the saints . . . and to know" (Ephesians 3:18,19).

"The righteous one knows [YADA] . . . but the wicked do not understand [BIN] knowledge [DAATH]" (Proverbs 29:7).

"By his knowledge shall My righteous servant make the many to be accounted righteous" (Isaiah 53:11).

"Righteousness delivers from death" (Proverbs 10:2).

"Through knowledge shall the righteous be delivered" (Proverbs 11:9).

"Abraham [the righteous "friend of God"] was saved on the day when he acquired knowledge" (Zadokite Fragment [CD] 16:6, MS. A].

"The Most High will be known by His holy ones" (Odes of Solomon 7:16).

"Make known to me therefore the interpretation of this vision for You know that my soul has always walked in Your Law, and from my earliest days I have not departed from Your wisdom" (2 Baruch 38:2-3).

"You have been enlightened because you have forsaken your own ways and applied your diligence to My Law" (2 Esdras 13:53,54; see also 2 Baruch 54:5; 2 Esdras 6:32-33).

"Now, therefore, hold fast in your heart everything that I command you . . . and then I will show you the judgment of My might, and My ways which are past finding out" (2 Baruch 20:3,4).

"With those who held fast the commandments of God . . . God established His covenant with Israel forever, revealing to them the hidden things" (Zadokite Fragment [CD] 3:12,13,14).

"Revelations [are] for those who pass through life virtuously" (3 Baruch 11:7, Greek Baruch).

"The secret of the Lord is for those who fear Him, He makes known to them His covenant" (Psalm 25:14).

"His secret is with the upright" (Proverbs 3:32, Literal Translation).

"The Lord God . . . reveals His secret to His servants the prophets" (Amos 3:7).

"The Most High has revealed many secrets to you because He has seen your righteous conduct" (2 Esdras 10:38,39).

"The mystery which has been hidden from the past ages and generations . . . has now been manifested to His saints" (Colossians 1:26).

"The soul of a holy man . . . discovers true things sometimes" (Sirach 37:18, Latin Vulgate Text).

"The righteous shall see" (Psalm 52:6).

"The righteous shall rejoice when he sees" (Psalm 58:10).

"The upright shall see it and rejoice" (Psalm 107:42).

"His servants . . . shall rise up and see great peace" (Jubilees 23:30).

"The righteous see it and are glad" (Job 22:19).

"Light is sown for the righteous" (Psalm 97:11, Literal Translation).

"The righteous always have light" (Proverbs 13:9, Greek Text).

Conversely

"The wicked do not know, neither will they understand, they walk in darkness" (Psalm 82:4,5).

"Their wickedness blinded them, and they knew not the mysteries of God" (Wisdom 2:21,22).

"The light of the wicked shall be put out" (Job 18:5; Proverbs 13:9).

"The wicked, their light is withheld" (Job 38:15).

"They shall walk like blind men, because they have sinned against the Lord" (Zephaniah 1:17).

They were "blinded through sins" (Testament of Joseph 7:5).

"Error and darkness had their beginning together with sinners" (Sirach 11:16, Greek Cursives 248,23,106,253; ibid., Old Latin and Syriac Texts).

"The evil one . . . his luminary is extinguished and has lost its light . . . for he is a son of darkness and not of light" (Testament of Job 10:14,15).

"The wicked have lost the use of their dominant part: their understanding, over which folly has shed profound darkness" (Philo, *De Providentia*, Fragment 2,20).

"Having the understanding darkened because of . . . lasciviousness . . . uncleanness with greediness" (Ephesians 4:18,19).

"Darkened through transgressions" (Testament of Levi 14:4).

"An evil eye . . . knows not" (Proverbs 28:22).

"Wickedness . . . seeing and not understanding" (Wisdom 4:14(15), Latin Vulgate).

"Confusion of wickedness" (1QS 3:2, Dead Sea Scrolls).

"They stumble about like mad men corrupting because there is no understanding in them" (Odes of Solomon 38:14,15).

They are "led astray" by "the foolish reasonings of their unrighteousness" (Wisdom 11:15; see also Romans 1:18,21-22).

"The wicked have not known the Mystery to come, and have not understood past things" (1QMyst 1:3 [Book of Mysteries], Dead Sea Scrolls).

"The wicked do not understand knowledge" (Proverbs 29:7).

"Evil men do not understand" (Proverbs 28:5).

"None of the wicked shall understand" (Daniel 12:10).

"They are wicked, having no understanding" (Isaiah 56:11, Greek Text).

The wicked are "void of counsel because there is no understanding in them" (Zadokite Fragment 7:18; Deuteronomy 32:28).

The wicked are "ever learning, but never attaining the knowledge of the Truth" (2 Timothy 3:7).

"Men who have lived dissolutely and unrighteously . . . they went astray very far in the ways of error . . . being deceived, as babes without understanding" (Wisdom 12:23,24).

"Our fathers . . . have committed iniquity . . . have done wickedly, our fathers . . . did not understand" (Psalm 106:6,7).

"Have all the workers of iniquity no knowledge?" (Psalm 14:4; 53:4).

Yes, because "by reason of . . . the wickedness of their ways . . . their knowledge shall forsake them" (Jubilees 23:9,11).

"The works of the ungodly are far from knowledge" (Proverbs 13:19, Greek Text).

"The wicked do not know any good" (Targum on Ecclesiastes 9:5).

"The wicked and . . . the workers of iniquity . . . do not understand the deeds of the Lord nor the works of His hands" (Psalm 28:3,5).

"The word of an unrighteous and wicked man is very dark" (Philo, *Q.Exod.* II.44).

"The words of his mouth are iniquity and deceit, he has ceased to understand" (Psalm 36:3).

"Separate yourself from the [wicked] nations . . . their works are unclean, and all their ways are a pollution and an abomination and foul . . . all their works are vanity and nothingness, they have no heart to understand" (Jubilees 22:16,17,18).

"The world . . . cannot understand these things . . . because the world is full of unrighteousness" (2 Esdras 4:26,27).

"When God became angry with the [wicked] inhabitants of the earth He commanded that their knowledge should depart" (Zadokite Fragment [CD] 11:4).

"The ungodly . . . err as regard the knowledge of God" (Wisdom 14:9,22).

"As for him who abhors doing the precepts of uprightness . . . his lot does not fall among those who are taught by God" (Zadokite Fragment [CD] 2:1,2,4, MS. B1)

"A man who is accustomed to disgraceful talk will not be instructed in wisdom all the days of his life" (Sirach 23:15, Syriac Text).

"The words of his mouth are iniquity and deceit, he has ceased to understand [SAKAL]" (Psalm 36:3).

"What Truth can come out of that which is false?" (Sirach 34:4).

"The framers of evil do not understand" (Proverbs 14:22, Greek Text).

"Sinners shall not see Wisdom" (Sirach 15:7).

"Wisdom will not enter a deceitful soul, nor dwell in a body that is enslaved to sin" (Wisdom 1:4).

"He who despises the Law shall not become wise" (Sirach 33:2).

"They who have loathed My Law . . . did not understand" (2 Esdras 9:11).

"Withdrawing from the Law of God blinds the inclination of the soul" (Testament of Judah 18:3).

"My Law they did not know by reason of their pride" (2 Baruch 48:40).

"Far from scoffers is Wisdom" (Sirach 15:8, Hebrew Text).

"The unrighteous . . . shall not understand" (Wisdom 4:16,17).

"Because of their sin You have hidden the fountain of understanding and the secret of Truth from them" (1QH 5:25,26, Dead Sea Scrolls).

"They have not known Me . . . and they have no understanding; they are wise to do evil, but to do good they have no knowledge" (Jeremiah 4:22; see also Amos 3:10).

"The Holy spirit of instruction will flee deceit and depart from thoughts that are without understanding, and will not abide when unrighteousness comes in" (Wisdom 1:5).

"The spirit of fornication . . . the spirit of insatiableness . . . the spirit of fighting . . . the spirit of obsequiousness and chicanery . . . the spirit of lying . . . the spirit of injustice . . . darkens a young man's understanding" (Testament of Reuben 3:3-8).

"The spirit of fornication has caused them to err" (Hosea 4:12).

"In fornication there is neither understanding nor godliness" (Testament of Reuben 6:4).

"Fornication . . . deceives the mind and understanding" (Testament of Reuben 4:6).

"Harlotry, and wine, and new wine, take away the understanding" (Hosea 4:11).

"He who commits adultery with a woman lacks understanding" (Proverbs 6:32).

"Your spouses when they commit adultery . . . do not understand" (Hosea 4:14).

"Passions . . . blinded his soul" (Testament of Judah 18:6).

"Anger . . . blinds his eyes . . . lying darkens his understanding" (Testament of Dan 2:4).

"Wrath . . . disturbs his understanding" (Testament of Dan 4:1,2).

"The spirit of hatred darkened my understanding" (Testament of Gad 6:2).

"Anger leads the mind to frenzy and does not allow understanding to work in men" (Testament of Simeon 4:8).

"Readiness to anger banishes understanding" (Evagrius Ponticus).

"There is blindness in anger . . . no angry man sees the face in Truth" (Testament of Dan 2:2, B, A, and S Texts).

"Bad temper is first of all foolish, impetuous and without understanding [APHRON]" (Shepherd of Hermas, *Mand.* V.2.34:4).

"The angry man: "vacillates in everything he does, being pulled here and there by the evil spirits and totally blinded from a good understanding" (Shepherd of Hermas, *Mand.* V.2.34:7).

"A man of violence does not receive understanding" (Sirach 32:18, Hebrew Text, MS. E [Genizah Fragment]).

"Malicious jealousy . . . confuses the understanding" (Testament of Simeon 4:9).

"Jealousy . . . blinded my understanding" (Testament of Simeon 2:7).

"Envy . . . does not allow understanding to work in men" (Testament of Simeon 4:8).

"As His ways are plain to the holy, so are they stumbling blocks to the wicked" (Sirach 39:24).

"He who is without understanding will not remain with wisdom, she will lie upon him as a mighty stone of trial" (Sirach 6:20,21).

"You do not understand for your sins weigh you down" (Shepherd of Hermas, *Sim.* IX.28,105:6).

"Your double-mindedness makes you unable to understand" (Shepherd of Hermas, *Vis.* III.10.18:9).

"Ungodliness brings darkness upon you and you cannot see" (Theophilus of Antioch, *Ad Autolycum* I.2).

"You did not hear, yes, you did not know . . . your ear was not opened, for I knew you would deal very treacherously" (Isaiah 48:8).

"There is no fidelity, nor mercy, nor knowledge of God in the land" (Hosea 4:1).

"You shall seek wisdom among the wicked, and you shall not find it" (Proverbs 14:6, Greek Text).

Because "far from the wicked is Wisdom's word and [far is] her knowledge from the proud" (11QPs ᵃ XVIII.15 [Psalm Scroll 154:15], Dead Sea Scrolls).

"Wisdom is far from pride, and men who are liars cannot remember her" (Sirach 15:8).

But "the wisdom of the wise nothing can take away, except the blindness of ungodliness and the callousness that comes from sin" (Testament of Levi 13:7).

"He was perfect and true, he departed from evil and understood [Job 28:28] the mysteries of the heavens, and was wise in divine things" (Second Targum [Sheni] to Esther, c.2).

*　　*

Woe to those who sin after having understood.

"A man who wanders from the way of understanding shall remain in the assembly of the dead" (Proverbs 21:16).

"They shall be tormented because, having understanding, they yet committed iniquity" (2 Esdras 7:72, Old Latin Codex Sangermanensis).

"Because he transgressed though he understood, yes, for this very reason he shall be tormented" (2 Baruch 15:6).

"He called heaven and earth to witness against them . . . for though they knew and had the Law reproving them, and the light in which nothing could err, they still sinned and transgressed" (2 Baruch 19:1,3).

"Fire shall consume their thoughts . . . the Judge shall come and will not tarry because each of the inhabitants of the earth knew when he was transgressing" (2 Baruch 48:39,40).

"A man shall utterly perish who having had the knowledge of the way of righteousness forces himself into the way of darkness" (*Epistle of Barnabas* 5:4).

"The greater the knowledge given to us, the greater the risk we incur" (First Clement 41:4).

"That servant who knew his lord's will and did not prepare himself nor did according to his will, he shall be beaten with many lashes" (St. Luke 12:47).

"To him who knows how to do good and does not do it, to him it is a sin" (St. James 4:17).

"Jesus said to them 'If you were blind, you would have no sin; but since you say 'we see,' your sin remains'" (St. John 9:41).

"They are without excuse; for although they knew God they did not honor Him as God, or give thanks to Him . . . though they knew God's decree that those who do such things deserve to die, they not only do them but approve those who practice them" (Romans 1:20,21,32).

"For if after we sin deliberately after receiving the knowledge of the Truth, there no longer remains a sacrifice for sins but a fearful prospect of judgment, and a fury of fire which will consume" (Hebrews 10:26,27).

"For if after they have escaped the defilements of the world through the knowledge of our Lord and Saviour Jesus Christ, they again are entangled in them and overpowered, the last state has become worse for them than the first. For it would have been better for them never to have known the way of righteousness than after knowing it to turn back from the holy commandment delivered to them" (2 Peter 2:20,21).

"I [Wisdom] . . . will reveal to him my secrets, but if he turns away I will forsake him and deliver him to the spoilers" (Sirach 4:18,19, Hebrew Text).

"There is a wise man who is wise for many but for himself is a fool" (Sirach 37:19, Hebrew Text).

"It is impossible to restore again to repentance those who have once been enlightened and have tasted the heavenly gift, and have become partakers of the Holy Spirit, and have tasted the goodness of the Word of God and the powers of the age to come, if they then commit apostasy, since they crucify the Son of God on their own account and hold Him up to contempt" (Hebrews 6:4-6).

"The one who does not know God, and does evil, receives some punishment for his evil, but the one who has come to know God ought not to do evil, but do good . . . those who have not known God and do evil are condemned to death, but the ones who have known God . . . and do evil, will be punished doubly and will die forever" (Shepherd of Hermas, *Sim.* IX.18.95:1,2).

"A righteous man understands [SAKAL]" (Proverbs 21:12).

But "when a righteous man turns away from his righteousness, and commits iniquity, and does the same abominable things that the wicked man does, shall he live? All his righteous deeds which he has done shall not be remembered; because of the treachery of which he is guilty and the sin which he has committed, he shall die" (Ezekiel 18:24).

"Our understanding is called a spring": "the spring of understanding [BINAH]" (Philo, *Fug.* 177; 1QH 5:26, Dead Sea Scrolls).

"Understanding [SEKEL] is a wellspring of life to him who has it" (Proverbs 16:22).

"Like a muddied spring or a polluted fountain is a righteous man who gives way before the wicked" (Proverbs 25:26).

*   *

The ancient Egyptians also knew that we shall not
be wise and understanding unless we are good.

"If you wish to be a wise man, and one sitting in council with your overlord, apply your heart to perfection" (Instruction of Ptah-Hotep 1.24, Prisse Papyrus, Paris [c. 3550 B.C.]).

UNDERSTANDING AND SALT

"He shall put a taste [referring to 'salt'] into it as does understanding into a man" (Sifre Vayikra N'dab. Par.12, c.14 [re Leviticus 2:13]; Yalkut Leviticus 454, Arukh [Complete ed. Kohut, 1878]).

"If his son is eager to learn and bright [literally "salted," i.e., understanding]" (Kiddushin 29b, BT).

"Have salt in yourselves, and be at peace [see "Peace and Understanding"] with one another" (St. Mark 9:50).

"Let there be understanding in you . . . in you let there be understanding" (Pesikta Rabbati, Piska 12.3).

"You are the salt of the earth; but if the salt becomes foolish [MŌRANTHĒ] with what shall it be salted?" (St. Matthew 5:13, Literal Translation).

"Let your speech always be with grace [see "Grace and Understanding"], seasoned, as it were, with salt [i.e., understanding], so that you may know how to answer [see "Answering and Understanding"] everyone" (Colossians 4:6).

SEEKING AND UNDERSTANDING

We should seek to understand.

"If you cry out for insight [BINAH], and lift up your voice for great understanding [TEBUNAH]; if you seek understanding as silver, and search for her as for hidden treasures, then you shall understand [BIN]. . . ." (Proverbs 2:3-4,5).

"Where is the place of understanding [BINAH]? Seeing that it is hidden from the eyes of all living, and kept hidden from the birds of the heavens" (Job 28:20,21).

"God understands the way to it, and He knows its place . . . He . . . searched it out" (Job 28:23,27).

"He [God] has found out all the way to understanding [EPISTĒMĒS]" (Baruch 3:36).

But "there is no searching of His great understanding [TEBUNAH]" (Isaiah 40:28).

"The sons of Agar who seek understanding [SUNESIN] upon earth, the merchants of Merran and Teman . . . the seekers of understanding [SUNESEŌS]" (Baruch 3:23).

"I, Daniel, had seen the vision, and sought for the understanding [BINAH]" (Daniel 8:15).

"See one who understands, and seek him out earnestly" (Sirach 6:35, Hebrew Text).

"Happy is he who has found understanding [PHRONĒSIN]" (Sirach 25:9).

To seek and find, is to understand, and also to know.

"Search and seek Wisdom and she shall be made known to you . . . in the end you shall find [i.e., understand] her" (Sirach 6:27,28).

"Despise me not and in the end you shall *find*" (Sirach 31:22, Greek Text).

"Despise me not and in the end you shall *understand*" (ibid., Hebrew Text).

"They who fear the Lord shall *find* judgment" (Sirach 32:16, Greek Text).

"They who fear the Lord shall *understand* judgment" (ibid., Hebrew Text).

"Wisdom . . . *found* the just man and preserved him blameless" (Wisdom 10:5, Greek Vaticanus Text).

"Wisdom . . . *knew* the just man and preserved him blameless" (ibid. 10:5, Greek Sinaiticus, Alexandrinus and Ephraemi Texts, and Latin Vulgate Text).

"The first man [Adam] did not know Wisdom perfectly, neither shall the last one find [i.e. understand] her out" (Sirach 24:28).

God's Understanding searches out that which is hidden.

"Known to God are all His works from the beginning of the world" (Acts 15:18).

"There is no creature that is not manifest in His sight, but all things are naked and laid bare before the eyes of Him to whom we must give account" (Hebrews 4:13).

"The eyes of the Lord are ten thousand times brighter than the sun; beholding all the ways of men, and thoroughly understanding [KATANOOUNTES] the most secret parts" (Sirach 23:19).

"He [God] searches out the deep and the heart for He has great understanding [TEBUNAH]" (Sirach 42:18, Hebrew Text).

"You cannot fathom the depths of the human heart" (Judith 8:14).

Because "the heart is deep beyond all things" (Jeremiah 17:9, Greek Text).

"But the Lord searches all hearts and understands the inclination of the thoughts" (1 Chronicles 28:9).

"He . . . has found Wisdom out with His understanding [SUNESEI]" (Baruch 3:32).

Understanding helps us not only to search things out, but also to seek and find hidden wisdom and knowledge.

"A rich man is wise in his own eyes, but a poor man who has understanding searches him out" (Proverbs 28:11).

"An eloquent man is known far and wide, but a man of understanding knows when he [the eloquent man] slips" (Sirach 21:7).

For "as the palate tries the taste of a thing so does an understanding heart the taste of a lie" (Sirach 36:24, Hebrew Text).

Yes, "as the palate tastes different kinds of venison so does an understanding [SUNETĒ] heart [detect] false speeches" (Sirach 36:19).

"The ear [of one who understands] tries words, as the mouth tastes meat" (Job 34:3).

"A man of understanding understands the word" (Sirach 33:3, Hebrew Text).

"Cannot my understanding [literally "taste"] understand [BIN] perverse things [i.e., detect them]?" (Job 6:30).

"One who understands proves the work of the worker" (Sirach 31:26b, Hebrew Text).

"The man of understanding recognizes the one who is before him, and spies out the sinner in a moment" (Sirach 21:7, Syriac Text).

Hence it is written in the book of Nehemiah 13:7:

> "I came to Jerusalem and found out [literally "understood"] of the evil that Eliashib did for Tobiah."

And in the book of Ezra 8:15:

> "I [Ezra] gathered them together . . . and I scrutinized [literally "understood"] the people and the priests, and found none of the sons of Levi among them."

"Understanding loves to learn and advance to full understanding, and its way is to seek the hidden meaning rather than the obvious" (Philo, *Decal.* 1).

"O my Understanding, you search . . . into the oracles" (Philo, *Det.* 13).

"I gave my heart [i.e., understanding] to seek and search out" (Ecclesiastes 1:13).

"I applied my heart to know [i.e., "to know Wisdom," as in 1:17], and to search and to seek out wisdom" (Ecclesiastes 7:25).

"I will . . . trace [i.e., seek with understanding] Wisdom out from the beginning of Creation, and bring into light the knowledge of her" (Wisdom 6:22).

"He [the understanding scribe] will seek out the wisdom of the ancients . . . he will seek out the hidden meaning of proverbs" (Sirach 39:1,3).

"Whoever occupies himself with the Law [searching through it with his understanding] . . . to him are revealed the secrets of the Law" (Kallah Rabbathi 54a).

"Wisdom . . . takes hold of those who *seek* her" (Sirach 4:11, Greek Text).

"Wisdom . . . takes hold of those who *understand* her" (ibid., Hebrew Text).

"And by their *searchings out* rulers of the people" (Sirach 44:4, Hebrew Text).

"And by their *understanding* [SUNESEI] . . . leaders of the people" (ibid., Greek Text).

Conversely

"There is no one who understands, there is no one who seeks after God" (Romans 3:11).

"They stumble about like mad and corrupted men since there is no understanding in them, neither do they seek it" (Odes of Solomon 38:15).

*   *

"The god Sia [Egyptian god of Understanding] who is in men's hearts, his eyes examine the hearts of all" (Cairo Papyrus No. 20538).

"He [Amenenhet IV] is Understanding [Sia] in men's hearts, and his eyes search out everyone" (Stele of Amenenhet IV [Cairo], Text found in K.Piehl's *Inscript. Hieroglyphiques*, series 3, pl.5-6, Uppsala, 1903).

"Thou art Thoth [the all-wise and understanding scribe of the gods] who lovest Truth, thou lookest into hearts" (Turin Tablet No. 101).

"Thoth, the knowing one who does search out the hidden things . . . he who looks through bodies and tests hearts" (Tomb of Nb-Wnnf, Transcription by K. Sethe).

"His heart [i.e., understanding] is like that of Thoth searching out the [secret] plans which they love" (LD 3.175A found in C.R. Lepsius' *Denkmäler aus Aegypten etc.,* Texts 1-5, Leipzig, 1913).

SHEPHERDS AND UNDERSTANDING

"I will give you shepherds after My own heart, who shall feed you with knowledge and understanding" (Jeremiah 3:15).

"He also chose David His servant and took him from the sheepfolds; from the tending of the ewes with suckling lambs, He brought him to shepherd Jacob His people, and Israel His inheritance. So he fed them according to the integrity of his heart and guided them by the great understanding [TEBUNAH] of his hands" (Psalm 78:70-72).

"David, the [shepherd] son of Jesse was wise, and a light like the light of the sun, and literate and understanding [BIN] and perfect in all his ways before God and men. And the Lord gave him an understanding [BINAH] and enlightened spirit" (11QPsª Col. XXVII.2-4 [Psalm 151], Dead Sea Scrolls).

"A shepherd with understanding" (Sumerian Hymn 23 1.10 [Sumerische Konigshymnen, Ed. W.P. Roemer, 1965]).

"Jesus said unto them . . . 'I am the good Shepherd'" (St. John 10:7,11).

"Jesus when He came saw many people, and was moved with compassion, because [He saw] they were like sheep without a shepherd, and so He began to teach them many things" (St. Mark 6:34).

For "Jesus Christ . . . is the Understanding of the Father" (St. Ignatius, *Epistle to the Ephesians* 3:2).

"The Lord shall . . . feed His flock with power [see "The Power and Strength of Understanding"]" (Micah 5:4, Greek Text).

Conversely

"His watchmen are blind, they know nothing, they are all dumb dogs unable to bark, sleeping lying down, loving to slumber. Yes, they are greedy dogs who are never satisfied. And they are shepherds who cannot understand [BIN]" (Isaiah 56:10-11).

"The shepherds have become brutish, and they have not sought the Lord; therefore they shall not understand [SAKAL], and all their flocks shall be scattered" (Jeremiah 10:21).

SILVER AND UNDERSTANDING

"If you . . . lift up your voice for Great Understanding [TEBUNAH], if you seek her as silver" (Proverbs 2:3,4).

"How much better it is to buy wisdom than gold, and to get understanding is rather to be chosen than silver" (Proverbs 16:16).

"Wisdom [as gold] is a defense [i.e., protection], and silver [as understanding] is a defense" (Ecclesiastes 7:12).

Because "Great Understanding [TEBUNAH] will watch [NATSAR] over you" (Proverbs 2:11).

"The Almighty . . . will He not understand [BIN]?" (Job 11:7,11).

"The understanding of the Almighty" (Judith 8:13, Greek Codex 58 and the Old Latin and Syriac Texts).

"The Almighty . . . He has understanding" (Sirach 42:17,18, Greek Sinaiticus and Alexandrinus Texts).

"The breath of the Almighty gives them understanding" (Job 32:8).

"The Almighty [who gives us understanding] shall be your defense, and you shall have plenty of silver [i.e., understanding]" (Job 22:25, KJV).

"Happy is the man . . . who gets great understanding [TEBUNAH], for its profit is better than the profit of silver and its gain than fine gold" (Proverbs 3:13,14).

"Gold is acquired by means of silver" (Baba Metzia 44a, BT).

"How much better it is to buy wisdom than gold" (Proverbs 16:16a).

But "a man without understanding [APHRONI] will not be able to buy wisdom" [because he has no 'silver' of understanding] (Proverbs 17:16, Greek Text).

"Receive my instruction [which will give you understanding] and not silver [itself]" (Proverbs 8:10).

"The divine revelations [which give us understanding into the mysteries of God] are often denoted by the term 'silver' " (St. Gregory, *Morals on the Book of Job* XVIII.45).

"How shall I be able to answer unless You make me to understand [SAKAL]?" (1QH 10:7, Dead Sea Scrolls).

For we need "understanding to answer" (Pesikta Rabbati, Piska 33.3).

"Let men of understanding answer [AMAR] me" (Job 34:34).

"If you have understanding, answer your neighbor" (Sirach 5:12).

"Silver [KESEPH] answers all [just as understanding does]" (Ecclesiastes 10:19).

"Close to the heart, which is the seat of understanding, God set the breasts" (Midrash Rabbah on Psalms 103.3).

God "who formed man out of a meager drop, brought him forth into the light of the world and provided nourishment [at the breasts] for him in the acquisition of understanding" (Testament of Naphtali 10:8, Hebrew Text, Codex 563, MS. Parma de Rossi [Ed. A. Wertheimer]).

"His breast [where the heart and understanding are] and arms [see "Right Hand and Understanding"] are of silver [KESEPH]" (Daniel 2:32).

SKILL AND UNDERSTANDING

"As a man's strength, so also is his work, and as his understanding [NOUS] so also is his skill [TECHNĒ]" Testament of Naphtali 2:6, Greek A Text).

"As the mind is to sense, so understanding [EPISTĒMĒ] is to skill [TECHNĒN]" (Philo, *Cong.* 144).

"And if Understanding [PHRONĒSIS] works; who of all who are, is a more skill-ful artisan [TECHNITIS] . . . ?" (Wisdom 8:6).

We know that it takes Wisdom to build [W/N:21-26].
And because good artisans have wisdom and understanding,
they have the skill to build well.

"A wise son knowing understanding [SEKEL] and insight [BINAH] that he may build a house for the Lord, and a house for his kingdom" (2 Chronicles 2:12).

"I was the first to build a boat to sail upon the sea, for the Lord gave me under-standing and wisdom" (Testament of Zebulon 6:1).

"To everyone who is understanding [SUNETO] in heart, I have given under-standing, and they shall build . . . the tabernacle of witness, and the ark of the covenant, and the propitiatory that is upon it, and the furniture of the tabernacle, and the altars, and the table and all its furniture, and the pure candlestick and all its furniture [all the work of artisans]" (Exodus 31:6-9, Greek Text).

*   *

Jesus "the carpenter [TEKTŌN], the son of Mary" (St. Mark 6:3).

Jesus "Christ, in whom are hidden all the treasures of wisdom and knowledge" (Colossians 2:2,3).

Jesus "Christ, the Power of God and the Wisdom of God" (1 Corinthians 1:24).

"All who heard Him [Jesus] were astonished at His understanding" (St. Luke 2:47).

*   *

Among the rabbis the Hebrew word CHARASH ("master carpenter") and the Aramaic word for "craftsman" [NAGGAR] became also words used to describe someone who really understood and could resolve mysterious things by joining (as in carpentering) pertinent texts together: "he linked together the words of the Torah with those of the prophets and those of the prophets with those of the hagiographers, and therefore the words of the Torah rejoiced as on the day they were revealed in the flames of Sinai" (Midrash Song of Songs Rabbah I.10.2; Midrash Leviticus Rabbah 16.2 re Rabbi Simeon ben Azzai).

Thus, if a difficult problem arose in their discussions the rabbis would ask: "Is there a master carpenter among us, or the son of a master carpenter who can solve the problem for us?" (Abodah Zarah 50b, BT; Qiddushin I.66a, JT).

"When a man who has understanding sees something either wholly or partially, he can build upon it and complete it" (Zohar Hadash [Bereshith], 4a).

UNDERSTANDING SOWS AND PLANTS

"Through counsel the understanding sows worthy, fitting, and persuasive things in those who are not discordant in aiming at the Truth" (Philo, *Q.Gen.* IV.56).

"The truly existent One planted the tree of life by His lucid understanding" (Philo, *Q.Gen.* I.55).

THE SPIRIT AND UNDERSTANDING

"You did give Your good Spirit to make them understand [SAKAL]" (Nehemiah 9:20).

"The Spirit which gives understanding" (Enoch 49:3b).

"The Spirit of understanding and of power" (Enoch 49:3c).

"The Spirit of understanding" (Testament of Judah 20:2).

"The Spirit of understanding of the Lord came upon me" (Testament of Levi 2:3).

"The Spirit of understanding and sanctification shall rest upon him" (Testament of Levi 18:7).

"God will make him . . . wise by means of the Spirit of understanding" (Psalms of Solomon 17:42).

"In whom the Spirit of God is . . . there is no one so understanding and wise" (Genesis 41:38,39).

"If the great Lord is willing, he shall be filled with the Spirit of understanding; he will pour forth words of wisdom and give thanks to the Lord in prayer" (Sirach 39:6).

"He has filled him with the Spirit of God, in wisdom, in great understanding [TEBUNAH], and in knowledge" (Exodus 35:31; 31:3).

"Be renewed in the spirit of your understanding [NOUS]" (Ephesians 4:23).

"The spirit of my understanding [BINAH] causes me to answer" (Job 20:3; see "Understanding and Answering").

"That which is precious [YAQAR] about the spirit of man is great understanding [TEBUNAH]" (Proverbs 17:27, Literal Translation).

"A spirit [PNEUMA] of understanding" (Job 15:2, Greek Text).

"In Wisdom there is an understanding spirit" (Wisdom 7:22).

"The spirit of wisdom and understanding [BINAH]" (Isaiah 11:2).

"My soul recovered the spirit of understanding" (2 Esdras 5:22).

"What is the spirit of flesh to understanding [BIN] all these things, and to understand [SAKAL] Your great secret of Truth?" (1QH 13:13,14, Dead Sea Scrolls).

"I Your servant know through the *Spirit* which You have given me" (1QH 13:19, Dead Sea Scrolls).

"I know by the *Spirit* which You have given me" (1QH Fragment 3:14, Dead Sea Scrolls).

"I know by Your *understanding* [BINAH]" (1QH 4:12, Dead Sea Scrolls).

"I know on the basis of Your *understanding* [BINAH]" (1QH 1:21, Dead Sea Scrolls).

"He who keeps the Law becomes master of the *spirit* thereof" (Sirach 21:11, Syriac Text).

"He who keeps the Law gets the *understanding* [ENNOĒMATOS] thereof [AUTOU]" (ibid., Greek Text).

"The understanding [PHRONĒMA] of the Spirit" (Romans 8:6).

"He shall examine him according to his *spirit* and deeds" (1QS 6:17, Dead Sea Scrolls).

"He shall examine him according to his *understanding* [SEKEL] and deeds" (1QS 6:14, Dead Sea Scrolls).

"Understanding [BINAH]" is called "the Spirit of God" (Zohar I.246b; ibid. II.238b-239a).

"Who has pondered [see "Pondering and Understanding"] the *Spirit* [RUACH] of the Lord?" (Isaiah 40:13, Hebrew Text).

"Who has known the *understanding* [NOUS] of the Lord?" (ibid., Greek Text).

Knowing that "Spirit" and "Understanding" are used synonymously, we shall understand what the Spirit of Christ means.

"Their minds were made dull, for to this very day the same veil remains [covering their understanding] when the Old Testament is read, because only through Christ is it taken away. Even to this day whenever Moses is read, a veil lies over their understanding; but whenever a man turns to the Lord, the veil is removed.

Now the Lord is the Spirit [i.e., Understanding]" (2 Corinthians 3:14-17; see Job 33:16, Greek Text, for the term 'unveiling of the understanding').

"For who has known the understanding ["Spirit" [RUACH] in the Hebrew Text] of the Lord? . . . but we have the understanding [NOUS] of Christ" (1 Corinthians 2:16; Isaiah 40:13).

"He [Jesus Christ] opened their understanding [NOUS] so that they might understand the Scriptures" (St. Luke 24:45).

Jesus "Christ, in whom are hid all the treasures of wisdom and knowledge" (Colossians 2:2,3).

"We know that the Son of God has come, and has given us understanding" (1 John 5:20).

"The Lord [Jesus Christ] will give you understanding in all things" (2 Timothy 2:7).

*   *

Since the "spirit" of man and "understanding" are synonymous, both are said to have been "formed."

"The Lord . . . forms the *spirit* of man within him" (Zechariah 12:1).

"The *spirit* which God forms for him" (1QH 4:31, Dead Sea Scrolls).

"The *spirit* which gives understanding" (Enoch 49:3).

"By what means can I obtain *understanding* unless You form it for me?" (1QH 10:6, Dead Sea Scrolls).

"I [the Lord] . . . formed the *understanding*" (Odes of Solomon 8:18).

"The Lord is also pleased . . . to form him with *understanding*" (Isaiah 53:11, Greek Text).

The Holy Spirit gives us understanding by instructing us and guiding us into all the Truth.

To "receive instruction" is to "learn understanding [SUNESIS]" (Sirach 8:8,9, Hebrew and Greek Texts respectively).

"The Holy Spirit whom the Father will send in My name, He shall teach you all things, and bring all things to your remembrance, whatsoever I have said to you" (St. John 14:26).

"The Spirit of Truth . . . He will guide you into all Truth" (St. John 16:13).

"The Holy Spirit shall teach you" (St. Luke 12:12).

"The Holy Spirit of instruction" (Wisdom 1:5).

"Instruction was given through the Holy Spirit" (Pesikta Rabbati, Piska 3.4 [re Psalm 89:1]).

"The Holy Spirit teaches, comparing spiritual things with spiritual" (1 Corinthians 2:13).

"I am gifted with understanding [SAKAL] . . . because of the Spirit that You have put in me" (1QH 12:11,12, Dead Sea Scrolls).

"I know because of the Holy Spirit which You have put in me" (1QH 16:1,2, Dead Sea Scrolls)

"The prophets revealed in His Holy Spirit" (1QS 8:16, Dead Sea Scrolls).

"The Mystery of Christ . . . is now revealed to His holy apostles and prophets by the Spirit" (Ephesians 3:4,5).

"The things which God has prepared for those who love Him . . . God has revealed them to us by His Spirit" (1 Corinthians 2:9,10).

"Teach me to do Your will for You are my God, Your Spirit is good [who shall teach me]" (Psalm 143:10).

Through "Your Holy Spirit from on high . . . men were taught the things that are pleasing to You" (Wisdom 9:17,18).

> *Since the Holy Spirit reveals all things, He is the Spirit of Knowledge and of Prophecy. The Holy Spirit shall convince us and enable us to convince others concerning His Truth.*

"Your counsel who has known, except when You give Wisdom and send Your Holy Spirit from above?" (Wisdom 9:17).

"The things of God no one knows except the Spirit of God" (1 Corinthians 2:11).

"For the Spirit searches all things, yes, even the deep things of God" (1 Corinthians 2:10).

"We have received . . . the Spirit which is of God, so that we may know the things which are freely given to us by God" (1 Corinthians 2:12).

"This is the Spirit of the Lord who does not lie, and who teaches the sons of men to know His ways" (Odes of Solomon 3:12).

"The Spirit rested upon them, and they prophesied" (Numbers 11:25, also v.26).

"The Spirit of the Lord will come upon you, and you shall prophesy . . . and the Spirit of God came upon him and he prophesied" (1 Samuel 10:6,10).

"And his father Zacharias was filled with the Holy Spirit, and he prophesied" (St. Luke 1:67).

"The testimony of Jesus is the Spirit of prophecy" (Revelation 19:10).

"The Spirit is poured out upon me, that I may show you everything that shall befall you" (Enoch 91:1).

"He [Isaiah] saw by an excellent Spirit what would come to pass . . . he showed the things that will happen at the end of time, and the hidden things before they came" (Sirach 48:24,25).

"You have blessed Your servant with the Spirit of knowledge" (1QH 14:25, Dead Sea Scrolls).

"When He [the Holy Spirit] comes, He will convince the world of sin, and of righteousness and of judgment" (St. John 16:8).

"Do not be anxious how or what you are to answer [see "Understanding and Answering"] or what you are to say; for the Holy Spirit shall teach you in that same hour what you ought to say" (St. Luke 12:11,12).

"You shall receive power when the Holy Spirit comes upon you, and you shall be My witnesses . . . to the ends of the earth" (Acts 1:8).

"Take not Your Holy Spirit from me . . . uphold me with Your noble Spirit then I will teach transgressors Your ways, and sinners shall be converted to You" (Psalm 51:11,12,13).

*   *

"Those who erred in spirit [RUACH] shall know [YADA] understanding [BINAH]" (Isaiah 29:24).

Those who believe in the Lord Jesus Christ receive
Understanding from Him. Thus, it is also through the
Lord that we receive the Holy Spirit of Understanding.

"Their minds were made dull, for to this very day the same veil remains [covering their understanding] when the Old Testament is read, because only through Christ is it taken away. Even to this day whenever Moses is read a veil lies over their understanding; but whenever a man turns to the Lord [Jesus] the veil is removed" (2 Corinthians 3:14-16).

"He [Jesus] opened their understanding [NOUS] so that they might understand the Scriptures" (St. Luke 24:45).

"We know that the Son of God [Jesus] has come and has given us understanding, in order that we might know Him who is true" (1 John 5:20).

"We have the understanding of Christ" (1 Corinthians 2:16).

"Why do you not ask of the Lord [Jesus] understanding and receive it from Him?" (Shepherd of Hermas, *Sim.* V.4.57:4).

"Ask the Lord [Jesus] to receive the insight to understand" (Shepherd of Hermas, *Sim.* IX.2.79:6).

"The Lord [Jesus] give you understanding in all things" (2 Timothy 2:7).

"Jesus stood and cried out, saying . . . 'he who believes in Me, as the Scripture said, out of his innermost being shall flow rivers of living water.' But this He spoke of the Spirit, whom those who believed in Him were to receive" (St. John 7:37,38,39).

"The Comforter, the Holy Spirit, whom the Father will send in My name [Jesus], He will teach you all things, and bring to your remembrance all that I have said to you" (St. John 14:26).

"I will ask the Father, and He will give you another Comforter, that He may be with you forever, that is the Spirit of Truth" (St. John 14:16).

"When the Comforter comes, whom I will send to you from the Father, that is the Spirit of Truth, who proceeds from the Father, He will bear witness concerning Me" (St. John 15:26).

"I tell you the Truth, it is to your advantage that I go away; for if I do not go away, the Comforter shall not come to you; but if I go, I will send Him [the Holy Spirit] to you" (St. John 16:7).

"Jesus . . . being therefore exalted at the right hand of God, and having received from the Father the promise of the Holy Spirit, He has poured out this which you see and hear" (Acts 2:32,33).

"Jesus said to them . . . 'receive the Holy Spirit' " (St. John 20:21,22).

STAND AND UNDERSTAND

"Hearken to this, O Job, stand ['AMAD] still and understand [BIN] the wonders of God" (Job 37:14).

"I stand ['AMAD] up and You understand [BIN] me" (Job 30:20).

"That this vermin that is man may be raised from the dust to Your secret of Truth, and from the spirits of perversity to Your understanding [BINAH], that he might stand ['AMAD] before You with the everlasting host" (1QH 11:12,13, Dead Sea Scrolls; see also Shekalim I.45d, JT).

"Let the counsel of your own heart *stand*, for there is no man more faithful to you than it" (Sirach 37:13, Greek Text).

"*Understand* [BIN] the counsel of your own heart, for who is more faithful to you than it?" (ibid., Hebrew Text).

"As timber girt and bound together in a building cannot be loosened by shaking [but continues standing], so the heart [i.e., understanding] that is established by well advised counsel shall not fear at any time [but shall stand fast]" (Sirach 22:16; see "Understanding Establishes" etc.).

"When he [Uriel the angel, v.28] saw that I lay on the ground as one dead, my understanding being collapsed, he grasped my right hand [see "The Right Hand and Understanding"] and strengthened me . . . and he said unto me: 'stand up like a man! and I will counsel you' " (2 Esdras 10:30,33; see "Man and understanding" and "Understanding and Counselling").

"If you can answer me [see "Understanding and Answering"] . . . stand up!" (Job 33:5).

"Do you see a man quick [see "The Quickness of Understanding"] in work? he shall stand before Kings" (Proverbs 22:29).

"Now I will arise [i.e., stand up], says the Lord, now I will be glorified, now I will be exalted. Now you shall see, now you shall understand" (Isaiah 33:10,11, Greek Text).

"Behold, My servant will understand [SAKAL], he shall be exalted and extolled [NASA, "lifted up"], and be very high . . . Kings shall shut their mouths because of him; for that which has not been told them they shall see, and that which they have not heard they shall understand [BIN]" (Isaiah 52:13,15).

"A servant who has understanding [SAKAL] shall be exalted" (Sirach 10:24, Hebrew Text).

"How . . . shall he answer his Maker, and how shall he understand [BIN] His works? and how shall he stand [if he has no understanding]?" (1QH 12:27,28, Dead Sea Scrolls).

"And the Lord shall stand . . . and feed His flock with power" (Micah 5:4, Greek Text; see "The Power and Strength of Understanding").

"The words of the Torah stand up [i.e., they let themselves be understood] for him who valorously gives them the labor they require to be understood" (Pesikta de Rab Kahana, Piska 12.5).

SUFFERING AND UNDERSTANDING

Ever since the Fall and expulsion from the Garden of Eden,
the lot of mankind is to labor and suffer in the field
of exile. Nevertheless, through the kindness of
the Lord, we receive understanding in the
midst of our tribulations to comfort
and strengthen us.

"Is not the life of man upon earth a state of trial?" (Job 7:1, Greek Text).

"Man is born to labor" (Job 5:7).

"Great travail is created for every man, and a heavy yoke is upon the sons of man" (Sirach 40:1).

"I have seen the travail, which God has given to the sons of man to be afflicted with" (Ecclesiastes 3:10).

"Man is land suffering" (*Epistle of Barnabas* 6:9).

"The understanding in us call it 'Man'" (Philo, *Cher.* 57; see "Man and Understanding").

Pain and Suffering help us to understand and to know.

"To whom has the *discipline* of wisdom been revealed and made manifest?" (Sirach 1:7, Latin Vulgate).

"To whom has the *understanding* [EPISTĒMĒ] of wisdom been made manifest?" (Sirach 1:7, Greek Cursives 23,55,70,106,253 and Old Latin Texts).

"Discipline and understanding [EPISTĒMĒS]" go together (Philo, *Q.Gen.* IV.103).

"Such is the discipline of wisdom, causing pain to produce understanding" (Clement of Alexandria, *Strom.* II.c.2).

Conversely: "All the undisciplined people void of understanding" (Sibylline Oracles III.670).

"From desolation to ruin and from pain to the blow and from travail to the billows ['of death' v.4] my soul [as a result] understood [BIN] Your marvels" (1QH 9:6,7, Dead Sea Scrolls).

"I will teach you by the hand of God" (Job 27:11).

"The Lord made me to understand [SAKAL] . . . by His hand upon me" (1 Chronicles 28:19).

"Day and night Your hand was heavy upon me . . . I [the Lord] will make you understand [SAKAL] and teach you in the way you should go" (Psalm 32:4,8).

"Give me understanding that I may learn Your commandments" (Psalm 119:73).

"It is good for me that I have been afflicted, that I may learn" (Psalm 119:71).

"He who has learned many things, shall show forth understanding" (Sirach 34:9, Latin Vulgate).

"Be understanding [EUPHRŌNESON] then, at last, O Croesus, taught by suffering" (Clement of Alexandria, *Exh.* III.43.4).

"Bow down your heart to great understanding [TEBUNAH]" (Proverbs 2:2, Literal Translation).

"He brought down [KANA = 'subdued,' 'brought low'] their heart [i.e., understanding] through suffering" Psalm 107:12).

"Every hour I suffer agonies of heart striving to understand" (2 Esdras 5:34).

"He extended to me a full cup which was full as it were with water, but the colour of it was like fire. And I took it, and drank and when I had drunk of it, my heart anguished forth [CRUCIABATUR] understanding" (2 Esdras 14:39,40, Latin Vulgate).

"I fasted seven days, mourning and weeping . . . then my soul recovered the spirit of understanding" (2 Esdras 5:21,22).

"Troubles have enlarged my heart" (Psalm 25:17 [see "Heart and Understanding" and "The Breadth and Depth of Understanding"].

"Your heart shall fear and be enlarged" (Isaiah 60:5).

"I will run the way of Your commandments when You shall enlarge my heart" (Psalm 119:32).

"Give me understanding and I shall keep Your Law, yes, I shall observe it with all my heart" (Psalm 119:34).

"He who pricks the heart makes it show her knowledge" (Sirach 22:19).

"He has driven a goad right through my heart to tell exactly all that is happening to men now and all that is to happen" (Sibylline Oracles IV.18-20).

"A sword shall pierce through thine own soul also, that the thoughts of many hearts may be revealed" (St. Luke 2:35).

"I understand . . . for God makes my heart soft [hard hearts do not understand] and the Almighty troubles me" (Job 23:15,16).

"The Almighty gives them understanding" (Job 32:8).

"The Almighty Lord . . . He has understanding" (Sirach 42:17,18, Greek Sinaiticus and Alexandrinus Texts).

"Vexation alone shall make you understand what you hear" (Isaiah 28:19, Old Latin and Latin Vulgate Texts).

"He delivers the poor in his affliction and opens their ears [to understand] in oppression" (Job 36:15).

"He opens the *ears* of men" (Job 33:16, Hebrew Text).

"He opens the *understanding* [NOUN] of men" (ibid., Greek Text).

"If they be bound in fetters and held in the cords of affliction, then . . . He opens their ears to instruction" (Job 36:8,9,10).

"When a dreadful alarm happens to fall upon men, in slumberings on the bed, then He opens [literally 'unveils'] the understanding of men" (Job 33:15,16, Greek Text).

"The wicked [who have persecuted the Psalmist, see vv.78,84-87,92] have waited for me to destroy me, but I will [through sufferings] understand [BIN] Your testimonies" (Psalm 119:95).

"I will expose her uncleanness . . . no one shall by any means deliver her out of My hand, and I will take away all her gladness . . . I will . . . make her desolate . . . to open her understanding [SUNESIN]" (Hosea 2:10,11,14,15, Greek Text).

Knowing that mourning and suffering enlarge and soften the heart so that it may understand all the more:

> "The heart of the wise is in the house of mourning; but
> the heart of fools is in the house of mirth" (Ecclesiastes
> 7:4).

"For sorrow is better than laughter [for the understanding], because by the sadness of the countenance the heart [i.e., understanding] is made better" (Ecclesiastes 7:3).

"It is better to hear the rebuke of the wise, than for a man to hear the song of fools" (Ecclesiastes 7:5).

For "he who hears reproof gets understanding" (Proverbs 15:32).

"And he who regards reproofs shall be made wise" (Proverbs 16:17, Greek Text).

"Reprove one who has understanding and he will understand [BIN] knowledge" (Proverbs 19:25).

Conversely: "One who is insensitive to reproach will never be instructed in wisdom" (Sirach 23:15, Syriac Text).

"Admonition is the censure of loving care and produces understanding" (Clement of Alexandria, *Paed.* I.9.76:1).

"I will reprove you, and set in order before your eyes, now understand this you who forget God" (Psalm 50:21,22).

"A reproof enters more into a man of understanding than a hundred blows into a fool" (Proverbs 17:10).

"Affliction regulated by Law breeds a perfect good, that most admirable thing: admonition [NOUTHESIA = TITHEMI ('putting in') of NOUS ('understanding')]" (Philo, *Cong.* 160).

"He *chastised* him" (Deuteronomy 32:10, Greek Text).

"He made him to *understand* [BIN]" (ibid. 32:10, Hebrew Text).

"Whoever loves chastisement loves knowledge, but he who hates reproof is brutish" (Proverbs 12:1).

He "is brutish in his knowledge" (Jeremiah 10:14; 51:17).

"He who chastises . . . shall He not correct? He who teaches man knowledge?" (Psalm 94:10).

"Who will set scourges over my thoughts, and the chastisement of wisdom over my heart, that they spare me not for my lack of knowledge [AGNOĒMASI]?" (Sirach 23:2).

"A fool though scourged knows not" (Proverbs 17:10, Greek Text).

"They have beaten me . . . and I knew it not" (Proverbs 23:35).

"In vain have I smitten your children and they have received no instruction" (Jeremiah 2:30; ibid. 5:3).

"A rod is for the back of him who is void of understanding" (Proverbs 10:13).

"Folly is bound up in the heart of a child but the rod of correction will drive it far from him" (Proverbs 22:15).

For "the rod and reproof give wisdom" (Proverbs 29:15).

"Happy is the man whom You do chasten O Lord, and teach out of Your Law" (Psalm 94:12).

"Behold, happy is the man whom God corrects, therefore do not despise the chastening [MUSAR] of the Almighty for . . . you shall know . . . you shall know" (Job 5:17,18,24,25).

"You have chastised me and I was chastised . . . surely after that I was turned, I repented, and after that I was made to know [YADA]" (Jeremiah 31:18,19).

"Has anyone said to God, 'I have borne chastisement; I will not offend You any more, do teach me what I do not see [and know]?' " (Job 34:31,32).

"He humbled you and let you be hungry . . . that He might make you know [YADA]" (Deuteronomy 8:3).

"Fifteen days after I had fasted and prayed much to the Lord, the knowledge of the writing was revealed to me" (Shepherd of Hermas, *Vis.* II.2.6:1).

"You shall also know in your heart [after being chastised] that, as a man chastises his son, so the Lord your God chastises you" (Deuteronomy 8:5).

"Your own wickedness will chastise you, and your apostasy will reprove you, know and see" (Jeremiah 2:19).

"A man of understanding [EPISTĒMŌN] will not complain when he is disciplined" (Sirach 10:25).

Nor will he object to "The disciplines of knowledge" (1QS 3:1, Dead Sea Scrolls).

"The *misery* of man is great upon him" (Ecclesiastes 8:6, Hebrew Text).

"The *knowledge* of man is great to him" (ibid., Greek Text).

"In much wisdom is much grief, and he who increases knowledge increases sorrow [because grief and sorrow give wisdom and knowledge]" (Ecclesiastes 1:18).

"Ungodly men denying knowledge of You were scourged by the strength of Your arm . . . that they might see and know" (Wisdom 16:16,18).

"Brought to know . . . by torment" (2 Esdras 9:12).

"Through the sufferings . . . knowing Him whom before they refused to know, they fully knew [EPEGNŌSAN = 'to fully know' and 'acknowledge'] the true God" (Wisdom 12:27).

"His limbs were much pained by a grievous bruising of the body . . . he lived in sorrow and in pain . . . by this means [the sufferings], being brought down from his great pride, he began to come to full knowledge [EPIGNŌSIN] by the scourge of God" (2 Maccabees 9:7,9,11).

"There appeared two other young men beautiful and strong, bright and glorious, and in comely apparel who stood by him . . . and scourged him [Heliodorus] without ceasing with many lashes. And Heliodorus suddenly fell to the ground . . . the same young men . . . said to him: 'give thanks to Onias the priest because for his sake the Lord has granted you life. And you having been scourged by God, declare unto all men the great works and power of God . . .' and he [Heliodorus] testified to all men the works of the great God, which he had seen with his own eyes" (2 Maccabees 3:26,27,33,34,35,36).

"Pain brings forth perception" (Philo, *L.A.* III.216).

"Behold, My [suffering] Servant shall understand [SAKAL], He shall be exalted and lifted up, and shall be very high. Just as many were astonished at Him, His appearance was so marred more than any man, and His form more than the sons of man. Thus shall He startle many nations, Kings shall shut their mouths because of Him; for that which has not been told them they shall see [and know], and that which they had not heard they shall understand" (Isaiah 52:13-15).

"A servant who has understanding [SAKAL] shall be exalted" (Sirach 10:24, Hebrew Text).

"He [the suffering servant] was despised and rejected by men, a man of sorrows, and knowing [YADA] suffering . . . He was despised, and we did not esteem Him. Surely He bore our infirmities and carried our sorrows; yet we considered Him stricken, smitten by God, and afflicted. But He was wounded for our transgressions, He was bruised for our iniquities; upon Him was the chastisement that made us whole . . . the Lord has laid on Him the iniquity of us all. He was oppressed and afflicted, yet He did not open His mouth; like a lamb that is led to the slaughter, and like a sheep that is silent before its shearers, He did not open His mouth . . . yet it was the will of the Lord to bruise Him and cause Him to suffer; if He shall render Himself as a guilt offering, He will see His offspring and prolong His days, and the will of the Lord shall prosper in His hand. He shall see the fruit of the labor of His soul and shall be satisfied, by His knowledge [gained through suffering] shall the Righteous One, My Servant, make the many to be accounted righteous" (Isaiah 53:3,4,5,6,7,10-11).

"The godly man . . . makes his sufferings contribute to the increase of his knowledge" (Corpus Hermeticum, Libellus IX.4b).

"Suffering leads to knowledge" (Herodotus I.207 [see also Aeschylus, *Ag.* 176ff, 249ff; Sophocles, *Oed. Col.* 7ff; Corpus Hermeticum I.4ff, 482; Irenaeus, *Adversus Haereses* I.4.5; Plotinus, *Enn.* IV.8,7]).

"Now brethren, we make known to you . . . that in a great ordeal of affliction . . . you abound in everything, in faith and utterance and knowledge" (2 Corinthians 8:1,2,7).

"When they were tried, though they were being disciplined in mercy, they thoroughly knew [EGNŌSAN] . . . for You did admonish and try them as a father" (Wisdom 11:9,10).

"What does he know who has not been tried?" (Sirach 34:9, Latin Vulgate).

"He who has not been tried, what manner of things does he know?" (Sirach 34:11, Latin Vulgate).

"He who has not been tried knows little" (Sirach 34:10, Greek Sinaiticus Text).

"I count all things to be loss compared to the excellency of the knowledge [GNŌSEŌS] of Christ Jesus my Lord, for whom I have suffered the loss of all things . . . that I may know Him" (Philippians 3:8,10).

"An agonizing conflict she [Wisdom] decided for him [Jacob] that he might know [GNŌ]" (Wisdom 10:12).

"My people have gone into captivity [to suffer] because they have no knowledge [DAATH]" (Isaiah 5:13).

"Misery will come suddenly upon you, I have caused you to be tried among nations and you shall know" (Jeremiah 6:26,27, Greek Text).

"The pains of a woman in labor shall come upon him, for he is an unwise son" (Hosea 13:13).

"Brought to a wiser understanding [SOPHRONISTHENTES] by the magnitude and number of successive punishments" (Philo, *Mos.* I.147).

"I will soon pour out My wrath on you, and spread My anger against you . . . I will punish you . . . My eye will not spare, nor will I have pity. I will punish you according to your ways . . . then you will know [YADA]" (Ezekiel 7:8,9).

"I will execute great vengeance upon them, with furious rebukes and they shall know [YADA]" (Ezekiel 25:17).

"When I have broken [through punishments] their wanton heart which has departed from Me and blinded their eyes . . . they shall know [YADA]" (Targum on Ezekiel 6:9,10, and Latin Vulgate and Syriac Texts).

"The days of visitation have come, the days of retribution have come, Israel shall know [YADA]" (Hosea 9:7).

"Let him repay [with punishment] the man himself, so that he will know [YADA]" (Job 21:19).

"He took the elders of the city and he took thorns of the wilderness and briers and with them [the thorns and briers as whips] he made the men of Succoth to know [YADA i.e., he painfully instructed them]" (Judges 8:16).

"I know [now, after punishment], O Lord, that Your judgments are right, and in faithfulness You have afflicted me" (Psalm 119:75).

"Before I was afflicted I went astray, but now I keep Your word" (Psalm 119:67).

"It is good for me that I have been afflicted, that I might learn" (Psalm 119:71).

"He who has learned . . . shall show forth understanding" (Sirach 34:9, Latin Vulgate).

"They were chastised so that they might be made holy" (2 Baruch 13:10).

"Disciplined . . . for our profit, that we might be partakers of His holiness" (Hebrews 12:10).

And have "the understanding of the holy ones" (Proverbs 2:11, Syriac Text).

"I have refined you . . . I have chosen you in the furnace of affliction" (Isaiah 48:10).

"They shall be known, who are My chosen, and they shall be tried as gold in the fire" (2 Esdras 16:73).

"God will purge by His Truth all the deeds of man refining for Himself some of mankind . . . to cleanse him . . . sprinkling upon him a spirit of Truth as purifying water to cleanse him from all untrue abominations . . . so as to give the upright understanding of the knowledge of the Most High and to the perfect of way understanding of the wisdom of the sons of heaven" (1QS 4:20,21,22, Dead Sea Scrolls).

"Many must be chosen out and thoroughly whitened, and tried with fire, and be made holy . . . and . . . shall understand" (Daniel 12:10, Greek Text).

"The furnace proves the potter's vessels, so the trial of a man is [revealed] in [the quality of] his reasoning" (Sirach 27:5).

"The fruit declares if the tree has been pruned, so is the utterance of the thought of the heart of man [the quality of a man's utterance reveals the discipline and training behind it]" (Sirach 27:6).

"If any one makes no mistakes in what he says he is a perfect man, able to bridle the whole body also" (St. James 3:2).

"Present your bodies as a living sacrifice [by self denial] holy, and acceptable to God which is your spiritual worship and . . . be transformed by the renewing of your understanding [thereby]" (Romans 12:1,2).

"Put off [by self denial] . . . the old man, which is corrupt in accordance to the deceitful lusts, and be renewed [through self denial] in the spirit of your understanding [NOOS]" (Ephesians 4:22,23).

"O Lord . . . give unto us the seed of a new heart and cultivation [by painful tilling and pruning] to our understanding whereby fruit may come" (2 Esdras 8:6, Syriac Text). "Have you cultivated your understanding? . . ." (Shabbath 31a, BT).

"Man is land suffering": "earth whose fruits are raised by labor" (*Epistle of Barnabas* 6:9; Testament of Issachar 5:5).

"Bread of *affliction*" (1 Kings 22:27; 2 Chronicles 18:26).

"Bread of *sorrow*" (Deuteronomy 16:3).

"Bread of *tears*" (Psalm 80:5).

"Bread of *understanding*" (Sirach 15:3; Greek and Hebrew Text).

"O King Nebuchadnezzar . . . you shall be driven from among men, and your dwelling shall be with the beasts of the field; and you shall be made to eat grass like oxen; and seven times shall pass over you, until you know [YADA] . . . that same hour the word was fulfilled upon Nebuchadnezzar. He was driven from among men, and ate grass like oxen and his [exposed] body was wet with the dew of heaven . . . at the end of the days I, Nebuchadnezzar, lifted my eyes to heaven and my knowledge returned to me" (Daniel 4:31,32,33,34).

In the book of Isaiah the Suffering Servant relates: "I gave my back to the smiters, and my cheeks to those who pulled out the beard; I did not hide my face from shame and spitting" (Isaiah 50:6). Although he suffered at the hands of his enemies, he did not get discouraged: "For the Lord God helps me, therefore I have not been confounded" (Isaiah 50:7). He was not confounded because in the midst of his sufferings: "the Lord God has given me the tongue of those who are taught, that I may know how to sustain with a [comforting] word him who is weary. Morning by morning He wakens my ear to hear as those who are learned. The Lord God has opened my ear and I was not rebellious, I did not turn backwards. I gave my back to the smiters. . . ." (Isaiah 50:4-6). For does not the Lord God open the ears of the oppressed and afflicted to comfort them with understanding?:

> "He delivers the poor in his affliction and opens their ears in oppression" (Job 36:15).

> "If they be bound in fetters and held in the cords of affliction then . . . He opens also their ears to instruction" (Job 36:8,9,10).

"Continue in prayer . . . praying for us that God may open up to us a door of utterance, so that we may speak forth the mystery of Christ, for which I am also in bonds: in order that I may make it clear in the way I ought to speak [St. Paul knew that the Lord opens up the understanding of those who are imprisoned for His sake] (Colossians 4:2,3-4).

"I Paul the prisoner . . . with all prayer and petition pray at all times in the Spirit . . . alert with all perseverance, making supplication for all the saints, and also for me, that utterance may be given to me that I may open my mouth boldly to make known the mystery of the Gospel, for which I am an ambassador in chains; that I may declare it boldly [with eloquence], as I ought to speak" (Ephesians 3:1; 6:18-20).

"Urge slaves to be subject to their masters, and to please them well in all things . . . showing good fidelity that they may adorn [with the knowledge and understanding received from their subjection] the teaching about God our Saviour in every respect" (Titus 2:9,10).

"Joseph was sold as a slave, whose feet they hurt with fetters, iron went into his soul; until what he had said came to pass the Word of the Lord tested him. The King sent and released him, the ruler of the peoples set him free; he made him lord of his house and ruler of all his possessions, to bind his princes at his will, and to teach his elders wisdom" (Psalm 105:17-22).

"Put your feet into Wisdom's fetters and your neck into her chain. Bow down your shoulder and bear her, and do not be grieved with her bonds. Come to her with all your soul, and keep her ways with all your strength . . . then her fetters will become for you a strong defense, and her chain a robe of glory" (Sirach 6:24-26,29).

"Put your neck under Wisdom's yoke and let your soul bear her burden" (Sirach 51:26, Hebrew Text).

"Her [Wisdom's] yoke was to me for glory" (Sirach 51:17, Hebrew Text).

"The words of the Torah stand up for him who valorously gives them the labor they require to be understood" (Pesikta de Rab Kahana, Piska 12.5).

"Chastisement is as fetters on the feet, and manacles on the right hand to one without understanding [ANOĒTOIS]" (Sirach 21:19).

But "Chastisement is to a man of understanding as an ornament of gold, and as a bracelet on the right arm" (Sirach 21:21).

Because "the very beginning of wisdom is the desire for discipline" (Wisdom 6:17).

"God decided to go and try for Himself a nation from the midst of another nation by trials, by signs, and by wonders, and by war, and by a mighty hand and by a stretched out arm, and by great terrors. All that the Lord God did for you in Egypt before your eyes, to you it was shown that you might know [YADA]" (Deuteronomy 4:34,35).

"Was not Abraham found faithful in trial?" (1 Maccabees 2:52).

"When he [Abraham] was proved, he was found faithful" (Sirach 44:20).

And thereby "Abraham [through his trial] . . . acquired knowledge" (Zadokite Fragment [CD] 16:6, MS. A).

"A man of understanding is faithful [one is called 'faithful' after he has been tried]" (Sirach 33:3, Latin Vulgate).

"Because you were acceptable to the Lord it was necessary that trial should prove you" (Tobit 12:13, Latin Vulgate).

"At first Wisdom chooses him, [then] she will bring upon him fear and dread and trial, and she will scourge him with the affliction of her discipline, till she try him by her Laws, and trust his soul. Then she will strengthen him and make a straight way to him, and give him joy. And she will disclose her secrets to him and will heap upon him treasures of knowledge and understanding" (Sirach 4:18-21, Latin Vulgate).

"I [Wisdom] will scourge him with chastisements until his heart is filled with me. Then I will return and direct him and reveal to him my secrets" (Sirach 4:17,18, Hebrew Text).

"Turn at my [Wisdom's] reproof, behold, I will pour my spirit on you and I will make my words known to you" (Proverbs 1:23).

Conversely, the undisciplined sybarites who live in luxury catering to every desire are without true knowledge and understanding because they do not accept chastening and have not experienced salutary suffering.

"One who lives in luxury . . . does as he pleases . . . and does not understand what he is doing" (Shepherd of Hermas, *Sim.* VI.5.65:3).

"See your Kings and your great ones, those who are clothed in soft garments, they shall not be able to understand the Truth" (Gospel of Thomas, Logion 78).

"Man who is held in honor [for his riches] . . . understands not" (Psalm 49:20).

"A rich man who is void of understanding" (Sirach 22:23, Greek Cursives 248,106).

"Men who have lived dissolutely and unrighteously . . . they went astray very far in the ways of error . . . being deceived as babes, without understanding [APHRONŌN]" (Wisdom 12:23,24).

"They [the rich] became insolent in their prosperity and they were without understanding" (Psalms of Solomon 1:6 [Von Gebhardt Transl.])

"Their riches concealed from them the Truth and darkened them [in their understanding]" (Shepherd of Hermas, *Sim.* IX.30.107:4).

"Those . . . mixed up in affairs of business and in wealth and in heathen friendships and many other affairs of this age — those who are absorbed in these things do not understand" (Shepherd of Hermas, *Mand.* X.1.40:4).

"Wealth has led astray the hearts [i.e., understanding] of princes" (Sirach 8:2, Hebrew Text).

"For men shall put on more adornments than a woman, and more coloured garments than a virgin, in royalty, grandeur, and in power, and in silver and gold and purple, and in splendor and in food they shall be poured out as water. Therefore they shall be wanting in doctrine and in wisdom" (Enoch 98:2,3).

"Because you say, 'I am rich and have become wealthy, and have need of nothing,' you know not that you are . . . blind" (Revelation 3:17).

"The newly rich . . . know nothing" (Philo, *Spec.* II.23).

"He who is grasping, even though he possesses things, is nevertheless dull of understanding" (Story of Ahikar 2:92, Armenian Text).

"They are greedy dogs who do not know satisfaction [i.e., they are insatiable], they are shepherds who do not know [YADA] how to understand [BIN], they all look to their own way, every one after his own gain, from the first even to the last. 'Come,' they say, 'let us get wine, and fill ourselves with strong drink; and tomorrow will be like today, even much better' " (Isaiah 56:11-12).

"Choice things [luxuries, delicacies] bestowed are a pollution for the soul, and for a man of knowledge [they are] a suffering in the inward parts [because he knows that they take away knowledge and understanding]" (Sirach 40:29,30, Hebrew Text).

"Where is the place of understanding? Man does not know the price thereof, neither is it found in the land of those who live daintily [SUAVITUR = 'full of delights,' 'carefree']" (Job 28:12,13, Latin Vulgate and Old Latin Texts).

For "there are no two things so utterly opposed as understanding [EPISTĒMĒ] and pleasures of the flesh" (Philo, *Deus.* 143).

"The understanding of the pleasure-loving man is blind" (Philo, *Q.Gen.* IV.245).

"The delightful experience of abounding pleasure is the ruin of the understanding" (Philo, *Agr.* 108).

"They . . . who give themselves to their lusts [are] as the horse and mule which do not have understanding" (Tobit 6:17, Latin Vulgate).

"Pleasures . . . bewitch the understanding" (Philo, *Spec.* I.9).

"Understanding is contrary to the flesh" (Corpus Hermeticum, *Libellus* X.10).

Since "understanding [EPISTĒMĒ] comes into being through estrangement from sensuality . . . it follows that the lovers of wisdom reject rather than choose sensuality" (Philo, *Cher.* 41).

The "lovers of pleasure rather than lovers of God . . . this sort are . . . ever learning and never able to come to the knowledge of Truth" (2 Timothy 3:4,6,7).

"O Understanding, if you do not prepare yourself, excising desires, pleasures . . .

follies, injustices and related evils, and if you do not adapt yourself to the vision of holiness, you will end your life in blindness unable to see the sun of understanding" (Philo, *Q.Exod.* II.51).

"The fascination of vice obscures the things that are good, and the wandering allurements of concupiscence perverts the innocent understanding" (Wisdom 4:12).

"Nothing else so constrains and oppresses the understanding as do desires for sensual pleasures" (Philo, *Q.Gen.* IV.177).

"Understanding starves when the senses feast, on the other hand it rejoices when they are fasting" (Philo, *Mig.* 204).

"Those who cram themselves with food and drink are most wanting in understanding, because the reason is drowned by the stuff brought in" (Philo, *De Providentia* 67).

"Understanding [PHRONĒSIS] and indulgence of the body cannot occupy the same quarters" (Philo, *L.A.* III.151).

"Pleasure endeavors to break up and destroy the way of life of the wise understanding" (Philo, *L.A.* III.189).

"Wine bibbing . . . gluttony . . . delicate living and excessive indulgence in food . . . mulct the most vital element: the understanding" (Philo, *Ebr.* 22,23).

As the Son of Man who understands all things, the Lord Himself underwent suffering.

"The Prophets searched carefully and sought to know what person or time the Spirit of Christ within them was indicating, when He predicted the sufferings of Christ and the glories that would follow" (1 Peter 1:10,11).

"From that time Jesus began to show His disciples that He must go to Jerusalem and suffer many things from the elders and chief priests and scribes and be killed, and on the third day be raised" (St. Matthew 16:21; see also St. Mark 8:31; St. Luke 9:22).

"What son is there whom his father does not chastise?" (Hebrews 12:7).

"It is written of the Son of Man, that He will suffer many things and be treated with contempt" (St. Mark 9:12).

"The Son of Man shall be betrayed to the chief priests and scribes, and they will condemn Him to death" (St. Matthew 20:18).

"The Son of Man will suffer at their hands" (St. Matthew 17:12).

"The Son of Man must be delivered into the hands of sinful men, and be crucified, and on the third day rise" (St. Luke 24:7).

"And He [Jesus] said to them, 'O foolish ones, and slow of heart to believe all that the prophets have spoken! Was it not necessary that the Christ should suffer these things and enter into His glory?" (St. Luke 24:25-26).

"Thus it is written, that the Christ should suffer and on the third day rise from the dead" (St. Luke 24:46).

"The Messiah shall be cut off, and shall have nothing" (Daniel 9:26).

"Christ Jesus . . . empties Himself, taking the form of a bondservant, being born in the likeness of men. And being found in human form He humbled Himself and became obedient unto death, even death on a cross" (Philippians 2:5,7-8).

"The things which God foretold by the mouth of all the prophets, that His Christ had to suffer, He [Jesus] thus fulfilled" (Acts 3:18).

"Paul . . . reasoned with them from the Scriptures, explaining and proving that the Christ had to suffer" (Acts 17:2,3).

"Christ, the Power of God and the Wisdom of God" (1 Corinthians 1:24).

"Christ, in whom are hidden all the treasures of wisdom and knowledge" (Colossians 2:2,3).

"Christ Jesus, whom God made our wisdom and our righteousness" (1 Corinthians 1:30).

> *Jesus, the Son of Man who suffered and died for us,*
> *understands all things, and gives understanding to*
> *those who believe in Him and suffer for His sake.*

"All who heard Him were astonished at His understanding and His answers" (St. Luke 2:47).

"Where did this man [Jesus] get this wisdom" (St. Matthew 13:54).

"All spoke well of Him, and wondered at the gracious words which proceeded out of His mouth" (St. Luke 4:22).

"The officers answered, 'no man ever spoke like this man [Jesus]!' " (St. John 7:46).

"All His adversaries were put to shame, and all the people rejoiced at all the glorious things that were done by Him" (St. Luke 13:17).

"When they heard it [what Jesus said], they marvelled" (St. Matthew 22:22).

"No one was able to answer Him a word, and from that day no one dared to ask Him any more questions" (St. Matthew 22:46).

"The Understanding [NOUS] and Word [LOGOS] of the Father is the Son of God [Jesus Christ]" (Athenagoras [c.A.D. 177], *Emb.* X).

"The Son is the Understanding, Word, and Wisdom of the Father" (ibid. XXIV).

"The Son of God: the creative Understanding" (Synesius, *Hymn to Christ*).

"Jesus Christ . . . His role is the Understanding of the Father" (St. Ignatius, *Epistle to the Ephesians* 3:2).

"The mind [GNŌMĒ] of God: Jesus Christ" (ibid.).

"Christ Himself is Wisdom" (Clement of Alexandria, *Strom.* VI.c.7).

"The Lord [Jesus] is the Truth, and Wisdom, and Power of God" (Clement of Alexandria, *Strom.* II.c.2; Ibid. IV.c.7; St. John 14:6).

"The Truth . . . its discovery is by the Son [Jesus Christ]" (Clement of Alexandria, *Strom.* I.c.20).

"The Son of the Father is . . . the door of knowledge" (St. Ignatius, *Epistle to the Philadelphians,* I.9).

"Set yourself earnestly to find Christ. For He said: 'I am the Door' which we who desire to understand God must discover" (Clement of Alexandria, *Exh.* I.10.2).

"Nothing is incomprehensible to the Son of God [Jesus Christ]" (Clement of Alexandria, *Strom.* VI.c.8).

"For who among men at all understood before His [Jesus'] coming what God is?" (*Epistle to Diognetus* 8:1).

"We worship Jesus through whom we know God" (Aphraates, *Demonstration* XVII.8).

"Men must be saved by learning the Truth through Christ" (Clement of Alexandria, *Strom.* V.c.13).

"We thank you holy Father, for Your holy name . . . and for the knowledge, and faith, and immortality which You have made known to us through Jesus Your Servant" (*Didache* 10:2).

"Jesus Christ through whom He [God] has called us from darkness into light and from ignorance into the knowledge of the glory of His name" (First Clement 59:2).

"Through Him [Jesus Christ] the eyes of our heart [i.e., understanding] have been opened" (First Clement 36:2).

"We cannot ourselves attain to this knowledge [of God]; it is the gift of God through His Son [Jesus]" (Clement of Alexandria, *Strom.* V.c.1).

"The Father loves the Son, and shows Him all that He Himself is doing" (St. John 5:20).

"O righteous Father, the world has not known You, but I have known You" (St. John 17:25; ibid. 8:55).

"No one has ever seen God, the only begotten Son [Jesus] who is in the bosom of the Father, He [Jesus] has made Him known" (St. John 1:18; ibid. 6:46).

"I [Jesus] speak that which I have seen with My Father" (St. John 8:38).

"I [Jesus] speak these things as the Father taught Me" (St. John 8:28).

"I and the Father are one" (St. John 10:30).

"The Father is in Me, and I am in the Father" (St. John 10:38).

"All that the Father has is Mine" (St. John 16:15).

"All things have been delivered to Me by My Father; and no one knows the Son except the Father, and no one knows the Father except the Son and any one to whom the Son chooses to reveal Him" (St. Matthew 11:27).

"All that I have heard from My Father I have made known to you" (St. John 15:15).

"The Law was given to us through Moses, but grace and Truth came into being through Jesus Christ" (St. John 1:17).

"His [God's] Son Jesus Christ our Lord . . . through whom we have received grace" (Romans 1:3,5).

"The grace of God which is given to you by Jesus Christ, so that in everything you are enriched by Him, in all speech and in all knowledge" (1 Corinthians 1:4,5).

"According to the riches of His [Jesus'] grace which He made to abound towards us in all wisdom and understanding making known to us the mystery of His will" (Ephesians 1:7,8,9).

"Grace which confers understanding [and] makes Mysteries plain" (*Epistle to Diognetus* 11:6,7).

"We know that the Son of God has come and has given us understanding, in order that we might know Him who is true" (1 John 5:20).

"He [Jesus Christ] opened their understanding [NOUN] so that they might understand the Scriptures" (St. Luke 24:45).

"We have the understanding [NOUN] of Christ" (1 Corinthians 2:16).

"Their minds were made dull, for to this very day the same veil remains [covering their understanding] when the Old Testament is read, because only through Christ is it taken away. Even to this day, whenever Moses is read, a veil lies over their understanding; but whenever a man turns to the Lord [Jesus] the veil is removed" (2 Corinthians 3:14-16).

"I [Jesus] will give you utterance and wisdom which none of your opponents will be able to resist or refute" (St. Luke 21:15).

"I extol Jesus Christ . . . who has granted you such wisdom" (St. Ignatius, *Epistle to the Smyrneans* 1:1).

"Whoever is a servant of God and has the Lord [Jesus Christ] in his heart may ask for understanding from Him and receive it, and interpret every parable, and with the help of the Lord those things spoken through the parables are made known to him" (Shepherd of Hermas, *Sim.* V.4.57:3).

"Ask the Lord [Jesus] to receive the insight to understand them" (Shepherd of Hermas, *Sim.* IX.2.79:6).

"Blessed is our Lord [Jesus] who has placed in us wisdom and understanding of His secrets" (*Epistle of Barnabas* 6:10).

"He [Jesus] circumcised our ears and hearts so that we might understand these things" (*Epistle of Barnabas* 10:12; 9:1,4).

"The Lord [Jesus] will give you understanding in all things" (2 Timothy 2:7).

"The Lord [Jesus] has made known to us . . . giving us also the first-fruits of the knowledge of things to come" (*Epistle of Barnabas* 1:7).

"Jesus . . . through Him the eyes of our heart have been opened; through Him our foolish and darkened understanding springs up to the light. Through Him the Lord has willed that we should taste immortal knowledge" (First Clement 36:2; Ephesians 4:13).

"The eyes of the understanding being opened by [Jesus] the Teacher who rose on the third day" (Clement of Alexandria, *Strom.* V.c.11).

422

"We thank you for the life and knowledge which you have made known to us through Jesus" (*Didache* 9:3).

"Jesus . . . who has put in us the implanted gift of His teaching" (*Epistle of Barnabas* 9:9).

"Where the Lord [Jesus] dwells, there is much understanding. Cleave then to the Lord and you will understand and perceive all things" (Shepherd of Hermas, *Mand.* X.1.40:6).

"His own wise counsel . . . He revealed it through His beloved Son [Jesus] and made known what had been prepared from the beginning, He granted us all things at once. [Through Him] He made us partakers of His benefits, and see and understand things which none of us could ever have expected" (*Epistle to Diognetus* 8:10,11).

"Why do you not ask of the Lord [Jesus] understanding and receive it from Him?" (Shepherd of Hermas, *Sim.* V.4.57:4).

"The godly Christian alone is rich and wise and of noble birth, and by these things he is God's image and also His likeness, having become through Jesus Christ righteous and holy and understanding [PHRONĒSEŌS] and in this measure like God" (Clement of Alexandria, *Exh.* XII.122.4).

"Through Jesus Christ our foolish and darkened understanding springs up to the light. By Him the Sovereign Lord wished us to taste the knowledge that is immortal" (Clement Alexandria, *Strom.* IV.c.17).

"The Lord [Jesus Christ] . . . is the Light and the true knowledge" (Clement of Alexandria, *Strom.* VI.c.1).

*　　*

"The Lord [Jesus Christ] having come alone into the world of understanding, enters by His sufferings" (Clement of Alexandria, *Strom.* V.c.6).

*　　*

"There is no limit to trials; but the man of understanding increases his knowledge by their means" (Ibn Gabirol, *Mibhar Ha-Peninim*).

TASTE AND UNDERSTANDING

"As the palate tries [BACHAN] the taste [TAAM] of a thing, so does an understanding [BIN] heart [try] the taste of a lie" (Sirach 36:24, Hebrew Text).

"Cannot my palate understand [BIN, i.e., 'taste'] perverse things [to detect and discard them]?" (Job 6:30).

"He takes away the *taste* [TAAM] of the aged" (Job 12:20, Hebrew Text).

He takes away . . . "the *understanding* [SUNESIN] of the elders" (ibid., Greek Text).

"The body's senses relish worldly enjoyments, but the soul's understanding relishes the sweetness of Christ" (*Letter of Philoxenus, [Bishop] of Mabbug to a Novice*, I.2 [c.A.D. 500), edited by Gunnar Olinder in *Göteborgs Högskolas Arsskrift*, XLVII [1941:21], p. 14).

TEACHING AND UNDERSTANDING

"He gave him [Moses] commandments . . . the Law of life and great understanding [EPISTĒMĒS-TEBUNAH] so that he might teach Jacob His covenants, and Israel His judgments" (Sirach 45:5, Greek and Hebrew Texts).

"There have been given to you counsel and understanding, that you may teach your sons" (Testament of Levi 4:5).

"There is a spirit in mortals, and the breath of the Almighty is that which *teaches*" (Job 32:8, Greek Text).

"There is a spirit in man, and the breath of the Almighty *gives understanding*" (ibid., Hebrew Text).

"By the word is wisdom known, and *teaching* by the word of the tongue" (Sirach 4:24, Greek Text).

"By the word is wisdom known, and *understanding* by the answer of the tongue" (ibid., Hebrew Text).

"Teach your children letters that they may have understanding" (Testament of Levi 13:1,2).

"Man would not have rightly understood My judgment, unless . . . I had taught him in understanding" (2 Baruch 15:5).

"You teach created things in the understanding of You" (2 Baruch 48:9).

"To depart from evil is understanding" (Job 28:28).

"Depart from evil and do good" (Psalm 34:14), "by 'do good' is meant the occupation with the Torah [with the understanding gained by departing from evil]" (Abodah Zarah 19b, BT; Midrash Rabbah on Psalms 1.6; see Job 28:28).

VOICE AND UNDERSTANDING

"Does not Wisdom cry [QARA`] out? and Understanding [TEBUNAH] put forth her voice [QOL]?" (Proverbs 8:1).

"If you have understanding [BINAH] hear this: give ear to the voice [QOL] of my words" (Job 34:16).

"Yes, if you cry out for insight, and lift up your voice [QOL] for great understanding [TEBUNAH]" (Proverbs 2:3).

"Hear my voice and understand" (2 Esdras 8:19).

"A voice will cry out at night which many will not understand but all will hear" (2 Esdras 5:7, Syriac Text).

"The Spirit of the Lord fills the world and that [i.e., His understanding] which contains all things [see "Understanding Encompasses"] has knowledge of the Voice" (Wisdom 1:7).

"God thunders [RAAM] with His voice [QOL] marvelously" (Job 37:5).

"The thunder of His power [or 'voice'] who can understand?" (Job 26:14; see sect. "Understanding gives Power — The Power and Strength of Understanding").

"Who can understand Your understanding?" (2 Baruch 75:3).

"Understanding [BINAH] is the source of the Voice" (Zohar I.74a).

WATCHING AND UNDERSTANDING

"The understanding [DIANOIAN] . . . is not quiescent, but unsleeping" (Philo, *Abr.* 162).

"O my Understanding, never show weakness or slacken . . . never either willingly or unwillingly close your eyes, because sleep is a blind thing, as watchfulness is a thing of keen sight" (Philo, *Mig.* 222)

"Sleep of the understanding is waking of sense, since the waking of the understanding is inaction of sense" (Philo, *Her.* 257).

"The understanding when awake throws [like the sun] the senses into shade" (Philo, *L.A.* II.30).

"This second epistle, beloved, I now write to you to thoroughly awaken [DIEGEIRŌ] your pure understanding [DIANOIAN]" (2 Peter 3:1).

"I bid you come and contemplate the universe and its contents, a spectacle apprehended not by the eye of the body but by the unsleeping eyes of the understanding [DIANOIAS]" (Philo, *Spec.* I.49).

"Be . . . understanding and vigilant" (Odes of Solomon 3:11).

"Watchfulness [GRĒGORĒSIS] and understanding [SUNESIS] were found in him [Daniel]" (Daniel 5:11,14, Greek Text).

"They shall greatly understand [TEBUNAH] as the Watchers (understand) His works" (4QMess. 2:16 [Messianic Text Fragments], Dead Sea Scrolls).

"Understand the counsel of your heart for there is no one more faithful to you than it. A man's heart [i.e., understanding] sets before him [the counsel of] opportune action more than seven watchmen on a watchtower" (Sirach 37:13-14, Hebrew Text; see also Baba Kamma 27b, BT, on the "watchfulness" of understanding).

"Those who understand it shall not sleep, but shall listen with the ear that they may learn this wisdom" (Enoch 82:3).

"Who is wise and will watch [SHAMAR] over these things? they will understand [BIN] the loving kindness of the Lord" (Psalm 107:43).

"Get understanding [BINAH] . . . do not forsake her and she shall keep [SHAMAR] you, love her, and she shall watch [NATSAR] over you" (Proverbs 4:5,6).

"Great Understanding [TEBUNAH] shall watch [NATSAR] over you" (Proverbs 2:11).

"O You *watcher* [NATSAR] of man" (Job 7:20, Hebrew Text).

"O You who *understand* [EPISTAMENOS] the understanding [NOUS] of man" (ibid., Greek Text).

"Who has given understanding [BINAH] to the cock [who is a 'watcher' par excellence]?" (Job 38:36).

"Blessed are You who have given the cock understanding to [watch and] distinguish between day and night" (Jewish Benediction on hearing a cock crow).

N.B. Roosters are traditionally good watchers: "like the cocks that tolerate no intruder" (Yebamoth 84a, BT). Hence, a watchtower near Caesarea was named "Fort Cock" (Targum Jerusalem to Deuteronomy 2:8; Tosefta Shebi IV.10). The word for "cock," in Job 38:36, is SEKVI from the Hebrew root SEKAH which means "to be on the look-out for," "to watch hopefully for." Thus, one of the Hebrew words for "prophet" or "seer" is SAKHIYYA [see Midrash Rabbah on Leviticus I.3 re 1 Chronicles 4:18; also Midrash Rabbah on Ecclesiastes IX.18 re 2 Kings 18:37]).

"I found a book of no small learning; therefore I thought it most necessary for me to bestow some diligence and travail to interpret it, applying much watchfulness [AGRUPNIAN] and understanding [EPISTEMEN] in that space of time to bring the book to an end, and set it forth for them" (Prologue to Sirach).

"Wise souls . . . kindle the light and rouse up the understanding" (Clement of Alexandria, *Strom.* V.c.3).

"A well instructed man of understanding [EPISTEMON] will be watchful" (Sirach 40:29).

THE WATERS, SPRINGS, AND RIVERS OF UNDERSTANDING, WISDOM, AND KNOWLEDGE

The Lord Himself is the Source of all Living Waters.

"The Lord [is] the fountain of living waters" (Jeremiah 17:13).

"With You is the fountain of life" (Psalm 36:9).

"My people . . . have forsaken Me, the fountain of living waters" (Jeremiah 2:13; Enoch 96:6).

"Jesus stood up and cried out saying: If any one thirst, let him come to Me and drink. He who believes in Me as the Scripture has said, 'out of his innermost being shall flow rivers of living water' " (St. John 7:37-38).

"Ho, every one who thirsts, come to the waters . . . come to Me" (Isaiah 55:1,3).

"Jesus said . . . 'whoever drinks of the water that I shall give him will never thirst; the water that I shall give him will become in him a spring of water welling up to eternal life" (St. John 4:13,14).

"He shall come down like rain upon the mown grass, as showers that water the earth. In His days shall the righteous flourish, and abundance of peace, as long as the moon endures" (Psalm 72:6-7).

"He showed me a pure river of water of life, clear as crystal proceeding from the throne of God and of the Lamb" (Revelation 22:1).

"The Lamb in the center of the throne . . . shall guide them to living fountains of waters" (Revelation 7:17).

We are to thirst for the Lord, and for His commandments, and righteousness.

"As the deer longs for the water brooks, so my soul longs for You, O God. My soul thirst for God, for the living God" (Psalm 42:1,2).

"O God . . . my soul thirsts for You, my flesh yearns for You as in a dry and thirsty land where there is no water" (Psalm 63:1).

"I stretch out my hands to You; my soul thirsts for You, as a parched land" (Psalm 143:6).

"I opened my mouth, and panted [with thirst] for I longed for Your commandments" (Psalm 119:131).

"Blessed are those who hunger and thirst for righteousness for they shall be filled" (St. Matthew 5:6).

"As newborn babes, desire the sincere milk of the Word, that you may grow thereby" (1 Peter 2:2).

The Waters of Understanding

"Understanding [SEKEL] is a wellspring of life to him who has it" (Proverbs 16:22).

"In the first place our understanding [NOUS] is called a spring" (Philo, *Fug.* 177).

"Those . . . athirst as they are for instruction settle down beside springs of understanding [EPISTEMAIS] which are able to water their souls and give them to drink" (Philo, *Fug.* 187).

"Abraham and Isaac dug wells: deep sources of understanding [EPISTEMAS] from which draughts of reason are drawn" (Philo, *Fug.* 200).

"Wisdom shall . . . give him the waters of great understanding [TEBUNAH] to drink" (Sirach 15:3, Hebrew Text).

"He makes understanding [SUNESIN] abound like the Euphrates, and like the Jordan at harvest time" (Sirach 24:26; see also Zohar III.65a-65b,135b,289b-290a).

O "Solomon . . . how wise you were in your youth! You overflowed like a river with understanding" (Sirach 47:13,14).

"The wise among the people . . . in them is the spring of understanding" (2 Esdras 14:46,47).

"Speech issues from the understanding as its spring" (Philo, *Mut.* 69).

"The soul which is thirsty for understanding" (Philo, *Q.Gen.* III.27) belongs to "the man who drew from the well of understanding [EPISTEMES]" (Philo, *Plant.* 168).

"O my soul, imbibe understanding" (2 Esdras 8:4).

"The understanding of a wise man shall abound like a fountain, and his thoughts like a spring of living waters" (Sirach 21:13, Syriac Text).

"Wisdom rains down insight [EPISTEMEN] and knowledge [GNOSIN] of understanding [SUNESIS]" (Sirach 1:19).

"The Creator freely gave man the Word, but the Understanding He sent down to earth as waters in a great basin" (Corpus Hermeticum, *Libellus* IV.4).

"Because of their sin, You have hidden the spring of understanding [BINAH] and the secret of Truth" (1QH 5:25-26, Dead Sea Scrolls).

"You have opened a spring in the mouth of Your servant . . . that he may proclaim them [the precepts] to creatures because of his [the servant's] understanding [the source of that spring]" (1QH 18:10,11, Dead Sea Scrolls).

"Out of his heart . . . poured forth great understanding [TEBUNAH]" (Sirach 50:27, Hebrew Text).

"My son, keep my counsel and understanding, and do not let them flow by [PARARREO] you" (Proverbs 3:21, Greek Text).

"Understanding [BINAH] is an everflowing stream" (Zohar I 74a; ibid. III.7b-8a,17a-17b,181a).

The Waters of Wisdom.

"From whence is it likely that an understanding thirsting for insight should be filled except by the wisdom of God, that never failing spring" (Philo, Post. 136).

"From wisdom, that Divine spring, she has drawn understanding" [EPISTĒMAS]" (Philo, Post. 138).

"The Divine spring which we declare to be the eternal wisdom of understanding [EPISTĒMAS]" (Philo, Q.Gen. IV.100).

"The Divine spring: this is wisdom" (Philo, Q.Gen. IV.94).

"The spring of Divine wisdom" (Philo, Det. 117).

"You have forsaken the spring of wisdom" (Baruch 3:12).

"This spring is the Divine wisdom" (Philo, Fug. 195).

"Wisdom . . . always opens her doors to those who thirst for the sweet water of her discourse" (Philo, Prob. 13).

"Wisdom is poured out like water" (Enoch 49:1).

"Souls endowed with good native ability [to understand] are likened to cisterns ready to receive wisdom as these [cisterns] receive water" (Philo, Fug. 176).

"She shall . . . give him the water of wisdom to drink" (Sirach 15:3).

"Take water from the Divine spring . . . from the pure and unfailing wisdom of God" (Philo, Q.Gen. IV.107).

"I saw the fountain of righteousness which was inexhaustible and around it were many fountains of wisdom, and all the thirsty drank from them and were filled with wisdom" (Enoch 48:1).

"The fountain of wisdom" (2 Esdras 14:47).

"Wisdom's thoughts are more vast than the sea, and her counsels more deep than the great ocean. I, Wisdom, have poured out rivers" (Sirach 24:39-40, Latin Vulgate).

"He created Wisdom and saw her, and numbered her and poured her out upon all His works" (Sirach 1:9).

"Wisdom is a vapour [ATMIS] of the power of God, and a clear effluence of the glory of the Almighty" (Wisdom 7:25).

"I [Wisdom] came out of the mouth of the Most High and covered the earth like a mist" (Sirach 24:3).

"They who fear the Lord understand His judgment and draw forth [as water] great wisdom with skill from their hearts" (Sirach 32:16, Syriac Text).

"The words of a man's mouth are as deep waters, and the spring of wisdom as a gushing stream" (Proverbs 18:4).

"Solomon, how wise you were in your youth, wisdom flowed like a river from your understanding" (Sirach 47:14, Syriac Text).

"When the great Lord wills, he shall be filled with the spirit of understanding, and he shall pour out [as water] wise sentences" (Sirach 39:6).

Because "the teaching of the wise is as a fountain of life" (Proverbs 13:14).

"Your scribes are filled with wisdom as channels of water" (Targum on the Song of Songs 7:5).

"My heart poured forth wisdom" (2 Esdras 14:40, Syriac Text).

"Let your house be a house of meeting for the wise . . . and drink with thirst their [wise] words" (Pirke Aboth 1:4).

For "wisdom rightly desires to give to another some of the drink which she has taken" (Philo, *Q.Gen.* IV.103).

"No man can fathom the words of the wise" (Midrash Rabbah on Numbers 14.4).

*   *

"The Word of God on high is the fountain of wisdom" (Sirach 1:5, Greek Cursives 248,23,55,70,106,253 and Latin Vulgate).

"They found it to be a dictum of God that it is the Divine Word from which all kinds of instruction and wisdom flow in a perpetual stream" (Philo, *Fug.* 137).

The Waters of Knowledge

"The earth shall be full of knowledge [DEAH] of the Lord, as the waters cover the sea" (Isaiah 11:9).

"The earth shall be filled with the knowledge [DAATH] of the glory of the Lord, as the waters cover the sea" (Habacuc 2:14).

"A wide sea of knowledge" (2 Esdras 14:47, Arabic¹ Text).

"The knowledge [GNOSIS] of a wise man shall abound like a flood" (Sirach 21:13 [see also Aboth R. Nathan 27a; Soferim 41b; Abodah Zarah 3b, BT; Midrash Rabbah on Genesis 97.3]).

"Within whose heart You have set understanding [BINAH] that he might open the spring of knowledge to all who understand" (1QH 2:18, Dead Sea Scrolls).

"You have created . . . the fountain of knowledge and power" (1QH 12:28,29, Dead Sea Scrolls).

"The fountain of knowledge" (2 Baruch 59:7).

"Knowledge will be revealed to them abundantly as the waters of the sea" (1QpHab. 11:1,2, Dead Sea Scrolls).

"He has filled me with words of Truth that I may proclaim Him, and like the flowing of waters Truth flows from my mouth. And my lips declare His fruits for He has caused His knowledge to abound in me" (Odes of Solomon 12:1-2,3).

Conversely

"The inner parts of a fool are like a broken vessel, and he will hold no knowledge as long as he lives" (Sirach 21:14).

"My people . . . have no knowledge . . . their multitude has dried up with thirst" (Isaiah 5:13).

The Ancient Babylonians also knew about the Waters of Understanding.

"O sage . . . where is the wise man of your standing? Where is the scholar who can oppose you? For your understanding is like a river whose spring never fails, an immense sea which knows no decrease" (Babylonian Tablet No. 35405, Lines 1,23-24, British Museum).

*Because Wisdom, Understanding, and Knowledge are found in good
teachers, instruction and excellent counsel pour forth
from their lips. Good teachers know that the Word
of God is the source of all life-giving water.*

"My teaching shall drop down as the rain, and My choice words [IMRAH pl.] shall distill as the dew, as the droplets upon the tender grass, and as showers upon the herb" (Deuteronomy 32:2).

"As the rain comes down and the snow from heaven . . . waters the earth and makes it bring forth and bud that it may give seed to the sower and bread to the eater, so shall My word be that goes forth out of My mouth [as rain]" (Isaiah 55:10,11).

"We will hearken unto Him at the least moisture [IKMADA] of His word" (Job 26:14, Greek Text).

"The words of the Torah [Teaching or Law of the Lord] are likened unto water" (Taanith 7a, BT).

"As waters give life to the world, so do the words of the Torah give life to the world" (Sifre 84a; ibid. 37cd [see also Berakoth 24a, 61b, BT; Sukka V.42, JT; ibid. 55a, BT; Erubin 54a, BT; Moed Katan 25b, BT; Sanhedrin 7a, BT; Abodah Zarah 3b, BT; Sifre Deuteronomy, Ekeb 48 (f.84a); Midrash Rabbah on Genesis 70.8; Midrash Rabba on Canticles I.2,3; Pesikta de Rab Kahana, Piska 5.6; Pesikta Rabbati, Piska 36.1; Tanna debé Eliyahu Rabbah, p. 105, Ed. Friedmann, 1902]).

"The well is the Torah" (Zadokite Fragment 8:6 [CD 6:4, MS. A]).

"Those who occupy themselves with the study of the Torah are as the well of living waters" (Targum on Canticles 4:15).

"All those who reject the commandments of God and forsake them . . . departed from the spring of living waters" (Zadokite Fragment 9:27,28 [CD 1:33,34, MS. B1]).

But "everyone who is occupied with the Torah . . . is made like a spring which ceases not, and like a stream that goes on getting stronger" (Pirke Aboth 6:1).

"If it shall please the great Lord, He will fill him with the spirit of understanding, and he will pour forth the words of his wisdom as showers" (Sirach 39:8,9, Latin Vulgate).

"My speech dropped upon them, and they waited for me as for the rain, and opened wide their mouth as for the latter rain" (Job 29:22,23).

"You, O my God, have put in my mouth as it were an abundant rain for all, and a spring of living waters which shall not run dry" (1QH 8:16,17, Dead Sea Scrolls).

"You have opened a spring in the mouth of Your servant . . . that he may pro-claim them [the 'precepts'] to creatures because of his understanding [BINAH], and be an interpreter of these things" (1QH 18:10,11, Dead Sea Scrolls).

"I have planted [the Word], Apollos watered [by his teaching], but God gives the increase" (1 Corinthians 3:6).

"We drink of your water [i.e., we assimilate your teaching]" (Ḥagigah 3a, BT).

"Rabbi Eleazar ben Arach [a very learned man] is as a full flowing spring" (Pirke Aboth 2:10).

"You [Solomon] . . . did overflow like the Nile with your instruction" (Sirach 47:14, Hebrew Text).

"He makes the teaching of knowledge appear . . . as the Gihon [river] in the time of vintage" (Sirach 24:27, Greek Cursive 248).

"With joy shall you draw water out of the wells of salvation" (Isaiah 12:3).

"You shall receive new instruction with joy from the chosen of righteousness" (Targum on Isaiah 12:3).

"The righteous . . . their teaching shall be received quickly as streams of water that flow in a thirsty land" (Targum on Isaiah 32:2).

"I did not cease from the instruction of my son, until I had filled him as with bread and water" (Story of Ahikar 1:15, Syriac A text and Arabic[1] Text).

"Counsel in the heart of man is like deep water, but a man of understanding will draw it out" (Proverbs 20:5).

"The fame of Your great goodness they shall pour forth [NABA`]" (Psalm 145:7).

"As a fountain gushes forth its water, so my heart the praise of the Lord" (Odes of Solomon 40:2).

Conversely, there are evil waters, and bad waters of lies.

"Woe unto those who seek to make deep their counsel from the Lord" (Isaiah 29:15).

In "the depths of Satan" (Revelation 2:24).

For "therein in the deeps are . . . the mights of pride [RAHAB]" (Sirach 43:25, Hebrew Text [Masada Scroll]).

"The dripper of lies . . . waters of falsehood" (Zadokite Fragment 1:10 [CD 1:14,15, MS. A.]).

"Place of evil waters [i.e., place of bad teaching]" (Pirke Aboth 1:11).

"Where the disciples . . . drink and die" (ibid.).

"The wicked are like a troubled sea, which cannot rest, whose waters cast up refuse and mud" (Isaiah 57:20).

*   *

The Spirit of the Lord is the Spirit of all Wisdom, Understanding Knowledge and Counsel. And as such He is poured upon us.

"The Spirit of the Lord shall rest on Him, the spirit of wisdom and understanding, the spirit of counsel and might, the spirit of knowledge and of the fear of the Lord" (Isaiah 11:2).

"Until the Spirit be poured upon us from on high" (Isaiah 32:15).

"I will pour out My Spirit upon all flesh" (Joel 2:28; Acts 2:17).

"I have poured out My Spirit" (Ezekiel 39:29).

"I will pour out My Spirit upon your seed, and My blessing upon your offspring" (Isaiah 44:3).

"On the Gentiles also was poured out the gift of the Holy Spirit" (Acts 10:45).

"You have poured forth Your Holy Spirit upon Your servant" (1QH 17:26, Dead Sea Scrolls).

"We were all made to drink of one Spirit" (1 Corinthians 12:13).

"He shall baptize you with the Holy Spirit" (St. Matthew 3:11; St. Mark 1:8).

"Unless one is born of water and the Spirit, he cannot enter into the Kingdom of God" (St. John 3:5).

"He will cause the Spirit of Truth to gush forth upon him like lustral water" (1QS 4:21, Dead Sea Scrolls).

"I will pour out upon the house of David and upon the inhabitants of Jerusalem, the Spirit of grace and of supplication, so that they will look on Me whom they have pierced and they will mourn for Him as one bitterly weeps over a first-born" (Zechariah 12:10, Literal Translation).

THE WAY OF UNDERSTANDING

"Forsake the foolish and live, and go in the way of understanding [BINAH]" (Proverbs 9:6).

"There were the giants born, who were famous of old, great in stature, skilled in war. God did not choose them, neither did He give them the way of understanding [EPISTĒMĒS]; so they were destroyed because they had no understanding, they were destroyed through their lack of counsel [ABOULIAN]" (Baruch 3:26-28).

"The man who wanders from the way of understanding shall remain in the congregation of the dead" (Proverbs 21:16).

"Young men have seen the light and dwelt upon the earth, but the way of understanding [EPISTĒMĒS] they have not known [because they have not asked the Lord to show them the way to it]" (Baruch 3:20).

"Where is the place of understanding [BINAH]? . . . God understands the way to it and He knows its place" (Job 28:20,23).

"Who has directed the Spirit of the Lord, or as His counselor has taught Him? With whom did He take counsel and who made Him understand [BIN] and taught Him in the path of judgment, and taught Him knowledge, and made Him know [YADA] the way of great understanding [TEBUNAH]?" (Isaiah 40:13-14).

WEAVING, NETS, AND UNDERSTANDING

"They brought him the Law [TORAH] and he wove it [i.e., he expounded it with understanding]" (Midrash Rabbah on Ruth 2.1).

"The Sanhedrin wove [expounded] with him the words of the Torah" (ibid.).

"Who has given women wisdom in weaving and understanding [EPISTĒMĒN] in embroidery?" (Job 38:36, Greek Text).

"Every wise-hearted [i.e., understanding] man among them who wrought the work of the tabernacle made ten curtains of fine twisted linen and blue and purple and scarlet" (Exodus 36:8).

O Solomon, "how wise you were in your youth, and, as a flood, filled with understanding" (Sirach 47:13,14 Greek Text).

"You [Solomon] did gather parables [in your net] like the sea through your understanding" (Sirach 47:15, Syriac Text).

"You shall rejoice in Wisdom, and her net shall become the foundation of your strength" (Sirach 6:28,29, Syriac Text; see "Understanding gives Power").

*   *

"Sia [Egyptian god of understanding] lord of abundance, great in fishing and fowling [with nets]" (Papyrus Leiden 237:12 ll.2-4 [Text found in *Denkmaler aus Aegypten und Aethiopien*, Ed. C.R. Lepsius, LD Text III. p.187]).

*   *

"My son, what is your work? He replied: I am a fisherman. I asked: my son, who told you to bring linen cord, weave it into nets, cast them into the sea, and bring fish up from the depths? He replied: My master, with regard to my work, understanding and knowledge were given me from Heaven" (Tanna debe Eliyahu Zuta, p. 195-196 [Ed. Friedmann]; see also Testament of Zebulon 6:1-3).

"WHO" AND UNDERSTANDING

"Where is Understanding [SUNESIS]? . . . who has found out her place? or who has come into her treasures?" (Baruch 3:14,15).

"Who can understand Your understanding?" (2 Baruch 75:3).

"Who is there who can understand the things of heaven?" (Enoch 93:12).

"Who, O Lord, my Lord, will understand Your judgment, or who will search out the profoundness of Your ways? Or who will think out the weight of Your path? Or who will be able to think out Your incomprehensible counsel? Or who of those who are born has ever found the beginning or end of Your wisdom?" (2 Baruch 14:8-9).

"Who can understand, O Lord, Your goodness? for it is incomprehensible" (2 Baruch 75:1).

"Who can understand his errors?" (Psalm 19:12).

"The thunder of His power who can understand?" (Job 26:14).

"Who is the wise man who can understand this?" (Jeremiah 9:12).

"Who is wise and understands these things? Who is understanding and knows them?" (Hosea 14:9).

"Who is wise and will keep these things? They will understand" (Psalm 107:43).

"Who is wise and understanding [EPISTĒMŌN] among you?" (St. James 3:13).

"Who then, is that faithful and understanding [PHRONIMOS] slave [DOULOS], whom his lord will set over his household?" (St. Matthew 24:45).

"Who then, is the faithful and understanding [PHRONIMOS] steward [OIKONOMOS], whom his lord will set over his household, to give them their portion of food in due season?" (St. Luke 12:42).

"Whom shall He make to understand what is heard?" (Isaiah 28:9).

"Unto whom has the understanding of Wisdom been made manifest? and who has understood her great experience?" (Sirach 1:7, Syriac and Sahidic Texts).

"Who does the same as Your marvelous deeds, O God? And who understands Your deep thought of life?" (2 Baruch 54:12).

"Who has given understanding and wisdom to everything that moves on the earth and in the sea?" (Enoch 101:8).

"Who will understand but one who is wise and discerning and loves the Lord [Jesus]?" (*Epistle of Barnabas* 6:10b).

"Blessed are they who by means of Him have understood everything, and have known the Lord in His Truth" (Odes of Solomon 12:13).

The very word "who" [MI in Hebrew] is called Understanding [BINAH] since insight is the highest point of human perceptions where only questions can be asked without any replies:

"Understanding [BINAH] is 'Who' " (Zohar I.85b-86a; ibid. II.139b-140a).

"Who [MI] denotes understanding [BINAH]" (Zohar III.27b-28a, Raya Mehemna).

WIFE, WOMEN, AND UNDERSTANDING

"Happy the husband of an understanding [SAKAL] wife" (Sirach 25:8, Hebrew Text).

"A friend and a companion will each give support at the right time, but an understanding [SAKAL] wife is above both" (Sirach 40:23, Hebrew Text).

"House and riches are inherited from fathers, and from the Lord is an understanding wife" (Proverbs 19:14).

"The grace of a wife delights her husband, and her understanding [EPISTĒMĒ] will fatten his bones" (Sirach 26:13).

"Abigail . . . was a woman of good understanding [SAKAL] and of a beautiful countenance" (1 Samuel 25:3).

"Do not despise an understanding woman, for her good grace is above pearls" (Sirach 7:19, Hebrew Text).

"A daughter who understands [PHRONIMĒ] shall bring an inheritance to her husband" (Sirach 22:4).

"You have ordered your life in wisdom and have called understanding: 'mother' " (2 Esdras 13:55, Syriac Text [see Targum on Proverbs 2:3]).

WINE AND UNDERSTANDING

"Do not miss the discourse of the aged . . . because from them you shall learn understanding" (Sirach 8:9).

"He who learns from the aged, to whom is he like? To one who eats ripened grapes and drinks old wine" (Pirke Aboth 4:26). Hence "a new vessel full of old wine" (ibid. 4:20) is a young man full of understanding.

"As for him who lacks understanding, Wisdom says to him: 'Come, eat of my bread and drink of the wine I have mingled' " (Proverbs 9:4,5).

"A life of wine and strong drink is sweet but better than both is a life of wealth of understanding" (Sirach 40:18, Hebrew Text, marginal reading).

Jewish legend holds that in the next world the righteous will drink a specially preserved wine called *yayin meshumar* (Zohar III.40a). This wine is Understanding [BINAH] (Zohar III.40a-40b [Tishby, p. 1211]).

Conversely

"I went by . . . the vineyard of the man void of understanding, and behold, it was all grown over with thorns, and nettles had covered the face thereof, and the stone wall thereof was broken down" (Proverbs 24:30,31).

*   *

"Wine that makes glad the understanding" (Homer's *Iliad* 3.246-247).

The Egyptian god Thoth was the Scribe of the gods by reason of his great wisdom and understanding. He was also known as "Thoth, lord of wine who drinks abundantly" (*Philae*, Phot. 1434). And since wine and understanding make the heart of man glad, Thoth was also known as "lord of gladness" (*Dendarah*, IV.78 [Text found in A. Mariette's, *Dendara* 5 Vols. Paris 1870 and Cairo 1875.]).

> *It is because "Wine gladdens the heart of man" (Psalm 104:15)*
> *that understanding is compared to good Wine [see "The*
> *Delights and Joys of Understanding"]. But drinking*
> *to excess results in loss of Understanding.*

"Wine bibbing . . . gluttony . . . excessive indulgence . . . mulct the vital element: the understanding" (Philo, *Ebr.* 22,23).

"Understanding and [over] indulgence of the body cannot occupy the same quarters" (Philo, *L.A.* III.151).

"Men who live dissolutely . . . went astray very far into the ways of error . . . being deceived as babes without understanding" (Psalms of Solomon 1:6, Von Gebhardt Transl.].

"They are greedy dogs who do not know satisfaction, they are shepherds who do not know [YADA] how to understand [BIN], they all look to their own way, every one after his own gain, and from the first even to the last. 'Come,' they say, 'let us get wine, and fill ourselves with strong drink' " (Isaiah 56:11,12).

"Jesus said: 'I stood in the midst of the world, and in the flesh I was seen by them, and I found all men drunk . . . and my soul grieved over the sons of men because they are blind in the heart [i.e. understanding]' " (*Oxyrrynchus Agrapha*, Logion 3, ll. 11-12 [*Gospel of Thomas*, Logion 28]).

WORK AND UNDERSTANDING

"He who gathers [working in the fields] in the summer is an understanding [SAKAL] son" (Proverbs 10:5).

"If understanding [PHRONĒSIS] works, who, of all who are, is a more skillful artisan? . . ." (Wisdom 8:6).

"Like a whetstone . . . the understanding [NOUS] . . . loves effort, and exercise sharpens its edge" (Philo, *Cong.* 25).

"In His hands are both we and our words, all insight and understanding [EPISTĒMĒ] of workmanship" (Wisdom 7:16).

Conversely

"Envy . . . leads the mind into frenzy and does not allow the understanding [SUNESIS] of man to work" (Testament of Simeon 4:8, Greek B, Armenian, and Slavonic I Texts).

In turn, Understanding helps us to understand the wonderful works of God.

"Hear all you who know righteousness and understand the works of God" (Zadokite Fragment [CD] 1:1,2).

"Now therefore children, hearken unto me and I will open your eyes to see and to understand the works of God" (Zadokite Fragment 3:1 [CD 2:14,15, MS. A]).

"Hearken unto this . . . and understand the wondrous works of God" (Job 37:14).

"What is he who is flesh to understand Your works?" (1QH 15:21, Dead Sea Scrolls).

"How is he who is dust and ashes to answer his Maker? And how is he to understand His works?" (1QH 12:27,28, Dead Sea Scrolls).

"Blessed is he who understands the Lord's works and glorifies the Lord God" (2 Enoch 42:14, B Text).

"You have given Your servant understanding of knowledge to understand Your marvels and Your works without number" (1QH 11:27,28, Dead Sea Scrolls).

"Make me to understand the way of Your precepts, and I shall speak of Your wondrous works [for I shall understand them]" (Psalm 119:27).

Because "through Your precepts I get understanding" (Psalm 119:104).

*   *

"He who fashions their hearts alike, He understands [BIN] all their works" (Psalm 33:15).

"The eyes of God are greater than ten thousand suns and He sees the ways of man and in the darkness He understands the face of their works" (Sirach 23:19, Syriac Text).

"God understood all their works" (Zadokite Fragment 1:10).

Conversely

"No one heeds Your wisdom and no one understands [BIN] Your mighty works" (1QH 10:2,3, Dead Sea Scrolls).

"The wicked and . . . the workers of iniquity . . . do not understand [BIN] the deeds of the Lord, nor the works of His hands" (Psalm 28:3,5).

WRITING AND UNDERSTANDING

"The Most High gave understanding to the five men, and they wrote" (2 Esdras 14:42).

"All this the Lord made me understand [SAKAL] in writing by [His] hand upon me" (1 Chronicles 28:19, Literal Translation).

"That they may read and understand, how there is no God but Me" (2 Enoch 36:1; ibid. 33:8, A Text).

"I have put all these things down in writing that you may read and understand" (2 Enoch 66:8, A Text).

"I am writing to you in very plain language that you may understand" (*Epistle of Barnabas* 6:5).

"In this book I have written the instruction of understanding [SUNESEŌS] and insight [EPISTĒMĒS]" (Sirach 50:27).

"From the very beginning I was assured, and when I had greatly understood [TEBUNAH] it, I set it down in writing" (Sirach 39:32, Hebrew Text, MS. B).

"I wrote . . . so that when you read you may understand my knowledge in the mystery of Christ" (Ephesians 3:3,4).

"Now go, write it before them on a tablet and note it in a book that it may be for the latter days forever and ever" (Isaiah 30:8).

"In the latter days you shall understand [BIN] it with understanding [BINAH]" (Jeremiah 23:20; 30:24).

*   *

"I will light the lamp of understanding in your heart, and it will not be extinguished until what you are to write is finished" (2 Esdras 14:25).

EPILOGUE

EPILOGUE

She rose early while it was still dark, and having performed her ablutions, knelt by the hearth, and kindled the fire, setting the kettle of water above it. Then, taking the distaff and spindle she sat by the fireside spinning, and pondering in her heart words uttered long ago: words that portended a throne for her Son, and a kingdom that was to endure forever. Her eyes wandered to the bed where He lay fast asleep, His strong hands upon His chest and His head to one side, turned towards her. She felt a tender longing to kiss His peaceful brow and caress the tousled locks of His hair, remembering the cold night, almost thirty years ago, when she brought Him forth and first held Him close to her bosom, then placed Him in a manger that was to be, of all things, a sign. She recalled the prophecy of old Simeon as He took the Child in His arms and said that He was to be a light to the Gentiles, and glory to God's people Israel. She smiled at the wonder of it all, for He was there, presently before her tranquilly asleep, her Yeshua, the village carpenter who did all things well with a quiet smile. These last two years she would now and then see Him by the window in deep reverie with a far-away look in His eyes, and she would then remember the anguish she felt long ago when they had lost sight of Him for three days, before they found Him in the Temple sitting in the midst of the teachers. She heard Him stir and sigh. Getting up, she took a small brand from the fire and lit the wick of the table lamp. The flame flared and revealed upon the boards: the wholly leavened dough in a kneading trough. Moistening the cloth, she covered the mass and lifted it into a basket ready to be taken to the baker early in the morning. She sensed His eyes upon her and met His gaze. It was then that she knew that this was to be the day He would part from her, the day He would set forth on a course that was to end on a hill ablaze by the rays of a noon-day sun.

She trembled, for she suddenly understood about the grain-manger, and about that which was covered on the table ready for the ordeal that would transform it into bread. He was now fully risen, winding the leather thongs around His arm and wrist in a deliberate majestic manner — like a prince girding himself before the contest. Placing the prayer shawl upon His head, He went to open the shutters and face the dawn. Impulsively, she took the dough and cradled it in her arms, then pressing it to her cheeks she kissed it. She left the house sobbing, taking the bundle with her to the village oven.

Outside, the first beams of the sun heralded the morning of salvation.

NOTES

ON THE PROLOGUE

In this allegorical story of the meeting and union of Wisdom and Understanding, Wisdom is portrayed as the beautiful daughter of a King. She is called Princess Hakima a name derived from the Hebrew word for "wise": Ḥakam. Being an extraordinarily wise little girl brought up in the palace quarters of the King's many foreign wives, she was able to learn their languages. Thus, she greeted each emissary in his own tongue when all of them came that day from their countries to render homage to the King.

We know that Wisdom does things profitably and well. She is also adept in testing the skill and understanding of those who seek her by presenting before them enigmas, mysterious puzzles, dark sayings and "the riddles of the wise" (Proverbs 1:6) for them to solve.

The labyrinth and entrance to Princess Hakima's palace faced east, the direction from which Understanding was to come with the dawn (see pp. 244-247). The first door was of silver, symbolic of understanding (see pp. 392-393) and the many globes reflected the rising sun. Among all the *varied* sizes there were *two* eye-sized globes set side by side as in a face to see the light of the rising "sun of understanding" (Wisdom 5:6, Latin Vulgate; Philo, *Q.Exod.* II.51) for "the rising sun reveals all things" (Sirach 42:16, Hebrew Text) to "the eyes of the under-standing" (Philo, *Q. Gen.* IV.51).

The first door of the Day led to the second door which was the door of the Night. Thus, stars were carved in the *identical* shields on the fragrant second door at the end of a dark passageway that was illuminated here and there by an occa-sional lamp hanging from the pillars. Scrutinizing the shields with the aid of a lamp, the discerning eye would see among all the *identical* stars, *one* that was *dif-ferent* because it had an extra ray of light uniquely carved in it.

Just as the first door of the Day and the second door of the Night represented the *heavens* (sun and stars), the opening of the second door led to an open courtyard of fountains and falling waters leading to the third door with the marvelously painted scene of a beautiful and fertile *Earth* ('mountains and valleys', 'cascading streams', 'green meadows', 'wild flowers', 'fields of grain', 'vineyards', 'orchards', 'a blue lake', 'a small village', 'shepherds', 'flocks', 'reapers', 'young maidens' and gatherers of 'fruits'). One of the painted fruits proferred itself to the hungry, and the hand that discerned the hidden mecha-nism behind it released the latch.

The door opened to an alcove laden with tables of fruits, pastries, sweet-meats, viands, wines and other delicacies to eat to the heart's content. The first door was for the *eyes* (no other metal reflects light better than *silver*), and the fourth door at the end of the alcove was built for the *ears*. Did not the fragrance of the second door, the cool breeze in the courtyard, and the food delight the other senses? It was time to delight the ears. Every *golden* (nothing is more sonorous than a golden bell) little bell in the panel of the fourth door, rang with the same note and pitch except one which had a distinctive sound, pulling on that little golden bell released the latch of the fourth door. Of course, the ringing of all the rest of the bells alerted the princess and her maidens to the coming of the one who understood.

Opening that portal he would find himself in a passageway that led to the somber fifth door upon which was depicted a stormy ocean scene with heavy rain-laden black clouds overhead, and waves below dashing against precipitous cliffs. From a lofty crag a high waterfall cascaded to the sea. Running one's finger along that aqueous bridge which united the waters above and the waters below, released the catch and opened the door.

Understanding knows that Wisdom endeavors to unite. "All scripture is inspired by God" (2 Timothy 3:16) and "everything that was written long ago in the Scriptures was meant to teach us something" (Romans 15:4). The same Holy Spirit who inspired those who wrote the books of the Old Testament also provided inspiration for those who wrote the New. In the Old Testament, *Genesis* was written much prior to the *Psalms* of King David, in turn all the Psalms were written much before the book of *Revelation* of the New Testament. We can see the thread of inspiration, which joins together these three works in the Holy Bible, if we commence with the narrative in Genesis concerning the creation of the firmament. On the second Day "God said, 'Let there be a firmament in the midst of the waters, and let it *separate* the waters which were under the firmament from the waters which were above the firmament.' And it was so. And God called the firmament Heaven. And the evening and the morning were the second Day" (Genesis 1:6-7). In all the other days it is always mentioned, after each act of creation, that is was: "good" (see Genesis 1:4, 10, 12, 18, 21, 25, 31) but not on the second Day. It was not bad that God divided the deep waters above from the deep waters below because He thereby created the firmament but nevertheless it is not written that it was "good" because in so doing He "separated" them.

Being separated from one another it may be said that the deep waters above and the deep waters below would miss each other. Hundreds of years later when King David composed the *Psalms* he was inspired to write in Psalm 42:7: "The deep [above] calls to the deep [below] at the roar of your waterfalls." Because there, in that bridge of water they would be able to meet and be *one* again.

Again, hundreds of years later when St. John the Evangelist in the island of Patmos received the vision of the new heavens and the new earth, he, in turn, saw and was inspired to write in the book of *Revelation:* "And I saw a new heaven and a new earth, for the first heaven and the first earth had passed away, and the sea was no more"

(Revelation 21:1). Because the waters were united and made one again, no longer separated from one another as in the days of the first earth. For had not the Lord prayed to the Father in heaven, "that they may all be one . . . that they may be made perfect in one" (St. John 17:21, 23).

When the fifth door opened it led to a large *clear glass* portal at the end of a small corridor. This sixth door was flanked on either side by a large wooden ox and an ass. The solid *transparent* glass door did not have a knob and seemed to be fixed on its hinges until someone who understood would discover the two small buttons each hidden somewhere in the carved ox and the donkey. Pressing on these activated the mechanism that made it easy to swing open the thick glass door.

Upon opening the sixth door a man would find himself facing a thick *black* fissureless curtain of the richest silk extending top to bottom from the ceiling to the floor. This was the seventh enigma, not a door but a thick *opaque* curtain completely blocking further access. The wise Princess stood directly behind it waiting to be seen and understood by someone who knew what to do.

Did not Wisdom build herself a house with *"seven* pillars"? (Proverbs 9:1). Princess Hakima, who through her wisdom designed the beautiful little palace, had *seven* enigmatic portals bar the entrance to her private chambers which were at the end of all those doors that could only be opened by someone who had understanding. The front of her palace and the first door faced east towards sunrise with all its connotations of Understanding (see pp. 244-247). The back of the palace, where the Princess stood behind the black curtain, faced west towards the sunset with its connotations of Knowledge*. Thus, whoever succeeded by his understanding to go through all the portals and pierce the veil behind which the wise Princess stood, would also find himself standing in that western quadrant

---

*Knowledge

The rising sun of understanding (see pp. 244-247) sets in the west, and there, it may be said to have acquired knowledge because it is written that "the sun *know*s the place of his setting" (Psalm 104:19) in the west. For darkness comes with his setting, and then although "day to day pours forth speech . . . night to night declares *knowledge*" (Psalm 19:2). Thus, one can "pass over to the coasts of Cyprus (to the *west*) and see [and "know," *vide* p. 259] and send to Kedar (to the *east*) and understand mightily" (Jeremiah 2:10). Furthermore, the eastern rising sun courses the heavens to set in the west making the rising sun of understanding become the setting sun of knowledge. For we do go from understanding to knowledge (see p. 149). "When the wise is made to understand [SAKAL], he receives knowledge" (Proverbs 21:11b) because "understanding loves to learn and advance to knowledge" (Philo, *Decal.* I.9). That is why "God . . . gives wisdom to the wise and [He gives] knowledge to those who know understanding" (Daniel 2:21; see sequences in Exodus 31:3; 35:31; 1 Kings 7:14; Psalm 119:125; Proverbs 5:1-2; Jeremiah 9:24; Sirach 1:19; 24:25-27 Sinaiticus and Greek Cursive 248; 1QH 2:18; 1:31; 7:26, 27; 12:11, 12, Dead Sea Scrolls; *Didache* 2:21). Truly, "the heart of him who has understanding seeks knowledge" (Proverbs 15:14). Hence, a man understanding the way to get to Wisdom would then desire to have knowledge of her.

of Knowledge. And there, in that place, he would have been able to know Wisdom and embrace her by his understanding. Remembering that the first door was full of *light* from the hundreds of silver globes reflecting the sun, it was only fitting that the last portal was *darkness* (the black silk curtain).

The strong young man who understood was called Yamin, a name which means "right hand" [YAMIN] in Hebrew, and is also a word of circumlocution for "understanding" (see pp. 369-371 re *The Right Hand and Understanding*). He was the youngest son, the Benyamin ("son of the right hand") of the family. When he was a young lad, his father, a landowner with many herds and flocks, would take him on long excursions over mountains and valleys teaching him all the natural lore he knew and also skill in archery. He loved to teach him because Yamin was an obedient and very attentive son with a great desire to hear the wise words of his father and to do them.

Through his understanding Yamin succeeded in opening all the secret five doors. And as he now stood before the sixth door made of transparent glass flanked by the carved full-sized ox and ass, he remembered that things become clear to us if we can really see and know, and hear and understand them. His hands felt the large eyes of the ox and the long ears of the donkey for the secret releases to the door which he knew would be there (see p. 259).

He then passed through. And immediately saw the thick black curtain that blocked his path to the wise princess standing behind it waiting for a man who understood. Dagger in hand, Yamin pierced the dark veil from top to bottom with his understanding (see pp. 94-95, 317-320). Then, in all her glory, the beauty of Wisdom was revealed, and she captured his heart.

*   *

456

ON THE COVER

The cover painting is of Jacob and his dream in Bethel of a ladder extending from the earth to heaven with the angels of God ascending and descending on it (Genesis 28:11-19). The Lord stands at the very top of the ladder which has twelve steps including the foundation which is the "fear of the Lord". Each step from the base up is engraved with the Hebrew words for: "The fear of the Lord", "Wisdom", "Basic Understanding", "Insight", "Skillful Understanding", "Great Understanding", "Knowledge", "the Lord's Knowledge", "Counsel", "Powerful Counsel", "Ability to Grasp the Truth", and "Truth" which are found in the section of the book regarding the Ladder of Understanding (see pp. 107-208).

The ladder leads to the Lord Jesus at the very top for He is "the Way, and the Truth and the Life" (St. John 14:6). The two evergreen trees, one on each side of the ladder, and the two pine cone fruits, symbolize the two needed to bear witness to the Truth, we can also see the twin stars in the upper right hand corner.

It is from Jacob that the line of the Messiah sprung forth. At the foot of Jacob are the palm branches and the fruitful olive branch symbolic of the Messiah. On the other side of the painting are the outlines of a thorny rose bush, and the ripe pomegranate which is the symbolic fruit of Israel. There is an old Jewish tradition that the angels ascending and descending on the ladder are angels going up to God with questions from us, and angels coming down with answers from Him who *is* Understanding. For it is written that "He [the Lord] gives to His beloved *in* sleep" (Psalm 127:2, Literal Translation). Thus, while the beloved is asleep, the Lord gives him the answer to what he desired to know. Jacob's left hand is under his head (see Song of Songs 2:6; 8:3), and his right hand of understanding (see pp. 369-371) is there for all to see, because it is always ready to embrace Wisdom.

The title of the God of *Abraham* is God *"Most High"* (see Genesis 14:19; Sirach 44: 19,20; Book of Jubilees 12:19; 13:16), who is God and giver of *Knowledge* (see Numbers 24:16; Sirach 42:18c [Hebrew] Masada Scroll, and Greek Ephraemi Texts; Ibid. 38:6, Latin Vulgate; 1QS10:11,12, Dead Sea Scrolls; Odes of Solomon 12:3,4;6:6,10-12; Sibylline Oracles, Fragment i. 4; Psalm 73:11).

Jacob's God: "the Mighty One of Jacob" (Psalm 132:2,5; Isaiah 49:26; 60:16; Genesis 49:24) is *"God Almighty"* (Genesis 48:3) who *is* the *"Lord [YHVH]"* who appeared at the top of the ladder to Jacob in his dream (Compare Genesis 28:13-19; 48:3; 35: 6-11). The *"Lord [YHVH]"* is also identified as being the *"Mighty One of Jacob"* in Psalm 50:1; 146:5 and Isaiah 60:16. In the Holy Scriptures: *"God Almighty"* is God and giver of *understanding* (Job 36:5; 32:8; 11:7,11; Sirach 42:17,18, Sinaiticus and

Alexandrinus Texts; Judith 8:13 Greek Codex 58, Syriac and Vetus Latina Texts). His people knew that "the *understanding* possessed by Bezaleel was from the *Almighty"* (Midrash Exodus Rabbah 48.4).

The Lord at the top of the ladder in the cover painting is Jesus the Messiah and the Son of Man* who is *Understanding* incarnate, and the giver of under-standing as well (see pp. 419-423 etc.). Long ago it was asked in the book of Proverbs concerning God: "What is His name, and what is His Son's name? Surely you know!" (Proverbs 30:4). We know that Abraham was the (grand) father of Jacob and that the God of Abraham is the Most High. In turn we know that Jacob is the (grand) son of Abraham and that the God of Jacob is the Almighty. We also hear about the "sons of the Most High" (Psalms 72:6; Sirach 4:10; St. Luke 6:35; Book of Jubilees 21:11), and about "the Most High Father" (Odes of Solomon 23:18 Syriac Text) but we do not find any references to "sons" or "daughters" of "the Almighty."

It is the prerogative of "sons" to understand (see pp. 220-224). Thus, as *"the* Son of the Most High" (St. Luke 1:32; 8:28; St. Mark 5:7) and *"the* Son of Man" (St. Matthew 9:6; 12:8; 13:41; 25:31; St. Mark 3:31; 14:62; St. Luke 5:24; 6:5; 21:27; St. John 6:53, 62 etc.), Jesus the Messiah understands all things. Moreover, being Himself *"the* Almighty" (Revelation 1:8; Ladder of Jacob 7:20; St. Ignatius, *Epistle to the Philippians* VII.1), Jesus is *also* the giver of understanding (pp. 419-423 etc.). We have seen that the Almighty is "the Lord [YHVH]" who appeared to Jacob in his dream. Therefore, the Almighty: "Jesus *is* the Lord" (1 Corinthians 12:3) as well. And as such He is standing at the top of the ladder that Jacob saw in his dream.

To the question asked in Proverbs 30:4 we can say that if God the *Most High* "is His [God's] name" (Proverbs 30:4) as *Father* then "His Son's name" (Ibid.) as *Son* is the *Almighty.* And Jesus the Almighty is the Son of the Most High "in whom are hidden all the treasures of wisdom and knowledge" waiting to be seen by sleeping Jacob-Israel.

M.J.D.   **A.M.O.**

---

*See *The Revelation of the Son of Man*, by Levi Khamor, Third Edition 1992, BenYamin Press, Geneva, N.Y. for a full discussion on "Man/Son of Man", "Knowledge and Understanding", "The Most High and the Almighty", "The Creator and Former", "Jacob-Israel", etc. (See back of book for additional information)

*   *

"Why do you not ask the Lord [Jesus] for understanding and receive it from Him?"
Shepherd of Hermas, *Sim.* V.4.57:4

"The Lord [Jesus] will give you understanding in all things."
2 Timothy 2:7

*   *

BIBLIOGRAPHY

BIBLIOGRAPHY

Abel, F.M. *Les Livres des Maccabées*. Paris, 1949.

Aistleitner, J. (ed.). *Die Mythologischen und Kultischen Texte aus Ras Schamra*. 2nd Edit. Budapest, 1964.

——— *Wörterbuch der Ugaritischen Sprache*. 4th Edit. Berlin, 1974.

Aland, K. and Aland, B. *The Text of the New Testament*. An introduction to the Critical Editions and to the Theory and Practice of Modern Textual Criticism. Leiden, 1987.

Aland, K.; Black, M.; Metzger, B. M. and Wikgren, A. (eds.). *The Greek New Testament*. Philadelphia, 1966.

Albeck, C., and Theodor, J., eds. *Bereshith [Genesis] Rabbah*. 3 vols. Jerusalem, 1965.

Armstrong, A. H. *Plotinus*. 6 Vols. [Loeb Classical Library]. Cambridge, Mass., 1966.

Arnaldez, R.; Mondesert, C.; Pouilloux, J. et al. *Les Oeuvres de Philon d' Alexandrie*. 35 vols. Paris, 1961ff.

Arndt, W. F. and Gingrich F. W. *A Greek-English Lexicon of the New Testament and Other Early Christian Literature*. Chicago, 1957.

Asensio, F. *Misericordia et Veritas, el Hesed y'Emet divinos*. Rome, 1949.

Ashlag, R. *Commentary to the Zohar*. 2 Vols. Jerusalem, 1961.

Assman, J. (ed.). *Agyptische Hymnen und Gebete*. Zurich-Munich, 1975.

Assyrian Dictionary (The) of the Oriental Institute of the University of Chicago. Vols. I-IX, XVI, XXI [A-M, S and Z]. Chicago, 1956ff.

Aucher, J. B. (ed.). *De Providentia* [Philo] I and II. [Latin Translation of the Armenian Text]. Paris, 1822).

Baars, W. (ed.). *Psalms of Solomon*. [Syriac, Peshitta]. Leiden, 1972.

Bacher, W. ed. *Die Agada der palastinischen Amoraer*. Strassburg, 1892.

——— *Die Agada der babylonischen Amoraer*. Strassburg, 1878.

——— *Die Agada der Tannaiten*. Strassburg, 1890.

Baer, S. and Delitzsch, F. *Liber Proverbium*. Leipzig, 1880.

Bardy G. (ed.). *Eusebe de Césarée:* Histoire Ecclesiastique. 3 Vols. [Sources Chretiens, 31,41,55]. Paris, 1952-58.

Barnstein, H. *The Targum Onkelos to Genesis.* London, 1896.

Barr, J. *Comparative Philology and the Text of the Old Testament.* Oxford, 1968.

Barthelmy, D. and Rickenbacher, O. *Konkordanz Zum Hebräischer Sirach mit Syrisch-Hebräischen Index.* Gottingen, 1973.

Bate, H. N. *The Jewish Sybylline Oracles.* New York, 1918.

Becker, J. *Gottesfurcht im Alten Testament.* [Analecta Biblica 25]. Rome, 1965.

Behrend, B. Z. (ed.). *Talmud Yerushalmi.* [Hebrew]. Krotoschim, 1866.

Ben Yehuda, E., *A Complete Dictionary of Ancient and Modern Hebrew.* 16 vols. Jerusalem, 1911-1959.

——— *Thesaurus Totius Hebraitatis.* 8 vols. London and New York, 1960.

Benedite, G. *Le Temple de Philae.* Paris, 1893-95.

Bensley, R. L. *The Missing Fragment of the Latin Translation of the Fourth Book of Ezra.* Cambridge, 1875.

Berlin, M., and Zevin, S.Y., eds. *Encyclopedia Talmudit.* 10 Vols. Jerusalem, 1946 et seq.

Berlin, N. Z. J., ed. *Sifre.* Jerusalem, 1959.

Berliner, A. *Targum Onkelos.* Berlin, 1884.

Bernard, J. H. (ed.). *The Odes of Solomon.* Cambridge, 1912.

Beyerlin, W. (ed.). *Near Eastern Religious Texts Relating to the Old Testament.* Philadelphia, 1978.

Bezold, C. *Babylonische-Assyrisches Glossar.* Heidelberg, 1926.

Bidawid, R. J., ed. *The Old Testament in Syriac According to the Peshitto Version* [Contains 2 Esdras in Syriac]. Leiden, 1966.

Bietenhard, H., ed. *Midrash Tanchumah B.* Bern, 1980.

Bigg, C. *The Clementine Homilies.* Oxford, 1890.

Bissing (von) F. W. *Altaegyptische Lebenweisheit.* Zurich, 1955.

Black, M., ed. *The Book of Enoch or 1 Enoch* [A New English edition with commentary and textual notes]. Leiden, 1985.

Blass, F., and Debrunner, A. *A Greek Grammar of the New Testament and Other Early Christian Literature.* Revised by R. W. Funk. Chicago, 1961.

Blunt, A. W. F. *The Apologies of Justin Martyr.* Cambridge, 1891.

Bogart, P. *L'Apocalypse Syriaque de Baruch.* 2 Vols. Paris, 1969.

Boeckh, A., ed. *Corpus Inscriptionum Semiticarum*. Paris, 1881.

Boman, T. *Hebrew Thought Compared with Greek*. London, 1960.

Bonnard, P. E. *La Sagesse en Personne Annoncée et Venue: Jesus Christ*. [Lectio Divina 44]. Paris, 1966.

Borger, R. *Babylonische-Assyrische Lesestücke I-III*. Rome, 1963.

Boström, G. *Proverbia Studien: die Weisheit und das fremde Weib in Sprached 1-9*. Lund, 1935.

Botterweck, J. G. and Ringgren, H. (eds.). *Theological Dictionary of the Old Testament*. Vols. I-VI. Grand Rapids, Michigan, 1974-80ff.

Box, G. H. and Landsman, J. L. (eds.). *The Apocalypse of Abraham*. London, 1918.

Box, G. H. (ed.). *The Testament of Abraham*. London, 1927.

——— (ed.). *The Ezra Apocalypse*. London, 1912.

Boylan, P. *Thoth, the Hermes of Egypt*. Oxford, 1922.

Braude, W. G. (ed.). *The Midrash on Psalms*. 2 Vols. New Haven, 1959.

——— *Pesikta Rabbati*. 2 Vols. New Haven, 1968.

Braude, W. G. and Kapstein I. J. *Pesikta de Rab Kahana*. Philadelphia, 1975.

——— *Tanna Debe Eliyahu*. Philadelphia, 1981.

Brederek, E. *Konkordanz zum Targum Onkelos*. [Beihefte zur Zeitschrift fur die Alttestamentliche Wissenschaft IX]. Berlin, 1906.

Brock, S. P. (ed.). *Testamentum Iobi*. Leiden, 1967.

Brockelmann, K. *Lexicon Syriacum*. Olms, 1928.

Brongers, H. A. "La Crainte du Seigneur," *Old Testament Studies* 5. (1948) pp. 150-173

Brown, F., Driver, S. R. and Briggs, C. A. *An English and Hebrew Lexicon of the Old Testament*. Oxford, 1959.

Brownlee, W. H. *The Dead Sea Manual of Discipline*. [Bulletin of the American Schools of Oriental Research, Suppl. Stud. Nos. 10-12]. New Haven, 1951.

Brugsch H. (ed.). *Hieroglyphisch-demotisches Wörterbuch*, 7 Vols. Leipzig, 1867-82.

——— *Religion und Mythologie der Alten Aegypten*. 2 Vols. Leipzig, 1885.

——— *Thesaurus Inscriptionum Aegypticarum*. 6 Vols. Leipzig, 1883-91.

Bryce, G. E. *A Legacy of Wisdom: The Egyptian Contribution to the Wisdom of Israel.* Lewisburg and London, 1979.

Buber, M. *For the Sake of Heaven.* Philadelphia, 1953, and New York 1966.

Buber, S. (ed.). *Midrash Tanchuma.* 4 Vols. Wilma, 1885.

——— *Midrash Tehillim.* Wilma, 1891.

——— *Pesikta de Rab Kahana.* Siebert, Lyck, 1868.

——— *Yalkut Makiri.* 2 Vols. Berdyczew, 1899.

Buck, A. De (ed.). *The Egyptian Coffin Texts.* 2 Vols. Chicago, 1935-38.

Buckley, T. A. *The Iliad of Homer.* [Literally Translated]. London, 1879.

Budge, E. A. W. *The Book of the Dead.* London, 1899.

——— *The Gods of the Egyptians.* 2 Vols. London, 1904.

——— *The Paradise of the Holy Fathers.* 2 Vols. London, 1907.

——— *The Literature of the Ancient Egyptians.* London, 1914.

——— *An Egyptian Hieroglyphic Dictionary.* 2 Vols. New York, 1978 [repr. of 1920 edit.].

——— (Trans.). *The [Syriac] Book of the Bee.* Oxford, 1886.

Burckhardt, J. L. *Arabic Proverbs.* London, 1817.

Burrows, M. and Trever, J. C. (eds.). *The Dead Sea Scrolls of St. Mark's Monastery.* 2 Vols. New Haven, 1950-1951.

Butterworth, G. W. *Clement of Alexandria with an English Translation.* [Loeb Classical Library.] London and New York, 1919.

Buxtorf, J. *Lexicon Chaldaicum, Talmudicum et Rabbinicum.* 2 Vols. Leipzig, 1869-75.

Camelot, T. (ed.). *Ignace d' Antioche: Lettres.* [Sources Chretiens 10.] 3rd edit. Paris, 1958.

Caminos, R. A. *Literary Fragments in the Hieratic Script.* Oxford, 1955.

Campbell, B. J. ed. *The Last Chapters of Enoch in Greek.* London, 1937.

Campbell, L. *Sophocles.* London, 1879.

Caquot, A. et al. *Textes Ougaritiques I: Mythes et legendes.* Paris, 1974.

——— *Les Rephaim Ougaritiques.* Paris, 1960.

Carmignac, J. *La Regle de la Guerre des fils de lumière contre les fils de ténèbres.* Paris, 1958.

——— *Les Textes de Qumran, II.* Paris, 1963.

Castellino, G. *Sapienza Babilonese.* Turin, 1962.

Causse, A. "Sagesse Egyptienne et sagesse Juive," *Revue d' Histoire et Philosophie Religieuses 9* (1929), pp. 149-169.

Ceriani, A. M. *Translatio Syra Pescitto Veteris Testamenti ex Codice Ambrosiano.* Milan, 1876.

Ceriani, A. M. ed. *Monumenta sacra et profana.* Vol. V, fasc. I. [Syriac Version of 2 Esdras in Codex Ambrosianus]. Milan, 1868.

Chabot, J. B.; Guide, J.; Hyvernat, B.; et al. *Corpus Scriptorum Christianorum Orientalium.* Paris, 1903.

Charles, R. H. (ed.). *The Apocrypha and Pseudepigrapha of the Old Testament.* 2 Vols. Oxford, 1913.

——— *The Apocalypse of Baruch.* Oxford, 1896.

——— *The Ascension of Isaiah.* London, 1909.

——— *The Assumption of Moses.* Oxford, 1897.

——— *The Book of the Secrets of Enoch.* Oxford, 1896.

——— *The Book of Enoch.* 2nd edit. Oxford, 1912.

——— *Jubilees.* Oxford, 1908.

——— *The Testaments of the Twelve Patriarchs with Greek, Armenian and Slavonic Variants.* Oxford, 1908.

——— *Fragments of a Zadokite Work.* Oxford, 1912.

Charlesworth, J. H. (ed.). *The Odes of Solomon.* Oxford, 1973.

——— *The Old Testament Pseudepigrapha.* 2 Vols. Garden City, 1983-85.

——— *The Pseudepigrapha and Modern Research.* [Septuagint and Cognate Studies 7.] Missoula, Mont., 1976.

Chassinat, E. *Le Temple de Dendara.* 4 Vols. Cairo, 1934-35.

Chevallier, M. A. *L'Esprit et le Messie dans le bas-Judaisme et le N.T.* Paris, 1958.

Churgin, P. *Targum Jonathan to the Prophets.* New Haven, 1927.

——— *Targum Ketuvim* [Hagiographa]. New York, 1945.

467

Churton, W. R. (ed.). *The Uncanonical and Apocryphal Scriptures.* London, 1884.

Cohen, A. *Ancient Jewish Proverbs.* London 1911.

Cohen, A. (transl.). *Ibn Gabirol: The Choice of Pearls.* (Mibar ha-Peninim). New York, 1925.

Cohen, A. *The Minor Tractates of the Talmud.* London, 1911.

Cohen, I. *Dictionary of Parallel Proverbs in English, German, and Hebrew.* London, 1961.

Colombo, D. "I 'pneuma sophias' eiusque actio in mundo in libro Sapientiae," *Studi Biblici Franciscani Liber Annuus 1,* (1950-51) pp. 107-160. Jerusalem.

Colson, F. H.; Whitaker, G. H. and Marcus, R. *Philo.* 12 Vols. [Loeb Classical Library Series]. London, 1929-1953.

Conybeare, F. C.; Harris, J. R. and Lewis, A. S. (eds.). *The Story of Ahiqar.* [Syriac, Arabic, Armenian, Greek and Slavonic Versions]. Cambridge, 1898.

———— *The Story of Ahiqar from the Aramaic, Syriac, Arabic, Armenian, Ethiopic, Old Turkish, Greek and Slavonic Versions.* Cambridge, 1913.

———— *Testament of Solomon.* [Jewish Quarterly Review (October 1898)]. Philadelphia.

Coogna, D. *Stories from Ancient Canaan.* Philadelphia, 1978.

Cosser, W. "The Meaning of 'Life' (Hayyim) in Proverbs, Job and Ecclesiastes", *Glasgow University Oriental Society Transactions 15,* (1953-54) pp. 48-53.

Couturier, G. P. Sagesse *Babylonienne et Sagesse Israelite.* Paris, 1962.

Coxe, A. C. *Dialogues of Justin, Philosopher and Martyr with Trypho, a Jew.* [Ante-Nicene Fathers, Vol. I].

Craig, J. A. *Assyrian and Babylonian Religious Texts.* 2 Vols. Leipzig, 1895-97.

Creuzer, F. *Plotinus.* 3 Vols. Oxford, 1835.

Dahood, M. J. *Proverbs and Northwest Semitic Philology.* Rome, 1963.

Danby, H. *The Mishnah.* Oxford, 1933.

Daniel, S. (ed.). *Philo - De Specialibus I et II.* Paris, 1975.

Davies, P. R. *1QM, the War Scroll from Qumram.* Rome, 1977.

Deane, W. J. (ed.). *The Book of Wisdom.* Oxford, 1881.

Deimel, A. *Sumerisches Lexicon und Akkadisch-Sumerisches Glossar.* 9 Vols. Rome, 1928-50.

Deissman, A. *Light from the Ancient East*. London, 1927.

Dekkers, E. and Gaar, A. *Clavis Patrum Latinorum*. Rome, 1961.

Delcor, M. *Les Hymnes de Qumran*. [Texte Hebreau]. Paris, 1962.

——— *Le Testament d'Abraham*. [Studia in Veteris Testamenti Pseudepigrapha II]. Leiden, 1973.

Delitzsch, F. *Das Salomonisch Spruchbuch*. Leipzig, 1873.

——— *Assyrisches Handwörterbuch* Leipzig, 1896.

Denis, A. M. (ed.). *Concordance de l'Apocalypse grecque du Baruch*. Louvain, 1967.

Denis, A. M., and de Jonge M., eds. *Pseudepigrapha Veteris Testamenti Graece*. Leiden, 1987.

Denis, A. M. and Janssens, Y. (eds.). *Concordance Latine du Liber Jubilaeorum sine Parva Genesis*. Louvain, 1973.

Denis O.P., Albert-Marie, and Janssens, d'Yvonne. *Concordance grecque des pseudépigraphes d'Ancien Testament*. Leiden, 1987.

Denzinger, H. *Ritus Orientalium, Coptorum, Syrorum et Armenorum*. 2 Vols. Wurzburg, 1863-64.

Derousseaux, L. *La Crainte de Dieu dans l'Ancien Testament. Rescherches d' exegese et d'histoire sur la racine yârê*. [Lectio Divina 63 (1970)].

Devaud, E. *Les Maximes de Ptahhotep*. [Papyrus Prisse]. Fribourg, 1918.

Diels, H. *Sibyllinische Blätter*. Berlin, 1890.

Dietrich, M. and Loretz, O. (eds.). *Konkordanz der Ugaritischen textzählungen*. [*Alter Orient und Altes Testament* 19 (144), 1972].

Dietzfelbinger, C. *Pseudo-Philon Liber Antiquitatum Biblicarum*. Tubingen, 1975.

Diez Macho, A. *Targum Palestinense Neofiti*, Madrid, 1968.

Di Lella, A. A. *The Hebrew Text of Sirach*. The Hague, 1966.

Dillmann, A. *Biblia veteris testamenti aethiopica*, 5: *Libri apocryphi* (The Ethiopic Version of Sirach is found in pp. 54-117 here). Berlin, 1894.

Donald, T. "The Semantic Field of the Rich and Poor in the Wisdom Literature of Hebrew and Akkadian," *Oriens Antiquus* 3, (1964) pp. 27-41.

Donner, H. and Rollig, W. (eds.). *Kanaanäische und Aramaische Inschriften*. 3 Vols. Weisbaden, 1962-64.

Dos Santos, E. C. *An Expanded Hebrew Index for the Hatch-Redpath Concordance to the Septuagint*. Jerusalem, n.d.

Driver, G. R. *Canaanite Myths and Legends*. [Old Testament Studies 3]. Edinburgh, 1956.

Dronke, G. *Die Religiosen und Sittlichen Vorstellungen des Aeschylus und Sophocles*. Leipzig, 1861.

Drubbel, A. *Wijsheid*. Roermond, 1957.

Drummond, J. *Philo Judaeus*. 2 Vols. London, 1888.

Duesberg, H. *Les Scribes Inspirés: Introduction aux Livres Sapientiaux de la Bible*. 2 Vols. Paris, 1939.

Duesberg, H. and Fransen, I. *Idem*. 2nd edit. revised. Maredsous, 1966.

Dupont-Sommer, A. *The Dead Sea Scrolls*. Oxford, 1952.

——— (ed.). *The Essene Writings from Qumran*. [English Translation by G. Vermes] Oxford, 1961.

Ebeling, G. and Meissner, B. (eds.). *Reallexicon der Assyrologie*. 3 Vols. Berlin, 1932-59.

Edersheim, A. (ed.). *Ecclesiasticus*. London, 1888.

Edwards, I. E. S. *Hieroglyphic Texts from Egyptiun Stelae etc. in the British Museum*. London, 1939.

Einspahr, B. *Index to Brown, Driver and Briggs Hebrew Lexicon*. Chicago, 1977.

Eisenstein, J. D. *Ozar Midraschim*. 2 Vols. New York, 1918.

Eisenstein, J. D., ed. *Bibliotheca Midraschica: a Library of 200 Minor Midrashim*. New York, 1915.

Emerton, J. A. (ed.). *The Peshitta of the Wisdom of Solomon*. Leiden, 1959.

Encyclopedia Judaica [German]. 10 vols. Berlin, 1928-34.

Encyclopedia Judaica. 16 vols. Jerusalem-New York, 1972.

Engnell, I. "Knowledge and 'Life' in the Creation Story," *Vetus Testamentum Supplements 3*, (1955) pp. 103-119). Leiden.

Enslin, M. S. *The Book of Judith*. New York, 1973.

Epstein, I. (ed.). *The Talmud Babli with Minor Tractates*. 35 Vols. London, 1935-52.

Epstein, J. N., ed. *Mebooth leSifruth haTannaim*. Jerusalem, 1957.

Epstein, J. N., ed. *Mekilta de Rabbi Simeon ben Jochai*. Jerusalem, 1955.

Epstein-Lewin, ed. *Midrash Tanchumah*. Jerusalem, 1967.

Erman, A. *Agypten und agyptisches Leben im Altertum.* 2 Vols. Tubingen, 1884-87.

——— *Die Literatur der Agypter.* Leipzig, 1923.

Erman, A. and Grapow, H. *Worterbuch der Aegyptischen Sprache.* 6 Vols. Leipzig, 1926-31.

Erpenius, T. *Proverbiorum Arabicorum Centuriae.* Leiden, 1614.

——— *Grammatica Arabica.* [Edited by Schultens, A.]. Leiden, 1767.

Etheridge, J. W. *The Targums of Onkelos and Jonathan ben Uzziel on the Pentateuch with the Fragments of the Jerusalem Targum from the Chaldee.* New York, 1968 [repr. of 1862 edit.].

Fairbarn, P. *The Typology of Scripture.* Philadelphia, 1859.

Falkenstein, A. and Soden (von) W. (eds.). *Sumerische und Akkadische Hymnen und Gebete.* Zurich-Stuttgart, 1953.

Fang Che-Yong, M. *Quaestiones theologicae selectae libri Sira.* Rome, 1963.

——— *De discrepantis inter textum Graecum et Hebraicum libri Ecclesiastici seu Ben Sira.* (Diss. man. scrip.). Rome, 1963.

Faulkner, R. O. (ed. and trans.). *The Ancient Egyptian Pyramid Texts.* Oxford, 1969.

——— *A Concise Dictionary of Middle Egyptian.* Oxford, 1962.

Feldman, F. *Das Buch der Weisheit.* Bonn, 1926.

Festugiere, R. P., ed. *La Revelation d'Hermes Trimegiste.* 4 vols. Paris, 1949-60.

Fichtner, J. *Gottes Weisheit.* Stuttgart, 1965.

Finkelstein, L., ed. *Siphra ad Deuteronium.* New York, 1969.

——— *Sifra: or Torat Kohanim According to Codex Asemani.* New York, 1956.

Fisch, S., ed. *Midrash Haggadol* [to Sefer Devarim]. Jerusalem, 1972.

Fischer, B. (ed.). *Sapientia Salomonis.* [Vetus Latina]. Beuron, 1977.

Fisher, L. R. (ed.). *Ras Shamra Parallels: Texts from Ugarit and the Hebrew Bible.* 2 Vols. [Analecta Orientalia 49 and 50]. Rome, 1972-75.

Fitzgerald, A. (ed. and trans.). *Synesius: Essays and Hymns.* 2 Vols. London, 1930.

Fitzmyer, J. A. *The Dead Sea Scrolls: Major Publications and Tools for Study.* Missoula, 1975.

Fleck, F. F. (ed.). *Testament of Solomon.* Berlin, 1837.

Frankfort, H. *The Cenotaph of Seti I at Abydos.* [Memoirs of the Egyptian Exploration Society 39]. London, 1933.

Freytag, G. W. *Arabum Proverbia*. 3 Vols. Bonn, 1831-43.

Freedman, H. and Simon, M. *The Midrash*. 10 Vols. London, 1961.

Friedlander, G., ed. *Pirqe Rabbi Eliezer*. London, 1916.

Friedlieb, J. *Die Sybyllinische Weissagungen*. Leipzig, 1852.

Friedmann, M. *Pesikta Rabbati*. Vienna, 1880.

——— *Seder Eliahu Rabba und Seder Eliahu Zuta*. Vienna, 1902.

Friedmann, M., ed. *Pesikta Hadta* [a Midrash]. Vienna, 1880.

Friedmann, M., ed. *Sifra, der alteste Midrasch zu Leviticus*. Breslau, 1915.

Friedmann, M., ed. *Sifre on Deuteronomy*. Vienna, 1864.

Gammie, J. G.; Brueggemann, W. A.; et al. *Israelite Wisdom: Theological and Literary Essays in Honor of Samuel Terrien*. Missoula, 1978.

Gardiner, A. H. *The Admonitions of an Egyptian Sage from a Hieratic Papyrus in Leiden*. Leipzig, 1909.

——— *Hymns to Amon from a Leiden Papyrus*. [Zeitschrift fur Agyptische Spruche und Altertumskunde 42, pp. 12-42]. Leipzig, 1905.

——— *Hieratic Papyri in the British Museum*. Vol. III. London, 1935.

Gebhardt (von), O. *Psalmoi Solomontos*. [Codex Casanatensis]. Leipzig, 1895.

Gemser, B. "Jir'at Jahwe in den Psalmen," *New Testament Studies 22*, (1939) pp. 140-152, Cambridge.

——— *Sprüche Salomos*. Tubingen, 1963.

Gerleman, G. *Studies in the Septuaginta. III: Proverbs*. Lund, 1956.

Gesenius, W. and Buhl, F. *Hebraisches und Aramäisches Handwörterbuch das Alte Testament*. Leipzig, 1921.

Geyer, J. *The Wisdom of Solomon*. London, 1963.

Gianotti, C. R. *The New Testament and the Mishnah* [A Cross Reference Index]. Grand Rapids, 1983.

Gibson, J. C. L. (ed.). *Canaanite Myths and Legends*. Edinburgh, 1977.

Gifford, E. H. (ed.). *Eusebius's Preparation for the Gospel*. 2 Vols. Oxford, 1903.

Gildemeister, I. *Esdrae Liber Quartus Arabice e Codice Vaticano*. Bonn, 1877.

Gillet, R. and Baudemaris (de), A. (eds.). *St. Gregoire Le Grand: Morales sur Job*. Paris, 1952.

Ginzberg, L. H. *Legends of the Jews.* 7 Vols. Philadelphia, 1909-1955.

Ginsburg, C. D. *Ketubim.* London, 1926.

Ginsburger, M., ed. *Pseudo-Jonathan* [Targum Jonathan ben Uzziel on the Pentateuch]. Berlin, 1903.

——— *Das Fragmententhargum* [Targum Jerusalem on the Pentateuch, Fragments]. Berlin, 1899.

Godley, A. D. (ed.). *Herodotus.* 4 Vols. [Loeb Classical Library]. London, 1920-25.

Goldin, J. (trans.). *The Fathers According to Rabbi Nathan.* [Yale Judaica Series Vol. X]. New Haven, 1955.

Goldschmidt, L. *Oznayim LaTorah. Konkordantsiyah leTalmud Babli.* [Subject Concordance to the Babylonian Talmud]. Copenhagen, 1959.

Gollancz, H. (trans.). *Shekel Hakodesh and Yesod Hayirah.* Oxford, 1919.

——— *Targum on the Song of Songs, and the Tappuach.* London, 1908.

Gonzalo Maeso, D. *La Sabiduria Biblica, su Concepto naturaleza y excelencia.* Granada, 1953.

Goodrick, A. T. S. *The Book of Wisdom.* New York, 1913.

Gordis, R. Koheleth: *The Man and His World.* New York, 1955.

Gordon, C. H. *Ugaritic Handbook.* [Analecta Orientalia XXV]. Rome, 1947.

——— *Ugaritic Manual.* [Analecta Orientalia XXXV]. Rome, 1955.

——— *Ugaritic Textbook.* [Analecta Orientalia XXXVIII]. Rome, 1965.

Graffin, R. (ed.). *Patrologia Orientalis.* 25 Vols. Paris, 1903-07.

——— *Patrologia Syriaca.* 3 Vols. Paris, 1894-1926.

Grant, R. M. *Thophilus of Antioch: Ad Autolycum.* Oxford, 1970.

Grant, R. M. and Graham H. H. (eds.). *The Apostolic Fathers: Vol II — First and Second Clement.* New York, 1965.

Grant, R. M. and Freedman, D. N. *The Secret Sayings of Jesus.* London, 1963.

Gray, G. B. *The Psalms of Solomon.* Oxford, 1913.

Gray, J. *The Keret Text in the Literature of Ras Shamra.* 2nd edition. Leiden, 1964.

Grebant, E. *Hymne a Ammon-Ra des papyrus Egyptiens du Musée de Boulaq.* Paris, 1874.

Greenup, A. W. *The Targum on the Book of Lamentations.* Sheffield, 1893.

Gregg, J. A. F. *The Wisdom of Solomon.* Cambridge, 1909.

Gressman, H. *Altoriental Texte und Bilder.* 2 Vols. Tubingen, 1909.

Grimm, C. L. W. *Das Buch der Weisheit.* Leipzig, 1860.

Grossfeld, B. *The Targum to the Five Megilloth.* New York, 1973.

Gruenhut, E. *Sefer ha Likkutim.* Berlin, 1903.

Grünhut, L. *Midrasch Shir ha Shirim.* Jerusalem, n.d.

Gry, L. *Les dires prophetiques d'Esdras.* [II Esdras]. 2 Vols. Pairs, 1938.

Guillamont, A.; Puech, H. C.; Quispel, G; Till, W. and Yassah, A. A. M. *The Gospel According to Thomas.* Leiden-New York, 1959.

Guillamont, A. and C. (eds.). *Evagrius Ponticus: Traité pratique.* 2 Vols. Paris, 1971.

Gunn, B. G. *The Instruction of Ptah-hotep.* London, 1906.

Gwynn, J., ed. *Demonstrations of Aphrahat* [Aphraates], *the Persian Sage.* Grand Rapids, 1955.

Hadas, M. (ed.). *The Third and Fourth Books of Maccabees.* New York, 1953.

——— *Aristeas to Philocrates.* New York, 1951.

Hadas, M. and Lebel, M. (eds.). *De Providentia I and II.* [Les Oeuvres de Philon d'Alexandrie 35]. Paris, 1973.

Hage, W. *Die Griechische Baruch-Apokalypse.* Tubingen, 1974.

Haiman, M., ed. *Sefer Torah, Ha-Ketubah, ve-Ha-Masorah`al Torah, Nebi'im ve-Ketubim,* [Index by Biblical passage, of comments on that biblical passage in Rabbinic literature]. 3 vols. Tel Aviv, 1965.

Hallevy, E. E. (ed.). *Midrash Rabbah.* 8 Vols. Tel Aviv, 1965.

Hamp, V. *Das Buch der Sprüche.* Wurzburg, 1949.

Hanhart, R. (ed.). *Iudith.* [Septuaginta Vetus Testamentum Graecum VIII, 4]. Gottingen, 1979.

Harper, R. F. (ed.). *Assyrian and Babylonian Letters.* Part I-XIV. Chicago, 1892-1914.

Harris, J. R. (ed.). *The Psalms of Solomon.* Cambridge, 1909.

Harris, J. R. and Mingana, A. (eds.). *The Odes and Psalms of Solomon.* 2 Vols. Manchester, 1916-1920.

Hart, F. J. A. and Mayor, J. B. (eds.). *Clement of Alexandria Miscellanies (Stromata) Book VII.* London-New York, 1902.

Hart, J. H. A. (ed.). *Ecclesiasticus — The Greek Text of Codex 248.* Cambridge, 1909.

Hartman, L. F. and Di Lella A. A. (eds.). *The Book of Daniel*. [The Anchor Bible Series 23]. Garden City, N.Y., 1978.

Haspecker, J. *Gottesfurcht bei Jesus Sirach*. Rome, 1967.

Hatch, E. and Redpath, H. A. *A Concordance to the Septuagint and the Other Greek Versions of the Old Testament including the Apocrypha*. 2 Vols. Graz, Austria, 1954.

Heidel, A. *The Gilgamesh Epic*. Chicago, 1954.

——— *The Babylonian Genesis*. Chicago, 1963.

Heinisch, P. *Das Buch der Weisheit*. Münster, 1912.

——— *Personifikationen und Hypostasen im Alten Testament und im alten Orient*. Münster, 1921.

——— *Die persönliche Weisheit des Alten Testament*. Münster, 1947.

Hennecke, E. *Neutestamentliche Apokryphen*. 2nd edit. Tubingen, 1924.

Hennecke, E. ed. *New Testament Apocrypha*. 2 vols. New York, 1963-65.

Herdner, A. *Corpus des Tablettes en Cuneiformes Alphabétiques Decouvertes a Ras Shamra, Ugarit*. 2 Vols. Paris, 1963.

Herkenne, H. *De Veteris Latinae Ecclesiastici Capitibus I-XLIII*. Leipzig, 1899.

Hertz, J. H. (ed.). *Pirke Aboth*. New York, 1945.

Hertzenauer, P. M. *Biblia Sacra Vulgatae*. Rome, 1914.

Higger, M. *The Seven Minor Tractates*. New York, 1930.

——— *The Additional Tractates*. New York, 1931.

Higger, M., ed. *Pirqe Rabbi Eliezer*. Horeb, VIII, 1944, 1948.

Hirsch, S. R. *Horeb*. 2 Vols. London, 1962.

Hoffman, D. *Mechilta de Rabbi Simeon ben Johai*. Frankfurt, 1905.

——— *Midrash Tannaim*. Berlin, 1908-09.

Hoftijzer, J. *Dictionaire des Inscriptiones Semitiques de l'Ouest*. Leiden, 1965.

Holm-Nielsen, S. *Hodayot: Psalms from Qumran*. Aarhus, 1960.

——— *Die Psalmen Salomos*. Göttersloh, 1977.

Horowitz, H. S. *Sifre on Numbers and Sifre Zuta*. Leipzig, 1917.

——— *Siphre Zuta*. Lodz, 1929.

——— *Sifre on Deuteronomy*. Berlin, 1939.

Horowitz, H. S. and Rabin, I. A. (eds.). *Mekilta de Rabbi Ishmael*. Frankfurt, 1931.

Hrozny, F. *Mythen von dem Gotte Ninrag*, [Ninib]. Berlin, 1903.

Hyman, A. *Toledoth Tannaim we Amoraim*. 3 Vols. London, 1910.

Imschoot (van) P. "Sagesse et esprit dans l'Ancien Testament," *Revue Biblique 47*, (1938) pp. 23-49. Paris.

Jaeger, W. "The Patristic Conception of Wisdom in the Light of Biblical and Rabbinical Research," *Studia Patristica* IV. pp. 90-106. Berlin.

James, M. R. *The Biblical Antiquities of Philo*. London, 1917.

——— *The Apocryphal New Testament*. Oxford, 1924.

Janssen, E. *Testament Abrahams*. Tubingen, 1974.

Jastrow, M. *Die Religion Babyloniens und Assyriens*. Giesen, 1905-21.

Jastrow, M. A. *A Dictionary of the Targumim, the Talmud Babli and Yerushalmi, and the Midrashic Literature*. New York, 1950.

Jcllinek, A. (ed.). *Alphabet de Rabbi Akiba*. [Beth ha-Midrash, Vol. III]. Leipzig, 1853-77.

Jellinek, A., ed. *Beth ha Midrash*. 6 vols. Leipzig, 1853-77.

Jequier, G. *Le Papyrus Prisse*. Paris, 1911.

Joly, R. (ed.). *Hermas: Le Pasteur*. 2nd edit. Paris, 1968.

Jonge (de), M. (ed.). *The Testaments of the Twelve Patriarchs*. Assen, 1953.

——— *Testamenta XII Patriarchum*. [Greek Text]. Leiden, 1964.

Jongelin, B. *Le Rouleau de la Guerre des Manuscrits de Qumran*. Assen, 1962.

Kahle, P. *Prolegomena to Kittel's Biblia Hebraica*. Leipzig, 1937.

Kapelrud, A. S. *Baal in the Ras Shamra Texts*. Copenhagen, 1952.

Kasher, M. M. (ed.). *Torah Shelemah*. 28 Vols. Jerusalem 1927-75ff.

Kasovsky, C. J., and B. *Concordance to the Targum Onqelos*. 5 vols. in 2. Jerusalem, 1939-40.

Kennedy, J. "Riches, Poverty and Adversity in the Book of Proverbs," *Glasgow University Oriental Society Transactions 12* (1944-46) pp. 18-22. Glasgow.

Khamor, L. *The Revelation of the Son of Man*, BenYamin Press, Geneva, N.Y., 1992.

Kidner, D. *The Proverbs*. London, 1964.

King, E. G. *The Yalkut on Zechariah*. Cambridge, 1882.

King, L. W. *The Seven Tablets of Creation*. [Luzac's Semitic Text and Translation Series Nos. 12 and 13]. London, 1902.

Kisch, G. *Pseudo-Philo's Liber Antiquitatum Biblicarum*. Notre Dame, Indiana, 1949.

Kittel, G. and Friedrich, G. (eds.). *Theological Dictionary of the New Testament with Index* [by Pitkin, R. E.], 10 Vols. Grand Rapids, Michigan, 1964-76.

Kittel, R. *Biblia Hebraica*. 3rd edit. Leipzig 1937.

Klijn, A. F. J. *Die Syrische Baruch-Apokalypse*. Tubingen, 1976.

Kmosko, M. (ed.). *Apocalypsis Baruch.* [Patrologia Syriaca 1:2, cols. 1056-1207]. Paris, 1926.

Knabenbauer, J. (ed.). *Ecclesiasticum cum Appendix Ecclesiastici Hebraeus*. Paris, 1902.

——— *Commentarius in Proverbis*. Paris, 1910.

Knibb, M. A. and Ullendorff, E. (eds.). *Ethiopic Book of Enoch: New edition in the light of the Aramaic Dead Sea Fragments*. 2 Vols. Oxford. 1978.

Koehler, L. and Baumgartner, W. (eds.). *Hebraisches und Aramaisches Lexicon zum Alten Testament*. Leiden, 1967.

Kohen, Rabbi Eliyahu. *Midrash Talpiyot*. Warsaw, 1875.

Kohler, K. (trans.). *The Testament of Job*. [Semitic Studies in Memory of Rev. Dr. Alexander Kohut, pp. 264-338]. Berlin, 1897.

Kohut, A. (ed.). *Arukh Completum*. 8 Vols. + Suppl. Vienna 1878-92.

Kohut, A.; Krauss, S.; et al. (eds.). *Complete Talmudic Targumic and Midrashic Lexicon*. New York, n.d.

Kraft, R. A. and Purintum, A. E., eds. and trans. *Paraleipomena Jeremiou*. Missoula, 1972.

Kramer, S. N. *Sumerian Mythology*. [Memoirs of the American Philosophical Society, 21]. Philadelphia, 1944.

——— *Sumerische Literarische Texte aus Nippur*. Berlin, 1961.

——— *The Sumerians*. Chicago, 1963.

Kuhn, K. G., ed. *Der Tannatische Midrasch Sifre zu Numberi*. Stuttgart, 1959.

Kuhn, K. G. (ed.). *Konkordanz zu den Qumran Texten*. Gottingen, 1960.

Kuhn, K. G., et al. *Nachtrage zur Konkordance zu den Quamran-texten*. RDQ IV, Heft 14. 1963.

Kurfess, A. *Sybillinische Weissagungen*. Berlin, 1951.

La Bonnardière, A. M. *Le Livre des Proverbs*. Paris, 1975.

Lachower, F., and Tishby, I. *Mishnat ha-Zohar*. 2 vols. Jerusalem, 1971.

Lagarde (de), P. *Libri Veteris Testamenti Apocryphi Syriace*. Leipzig-London, 1861.

——— *Die Weisheiten der Handschrift von Amiata* (Mittheilungen 1). Göttingen, 1884. [Codex Amiatinus Old Latin Text of Sirach is found in pp. 283-378].

——— *Aegyptiaca*, Göttingen, 1883. [Coptic version of Sirach found in pp. 107-206].

Lake, K. (ed.). *The Apostolic Fathers*. 2 Vols. Cambridge, Mass., 1946.

Lambert, W. G. *Babylonian Wisdom Literature*. Oxford, 1960.

Lambert, W. G. and Millard, A. R. (eds.). *Babylonian Literary Texts*. London, 1965.

Lampe, G. W. H. *Patristic Greek Lexicon*. Oxford, 1968.

Langdon, S. *Sumerian and Babylonian Psalms*. Paris, 1909.

——— *Babylonian Liturgies*. [Library of Ashurbanipal]. Paris, 1913.

——— *Babylonian Wisdom*. [Babyloniaca VII. (1923) pp. 129-229]. Paris.

Langhe (de), R. *Les Textes de Ras Shamra - Ugarit et leurs rapports avec le milieu de l'Ancien Testament*. 2 Vols. Paris, 1945.

Lapide, C. A. and Crampon, A. (eds.). *Commentaria in Scripturam Sacram*. Vols. V and VI [Proverbs], and Vols. IX and X [Ecclesiasticus]. Paris, 1860.

Larcher, C. *Etudes sur le Livre de la Sagesse*. Paris, 1969.

Lau, R. J. and Langdon, S. (eds.). *The Annals of Ashurbanipal*. [Semitic Study Series 5]. Leiden, 1903.

Lauterbach, J. Z. *Mekilta de Rabbi Ishmael*. 3 Vols. Philadelphia, 1933-35.

Leaney, A. R. C. *The Rule of Qumran and its meaning*. Philadelphia, 1966.

Lebin, B.M., ed. *Otzar haGaonim*. 13 vols. Haifa and Jerusalem, 1928-43.

Leclant, J. et al. *Les Sagesses du Proche-Orient Ancien*. Paris, 1963.

Lee, S. *Vetus Testamentum Syriace*. London, 1823.

Leemhuis, F., Klijn, A. F. J. and Van Gelder, G. J. H. eds. *The Arabic Text of the Apocalypse of Baruch* [Parallel English and Syriac Translations of the Arabic Text]. Leiden, 1986.

Leisegang, I. *Philonis Alexandrini Opera Supersunt, Indices*. [Concordance to Philo]. Berlin, 1926.

Lepsius, C. R. *Denkmaler aus Aegypten und Aethiopien*. 6 Vols. Leipzig, 1897-1913.

478

Levertoff, P. P., trans. *Midrash Sifre on Numbers*. London, 1926.

Levi, I. (e.d). *L'Ecclesiastique. Texte Hebreu*. Paris, 1898.

——— *The Hebrew Text of Ecclesiasticus*. [Semitic Study Series No. III]. Leiden, 1969.

Levine, E. (ed.). *The Aramaic Version of Lamentations*. New York, 1976.

——— *The Aramaic Version of Qohelet*. New York, 1978.

Levy, J *Wörterbuch über die Talmudim und Midraschim*. 4 Vols. Darmstadt, 1924.

Levy, J. *Wörterbuch über die Talmudim und Midrashim*. 4 Vols. Darmstadt, 1963, [repr. of Leipzig, 1875-89 edit.].

——— *Chaldaische Wörterbuch über die Targumin*. 2 Vols. Koln, 1959.

Lexa, F. *Papyrus Insinger*. 2 Vols. Paris, 1926.

Licht, J. *The Thanksgiving Scroll*. [Hebrew]. Jerusalem, 1957.

Liddell, H. G. and Scott, R. (eds.). *A Greek-English Lexicon*. Oxford, 1940.

Lieberman, S., ed. *Midrash Debarim [Deuteronomy] Rabbah*. 2nd ed. Jerusalem, 1964.

Lightfoot, J. B. and Harmer, J. (eds.). *The Apostolic Fathers*. 2 Vols. New York, 1891.

Liplin, L. A. *The Akkadian Language*. Moscow, 1973.

Lobel, E. and Roberts, C. H. *The Oxyrhyncus Papyri*. London, 1954.

Lohse, E. *Die Texte aus Qumran*. [Hebrew and German]. Munich, 1964.

Lonergan, J. F. L. *Insight: A Study of Human Understanding*. San Francisco, 1978.

Mai, A. (ed.). *The Testament of Job*. [Scriptorum Veterum Nova Collectio Vol. VII (Greek-Latin)]. Rome, 1833.

Malan, S. C. (ed.). *The Book of Adam and Eve*. Edinburgh, 1882.

——— *Original Notes on the Book of Proverbs*. 3 Vols. London, 1889-93.

Malfroy, I. "Sagesse et Loi dans le Deuteronome," *Vetus Testamentum 15* [(1965) pp. 49-65]. Leiden.

Mandelbaum, B. *Pesiqta de Rab Kahana*. [Hebrew]. 2 Vols. New York, 1962.

Mandelkern, S. *Veteris Testamenti Concordantiae Hebraicae atque Chaldaicae*. 2 Vols. Graz, 1955.

Mansoor, M. *The Thanksgiving Hymns*. Leiden, 1961.

Mapsik, C. ed. *Le Zohar*. 2 vols. La Grosse, 1984.

Marcus, R. "The Tree of Life in Proverbs," *Journal of Biblical Literature 62* (1943) pp. 117-120.

——— "Tree of Life in Essene Tradition," *Journal of Biblical Literature 74* (1955) p. 274.

Margolioth, M. *Zohar: With Commentaries*. [Hebrew]. 3 Vols. Jerusalem, 1964.

——— *Encyclopedia of Talmudic and Geonic Literature*. 2 vols. Tel Aviv, 1946.

Margolis, R. (ed.). *Tikkunei Zohar*. Jerusalem, 1978.

——— *Zohar*. 3 Vols. [Hebrew]. Jerusalem, 1940-46.

——— *Zohar Chadash* ['New' Zohar; a commentary on Canticles]. Jerusalem, 1978.

Margollioth, E., ed. *Pesikta Rabbati de Rab Kahana*. Warsaw, 1893.

Margulies, M., ed. *Midrash Wayyikra [Leviticus] Rabbah* 5 vols. Jerusalem, 1953-60.

Mariette, A. *Les Papyrus Egyptiens du Musée de Boulaq*. 3 Vols. Paris, 1871-76.

——— *Abydos*. 2 Vols. Paris, 1869-80.

——— *Denderah*. 4 Vols. Cairo, 1875.

Marrou, H. I. and Harl, M. (eds.). *Clement d'Alexandrie*. Paris, 1960.

Martin, F. *Textes religieux assyriens et babyloniens*. [Bibliotheque de l'Ecole des hautes Etudes sciences philosophique et historique. Fasc. 130]. Paris, 1900.

Mayer, G. *Index Philoneus*. Berlin, 1974.

McCown, C. C. (ed.). *The Testament of Solomon*. Leipzig, 1922.

McKane, W. *Prophets and Wise Men*. [Studies in Biblical Theology 44 (1965-66)]. London.

——— *Proverbs: A New Approach*. London, 1970.

Meek, T. J. *Cuneiform Bilingual hymns, Prayers, and Penitential Psalms*. [Beiträge zur Assyrologie und semitischen Sprachwissenschaft 6:1 (1913) pp. 1-127]. Strassburg.

Melamed, R. H. *The Targum to Canticles*. Philadelphia, 1921.

Mercer, S. A. B., ed. *The Tell-El-Amarna Tablets*. 2 vols. Toronto, 1939.

Metzger, B. M. *An Introduction to the Apocrypha*. Oxford, 1957.

——— *New Testament Studies* [Philological, versional and patristic]. Grand Rapids, 1980.

——— (ed.). *The Apocrypha (RSV)*. [The Oxford Annotated Apocrypha]. New York, 1965.

Migne, J. P. *Patrologia cursus completus: Series Latina.* 221 Vols. Paris, 1844-66.

——— *Patrologia cursus completus: Series Graeca.* 161 Vols. Paris, 1857-66.

Midraot Gedolot (Hebrew Text of the Bible with Targum and Commentaries of Rashi, Ibn Ezra, Ramban, and Sforno). New York, Pardes Publishing Co., 1951.

Milik, J. T. and Black, M. (eds.). *The Book of Enoch.* [Aramaic Fragments of Qumran Cave 4]. Oxford, 1976.

Mingana, A. *The Apocalypse of Peter.* Cambridge, 1931.

Mondesart, C. *Clement d'Alexandrie.* Paris, 1949.

Montefiore, C. G. and Loewe, H. A. (eds.). *A Rabbinic Anthology.* London, 1938.

Montgomery, J. and Harris, Z. A. *The Ras Shamra Mythological Texts.* [Memoirs of the American Philosophical Society 4]. Philadelphia, 1935.

Montgomery, J. W. "Wisdom as Gift," *Interpretation 15* (1961) pp. 43-57. Richmond, Va.

Morfill, W. R. (trans.). and Charles, R. H. (ed.). *The Book of the Secrets of Enoch.* [2 Enoch]. Oxford, 1986.

Morrish, G. *A Handy Concordance of the Septuagint, Giving Various Readings from Codices Vaticanus, Alexandrinus, Sinaiticus, and Ephraemi.* London, repr. 1970.

Moscati, S. "La radice semitica ' mr." [*Biblica 27* (1946) pp. 115-126]. Rome.

——— *An Introduction to the comparative Grammar of the Semitic Languages.* Weisbaden, 1964.

Mras, K. (ed.). *Praeparatio Evangelica of Eusebius.* Paris, 1954-56.

Munk, L., ed. *Targum Sheni* [On Esther]. Berlin, 1876.

Murphy, R. E. *Seven Books of Wisdom.* Milwaukee, 1960.

Murray, A. T. *Homer: Iliad.* 2 Vols. [Loeb Classical Library]. London, 1924-25.

Myers, J. M. *I and II Chronicles.* [Anchor Bible Series Vols. 12 and 13]. Garden City, N. Y., 1965.

——— *Ezra-Nehemiah.* [Anchor Bible Series Vol 14]. Garden City, N.Y., 1965.

——— *I and II Esdras.* [Anchor Bible Series Vol. 42]. Garden City, N.Y., 1974.

Nau, F. *Histoire et Sagesse d'Ahikar l'Assyrian.* Paris, 1909.

Naville, E. *Das Agyptische Todtenbuch der XVIII bis XX Dynastie.* Berlin, 1886.

Nikiprowetzky, V. *Le Troisieme Sibylle.* [Etudes Juives IX (1970)]. Paris.

Noah, M. M. (trans.). *Sefer ha Yashar.* New York, 1840.

Nock, A. D. and Festugière, M. (eds.). *Corpus Hermeticum.* 4 Vols. Paris, 1945-54.

Noy, Dov. [Neumann, D.] *Motif-Index of the Talmudic Midrashic Literature.* Ann Arbor, 1954.

Odeberg, H. (ed.). *Third [3rd] Enoch or The Hebrew Book of Enoch.* Cambridge, 1928.

Oesterley, W. O. E. *The Wisdom of Egypt and the Old Testament.* London, 1927.

Oesterley, W. O. E. (ed.). *Ecclesiasticus.* Cambridge, 1912.

Oesterly, W. O. E., ed. *II Esdras.* London, 1933.

Olinder, G. (ed.). *Letter of Philoxenus of Mabbug to a Novice.* [Göteborg Hogskolas Arskrift XLVII (1941:21]. Goteborg, 1941.

Olivier, B. *La Crainte de Dieu comme valeur religieuse de l'Ancien Testament.* Bruxelles, 1960.

Owen, W. B. (ed.). *Athenagoras with Explanatory Notes.* New York, 1904.

Payne Smith, R. *Compendious Syriac Dictionary.* Oxford, 1957.

Payne Smith, R. *Thesaurus Syriacus.* Oxford, 1957.

Pereman, J. *The Book of Assyro-Babylonian Proverbs.* [Cuneiform Texts with Hebrew Translation]. Tel Aviv, 1947.

Perrot, C. and Bogaert, P. M. (eds.). *Pseudo-Philon: Les Antiquités Bibliques.* Paris, 1976.

Peters, N. (ed.). *Das Buch Jesus Sirach.* Freiburg, 1956.

Petit, F. (ed.) *L'Ancienne version latine des Questions sur la Genèse de Philon d'Alexandrie.* [Texts und Untersuchungen 113,114]. Berlin, 1973.

——— *Quaestiones in Genesim et in Exodum: Fragmenta Graeca.* Paris, 1978.

Petrie, W. M. F. *Koptos.* London, 1896.

Philonenko, M. (ed.). *Joseph and Asenath.* [Studio Post Biblica XIII]. Leiden, 1968.

Picard, J. C. (ed.) *Apocalypsis Baruch Graece.* Leiden, 1967.

Porteus, N. W. "Royal Wisdom," *Vetus Testamentum Supplement 3* (1955) pp. 247-261. Leiden.

Power, E. "A Study of the Hebrew Expression 'Wide of Heart'," *Biblica 1* (1920) pp. 59-75. Rome.

Priest, J. F. "Where is Wisdom to be Placed?", *Journal of Bible and Religion 31* (1963) pp. 275-282. Philadelphia, Pa.

Pritchard, J. B. (ed.). *Ancient Near Eastern Texts relating to the Old Testament*. 3rd edit. Princeton, 1969.

Rabin, C. (ed.). *The Zadokite Documents*. Oxford, 1954.

Rabbinowicz, R. N. N. *Dikdukei Soferim*. 15 Vols. Munich, 1867-86.

Rabinowitz, I. "The Qumran Hebrew Original of Ben Sira's Concluding Acrostic of Wisdom", *Hebrew Union College Annual*, Vol XLII (1971) pp. 173-194. Cincinnati.

Radford, L. B. (ed.). *The Epistle to Diognetus*. London, 1908.

Rahlf, A. (ed.). *Septuaginta*. 2 Vols. Stuttgart, 1935.

Rankin, O. S. *Israel's Wisdom Literature*. Edinburgh, 1936.

Rawlinson, H. C. *The Cuneiform Inscriptions of Western Asia*. 5 Vols. London, 1861-84.

Reider, J. *The Book of Wisdom*. New York, 1957.

Reisner, G. *Sumerische-Babylonische Hymnen*. Berlin, 1896.

Reitzenstein, R. *Poimandres*. Leipzig, 1904.

Ringgren, H. *Word and Wisdom: Studies in the Hypostatization of Divine Qualities and Functions in the Ancient Near East*. Lund, 1947.

——— *Sprüche*. Gottingen, 1967.

Roberts, A.; Donaldson, J. and Menzies, A. (eds.). *The Ante-Nicene Fathers*. 9 Vols. Grand Rapids, 1974-75.

Robinson, J. A. (ed.). *Barnabas, Hermas, and the Didache*. London, 1920.

——— *Irenaeus: Demonstration of the Apostolic Preaching*. London, 1920.

Robinson, J. M. (Dir.) et al. *The Nag Hammadi Library in English* [Nag Hamadi Library Gnostic Texts]. New York, 1984.

Robinson, T. *The Evangelists and the Mishna*. London, 1859.

Rochais, H. M. (ed.). *Livre D'Etincelles*. 2 Vols. Paris, 1961-62.

Rogers, R. W. *Cuneiform Parallels to the Old Testament*. New York, 1926.

Roth, W. "The Relation between the Fear of the Lord and Wisdom", *Beth Mikra* 25, (1980), pp. 150-162. Jerusalem.

Rowley, H. H. *The Zadokite Fragments and the Dead Sea Scrolls*. Oxford, 1952.

Rudolph, W. (ed.). *Vom Buch Kohelet*. Münster, 1959.

Rüger, H. P. *Text und Textform im Hebraischen Sirach*. Berlin, 1970.

Ryle, H. E. and James, M. R. (ed. and trans.). *Psalms of Solomon*. Cambridge, 1891.

Rzach, A. *Oracula Sibyllina*. Leipzig, 1891.

Saldarini, A. J., ed. *The Fathers according to Rabbi Nathan* [Version B]. Leiden, 1975.

Saltman, A., ed. *Pseudo Jerome. Questiones* [on the Book of Samuel]. Leiden, 1975.

Sander, C. F. *Aegyptische Leveregler*. Copenhagen, 1952.

Sanders, J. A. (ed.). *The Psalms Scroll of Qumran Cave 11*. Oxford, 1965.

Sauer, G. *Die Sprüche Agur*. [Beitrage zur Wissenschaft vom Alten und Neuen Testaments LXXXIV (1963)]. Stuttgart.

Savignac (de) J. "La Sagesse en Proverbes VIII, 22-31", *Vetus Testamentum*. 12 (1962) pp. 211-215. Leiden.

Schaff, P. (ed.). *Nicene and Post-Nicene Fathers*. First Series, 9 Vols. Grand Rapids, 1975.

Schaff, P. and Wace, H. (eds.). *Nicene and Post-Nicene Fathers*. Second Series, 14 Vols. Grand Rapids, 1974-76.

Schechter, S. *Fragments of a Zadokite Work*. Cambridge, 1910.

——— *Aboth de Rabbi Nathan*. Vienna, 1887.

——— *The Wisdom of Ben Sira: Portions of the Book Ecclesiasticus from Hebrew Manuscripts in the Cairo Geniza Collection*. Cambridge, 1899.

Schenke, W. *Die Chokma (Sophia) in der Judischen Hypostasen-spekulation*. Kristina, 1913.

Schleussner, J. F. *Opuscula critica ad versiones graecas Vetus Testamentum pertinentia*. Leipzig, 1812.

——— *Novus Thesaurus philologico-criticus, sive lexicon in LXX et reliquos interpretes graecos ac scriptores apocryphos Veteris Testamenti*. Leipzig, 1820-21.

Schodde, G. H. (ed.) *Book of Jubilees*. Oberlin, Ohio, 1888.

Schüpphaus, J. (ed.). *Die Psalmen Salomos*. Leiden, 1977.

Schwab, M. *Le Talmud de Jerusalem*. 6 Vols. Paris, 1960.

Scott, W. (ed.). *Hermetica, The Ancient Greek and Latin Writings which contain Religious and Philosophical Teachings ascribed to Hermes Trimegistus*. 3 Vols. Oxford, 1924-26.

Segal, M. S. *Sefer Ben Sira ha-Shalem*. Jerusalem, 1959.

Sethe, K. *Die altägyptischen Pyramid-texte*. 4 Vols. Leipzig, 1908-22.

Simpson, W. K. (ed.). *The Literature of Ancient Egypt: An Anthology of Stories, Instructions and Poetry.* New Haven, 1971.

Smend, R. *Die Weisheit des Jesus Sirach.* Berlin, 1906.

——— *Griechisch-Syrisch-Hebräischer Index zur Weisheit Des Jesus Sirach.* Berlin, 1907.

Snyder, G. F. (ed.). *Shepherd of Hermas.* [The Apostolic Fathers, Vol. 6]. Edited by R. M. Grant]. New York, 1968.

Soden (von), W. *Akkadische Handwörterbuch.* Wiesbaden, 1959.

Sperber, A. *The Bible in Aramaic.* [The Targums]. 4 Vols. London, 1959.

Sperlin, H.; Simon, M. and Abelson, J. *Zohar.* [English Translation]. 5 Vols. London, 1950.

Sprenger, N. *Konkordanz zum Syrischen Psalter.* Wiesbaden, 1976.

Srawley, J. H. *The Epistles of St. Ignatius of Antioch.* London, 1935.

Stählin, O. *Clement of Alexandria.* [Stromata-Books I-IV, found in: Die griechischen Christlichen Schriftsteller, Vols. 15-17]. Leipzig, 1897.

Starcky, J. (ed.). and Abel, F. M. (trans.): *Les Livres des Maccabées.* Paris, 1961.

Stenning, J. F. *The Targum of Isaiah.* Oxford, 1949.

Stephanus, H. *Thesaurus Linguae graecae.* Paris, 1831-65.

Stone, M. E. (ed.). *Testament of Levi.* [English Translations of the Armenian Text]. Jerusalem, 1969.

——— *Jewish Writings of the Second Temple Period.* Philadelphia, 1984.

——— (ed. and trans.). *The Armenian Version of IV Ezra.* [University of Pennsylvania Armenian Text and Studies 1]. Missoula, 1979.

Storr, F. *Sophocles.* 2 Vols. [Loeb Classical Library]. London, 1928-1939.

Strack, H. L. *Die Sprüche Salomos.* Monaco, 1888.

Strafforello, G. *La Sapienza del Mondo.* 3 Vols. Turin, 1883.

Strawley, J. H., ed. *The Epistles of St. Ignatius of Antioch.* London, 1935.

Stuart, M. *Commentary on the Book of Proverbs.* London, 1852.

Sukenick, E. L. *Osar hammegiloth Haggezanoth.* [Hebrew Text of 1QH and Fragments]. Jerusalem, 1954-57.

Sukenick, E. L. *The Dead Sea Scrolls of the Hebrew University.* Jerusalem, 1955.

Suys, E. *La Sagesse d'Ani.* [Analecta Orientalia II (1935)]. Rome.

485

Swete, H. B. (ed.). *The Psalms of Solomon [Greek Text] with the Greek Fragments of the Book of Enoch.* Cambridge, 1899.

——— *The Old Testament in Greek.* 3 Vols. Cambridge, 1909-22).

Tallqvist, K. L. *Cuneiform Texts from Babylonian Tablets in the British Museum.* 41 Vols. London, 1896-1931.

——— *Babyloniska hymner och böner.* Helsingfors, 1953.

Taylor, C. (ed.). *Sayings of the Jewish Fathers.* [Pirke Aboth]. Cambridge, 1897.

——— *The Oxyrhyncus Sayings of Jesus found in 1903.* Oxford, 1905.

Tedesche, S. S *A Critical Edition of I Esdras.* New Haven, 1928.

Terry, M. S. (trans.). *The Sibylline Oracles.* 2nd edit. London, 1899.

Thackeray, H. J. (ed.). *The Letter of Aristeas.* [Greek Text]. Found in the Appendix to H. B. Swete's: *The Introduction to the Old Testament in Greek.* Cambridge, 1902.

Thureau-Dangin, F. *Le Syllabaire Accadien.* Paris, 1926.

Tishby, I., ed. *The Wisdom of the Zohar.* Translated by D. Goldstein. Oxford University Press [Litman Library of Jewish Civilization]. Oxford, 1988.

Torczyner, H. *The Lachish Letters* [Tell-el-Amarna]. Jerusalem, 1938.

Tov, E. (ed.). *The Book of Baruch also called 1 Baruch.* [Pseudepigrapha Series 6]. Missoula, 1975.

Toy, C. H. *The Book of Proverbs.* Edinburgh, 1899.

Tur-Sinai, N. H. *Mishle Selomoh.* [Book of Proverbs]. Tel Aviv, 1950.

——— *The Book of Job: A New Commentary.* Jerusalem, 1967.

Vaccari, A. *La Sapienze.* [Found in *La Sacra Biblia a cura del Pont. Inst. Biblico.* pp. 131-175].

Vaillant, A. *Le Livre des Secrets d'Henoch.* [2 Enoch]. Paris, 1952.

Van den Born, A. *Wijsheid Van Jesus Sirach.* Roermond, 1968.

Van Dijk, J. J. A. *La Sagesse Sumero-Accadienne.* Leiden, 1953.

Van Erpe, T. [see Erpenius, T.]. *Arabic Grammar.* Leiden, 1614.

Van Der Weiden, W. A. *Le Livre des Proverbes: Notes Philologiques.* [Biblica et Orientalia 23 (1970)]. Rome.

Van Zijl, J. B. *A concordance to the Targum of Isaiah.* [Aramaic Studies 3 (1979)]. Missoula.

Vattioni, F. "Saggezza e Creazione in Proverbs 3:19-20", *Augustinianum 6* (1966) pp. 102-105.

——— "L'Albero della Vita", *Augustinianum 7* (1967) pp. 133-144. Rome.

——— *Ecclesiastico [Sirach]: testo ebraico con apparato critico e versione greca latina e siriaca.* Naples, 1968.

Violet, B. *Die Esra-Apokalypse [II Esdras].* Leipzig, 1910.

Virolleaud, C. (trans.). *Baal Text I*.* [Syria Vol. XV (1934) pp. 305-336]. Paris.

Visotzky, B.L. (ed.) *The Midrash on Proverbs.* New Haven, 1992.

Volten, A. *Zwei Altägyptische Politische Schriften, Die Lehre für König Merikare.* [Analecta Aegyptica, IV (1945)]. Copenhagen.

Wachsman, A. *Hanothen Bajam Derech.* [Talmudic Lexicon]. Budapest, 1938.

Wadsworth, M. *The Liber Antiquitatum Biblicarum of Pseudo-Philo.* [D. Phil. diss., Oxford University, 1975.

Wahl, O. (ed.). *Apocalypsis Esdrae. Apocalypsis Sedrach. Visio Beati Esdrae.* [Pseudepigrapha Veteris Testamenti Graece, IV]. Leiden, 1977.

Walton, B. *Biblia Sacra Polyglotta.* [Hebrew, Greek, Latin, Aramaic, Syriac, Arabic and Geez]. 6 Vols. London, 1964-65 repr. of 1657 edition.

Weir, Smyth, H. *Aeschylus.* 2 Vols. [Loeb classical Library]. London.

Weiss, I. H., ed. *Sifra on Leviticus.* Vienna, 1862.

Wensinck A. J. (trans.). *St. Isaac the Syrian [Isaac of Nineveh], Mystic Treatises.* Amsterdam, 1923.

Wernberg-Møller, P. *The Manual of Discipline.* [IQS]. Leiden, 1957.

Wertheimer, S. A., ed. *Batte Midrashot.* 4 vols. Jerusalem, 1893-97.

Wertheimer, S. A., ed. *Leket Midrashim.* Jerusalem, 1904.

Wertheimer, S. A., ed. *Otzar Midrashim.* 2 vols. Jerusalem, 1913-14 [revised and edited by his grandson A. J. Wertheimer].

Whiston, W., trans. *The Works of Flavius Josephus.* New York, 1853.

Whybray, R. N. *Wisdom in Proverbs: The Concept of Wisdom in Proverbs 1-9.* [Studies in Biblical Theology 45]. London, 1965.

Wilcke, C. *Das Lugalbanda-Epos.* Berlin, 1969.

Winter, M. M. (ed.). *A Concordance to the Peshitto Version of Ben Sira.* [Monographs of the Peshitto Institute 2]. Leiden, 1976.

Wise, S. S. (trans.). *Gabirol's Improvement of the Moral Qualities.* New York, 1902.

Wolfson, H. A. *Philo.* 2 Vols. Cambridge, Mass., 1947.

Wünsche, A. *Pesikta de Rab Kahana.* Leipzig, 1885.

Yadin, Y. *The Scroll of the War of the Sons of Light against the Sons of Darkness.* [IQM]. Oxford, 1962.

——— *The Ben Sira Scroll from Masada.* Jerusalem, 1965.

Yahuda, I. B. *Proverbia Arabica.* 2 Vols. Jerusalem, 1932-34.

Yohai ben, S. *Tikkune Zohar.* Livorno, 1854.

Zába, Z. *Les maximes de Ptahhoptep.* Prague, 1956.

Zerafa, P. P. *The Wisdom of God in the Book of Job.* Rome, 1978.

Ziegler, J. "Chokma, Sophia, Sapientia", *Würzburger Universitätsreden 32* (1961). Wurtzburg.

——— (ed.). *Sapientia Salomonis.* [Septuaginta Vol. XII,1]. Göttingen, 1962.

——— *Sapientia Iesu Filii Sirach.* [Septuaginta Vol. XII,1]. Göttingen, 1965.

Zimmer, F. *Akkadische Fremdwörter als Beweis für babylonischen Kultureinfluss.* Leipzig, 1917.

Zimmermann, F. *The Book of Tobit.* New York, 1958.

Zohrab, J. *Armenian Bible.* Venice, 1805.

Zorell, F. *Lexicon Hebraicum et Aramaicum Veteris Testamenti.* Rome, 1968.

REFERENCE INDEX

510

Sirach, *Hebrew*

Acts

OLD TESTAMENT PSEUDEPIGRAPHA

Apocalypse of Abraham

Apocalypse of Moses

Ascension of Isaiah

Assumption of Moses

2 Baruch [Syriac]

1QH Fragments

1QM [War Scroll]

PHILO

TARGUMS

EARLY CHRISTIAN AND PATRISTIC WRITINGS

NON-ISRAELITE ANCIENT TEXTS

Egyptian Hieroglyphs and Papyri

Mesopotamian, Babylonian and Ugaritic Texts

ACKNOWLEDGEMENTS

Many thanks to Rev. Daniel Twomey, Dr. Gilbert and Bonnie Lavoie, Solomon Bloomfield, Lila Olsen, Don Gorla, Dr. Anthony and Patricia Barraco, Dr. John and Ann Lipinski, James and Bobbie Sansone, Peter Malavenda, Dr. Francis and Sonia Cudjoe, Mary Lee DeGemmis, Florence Maron, Kerry and Paulette Wares, Keith and Monique Gallant, and Donnie J. Martin for their kind help and prayers.

Also From BenYamin Press

The Revelation of The Son of Man
Levi Khamor

Assembling with amazing mastery of sources a vast array of texts from the Bible, the Apocrypha and Pseudepigrapha, the Dead Sea Scrolls, Rabbinic writings, and ancient Egyptian and Babylonian texts, the author weaves a marvelous tapestry disclosing the biblical view of human origin and destiny.

In revealing what Jesus meant by the term "the Son of Man," Levi Khamor helps us grasp the wisdom behind the pre-existent Messiah's choice of Bethlehem to be his birthplace, Galilee to be the locale of his domicile, and carpentry to be his particular avocation. We shall know why it had to be from the tribe of Judah that the Messiah-Son of Man would trace his descent, and in turn be heralded by a Levite: John the Baptist. We shall understand why, as the Son of Man, the Messiah spoke in parables, and why he was to suffer and die. Levi Khamor also enables us to perceive the terms "Creator" and "Former", "the Most High" and "the Almighty", "Man" and "the Son of Man", and "Jabob" and "Israel" in a new light. The hoard of hidden treasures in the Holy Scriptures that *The Revelation of the Son of Man* discovers and brings to light are inexhaustible.

Paperback, 343 pages	ISBN 0-9627925-0-0	**$15.95**
Hardcover, " "	ISBN 0-9627925-1-9	**$23.95**

BOOK REVIEWS

A very learned work, amazing in its mastery of sources.

Daniel J. Harrington, S.J., Ph.D., D.S.S.
Professor of New Testament
Weston School of Theology
Cambridge, Massachusetts

Levi Khamor is both a Scriptural and rabbinic scholar. I found *The Revelation of the Son of Man* so fascinating that I was unable to put it down. I also found that I had great difficulty reading this book systematically, because I wanted to keep dipping into the next chapter and then the next, as I was so interested in finding the many gems that he had uncovered through his incredible research . . .

Editor — **The Hebrew Christian,** the quarterly
publication of the International Messianic
Jewish (Hebrew Christian) Alliance.

A fascinating work . . . brilliant union of biblical scholarship and religious fervor . . . the erudition will not deter the readers, it will attract them. The author's love for the Jewish Messiah burns through the pages . . .

Paul Hallett
The National Catholic Register

The Revelation of the Son of Man is a truly remarkable book. The author shows Jesus of Nazareth to be unmistakably the looked-for Messiah . . . the research required in its writing is without parallel . . . one might read and study the book almost indefinitely without exhausting the store of treasures it reveals.

Edith Myers
Books-in-Review

This book on Jesus Christ, the Son of Man, is a work of understanding and of love. It is full of riches, coming from the Bible (Old Testament and New Testament), as read in a community of living faith. A special trait of this work can be seen in the various and rich quotations borrowed from the Jewish heritage, bringing thus new perspectives to our Christian reading of the Word of God . . .

The rich variety of quotations found here is based on an accurate selection of Hebrew and Greek terms used in the biblical texts: they center on the person of Our Lord, Jesus Christ; they lead us to Him, our Savior, the Anointed One, who is the Messiah, the only Son of God who has revealed to us the Father (see John 1:18).

Professor Leo Laberge, O.M.I., Ph.D., D.S.S.
Professor of Old Testament
University of St. Paul
Ottawa, Canada

Confronted today by the denials and doubts of unbelieving neo-modernist Scripture scholars who continue to sap the foundations of Christian belief, what a relief it is to turn to a book by an erudite scholar who is both a believer and biblicist. I refer to *The Revelation of the Son of Man* by Levi Khamor . . . This book is remarkable for its mastery of Hebrew thought patterns and Rabbinic literature — both of which are utilized in demonstrating that the historical Jesus is the fulfillment of Jewish prophecy and expectation . . . *The Revelation of the Son of Man* is a marvelous vindication of faith in our Lord as the Eternal Son become man for our salvation.

James Likoudis
President, Catholics United for the Faith

I am honoured to have been invited to write a few lines to Levi Khamor's scholarly confession of faith. *The Revelation of the Son of Man* is a remarkable spiritual commentary upon the life of Jesus . . . The author brings to his labour a mastery of classical Judaica; biblical, rabbinic and intertestamental sources. With these, Levi Khamor blends faith and scholarship to his ultimate goal which is to establish Jesus as The Messiah . . .

Rabbi N. Saul Goldman
Temple Shalom--Pompano Beach, Florida

This remarkable book is a sustained study and meditation on the basic questions of human existence and on Jesus (or Yeshua) as the Son of Man. It draws on a vast range of literature: not only the whole of Christian Scripture, including the deuterocanonical books, but also the inter-Testamental literature, including the Dead Sea Scrolls, and the early Christian fathers. A special feature is the extensive use of Jewish sources to shed light on Scripture . . . this book offers a unique compilation of rabbinic parallels.

. . . The writer, throughout, seeks to uncover the hidden, spiritual significance of Scripture and he illuminates the meaning of key terms and concepts by extensive cross-references and comparisons. New light is shed on numerous texts and passages of the Bible.

. . . One has the feeling that this work is the product not just of lengthy study but also of lengthy meditation and of a life deeply committed to the service of God. Those who want to explore the hidden depths of Scripture will find this book an almost inexhaustible treasure house.

Professor Charles H. Scobie, Ph.D.
Head of the Dept. of Religious Studies
Mount Allison University
Sackville, New Brunswick
Canada

Levi Khamor's meditation and study have produced something unique in *The Revelation of the Son of Man*. This great labor displayed with perfect clarity provides an authoritative commentary on Jesus as the Son of Man: the personification of understanding, of labor, suffering, service and humility. He fully vindicates the historical Jesus as the Messiah of the Jews.

Professor J.D.M. Derrett, Ph.D., LL.D., D.C.L. (Oxford)
Professor Emeritus of Oriental Law
University of London, England
Author of **Law in the New Testament,**
Midrash in Action as a Literary Device,
Midrash, the Composition of the Gospels
and Discipline, *etc.*

I render homage to the prodigious erudition and the profound faith
that inspires this immense work.

François Dreyfus, O.P., Ph.D.
Professor of Biblical Studies
Ecole Biblique et Archéologique
de Jérusalem, Israël

The Revelation of The Son of Man – ISBN 0-9627925-0-0
and
The Book of Understanding – ISBN 0-9627925-3-5

Available from:
BenYamin Press
469 Snell Road
Geneva, NY 14456
Fax (315) 789-6000

Please enclose $2.00 for the first book and 50¢ for each additional book
to cover shipping/handling costs. Thank you.

Notes

Notes

Notes

Notes

the pain of exercise
effort; work up a sweat
discipline